The Law Corporate Social Responsibility Deskbook

Practical Guidance for Corporate Counsel and Law Firms

EDITORS
Alan S. Gutterman • Margaret M. Cassidy
Travis Miller • Ashley C. Walter

AMERICAN BAR ASSOCIATION
Business Law Section

Cover design by Catherine Zaccarine.

The materials contained herein represent the opinions of the authors and/or the editors, and should not be construed to be the views or opinions of the law firms or companies with whom such persons are in partnership with, associated with, or employed by, nor of the American Bar Association or the Business Law Section unless adopted pursuant to the bylaws of the Association.

Nothing contained in this book is to be considered as the rendering of legal advice for specific cases, and readers are responsible for obtaining such advice from their own legal counsel. This book is intended for educational and informational purposes only.

© 2019 American Bar Association. All rights reserved.

No part of this publication may be reproduced, stored in a retrieval system, or transmitted in any form or by any means, electronic, mechanical, photocopying, recording, or otherwise, without the prior written permission of the publisher. For permission contact the ABA Copyrights & Contracts Department, copyright@americanbar.org, or complete the online form at http://www.americanbar.org/utility/reprint.html.

Printed in the United States of America.

23 22 21 20 19   5 4 3 2 1

ISBN: 978-1-64105-500-0

Discounts are available for books ordered in bulk. Special consideration is given to state bars, CLE programs, and other bar-related organizations. Inquire at Book Publishing, ABA Publishing, American Bar Association, 321 N. Clark Street, Chicago, Illinois 60654-7598.

www.shopABA.org

Table of Contents

Editors' Note		xi
Chapter 1:	**Evolution of Corporate Social Responsibility**	**1**
I.	Regulating Manufacturing Operations and Point Sources	2
II.	Regulating Products and Product Waste Streams	4
III.	Behavioral Regulations and Mandatory Corporate Disclosure	5
IV.	The Need for a CSR Law Practitioner's Manual	6
Chapter 2:	**ESG, Sustainability, and CSR: Governance and the Role of the Board**	**9**
I.	Introduction	9
II.	The Legal Framework	10
III.	Why Boards Should Care about ESG	11
IV.	Recent Trends Influencing Governance on ESG	13
	A. Board Composition and Diversity	13
	B. Disclosure and ESG Ratings	14
	C. Increased Stakeholder Engagement	14
	D. Shareholder versus Stakeholder Models of Corporate Governance	15
V.	Components of the ESG Governance Framework	16
	A. Board Oversight	16
	B. Partnership with Management	17
	C. Board Composition and Capacity	18
	D. Shareholder and Stakeholder Engagement	18
VI.	Challenges and Opportunities for Boards of Directors and Management Teams	19
	A. Reconciling the Growth of ESG Metrics and Ratings with the Needs of the Company	19
	B. Ensuring Adequate, Accurate, and Timely Disclosures	20
	C. Capitalizing on ESG Risks and Opportunities	20
VII.	Practical Tips for Boards of Directors	21
	A. Articulate Clear Goals and Approaches on ESG Issues	21
	B. Determine Approach to Stakeholder Engagement and Maintain Consistent Messaging	21
	C. Build Human Capital to Manage ESG over the Long Term	21

VIII.	Case Studies		22
	A.	Salesforce.Com: Integrating ESG into Its Business Strategy	22
	B.	Peabody Energy and Exxon Mobil: The Disclosure of Material Climate Change Risks	23
IX.	Summary and Takeaways		25
X.	Practitioner's Resources Library		25
	A.	Articles	25
	B.	Books and White Papers	26
	C.	Reporting and Disclosure Standards	26

Chapter 3: Stakeholder Engagement — 29

I.	Introduction		29
II.	Legal and Regulatory Requirements		30
	A.	Discerning the Best Course of Action	31
	B.	Which Course of Action Is Best?	32
III.	General Best Practices in Stakeholder Engagement		34
	A.	Setting Goals	35
	B.	Stay Engaged	36
	C.	It's a Long Road	36
	D.	General Guidelines for Expectations and Logistics	37
IV.	Specific Preparation Needed to Effectively Dialogue and Techniques to Gauge Progress and Resolve Impasses		37
	A.	Subject Matter Experts Add Value to and Help Cultivate Trust in the Stakeholder Engagement Dialogue	38
	B.	Cultivating Trust on Dialogue Day: Behavioral Ground Rules	39
	C.	Cultivating Trust on Dialogue Day: Role of the Team Leader	40
	D.	Cultivating Trust on Dialogue Day: Corporate Representatives Must Be Flexible	40
	E.	Conclude Each Dialogue Day with an Action Plan	40
V.	Resolving Impasses		41
VI.	When to Know It's Time to Conclude the Dialogue: You Will Know		42
VII.	Summary and Takeaways		42
VIII.	Practitioner's Resources Library		43
	A.	Articles	43
	B.	Books and White Papers	44
	C.	Instruments and Standards	44
	D.	Reporting	44

Chapter 4: Reporting and Disclosure — 45

I.	Introduction		45
II.	A Framework for Thinking about CSR Disclosure		45
	A.	Types of CSR Disclosures	45
	B.	Disclosure Drivers	48
III.	Instruments, Frameworks, Standards, Guidance, and Regulations		50
	A.	Broad-Based Multilateral "Soft Law" Instruments	50
	B.	Broad-Based Voluntary Disclosure Frameworks and Standards	54
	C.	Issue-Specific CSR Disclosures	58

	IV.	The Evolving Litigation and Enforcement Landscape	69
	V.	Parting Thoughts—Keeping the Big Picture in Mind	70

Chapter 5: Environment — 71

	I.	Introduction	71
	II.	Global Legal and Regulatory Issues	71
		A. The London Convention	72
		B. The Montreal Protocol	72
		C. The Paris Accord	72
	III.	U.S. Federal Legal and Regulatory Requirements	73
		A. Clean Air Act	74
		B. Clean Water Act	76
		C. Safe Drinking Water Act	77
		D. Resource Conservation and Recovery Act	79
		E. Comprehensive Environmental Response, Compensation, and Liability Act	81
		F. The Toxic Substances Control Act	84
		G. Hazardous Materials Transportation Act	86
		H. The Endangered Species Act	87
	IV.	State and Local Legal and Regulatory Requirements	89
		A. State Participation in CERCLA	89
		B. Electronic Waste	89
		C. Air Quality/Emissions	90
		D. Wetlands Permitting	90
		E. Local Legal and Regulatory Requirements	90
	V.	Voluntary Environmental Standards for Businesses	91
	VI.	Recent Environmental Litigation Trends	92
	VII.	Summary and Takeaways	94

Chapter 6: Labor and Supply Chain Practices — 97

	I.	Introduction	97
	II.	Legal and Regulatory Requirements	98
		A. U.S. Labor and Employment Laws	98
		B. Human Trafficking and Labor Exploitation Laws and Regulations	102
		C. Global Labor and Employment Laws and Regulations	104
	III.	Voluntary Standards, Norms, and Guidelines	105
	IV.	Compliance	107
		A. Employment Laws and Practices	107
		B. Forced Labor	115
	V.	Labor Issues in the Supply Chain	119

Chapter 7: Product and Customer Responsibility — 123

	I.	Introduction	123
	II.	Legal and Regulatory Requirements—Customer Health and Safety	124
		A. Consumer Product Safety Commission (CPSC)	124
		B. Food and Drug Administration (FDA)	128

	C.	The National Highway Traffic Safety Administration (NHTSA)	131
	D.	The Federal Communications Commission (FCC)	133
III.	Legal and Regulatory Requirements—Marketing and Labeling		135
	A.	Federal Trade Commission (FTC)	135
	B.	Food and Drug Administration (FDA)	138
IV.	Legal and Regulatory Requirements—Customer Privacy		140
	A.	FTC and Current Federal Legal Approaches to Privacy	140
	B.	U.S. State Law Approaches	143
	C.	European Union's General Data Protection Regulation	144
	D.	Additional EU Privacy Frameworks	147
	E.	Other International Laws and Regulations	148
	F.	Relevant Voluntary Standards	149
V.	Privacy Governance, Compliance, and Practice Tools		149
VI.	Additional Reporting Considerations		150
VII.	Summary and Takeaways		151
VIII.	Practitioner's Resource Library		151
	A.	Customer Health and Safety	151
	B.	Marketing and Labeling	152
	C.	Customer Privacy	152

Chapter 8: Community Engagement and Investment — 155

I.	Introduction		155
II.	Legal and Regulatory Requirements		157
	A.	Structuring Corporate Philanthropy Initiatives	157
	B.	Charitable Contributions	158
	C.	Corporate Volunteer Programs	159
	D.	Events	160
	E.	Community Consultation Requirements	161
	F.	Fair Labor Standards	161
III.	Voluntary Standards, Norms, and Guidelines		162
IV.	Governance and Compliance		164
	A.	Strategies and Policies	165
	B.	Community Engagement	165
	C.	Measurement and Assessment	166
	D.	Reporting	167
V.	Practicing Community Involvement		168
	A.	Community Development	168
	B.	Community Investment	169
	C.	Community Partnering	171
	D.	Start-Ups and Small Businesses	172
VI.	The Case for Community Engagement and Investment		172
VII.	Summary and Takeaways		173
VIII.	Practitioner's Resources Library		175
	A.	Articles	175
	B.	Books and White Papers	175
	C.	Instruments and Standards	175
	D.	Reporting	176

Chapter 9: Corporate Social Responsibility and Indigenous Rights — 177

- I. Introduction — 177
- II. Legal and Regulatory Requirements—Indigenous Rights — 178
  - A. Overview of Aboriginal Law in Canada — 178
  - B. Indigenous Rights Abroad — 184
- III. Norms, Standards, and Guidelines — 188
  - A. General Considerations: Indigenous and Human Rights — 188
  - B. The Role of International Standards and Guidelines — 188
  - C. International Standards in Canadian Policy: Industry Guidance in the Extractive Sector — 193
  - D. Additional Resources — 194
- IV. Trends — 195
- V. Best Practices — 196
- VI. Summary and Takeaways — 197

Chapter 10: Building a CSR Program through an Ethics and Compliance Program — 199

- I. Introduction — 199
- II. Sources of Legal Requirements for Corporate Ethics and Compliance Programs — 200
  - A. Overview of Legal Requirements: Consistent across Jurisdictions and across Standard-Setting Organizations — 200
  - B. Sources of Laws Requiring Reporting, Encouraging Reporting, and Incentivizing Employees to Report — 205
- III. Developing and Implementing an Ethics and Compliance Program — 209
  - A. Governance, Leadership, and Resources — 210
  - B. Risk Assessment — 213
  - C. Code of Conduct, Policies, Procedures — 214
  - D. Training and Communications — 216
  - E. Internal System to Report Concerns — 217
  - F. Monitoring and Auditing — 218
  - G. Responding and Remediating — 219
  - H. Managing Third Parties: Assessing Risk, Conducting Due Diligence, and Mitigating Risk — 220
- IV. Uber's Steps to Develop an Ethical Culture — 227
  - A. Overview — 227
  - B. Conducting a Risk Assessment — 227
  - C. Ousted Uber Leadership — 228
  - D. New Leadership Brought In — 229
  - E. Communicating Expectations — 230
  - F. Settling Up with Regulators and Others — 231
- V. Summary and Takeaways — 232

Chapter 11: Impact Investing — 233

- I. Introduction — 233
- II. Impact Investment Instruments — 234
  - A. Convertible Debt — 234

		B.	Preferred Equity	235
		C.	SAFEs	236
		D.	Bonds	236
	III.	Impact Investor Structures		237
		A.	For-Profit Funds Designed to Promote Impact	237
		B.	Foundations	240
		C.	Hybrid Funds	242
	IV.	Impact Measurement and Reporting		243
		A.	ESG Factors for Existing Public Companies	243
		B.	Integrated Reporting	244
		C.	New Corporate Forms	244
		D.	New Delaware Statutes	245
	V.	Summary and Takeaways		245
	VI.	Practitioner's Resource Library		245
		A.	List of Relevant Organizations	245
		B.	Articles and Reports	246

Chapter 12: Alternative Legal Entities — 249

	I.	Introduction		249
	II.	Overview		251
		A.	Understanding the Driving Forces behind the Proliferation of the New Corporate Forms	251
		B.	Marrying Nonprofits with For-Profits (Hybrid or Tandem Structures)	251
		C.	Overview of the New Types of Alternative Legal Entities—L3C, SPC/PBC, Benefit Corporations, Benefit LLCs	252
	III.	Hybrid (Tandem) Entities		253
		A.	Overview	253
		B.	Benefits of Hybrid Structures	254
		C.	Legal and Practical Issues with Hybrid Structures	254
		D.	General Requirements and Best Practices for Hybrid Structures	255
		E.	Hybrid Fund Structures	257
	IV.	For-Profit Entities		258
		A.	Overview	258
		B.	Benefit Corporation	258
		C.	Certain State Differences	261
	V.	Summary and Takeaways		268
	VI.	Practitioner's Resource Library		269
		A.	Articles	269
		B.	Books and White Papers	270
		C.	Instruments and Standards	270
		D.	Reporting	270

Chapter 13: Cybersecurity Risk Management Is a Corporate Responsibility — 271

	I.	Introduction — 271
	II.	What Is Cybersecurity? — 271

III.	Which Companies and Organizations Are Affected?		273
	A.	Critical Infrastructure	273
	B.	Regulated Industries	274
IV.	Sources of Law		275
	A.	Key Statutes	275
	B.	Regulation of Federal Systems	276
V.	Regulation of Federal Contractors		277
VI.	Regulation of the Private Sector		278
VII.	State Laws and Enforcement		278
VIII.	"Soft" Law		279
	A.	Where Does Soft Law Come From?	279
IX.	Global Challenges		284
	A.	Asia	285
	B.	Europe	285
X.	How Should a Responsible Organization Manage Cybersecurity Risk?		287
	A.	Key Task: Risk Management and Planning	287
	B.	Key Task: Handling Incidents	288
	C.	Key Task: Handling Vulnerabilities in Products, Services, or Websites	289
	D.	Key Task: Establishing and Maintaining Privilege	290
	E.	Key Task: Communicating with Customers and Others	291
	F.	Key Task: Information Sharing and Interacting with Government	292
	G.	Key Task: Handling Investigations and Litigation	294
XI.	Summary and Takeaways		295
XII.	Practitioner's Resource Library		295
	A.	Select Federal Guidance and Resources	295
	B.	Select Private Sector Guidance and Resources	296

Chapter 14: Working with Governments — 299

I.	Introduction		299
II.	The Case for CSR When Working with Governments		300
III.	Select Laws and Regulations When Working with Governments		302
	A.	Overview	302
	B.	Bribery	304
	C.	Gifts/Gratuities/Entertainment	304
	D.	Political Activity—Campaign Contributions and Lobbying	305
	E.	Conflicts of Interest Laws	307
	F.	Procurement Laws	308
	G.	Trade Sanctions and Export Regulations	309
IV.	Standards and Guidance When Working with Governments		310
	A.	Overview	310
	B.	International Organization for Standardization (ISO)	311
	C.	The Organisation for Economic Co-operation and Development (OECD)	311
	D.	United Nations Convention against Corruption	312
V.	Governance and Compliance When Working with Governments		312
	A.	Developing a CSR Program for Working with Governments	312

	B.	Developing a Strategic View to Compliantly Work with Governments	313
	C.	External Engagement	315
VI.		Summary and Takeaways	317

About the Editors   **319**
About the Authors   **321**
Index   **331**

Editors' Note

Corporate social responsibility (CSR) was once a voluntary exercise taken up by companies for business reasons ranging from reduced energy costs, to increased competitiveness in the market for talent, to improved corporate morale. With the recent advent of CSR laws and regulations, legal practitioners have been confronted by unique and burdensome CSR-related legal requirements, and CSR initiatives that were previously entirely voluntary have become inherently legal. Companies now face significant legal penalties, measurable litigation risk, and meaningful public relations fallout if they fail to address these requirements. In-house counsel face the prospect of having to "cut twice" if CSR programs are not designed and implemented with reference to existing, pending, and proposed CSR-related legal requirements.

One could reasonably make the case that the increasing frequency with which in-house and outside counsel have been confronted with legal issues that in one way or another implicate CSR concerns is one of the most notable legal trends of the past decade. Such issues can arise in disparate contexts ranging from supply chain compliance requirements related to minerals sourcing or anti-trafficking, to investor inquiries regarding environmental, social, and governance performance, to board governance regarding sustainability issues. The issues typically span various legal practices areas such as securities law, corporate governance, compliance, commercial law, labor law, and trade law, among others; indeed, it is difficult to find an area of the law or legal practice that is not in some way impacted by CSR considerations. Moreover, the issues are frequently fairly unique when compared to the matters typically addressed by corporate practitioners and require unique expertise; there is little in a business attorney's repertoire that lends itself to reporting on the tracing of minerals back to their sources in the Great Lakes region of Africa, or assessing whether a company should consider transitioning to one of a variety of alternative corporate forms that incorporate social goals. While there may be similarities among CSR issues in terms of the substantive concepts involved and the legal expertise required, it has historically been the case and continues to be the case today that it is difficult for a lawyer to acquire the knowledge and gain the experience required to effectively address them. As a result, in-house attorneys often manage these issues by involving operational teams within the business (e.g., supply chain, procurement, social responsibility), analogizing from their own legal backgrounds, and/or seeking input from outside counsel (even if such legal counsel has no specific expertise itself).

The need for guidance is rendered even more acute by the fact that although the number of CSR-specific legal positions is increasing, and although the number of law firms with dedicated CSR practice groups continues to grow, in many if not most cases, CSR law has no clear home within a business or law firm. CSR-related legal issues are too often handed off to the in-house corporate, compliance, or commercial attorney who draws the short straw, and law firm management too frequently fails to recognize the business case for a CSR practice. Clear and concise guidance is even more critical in the absence of institutional structure, as in-house and outside counsel will not receive the full benefit of repetition, precedent, peer benchmarking, market norms, and organizational knowledge. Furthermore, if any front-runner has begun to emerge, it is the legal department that is frequently being identified as the most appropriate home for CSR risk management and compliance, given lawyers' key role in enterprise risk management generally and their involvement in many of the work streams impacted by CSR developments, such as disclosure, governance, and contracting, to name a few.

Despite this need, there has yet to be a text published with the goal of providing an informed, sophisticated, but above all, eminently *useful* overview/survey of the various CSR-related legal issues that confront in-house and outside counsel on a regular basis. This text, which contains the distillation of the expertise and experience of many skilled attorneys, aims to fill this void in existing practitioner-focused legal guidance, particularly where institutional resources may be limited. This project presented many challenges, chief among them: (i) the small number of experts nationwide; (ii) the constantly changing legal landscape, with the consequence that content can quickly become stale or superseded; and (iii) the vast diversity of issues and related legal regimes that may reasonably be included within the bounds of CSR and CSR law, with some disagreement regarding where to draw the line.

The editors have attempted to overcome these challenges by (i) seeking out and soliciting contributions from the "short list" of experts, with a great deal of success, (ii) considering CSR's trends and trajectory in selecting topics that are relevant today and that the editors believe will continue to be relevant for years to come, with subsequent editions and online updates planned to address new legal and business issues that arise, and (iii) adopting an extremely broad and inclusive definition of CSR in an effort to provide a text that can serve as a practitioner's sole and comprehensive reference material on the topics addressed herein.

Indeed, in some cases—for example, the content relating to board governance, community relations, stakeholder engagement, and aboriginal rights—the chapters contained herein may be the first fulsome practice-oriented resources published on a particular topic. The editors are pleased to be able to offer such rare and specialized expertise regarding topics that are garnering an increasing amount of attention from corporate boards, corporate managers, and in-house counsel, and are immensely grateful for the efforts of the authors in preparing such contributions; the expertise may be niche in the sense that there are few who possess it, but it is by no means niche in terms of its applicability or relevance—these issues now impact a broad range of businesses, and in many ways.

As noted above, there will undoubtedly be some discussion and debate regarding the concept of CSR adopted by the editors and the authors, the nomenclature used throughout the book, and the decisions regarding what subject matter to include and what subject matter to exclude. Various labels abound—CSR, ESG, sustainability, human rights, business integrity, corporate/environmental stewardship—each reflecting a specific perspective and interpretation. Corporate adoption of one or the other descriptor may be a function of industry/peer practice, geographic location, institutional inertia, "tone at the top," strategic objectives, or any combination of the foregoing. Furthermore, there is as much if not more variety in opinions regarding the taxonomy of topics or issues that should be properly included under the heading of CSR law, and so here, too, there will likely be disagreement. Certain topics are clearly squarely within the province of CSR law (e.g., nonfinancial reporting, conflict minerals sourcing, combating trafficking in persons, alternative corporate forms) and others clearly implicate CSR issues (e.g., environment, health and safety, board governance, stakeholder engagement); for topics outside of these categories, the litmus test used by the editors in assessing whether appropriate for inclusion was whether such topic had substantive or practice-related themes in common with CSR law. Thus, the Foreign Corrupt Practices Act is included due to the common substantive theme of corruption and the similarity in the due diligence measures employed. The editors do not believe themselves to have been overly inclusive in this regard, as there exist other well-regarded taxonomies of CSR issues that include topics the editors opted not to address here, such as tax policy and technology transfer.

One topic that was not given its own chapter but that deserves attention here is the recent elevation of corporate social *purpose*. An increasing number of investors, companies, and thought leaders are taking the position that (i) companies must have a social purpose, (ii) companies must articulate and execute on this social purpose, and (iii) companies must measure and report on their achievement of/performance against this social purpose; and while this exercise involves CSR, it is not the same as CSR. Various versions of this thesis have been articulated recently by Larry Fink, CEO of BlackRock; Bill McNabb, chairman of Vanguard; Jana Partners and CalSTRS; the law firm Wachtell Lipton; Deloitte; and the British Academy's Future of the Corporation project, led by Colin Mayer, the Peter Moores Professor of Management Studies at Oxford University's Saïd Business School. This trend captures both the challenge and the opportunity afforded lawyers as a result of the emergence of CSR law: on the one hand, lawyers are left to wrestle with how to integrate these considerations into existing corporate governance and compliance structures; but on the other, they are also uniquely qualified to serve as invaluable advisors in helping clients navigate these issues and well positioned to play a significant role in the ongoing articulation and implementation of social purpose within corporations.

In the editors' view, this is the lawyer's charge when it comes to CSR and its impact on business—to help clients successfully traverse this brave new world. It is our hope that this book can support you in this effort by filling a major void in existing legal literature and providing a powerful tool for engaging in this important enterprise.

Chapter 1

Evolution of Corporate Social Responsibility

Travis Miller

Modern society relies on manufacturing and industrialization to transform cultures and their economies from agrarian societies to modern economies.[1] These industrial revolutions have materialized across many countries and created a divide between economies that have undergone this process (first-world economies) and those still undergoing the transition (second- and third-world economies).[2] During the transition, the society in question tends to focus on the rapid creation of wealth that often coincides with industrialization.[3]

To support these transitions, governments condone the creation of corporations and business entities that can accumulate sufficient resources and infrastructure at a relatively low risk.[4] However, local governments and the associated regulation are often not prepared to manage these new industrial processes safely and in an environmentally and socially conscious manner. As a result, industrial pollution and labor exploitation

---

1. Richard D. Fitzgerald, *The Social Impact of the Industrial Revolution*, GLOBAL ISSUES IN CONTEXT, http://find.galegroup.com/gic/infomark.do?&idigest=fb720fd31d9036c1ed2d1f3a0500fcc2&type=retrieve&tabID=T001&prodId=GIC&docId=CX3408502115&source=gale&userGroupName=itsbtrial&version=1.0 (last visited Mar. 30, 2016) (providing an overview of NEIL SCHLAGER, SCIENCE and Its TIMES: UNDERSTANDING THE SOCIAL SIGNIFICANCE OF SCIENTIFIC DISCOVERY, 378–81 (Josh Lauer, 1st ed. 2000)).

2. *See* ONE WORLD NATIONS ONLINE, www.nationsonline.org/oneworld/third_world_countries.htm (last visited Mar. 30, 2016).

3. Fitzgerald, *supra* note 1.

4. *See* Melvin A. Eisenberg, *Corporate Law and Social Norms*, 99 COLUM L. REV. 1253 (1999).

often occur before legal controls are implemented to prevent, reduce, or eliminate the adverse effects of industrialization.[5]

These corporate social responsibility (CSR) laws often carry sweeping mandates that obligate corporations and individuals to modify practices and behaviors. Moreover, the same corporate entities that obtained wealth during the jurisdiction's industrial revolution are called upon to manage and fund remediation caused by their actions.[6] Industries are then forced to respond by adapting their manufacturing processes, making new mandatory disclosures, and implementing complex supply chain management systems to deal with these shifting economic realities.[7] These external regulatory mandates form the basis of this book.

The pattern of industrial innovation, the corresponding environmental and behavioral regulations, and industry's reaction have become increasingly visible over the last several decades.[8] Accordingly, when attempting to predict, plan for, and invest in the compliance infrastructure for managing the regulations of tomorrow, there is great value in assessing and understanding the principles affecting the current regulatory environment.[9] Applying these constructs to a business's internal activities, emerging cases, and regulatory regimes offers insight and the ability to plan and manage the impact businesses face from a swelling number of global environmental controls.[10] This introductory chapter provides a background concerning three core regulatory movements that have driven and established a new area of legal practice, corporate social responsibility law.

I. REGULATING MANUFACTURING OPERATIONS AND POINT SOURCES

"Prior to the 1960s, environmental law did not exist as a discrete domestic and international legal category."[11] Humanity, as a species, has long considered its relationship with the natural world to be one of competition, whereby our principal objective was to overcome and domesticate the natural world.[12] However, as humanity accomplished this

---

5. ROBERT OLSON, ENVIRONMENTALISM AND THE TECHNOLOGIES OF TOMORROW: SHAPING THE NEXT INDUSTRIAL REVOLUTION 1–2 (Robert Olson & David Rejeski eds., 2d ed. 2004).

6. *See generally* Donald J. Kochan, *Corporate Social Responsibility in a Remedy-Seeking Society: A Public Choice Perspective*, 17 CHAPMAN L. REV. 413 (2014).

7. Daniel Berliner et al., *Governing Global Supply Chains: What We Know (and Don't) about Improving Labor Rights and Working Conditions*, 11 ANN. R. LAW & SOC. SCI. 193 (2015).

8. *See* Eric Orts, *A Reflexive Model of Environmental Regulation*, 5 BUS. ETHICS Q. 779 (1995), http://law.uh.edu/faculty/thester/courses/Emerging%20Tech%202011/orts%20on%20reflexive%20environmental%20law.pdf.

9. *See* Eric W. Orts, *Reflexive Environmental Law*, 89 Nw. U. L. REV. 1227, 1229 (1995).

10. *See* JOSEPH F. C. DIMENTO, THE GLOBAL ENVIRONMENT AND INTERNATIONAL LAW (1st ed., University of Texas Press, 2003).

11. DAN TARLOCK, ENVIRONMENTAL LAWS AND THEIR ENFORCEMENT 1 (A. Dan Tarlock & John C. Dernbach eds., 2001), http://www.eolss.net/sample-chapters/c04/e4-21-01.pdf [hereinafter ENVIRONMENTAL LAWS].

12. *See* DONALD G. KAUFMAN & CECILIA FRANZ, BIOSPHERE 2000: PROTECTING OUR GLOBAL ENVIRONMENT 7 (3rd ed. 2000), https://books.google.com/books?id=xBG99KR52mgC&pg=PA23&lpg=PA23&dq=people+believe+they+are+not+part+of+the+natural+world&source=bl&ots=S2SRv9C5kw&sig=HksfcDuPnNkWmSEO4armMTcJEqs&hl=en&sa=X&ved=0CDkQ6AEwBDgKahUKEwj2_PugmdLIAhVXW4gKHfjdBh8#v=onepage&q=people%20believe%20they%20are%20not%20part%20of%20the%20natural%20world&f=false.

objective and achieved its goals of controlling the environment and redirecting resources for society's use, the ensuing results shaped the concept that it was humanity's obligation to protect the natural world.[13] As a result, environmental law emerged and established a series of rules of engagement governing human and societal interaction with the natural world.

This first environmental movement focused on land conservation and point-source waste reduction based on the preservation of the "commons" for future generations.[14] The conservation movement took hold in reaction to the United States' industrial revolution following the consequences of industrial facilities: specifically, the resulting material use and chemical processing that created waste streams that flowed into point-source channels.[15] These point source channels of highly concentrated waste resulted in negative impacts on the populations near these facilities.[16]

The United States led in this area and passed highly complex technical regulations to control and modify the behavior of manufacturers.[17] To escape the costs of compliance and the impacts of the local populations' propensity toward NIMBYism,[18] corporations moved production to more welcoming and less-regulated jurisdictions and expanded industrialization globally.[19] The resulting outsourcing and migration of production reduced the net cost of corporate compliance and the impact of facility pollution on the local populous.[20] However, the burden of the pollution did not disappear, but rather shifted to unregulated jurisdictions, in second- and third-world economies. Without the tax and fee revenue from local jobs and permitting costs, many local governments did not have funds available to manage the waste streams from the finished goods and legacy cleanup efforts.[21] To compensate and adapt to this phenomenon, regulation was expanded to control the actual product through product stewardship-based legislation.[22]

---

13. *Id.* at 12.
14. Garrett Hardin, *The Tragedy of the Commons*, 162 SCIENCE 1243, 1243–48 (1968).
15. *See* U.S. GEOL. SURVEY, *Point Source Pollution* (Aug. 4, 2015, 2:26 PM), http://toxics.usgs.gov/definitions/point_source.html.
16. *See* William L. Andreen, *Water Quality Today—Has the Clean Water Act Been a Success?*, 55 ALA. L. REV. 537, 554 (2004).
17. *See generally* U.S. ENVTL. PROT. AGENCY, LAWS & REGULATIONS, http://www.epa.gov/laws-regulations (last visited Mar. 31, 2016).
18. Denis J. Brion, *An Essay on LULU, NIMBY, and the Problem of Distributive Justice*, 15 B.C. ENVTL. AFF. L. REV. 437, 438 (1988) (NIMBY stands for "not in my back yard").
19. Travis Miller, *Know Thy Product: The Global Expansion of Product Stewardship's Impact*, GEO. INT'L ENVTL. L. REV. Online 1 (2015), http://gelr.org/2015/05/08/know-thy-product-the-global-expansion-of-product-stewardship-laws-impact-on-environmental-law-georgetown-international-environmental-law-review/#_ftn2 (last visited Mar. 31, 2016). *See also* Dion Wiggins & Diane Morello, *Outsourcing Backlash: Globalization in the Knowledge Economy*, GARTNER (July 31, 2003), https://www.gartner.com/doc/405776/outsourcing-backlash-globalization-knowledge-economy.
20. *See* Alex L. Wang, *Regulating Domestic Carbon Outsourcing: The Case of China and Climate Change*, 61 UCLA L. REV. 2018, 2022 (2014).
21. *See generally* Allen Blackman, *Colombia's Discharge Fee Program: Incentives for Polluters or Regulators?* 90 J. ENVTL. MGMT. 101 (2009), http://www.sciencedirect.com/science/article/pii/S0301479707003398 (last visited March 31, 2016).
22. Noah Sachs, *Planning the Funeral at the Birth: Extended Producer Responsibility in the European Union and the United States*, 30 HARV. ENVTL. L. REV. 51, 90 (2006).

II. REGULATING PRODUCTS AND PRODUCT WASTE STREAMS

The second environmental movement has developed since the early 1990s and has focused on the regulation of the product. Product regulations can be seen as a direct consequence of globalization and outsourcing.[23] The product compliance phenomenon was driven to a large extent by an increase in the cost of domestic production in first-world economies and the subsequent shifting of manufacturing operations to alternative jurisdiction.[24] As a result, developed economies' point-source regulations became increasingly ineffective at combating pollution on a global scale as the origin of the pollution became more diffuse.[25] The resulting inability to regulate the manufacturing process and the loss of manufacturing jobs served as an impetus for governments to establish new regulatory regimes focused on product stewardship.[26]

The European Union (EU) leads the product compliance movement by institutionalizing a regional regulatory framework centered on the product's entry into the market of the regulating state.[27] The EU's initial foray into product stewardship[28] regulation came from the necessity of waste stream management: Europe had reached a critical point where the influx of heavily packaged foreign products into the local market had overwhelmed its waste management system.[29] As production had migrated away from European sites, there was no clearly established domestic actor that regulation could target to influence the toxicity of batteries,[30] effectively manage the influx of electronic waste,[31] or reduce the volume of packaging materials encasing everyday products.[32] Accordingly, the EU instituted a new regulatory regime based upon the environmental constructs of the "polluter pays principle."[33]

---

23. *See Green Paper and Related Documents*, EUROPEAN COMM'N, http://ec.europa.eu/environment/ipp/2001developments.htm (last visited Mar. 31, 2016); *see also* Nicole C. Kibert, *Extended Producer Responsibility: A Tool for Achieving Sustainable Development*, 19 J. LAND USE, 503, 510–11 (2004).

24. *See* Fred Hoerger et al., *The Cumulative Impact of Health, Environmental, and Safety Concerns on the Chemical Industry during the Seventies*, 46 DUKE L. & CONTEMP. PROBS. L. REV. 60, 62–63, 93 (1983), http://scholarship.law.duke.edu/cgi/viewcontent.cgi?article=3726&context=lcp (last visited Apr. 3, 2016).

25. *See* David Zaring, *Agriculture, Nonpoint Source Pollution, and Regulatory Control: The Clean Water Act's Bleak Present and Future*, 20 HARV. ENVTL. L. REV. 515, 515–17 (1996).

26. Kibert, *supra* note 23, at 510–11.

27. *See generally* Aaron Ezroj, *Extended Producer Responsibility Programs in the European Union: In Search of the Optimal Legal Basis*, 20 COLO. J. INT'L ENVTL. L. & POL'Y 199 (2009).

28. *Extended Producer Responsibility*, THE EUROPEAN ORGANIZATION FOR PACKING AND THE ENVIRONMENT, http://www.europen-packaging.eu/policy/9-extended-producer-responsibility.html (last visited Mar. 31, 2015).

29. Ezroj, *supra* note 27, at 221.

30. Council Directive 2013/56, 2013 O.J. (L 329) 5–9 (EU).

31. Council Directive 2012/19, 2012 O.J. (L 197) 38 (EU).

32. Council Directive 85/339, 1985 (EC).

33. Michael Cardwell, *The Polluter Pays Principle in European Community Law and Its Impact on United Kingdom Farmers*, 59 OKLA. L. REV. 89, 90–91 (2006).

The resulting regulation instituted a program of assessing fees to manufacturers and importers of products based upon the quantity of materials from imported products that entered the waste stream.[34] While impactful economically, the mindset shift toward a "precautionary principle"[35] would have substantially greater long-term implications. The most visible and tangible implication of product stewardship emerged from the propensity of the top-level original equipment manufacturer (OEM) to flow down regulatory inquiries onto the supply chain.[36] By engaging in this form of supply chain transparency initiative, as a format of choice for compliance, OEMs created an inherent need to know one's supplier and its respective businesses.[37] As either an inadvertent or perhaps a natural consequence, this business format allowed both nongovernmental organizations (NGOs) and later regulators to envision other social responsibility initiatives that could fit neatly within the scope of these supplier surveys.[38] Through advocacy and policy positioning, supply chain transparency initiatives aimed at combating societal ills were born and placed upon the manufacturer, with an expectation that manufacturers would assess and eradicate non-desirable activities on a global scale.[39]

III. BEHAVIORAL REGULATIONS AND MANDATORY CORPORATE DISCLOSURE

CSR has long been a vague and amorphous concept.[40] As a result of the divergent viewpoints concerning what CSR constitutes, industrial practices have emerged that seek to standardize and articulate a corporation's social practices.[41] In response, numerous corporations have published robust CSR reports, codes of conduct, and aspirational goals stating their respective intent to improve the environment and the human condition.[42] The emergence of these documents has driven increased scrutiny by

---

34. Ezroj, *supra* note 27, at 220.

35. *See generally* JOAKIM ZANDER, THE APPLICATION OF THE PRECAUTIONARY PRINCIPLE IN PRACTICE: COMPARATIVE DIMENSIONS (Cambridge University Press, 2010).

36. *See* The Conflict-Free Sourcing Initiative, *Five Practical Steps to Support SEC Conflict Minerals Disclosure* (2015), http://www.conflictfreesourcing.org/media/docs/CFSI%20White%20Paper-Conflict%20Minerals%20Disclosure-Feb%202015.pdf (last visited Mar. 31, 2016).

37. *Id.*

38. *See* Jane Nelson, *The Operation of Non-Governmental Organizations (NGOs) in a World of Corporate and Other Codes of Conduct* (2007), http://www.hks.harvard.edu/m-rcbg/CSRI/publications/workingpaper_34_nelson.pdf (last visited Mar. 31, 2016).

39. *Id.*

40. *See* Peter Nobel, *Social Responsibility of Corporation*, 84 CORNELL L. REV. 1255, 1255–56 (1999), http://scholarship.law.cornell.edu/clr/vol84/iss5/4/.

41. *See* Noam Noked, *The Corporate Social Responsibility Report and Effective Stakeholder Engagement*, HARVARD LAW SCHOOL FORUM ON CORPORATE GOVERNANCE AND FINANCIAL REGULATION (Dec. 28, 2013), https://corpgov.law.harvard.edu/2013/12/28/the-corporate-social-responsibility-report-and-effective-stakeholder-engagement/.

42. *See generally* JOHN W. HOUCK & OLIVER F. WILLIAMS, IS THE GOOD CORPORATION DEAD? (Rowman & Littlefield, 1996); J.E. PARKINSON, CORPORATE POWER AND RESPONSIBILITY (Clarendon Press, 1993).

stakeholder groups demanding their publication and further levels of transparency.[43] As discrepancies between the published work and the actual practices came to light, NGOs cried foul, eventually drawing the attention of governmental authorities.[44]

The resulting regulations mandated that if a company makes a statement, it has to be a truthful one.[45] Further, the laws shifted voluntary company disclosures to mandatory disclosures concerning specific unpalatable behaviors. The implications of globalization and the moral imperatives consumers and stakeholder communities began to superimpose upon corporate practices compounded these declaration risks.[46] As a result, the corporation or firm and its outsourcing partners were perceived as a whole in the context of the law and the mind-set of society.[47] Consequently, the choice of the corporation or firm to globalize its operations, and the corresponding challenges associated with gaining transparency concerning the behaviors of highly diversified operations, has emerged as a core regulatory challenge since 2010.[48]

IV. THE NEED FOR A CSR LAW PRACTITIONER'S MANUAL

The history of the aforementioned CSR movement combined with the current globalization trend focused on outsourcing has created increasingly challenging new obligations for companies around the globe and legal counsel supporting and interpreting these laws.[49] The respective calls to action have evolved into an established obligation for corporations to maintain a comprehensive approach to questions of social responsibility and balance continuously competing interests.[50] The format of these comprehensive approaches is to institutionalizing social responsibility initiatives in the form of international data collection exercises, structured implementations of robust codes of conduct, and the drafting and regular publication of non-financial disclosure reports highlighting the organizations' due diligence efforts and detected issues.[51]

---

43. Tiffany Derville Gallicano, *A Critical Analysis of Greenwashing Claims*, 5 PUB REL. J. 3 (2011), http://www.prsa.org/Intelligence/PRJournal/Documents/2011Gallicano.pdf.

44. INT'L INST. FOR SUSTAINABLE DEV., THE RISE AND ROLE OF NGOS IN SUSTAINABLE DEVELOPMENT, https://www.iisd.org/business/ngo/roles.aspx (last visited Mar. 31, 2016).

45. *See* Michelle Diffenderfer & Keri-Ann C. Baker, *Greenwashing: What Your Client Should Know to Avoid Costly Litigation and Consumer Backlash*, 25 NAT. RES. & ENV'T 21 (2011), http://www.americanbar.org/publications/gp_solo/2011/september/greenwashing_what_your_clients_should_avoid.html.

46. BUSINESS ETHICS: A EUROPEAN APPROACH 5–6 (Brian Harvey ed., 1994) ("Whatever the fine points of argument about the appropriateness of expecting moral responsibility from the legal entities we call corporations, it is certain that moral responsibility will be ascribed to them by those affected by their operations.").

47. *See* Nobel, *supra* note 40, at 1256.

48. *See* Lauma Skruzmane, *Globalization's New Face—Corporate Social Responsibility*, JAPAN FOREIGN TRADE COUNCIL ESSAY COMPETITION (2005), http://www.jftc.or.jp/discourse/data/second_1.pdf (last visited Mar. 31, 2016).

49. Kilian Moote, *SB 657 in Review: Why Businesses Have a Stake in Supply Chain Transparency*, SUSTAINABLE BRANDS (Oct. 19, 2015), http://www.sustainablebrands.com/news_and_views/stakeholder_trends_insights/kilian_moote/sb_657_review_why_businesses_have_stake_supp.

50. Nobel, *supra* note 40, at 1256.

51. *See generally* HOUCK & WILLIAMS, *supra* note 57; PARKINSON, *supra* note 57.

However, CSR laws, the regulatory authorities, and the public are responding to these institutionalized data-gathering and reporting practices by demanding greater action and accountability.[52] International companies are finding that their disclosures are subject to continually increasing scrutiny by a wide diversity of stakeholders who believe that corporate responsibility extends beyond the pursuit of profit.[53] Through this lens, both regulators and an increasingly informed customer base are placing pressure on corporate actors, demanding that a corporation be held accountable for the information released in their disclosure statements and that corporations implement socially conscious practices to avoid significant liabilities.[54]

Management of these escalating risks will require adaptation by industry and well-informed corporate counsel who can respond proactively to these challenges.[55] Corporate actors can no longer view CSR and supply chain transparency initiatives as a strategic marketing or public relations function.[56] Rather, corporations must analyze the supply chain's activities as a compliance obligation that demands the same level of scrutiny as the now ingrained internal functions of environmental, health, safety, quality, and compliance programs.[57] Practically, in spite of the altruistic goals of product stewardship and supply chain transparency goals, citizen calls to action concerning the highly publicized implications of corporate conduct have emerged as they did in the past with environmental regulations.[58] As a consequence, we can gain perspective and insight into the likely future of the most recent environmental movement based upon the historical pattern of public reaction to environmental laws. In that vein, the enforcement of these emerging regulations will strengthen and drive increased liability and costs onto corporate actors.[59]

In this context, the regulated community is entering the enforcement stage of emerging legal structures that warrant increased attention by counsel and senior executives.[60]

---

52. *See* Miriam A. Cherry & Judd F. Sneirson, *Beyond Profit: Rethinking Corporate Social Responsibility and Greenwashing after the BP Oil Disaster*, 85 TUL. L. REV. 983 (2011).

53. *See* ENVIRONMENTALISM and the TECHNOLOGIES of TOMORROW: SHAPING the NEXT INDUSTRIAL REVOLUTION 1–2 (Robert Olson & David Rejeski eds., 2003).

54. *See* Kochan, *supra* note 6, at 437 (discussing ways in which CSR advocates seek to influence corporate actors and hold them accountable).

55. *See* Sol Picciotto, *Introduction: Reconceptualizing Regulation in the Era of Globalization*, 29 J.L. & SOC'Y 1, 6 (2002) (describing suggestions for change in management that includes recognizing environmental concerns).

56. *See* Henri Servaes & Ane Tamayo, *The Impact of Corporate Social Responsibility on Firm Value: The Role of Customer Awareness*, 59 MGMT. SCI. 1045, 1058 (2013), http://faculty.london.edu/hservaes/ms2013.pdf (recognizing that CSR activities enhance firm value in limited situations).

57. *See* Lee Godden, et al., *Law, Governance and Risk: Deconstructing the Public-Private Divide in Climate Change Adaptation*, 36 UNSW L.J. 224, 231–233 (2013).

58. *See* Gábor Kecskés, *The Societal Effects of Environmental Disasters in International Environmental Regulation* (2014), http://papers.ssrn.com/sol3/papers.cfm?abstract_id=2432691 (last visited Apr. 2, 2016) (discussing impacts of environmental regulations implemented after natural disasters).

59. Moote, *supra* note 49 (suggesting that, based on the "global demand from consumers, governments, and investors ... for more transparency and accountability in corporate supply chains," failing to address problems in the business's supply chain is "a business risk not worth taking").

60. *See* KECSKÉS, *supra* note 58 (discussing *ex ante* and *post facto* regulation being implemented in response to environmental disaster).

The emerging regulatory regimes targeted at product stewardship (RoHS,[61] REACH,[62] conflict minerals) and the regulation of supply chain disclosures (Modern Slavery Act, FTC Green Marketing Guide,[63] California Transparency in Supply Chains Act) will drive these liabilities.[64] These regulations' end goal is to place the same burden and scrutiny onto the brand owner as exists for domestically produced products.[65] As such, it is both prudent and necessary for corporations to evaluate their manufacturing strategies and conclude whether the associated cost advantages of outsourcing production to other regions outweigh the burdens of the new regulatory demands.

This contemporary CSR landscape will continue to evolve and adapt to manage the norms of a more globalized world and diversified industrial sector. Consequently, the status of international human rights and the responsibility of protecting workers across the globe are a concern not only to governments but also to consumers and investors, and hence to business. The major policy changes associated with making CSR-related claims and the availability of information concerning business practices require corporations to perform increased due diligence. Moreover, greater demand for ethical products has increased the potential liability for organizations that fail to properly vet their CSR initiatives. Businesses must adapt to a future of regulatory-mandated CSR and supply chain transparency. In so doing, corporate actors and the counsel that support them must acknowledge, understand, and be capable of anticipating and accounting for the costs of compliance to reap the ample rewards of proactive good corporate citizenship.

---

61. Directive 2002/95/EC of the European Parliament and of the Council of January 27, 2003, on the restriction of the use of certain hazardous substances in electrical and electronic equipment, http://eur-lex.europa.eu/legal-content/EN/TXT/?uri=CELEX:32002L0095.

62. Regulation (EC) No. 1907/2006 of the European Parliament and of the Council of December 18, 2006, concerning the Registration, Evaluation, Authorisation and Restriction of Chemicals (REACH), establishing a European Chemicals Agency, amending Directive 1999/45/EC and repealing Council Regulation (EEC) No. 793/93 and Commission Regulation (EC) No. 1488/94 as well as Council Directive 76/769/EEC and Commission Directives 91/155/EEC, 93/67/EEC, 93/105/EC and 2000/21/EC, http://eur-lex.europa.eu/legal-content/EN/TXT/?uri=CELEX:32006R1907.

63. *See* Federal Trade Commission, Green Guides Website: https://www.ftc.gov/news-events/media-resources/truth-advertising/green-guides (last visited July 18, 2016).

64. *See* Wiggins & Morello, *supra* note 19 (discussing outsourcing patterns in industry).

65. *See* Erika C. Collins & Larissa Boz, *Full Disclosure: An Overview of Global Supply Chain Regulations*, PROSKAUR (Mar. 3, 2016), http://www.internationallaborlaw.com/2016/03/03/full-disclosure-an-overview-of-global-supply-chain-regulations/?utm_source=Mondaq&utm_medium=syndication&utm_campaign=View-Original.

Chapter 2

ESG, Sustainability, and CSR: Governance and the Role of the Board

David M. Silk, Sabastian V. Niles, and Carmen X.W. Lu

I. INTRODUCTION

The last few years have witnessed a tremendous increase in focus on, understanding of, and debate about the role of public and private companies with respect to environmental, social, and governance (ESG) issues, including the responsibilities of those companies to their employees, customers, suppliers, communities, and other stakeholders in addition to their shareholders (commonly referred to as "corporate social responsibility" or "CSR" issues). The growing focus on ESG and CSR issues evolves both from the concept of the "triple bottom line," which calls for companies to consider social and environmental costs of doing business,[1] and from the recognition that long-term corporate sustainability requires a commitment to more than short-term bottom-line profitability. A wide variety of concerns are covered by this debate, including sustainability, climate change risk management, resource management, diversity and inclusion, human rights, community relations, consumer and product safety, political lobbying, board composition, and shareholder engagement. As the debate has blossomed, so too has the understanding of

---

1. See J. ELKINGTON, CANNIBALS WITH FORKS: THE TRIPLE BOTTOM LINE OF 21ST CENTURY BUSINESS (John Wiley & Sons Ltd., 1997).

the importance of board oversight and governance in the management of each individual company's approach to and handling of these issues. Many institutional investors and a growing number of activist investors now recognize that proper board oversight and management of ESG risks and opportunities are critical for long-term value creation. As Larry Fink, chairman and CEO of BlackRock, reiterated in his 2018 letter to CEOs a "company's ability to manage environmental, social and governance matters demonstrates the leadership and good governance that is so essential to sustainable growth, which is why we are increasingly integrating these issues into our investment process."[2]

This chapter provides an overview of the legal framework governing board oversight of ESG concerns and explains why, beyond the bare legal requirements, ESG governance matters. It also examines the recent trends affecting ESG governance, outlines the components of ESG governance, and highlights ESG-related challenges facing boards and management teams. Finally, this chapter provides practical tips for boards in addressing ESG issues and case studies on how companies have approached their ESG concerns.

II. THE LEGAL FRAMEWORK

The core component of the board's role in addressing ESG concerns is ensuring that the board has met its fiduciary duties to the company and its shareholders through proper oversight. Under the business judgment rule, courts will not second-guess the decisions of boards made with due care and in good faith. The Delaware courts have taken the lead in formulating the national legal standard with respect to board oversight: as a basic rule, directors may be liable for a failure of board oversight only where there is "sustained or systemic failure of the board to exercise oversight—such as an utter failure to attempt to assure a reasonable information and reporting system exists."[3] The Delaware courts reaffirmed this standard in recent decisions where they have held that director liability for failure to monitor business risks arises only where there has been a "sustained or systemic failure" to exercise oversight.[4] While the current case law makes it difficult for plaintiffs to establish a breach of fiduciary duty by the board for failure to exercise proper oversight, boards are well advised to adhere to reasonable and prudent practices and should not structure their oversight policies around the minimum required to satisfy Delaware's business judgment rule. As ESG issues increasingly draw the attention of investors and impact a company's bottom line, it is important that boards remain informed and receive timely updates about the ESG issues affecting their companies.

---

2. L. Fink, *Larry Fink's 2018 Letter to CEOs: A Sense of Purpose,* BLACKROCK, https://www.blackrock.com/corporate/investor-relations/2018-larry-fink-ceo-letter.

3. *In re* Caremark Int'l Inc. Derivative Litig., CA No. 13670, 698 A.2d 959, 971 (Del. 1996).

4. Mem. Op. at 52, *In re* Goldman Sachs Grp., Inc. S'holder Litig., CA No. 5215 (Del. Ch. Oct. 12, 2011).

III. WHY BOARDS SHOULD CARE ABOUT ESG

ESG issues have become critically important to institutional investors in recent years. BlackRock, State Street, and Vanguard, three of the world's largest institutional investors, have all indicated that boards should spearhead efforts to incorporate ESG considerations into their companies' long-term business strategies and stay abreast of ESG-related trends. A number of activist investors have also indicated an interest in ESG. In 2018, activist firm ValueAct Capital launched the ValueAct Spring Fund,[5] which focuses on promoting environmental and social goals among its portfolio companies. The Spring Fund follows in the steps of similar moves by activist firms JANA Partners and Blue Harbor Group.

The growing interest in ESG among institutional investors and activist firms is driven by significant interest at the investor level: approximately $23 trillion are now invested according to ESG principles, and the volume of ESG investments in the United States has grown over 200 percent in the past decade.[6] ESG exchange-traded funds (ETFs) now hold over $11 billion in assets and 22 ESG-themed ETFs were launched in 2016–2017.[7] In the United States, women and millennials are driving interest in ESG investing. Recent surveys by U.S. Trust[8] and Morgan Stanley[9] found that more than 70 percent of women and 84 percent of millennials agreed that ESG factors are important considerations when making an investment. It is estimated that women now have decision-making control over an estimated 40 percent of all investable assets in the United States and some $30 trillion will pass from baby boomers to the younger generation over the next half century.[10]

Institutional investors are also paying attention to changes in the global regulatory landscape: the European Union is currently considering legislation that would require institutional investors, including pension funds and insurance companies, to demonstrate how their investments align with ESG concerns.[11] Countries including Japan, Germany, and the Netherlands have already introduced new regulations whose objective is to promote sustainable investment among asset managers.[12]

---

5. D. Faber, *The Faber Report: Jeff Ubben's ValueAct Launching Fund with Social Goals, Following Similar Moves by Jana, BlackRock,* CNBC (Jan. 19, 2018), https://www.cnbc.com/2018/01/19/jeff-ubbens-valueact-launching-fund-with-social-goal.html.

6. *Sustainable Investing Is Moving Mainstream,* J.P. MORGAN GLOBAL RESEARCH REPORT ON ESG (Apr. 20, 2018), https://www.jpmorgan.com/global/research/esg.

7. *Id.*

8. 2018 U.S. Trust Insights on Wealth and Worth Overview, Bank of America (June 2018).

9. Sustainable Signals, Asset Owners Embrace Sustainability, Morgan Stanley (June 2018).

10. *Morningstar Magazine,* Morningstar (Dec./Jan. 2018).

11. *Commission Legislative Proposals on Sustainable Finance,* EUROPEAN COMMISSION (May 24, 2018), https://ec.europa.eu/info/publications/180524-proposal-sustainable-finance_en.

12. *Sustainable Finance Moves into the Regulatory Mainstream,* KPMG (June 2018), https://home.kpmg.com/content/dam/kpmg/xx/pdf/2018/05/sustainable-finance.pdf.

Investor interest in ESG issues also reflects academic studies, some of which suggest that investments that take into account ESG factors can lead to long-term value creation. A 2015 meta-study by Deutsche Bank and the University of Hamburg revealed that 90 percent of studies indicated a positive correlation between a company's performance on ESG metrics and corporate financial performance.[13] Similarly, a study by Morgan Stanley in 2015 of mutual funds found that investments that focused on sustainability usually matched or exceeded the performance of traditional investments.[14]

While researchers continue to explore the relationship between ESG investing and investment returns, investors have already begun integrating ESG metrics into their investment decisions. According to Morrow Sodali's 2018 Institutional Investor Survey, over half of the 49 global institutional investors surveyed—managing a combined $31 trillion in assets—incorporated ESG policies into their investment decisions and all were signatories to the Principles for Responsible Investment, a UN framework setting forth a road map for incorporating environmental, social, and corporate governance issues into investment practices.[15] A 2015 CFA Institute survey of members working as portfolio managers and research analysts found that 57 percent assessed ESG factors in the whole investment analysis and decision-making process, while 36 percent looked to ESG factors for exclusionary screening.[16] Many large institutional investors also offer products that specifically target ESG factors. For example, in 2015, BlackRock launched the BlackRock Impact U.S. Equity Fund, a mutual fund catering to those who wish to exclusively invest in companies that meet certain measurable social and environmental outcomes. Barclays, meanwhile, launched the Women in Leadership Exchange Traded Notes in 2014, designed to provide investors with exposure to companies with female representation on their boards and management.[17]

With large institutional shareholders (and activist funds) incorporating ESG metrics into their investment decisions, the spotlight has naturally turned to how companies—notably their boards—are managing ESG issues. Investors are now looking to boards to set the right tone from the top and to develop long-term strategies for managing ESG risks and opportunities. Investors are also increasingly considering a company's ESG performance as a proxy for good governance. In response, independent governance organizations, including Institutional Shareholder Services (ISS), are measuring companies on their ESG performance. By taking charge of their companies' ESG concerns, boards can build rapport with their shareholders and boost investor confidence.

---

13. *ESG & Corporate Financial Performance: Mapping the Global Landscape*, DEUTSCHE ASSET & WEALTH MANAGEMENT (Dec. 2015), https://institutional.dws.com/content/_media/K15090_Academic_Insights_UK_EMEA_RZ_Online_151201_Final_(2).pdf.

14. *Sustainable Reality: Understanding the Performance of Sustainable Investment Strategies*, MORGAN STANLEY INSTITUTE FOR SUSTAINABLE INVESTING (Mar. 2015), https://www.morganstanley.com/sustainableinvesting/pdf/sustainable-reality.pdf.

15. *Institutional Investor Survey*, MORROW SODALI (2018), https://www.morrowsodali.com/attachments/1517483212-IIS_2018_final.pdf.

16. M. Orsagh, *CFA Institute Survey: How Do ESG Issues Factor into Investment Decisions?*, CFA INSTITUTE (Aug. 17, 2015), https://blogs.cfainstitute.org/marketintegrity/2015/08/17/cfa-institute-survey-how-do-esg-issues-factor-into-investment-decisions.

17. *Product Summary: Barclays Women in Leadership ETN*, BARCLAYS (2018), http://www.etnplus.com/US/7/en/details.app?instrumentId=269035.

IV. RECENT TRENDS INFLUENCING GOVERNANCE ON ESG

There are a number of trends that boards may wish to consider when addressing ESG issues. These trends are driven by several factors, including investor priorities, regulatory developments, and current events. The key trends include growing investor scrutiny of board composition, the proliferation of ESG disclosure frameworks and ratings, continued growth in shareholder engagement with boards and management on ESG issues, and a shift from the shareholder to stakeholder view of corporate governance.

A. Board Composition and Diversity

A key ESG concern for investors is board composition. According to Morrow Sodali's 2018 survey[18] of institutional investors, respondents ranked board skills and expertise as the most important ESG issue for further engagement with companies, ahead of climate risk disclosure and cybersecurity risk. Investors want boards to have the appropriate balance of skills, experience, independence, and knowledge, and want companies to disclose detailed information on board composition to shareholders. Investors are also calling for companies to maintain a formal, transparent, and continuous process for monitoring the composition of their boards and to ensure regular board refreshment.[19]

Diversity, in particular gender diversity on boards, is also a hot-button ESG issue.[20] The SEC is currently considering introducing new rules that would require companies to describe in their proxy statements the extent to which their boards are diverse and to disclose the racial, gender, and ethnic composition of their boards.[21] The new proposals would expand on proxy rules introduced by the SEC in 2009, which require companies to disclose how boards consider diversity when identifying director nominees.[22] Meanwhile, the Office of the New York City Comptroller last year launched its Boardroom Accountability Project 2.0[23] to boost the number of women and minorities on boards. Since the project's launch in September 2017, more than 85 companies

---

18. *Institutional Investor Survey*, *supra* note 15.
19. *See, e.g.*, R. Kumar, *Addressing the Need for Board Refreshment and Director Succession in Investee Companies*, State Street Global Advisors (Nov. 2017), https://www.ssga.com/investment-topics/environmental-social-governance/2017/Addressing-the-Need-for-Board%20Refreshment-in-Investee-Companies.pdf.
20. S. Krouse, *BlackRock: Companies Should Have at Least Two Female Directors*, Wall Street Journal (Feb. 2, 2018), https://www.wsj.com/articles/blackrock-companies-should-have-at-least-two-female-directors-1517598407.
21. Recommendation regarding Disclosure of Board Diversity, *SEC Advisory Committee on Small and Emerging Companies* (Dec. 2016), https://www.sec.gov/info/smallbus/acsec-board-diversity-recommendation.pdf.
22. L. Aguilar, *Commissioner, U.S. SEC, Speech at Agenda Luncheon Program, Board Diversity: Why It Matters and How to Improve It* (Nov. 4, 2010), https://www.sec.gov/news/speech/2010/spch110410laa.htm.
23. Comptroller Stringer, *NYC Pension Funds Launch National Boardroom Accountability Project Campaign—Version 2.0*, https://comptroller.nyc.gov/services/financial-matters/boardroom-accountability-project/boardroom-accountability-project-2-0.

have refreshed their boards to improve diversity and to increase the transparency of nomination procedures. The Office of the New York City Comptroller is not alone in its push for boardroom diversity: during the past proxy season, State Street voted against 511 companies whose director slates failed to include any women. The move reportedly prompted 152 companies that previously had all-male boards to add at least one female director.[24]

B. Disclosure and ESG Ratings

As ESG becomes integrated into investment decisions and business strategies, companies and investors have focused attention on disclosing and measuring ESG performance. While there currently is no universally accepted set of benchmarks for measuring ESG performance, ESG disclosure frameworks such as the Sustainability Accounting Standards Board (SASB), the Global Reporting Initiative (GRI), and the International Integrated Reporting Council (IIRC) have proliferated in recent years. In addition, several stock exchanges, including the London and Hong Kong Stock Exchanges, have set forth guidance on ESG reporting. A report by the Governance & Accountability Institute revealed that the number of S&P 500 companies reporting on their ESG performance grew from 53 percent in 2012 to 85 percent in 2017.[25] Companies have also come under pressure to disclose ESG risks, notably climate change risk, as part of their periodic SEC filings.[26]

Companies are also being rated on their ESG performance. In February 2018, ISS announced the launch of its Environmental and Social QualityScore, which measures the quality of corporate disclosures on environmental and social issues, including sustainability governance, and identifies disclosure omissions. ISS's expectations on ESG disclosure practices are based on specific environmental and social risks identified for each industry and reflect standards and recommendations from groups including GRI, SASB, and the Task Force on Climate-Related Financial Disclosures. ISS is entering an already crowded field of ESG-ratings agencies: Bloomberg, Dow Jones, MSCI, RepRisk, Sustainalytics, Corporate Knights Global, and Thomson Reuters already provide assessments of ESG performance.

C. Increased Stakeholder Engagement

Board engagement on ESG issues remains a priority for shareholders. In 2017, 72 percent of S&P 500 companies disclosed engagement with shareholders, up from 6 percent

---

24. R. Vlastelica, *More Than 150 Companies Have Added Women to Their Previously All-Male Boards: State Street*, MARKETWATCH (Mar. 8, 2018), https://www.marketwatch.com/story/more-than-150-companies-have-added-women-to-their-previously-all-male-boards-state-street-2018-03-07.

25. *Flash Report: 85% of S&P 500 Index Companies Publish Sustainability Reports in 2017*, GOVERNANCE & ACCOUNTABILITY (G&A) INSTITUTE (Mar. 20, 2018), https://www.ga-institute.com/press-releases/article/flash-report-85-of-sp-500-indexR-companies-publish-sustainability-reports-in-2017.html.

26. *See, e.g.*, *SEC Sustainability Disclosure Search Tool*, CERES (May 31, 2018), https://www.ceres.org/resources/tools/sec-sustainability-disclosure-search-tool.

in 2010, and 29 percent of companies disclosed engagement involving directors, up from 25 percent in 2016.[27] Certain major institutional investors have now begun setting annual engagement priorities covering ESG issues. BlackRock, for example, has made shareholder engagement a centerpiece of its investment strategy, noting that "many of our engagements are triggered because companies have not provided sufficient information in their disclosure to fully inform our assessment of the quality of governance, including the exposure to and management of environmental and social factors."[28] BlackRock's key engagement priorities for 2018 include governance, corporate strategy, compensation, climate risk disclosure, and human capital.[29] State Street has also released similar global guidelines on proxy voting and engagement principles, which focus on issues including compensation, accounting and audit-related issues, capital structure, and environmental and social issues.[30]

D. Shareholder versus Stakeholder Models of Corporate Governance

At a structural and societal level, the focus on ESG concerns, as part of a renewed focus on the need for long-term value creation, has led to a reexamination of the relationship among corporations and their constituents. Larry Fink made this shift clear when he stated in his 2018 letter to CEOs that "companies must benefit all of their stakeholders, including shareholders, employees, customers, and the communities in which they operate."[31] Fink's letter echoed principles outlined in the New Paradigm of Corporate Governance, issued by the International Business Council of the World Economic Forum, which endorses the view that companies ought to take into account a "broader group of stakeholders, including employees, suppliers, customers, creditors and the community."[32] The New Paradigm seeks to recalibrate the relationship between public corporations and their major institutional investors and conceives of corporate governance

---

27. *Ernst & Young Center for Board Matters: Board Matters Quarterly*, ERNST & YOUNG (June 2017), https://www.ey.com/Publication/vwLUAssets/EY-board-matters-quarterly-june-2017/$FILE/EY-board-matters-quarterly-june-2017.pdf.

28. A. Friedman, R. McCormick, C. Spitler, & R. Zvinuska, *BlackRock's 2017–2018 Engagement Priorities*, THE HARVARD LAW SCHOOL FORUM ON CORPORATE GOVERNANCE AND FINANCIAL REGULATION (Mar. 17, 2017), https://corpgov.law.harvard.edu/2017/03/17/blackrocks-2017-2018-engagement-priorities.

29. *BlackRock Investment Stewardship Engagement Priorities for 2018*, BLACKROCK (Mar. 2018), https://www.blackrock.com/corporate/literature/publication/blk-stewardship-2018-priorities-final.pdf.

30. *Global Proxy Voting and Engagement Principles*, STATE STREET GLOBAL ADVISORS (Mar. 2018), https://www.ssga.com/investment-topics/environmental-social-governance/2018/03/Global-Proxy-Voting-and-Engagement-Principles-2018.pdf.

31. L. Fink, *Larry Fink's 2018 Letter to CEOs: A Sense of Purpose*, BLACKROCK, https://www.blackrock.com/corporate/investor-relations/2018-larry-fink-ceo-letter.

32. M. Lipton, S. Rosenblum, S. Niles, S. Lewis, & K. Watanabe, *The New Paradigm: A Roadmap for an Implicit Corporate Governance Partnership between Corporations and Investors to Achieve Sustainable Long-Term Investment and Growth*, WORLD ECONOMIC FORUM (Sept. 2, 2016), http://www.wlrk.com/docs/thenewparadigm.pdf.

as a collaboration among corporations, shareholders, and other stakeholders working together to achieve long-term value and resist short-termism. In this framework, if a corporation and its board and management team are diligently pursuing well-conceived strategies that were developed with the participation of independent, competent, and engaged directors, and its operations are in the hands of competent executives, it is contemplated that investors will support the corporation and refuse to support short-term financial activists seeking to force short-term value enhancements without regard to long-term value implications. As part of their stewardship role, institutional investors would be expected to work to understand corporations' strategies and operations and engage with them to provide corporations with opportunities to understand the investors' opinions and to adjust strategies and operations in order to receive the investors' support.

Alongside discussions of new frameworks for stakeholder relations, several states have adopted "benefit corporation" statutes that explicitly enable corporations to pursue societal benefits in addition to or in lieu of maximization of shareholder value. These types of provisions have been adopted by at least 34 states, including Delaware, and provide an alternative that companies can voluntarily follow to strike an appropriate balance between the interests of shareholders and other stakeholders. And more recently, the Accountable Capitalism Act proposed by Senator Elizabeth Warren seeks to federalize all public corporations with revenues in excess of $1 billion and aims to restructure these corporations such that business decisions take into account the needs of a wide range of employee and community stakeholders.

V. COMPONENTS OF THE ESG GOVERNANCE FRAMEWORK

A. Board Oversight

In satisfying both their fiduciary duties and the desire of investors to ensure that companies are fully engaged on ESG matters, boards may wish to pay particular attention to the following issues: board composition; the identification and disclosure of ESG risks and opportunities; regulatory compliance; and shareholder and stakeholder engagement. As the public conversation on the role of companies in addressing ESG issues continues to evolve, boards should consider how their risk oversight role specifically applies to various ESG-related risks. In large part, the board's function in overseeing management's identification and assessment of material ESG-related risks, such as supply chain disruptions, energy sources and alternatives, labor practices, and environmental impacts, involves both issue-specific and company-specific application of general risk oversight practices. However, as the public and investors scrutinize how companies address ESG issues, the board, working with management, should make a particular effort to ensure that its risk oversight role is satisfied with regard to various ESG risks. As part of this process, management should identify whether there are any emerging ESG issues or trends that could materially impact the company's ability to create long-term sustainable value and consider how best to allocate corporate resources toward managing the most critical ESG risks.

In considering how to allocate responsibility for oversight of ESG issues, boards can generally take one of three approaches: (i) oversight at the full board level, (ii) oversight through one of its standing committees, or (iii) oversight through a separately chartered committee dedicated to ESG issues. Some companies have formalized board- or committee-level review of these matters, especially as to those posing material risks to the business, and reference such reviews in committee charters and board-level governance guidelines. Doing so is a company-specific decision; review of these topics does not need to be delegated to a committee and may be considered by the board as a whole. To the extent that ESG matters are covered in committee charters, it is important that they be considered by the committee on a timely basis and reported to the full board. Currently, most boards continue to oversee ESG issues through current standing committees or at the full board level. According to the National Association of Corporate Directors' 2017 Director Compensation Report issued last year, a survey of 1,400 public companies showed that only slightly more than 5 percent of boards have designated committees specifically to address ESG issues. Still, boards should be aware that certain institutional investors such as Vanguard now expect boards to "seek out third-party perspectives and information instead of relying solely on the opinions of management" and to be "actively evaluating [sustainability] issues and integrating sustainability risks—and related business opportunities—into their strategic decision-making."[33]

B. Partnership with Management

To ensure proper oversight of ESG risks, the board and management should be aligned on the company's ESG goals and oversight processes. The board should take the lead, but also work closely with management, to set the tone at the top. ESG matters often have important reputational impacts and significant public, investor and stakeholder relations dimensions. The board may wish to consider working closely with management to identify which ESG issues are most pertinent to the company's business and major stakeholders and to oversee the implementation of appropriate policies and processes for assessing, monitoring, and managing material ESG risks and opportunities. In addition, the board may wish to work with management to determine how best to integrate ESG risks and opportunities into strategic and operational planning, crisis preparedness and risk management, investor and stakeholder communications, budgets, resource allocation, and incentive structures.

ESG risks are dynamic and the priorities of investors and other stakeholders continue to evolve. For these reasons, the board would be well advised to monitor and regularly review the company's ESG performance. In particular, management should periodically monitor the level of ESG disclosure by competitors and market cap peers pursuant to disclosure standards organizations with significant industry backing (such as SASB, GRI, and IIRC) and determine, in consultation with the board, the company's disclosure

---

33. *Investment Stewardship 2018 Annual Report, Vanguard* (2018), https://about.vanguard.com/investment-stewardship/perspectives-and-commentary/2018_investment_stewardship_annual_report.pdf.

posture with respect to these or other emerging approaches. A board may also consider tracking the overall progress of the company's ESG goals and ensuring that the company has established objective, measurable criteria for assessing its progress.

C. Board Composition and Capacity

The board should also be cognizant of its own skill set with respect to ESG. A handful of large companies in high-profile ESG areas have appointed directors who are also experts on ESG issues. For example, ExxonMobil last year elected climate scientist Susan Avery to its board and in 2012 ConocoPhillips named Jody Freeman, who previously served as an independent consultant to the National Commission on the Deepwater Horizon Oil Spill, to its board. Institutional investors such as BlackRock actively encourage boards to be familiar with ESG issues relating to their companies.[34] Not every director or member of senior management can be an ESG expert, and it is not currently mainstream practice for boards to recruit specific ESG experts as directors. Still, directors and appropriate company personnel should educate themselves on the key ESG issues facing the company and be able to converse comfortably on those issues that matter or present significant risks. Well-resourced companies are also increasingly developing specialized in-house expertise and updating internal reporting and business unit structures to have greater capacity in these areas.

The board should also consider its composition in light of ESG best practices. As discussed in Section IV.A, the diversity of the board itself is seen by many investors and reporting bodies as a stand-alone ESG issue. GRI considers board diversity as part of its data on a company's public disclosures, and the SEC requires similar disclosures on whether, and if so how, companies have considered diversity in identifying director nominees.[35] Directors should first and foremost possess a diversity of skill sets: qualifications that are aligned with the company's strategic goals, stakeholders, and risk oversight goals. Investors and ratings agencies are also looking at whether there is diversity (notably gender diversity) within the board, board refreshment practices, composition of board committees, director interlocks and conflicts, and tenure.

D. Shareholder and Stakeholder Engagement

The board, together with management, plays an important role in guiding the company's public messaging and engagement with shareholders and other stakeholders on ESG issues. The board should be informed about the company's approach to dealing with investor requests for ESG-related engagement, external disclosure and reporting of the company's approach, response, and progress on these matters. In determining what kind

---

34. *21st Century Engagement: Investor Strategies for Incorporating ESG Considerations into Corporate Interactions*, BLACKROCK (Mar. 31, 2015), https://www.blackrock.com/corporate/literature/publication/blk-ceres-engagementguide2015.pdf.

35. Recommendation regarding Disclosure of Board Diversity, *supra* note 21.

of external communication and, as determined appropriate by the company, what kind of reporting will be pursued, companies should develop a view on whether sustainability information, corporate responsibility initiatives, and progress will be publicly shared on the company's website or in other forums and periodically monitor actions taken by industry peers. In some cases, companies will embrace appropriate public reporting on specific ESG issues over acceptable time frames. Companies will also have to deal with pressure to set—and disclose—specific goals and targets. When constructively avoiding premature, immaterial, or duplicative disclosures, or those that involve unwarranted time, effort, or cost, it is prudent to also recognize that a complete lack of transparency is unlikely to be a sustainable approach over the long term. In the current environment, disclosure of the right kind may be viewed as an opportunity instead of just as a cost. Communications on ESG strategy need not be limited to annual or quarterly reports but can extend to sustainability reports and presentations and letters to investors.

VI. CHALLENGES AND OPPORTUNITIES FOR BOARDS OF DIRECTORS AND MANAGEMENT TEAMS

The growing importance of ESG presents multiple challenges—and opportunities—for boards. We identify below what we believe will be key challenges for boards in the next few years.

A. Reconciling the Growth of ESG Metrics and Ratings with the Needs of the Company

Companies should be prepared for more third-party information requests from emerging ESG-ratings services and existing providers (e.g., the proxy advisory firm ISS's new Environmental & Social QualityScore and accompanying list of 300-plus questions for companies to complete). Some of these entities seek to impose on public companies the burden of providing data for third-party, subscription-based services. The products and any asserted benefits of ESG-ratings services should be assessed carefully, especially those that fail to demonstrate consistent quality and accuracy. Management should be selective when allocating resources toward such services, including as to error-checking, and should consider whether increased investment in the company, improved positioning, or other benefits will in fact result. Boards may wish to follow the approaches taken by major institutional investors and decide whether it makes sense to integrate those metrics into internal assessments of the company's ESG performance. State Street,[36]

---

36. K. Kastiel, *ESG Risks and Opportunities Facing Investee Companies*, THE HARVARD LAW SCHOOL FORUM ON CORPORATE GOVERNANCE AND FINANCIAL REGULATION (Nov. 30, 2014), https://corpgov.law.harvard.edu/2014/11/30/esg-risks-and-opportunities-facing-investee-companies.

for example, notes that the factors it uses to analyze companies include the quality of the company's ESG disclosure, the relative performance of a company's sustainability program compared to that of its peers, the underlying economics of its sustainability initiatives, and the level of board involvement and oversight on the company's sustainability practices.

B. Ensuring Adequate, Accurate, and Timely Disclosures

Another challenge for boards is ensuring accurate, timely, and comprehensive disclosure of material ESG risks. In light of the ever-evolving regulatory and disclosure landscape, boards will need to work with management to stay abreast of both internal ESG reporting and external disclosure requirements. This task is particularly important for companies with a global presence, where a variety of ESG disclosure guidelines have been introduced in recent years. In the United States, legal reporting requirements on ESG are still guided by the SEC's materiality standards. In Europe, however, legal obligations surrounding ESG disclosure are evolving more rapidly. The European Commission has recently proposed new rules that will require institutional investors to disclose the sustainability or climate impact of their products and portfolios.[37] The proposed rules, if implemented, would require asset managers, pension funds, and insurers to report on procedures to integrate ESG risks into their investment and advisory processes, and the extent to which these risks are expected to have an impact on financial returns. Meanwhile, an increasing number of stock exchanges, including the London Stock Exchange, the Nasdaq, and the Singapore Exchange, have issued guidelines on ESG disclosures.[38]

C. Capitalizing on ESG Risks and Opportunities

For a long time, many companies have regarded ESG issues as "softer" concerns that did not have a meaningful impact on business. Not anymore. Today, companies are being pressed to find ways to integrate ESG into their business mission. Boards and management may be increasingly asked to search for opportunities that align ESG investments with the company's business strategy and long-term viability. In the process, the board and management will have to make trade-offs, engage in potential disruptions to the company's business, and adopt an innovative mind-set.

Boards should appreciate that in some industries and sectors, sustainability and other ESG initiatives may have clear (and positive) impacts on a company's bottom line and may provide business benefits and competitive advantages over peers; in other businesses

---

37. S. Rust, *European Commission Unveils Sustainable Finance Legislative Proposals*, IPE (May 24, 2018), https://www.ipe.com/news/esg/european-commission-unveils-sustainable-finance-legislative-proposals/10024869.article.

38. *See, e.g., Seven Stock Exchanges Launch ESG Reporting Guidance*, SUSTAINABLE STOCK EXCHANGES (Mar. 23, 2017), http://www.sseinitiative.org/home-slider/shanghai-stock-exchange-joins-united-nations-sustainability-initiative.

and contexts, the impact may be less clear, certain, or measurable. Companies should consider the value proposition of these kinds of initiatives relative to other business priorities and opportunities. The calculus for this, however, will continue to develop, especially as more institutional investors consider sustainability as an investment priority and more companies take a proactive but targeted approach to these issues.

VII. PRACTICAL TIPS FOR BOARDS OF DIRECTORS

While boards should strive to develop an approach to managing ESG issues that best suits the needs of their particular company, below are some high-level suggestions on how boards may wish to focus their attention.

A. Articulate Clear Goals and Approaches on ESG Issues

Boards should be aware that sustainability has become a major, mainstream governance topic that encompasses a wide range of issues, including a company's long-term durability as a successful enterprise, climate change and other environmental risks and impacts, systemic financial stability, management of human capital, labor standards, resource management, and consumer and product safety, and consequently, boards should consider how the company presents itself with respect to these matters. Boards should work with management to focus on a company's ESG goals by considering what are the most important risks and opportunities facing the company and assessing their connection to ESG matters.

B. Determine Approach to Stakeholder Engagement and Maintain Consistent Messaging

If faced with an activist investor sounding ESG-linked themes, leverage prior preparedness and apply best practices to respond. If faced with a shareholder proposal addressing these matters, have an appropriate governance process for considering the proposal, its business implications, and the company's options, including as to negotiating a withdrawal of the proposal on acceptable terms, pursuing legitimate exclusion under SEC rules, or taking the proposal to a shareholder vote (while recommending for, against, or taking no position on it) and securing investor support. In some situations, companies may want to present shareholders with a more preferable, management-backed approach or proposal. Tailored, company-specific approaches to these issues are significantly better than simply taking a one-size-fits-all, overly rigid approach.

C. Build Human Capital to Manage ESG over the Long Term

Well-resourced companies are increasingly developing specialized in-house expertise and updating internal reporting and business unit structures. In such cases, the board should ensure that in-house experts are integrated throughout the company's value chain and report regularly to the board and management.

VIII. CASE STUDIES

A. Salesforce.Com: Integrating ESG into Its Business Strategy

Salesforce.com, an on-demand customer relationship management technology company based in San Francisco, was recently named by Calvert Research and Management as one of the most sustainable companies among the 1,000 largest publicly traded companies in the United States.[39] In compiling its rankings, Calvert reviewed more than 300 performance indicators to measure performance in five key stakeholder categories: shareholders, employees, customers, community, and planet.[40] The rankings took into account the financial materiality of each stakeholder category within a company's industry peer group.[41]

Salesforce publishes an annual stakeholder report that discloses its approach to ESG issues and highlights how the company has integrated ESG concerns into core parts of its business, beginning with its company culture and extending to its governance structure, sustainability and philanthropic initiatives, and labor and workforce policies. The company has also developed internal processes for monitoring and reporting its performance on a variety of ESG metrics.[42] In his 2018 letter to investors, CEO Marc Benioff reiterated the importance of the company's commitment not just to its shareholders but to the community at large: "Truly great companies care about all of their stakeholders—employees, customers, partners, shareholders, the communities where we live and work, and the environment that sustains us."[43]

While the precise ranking measurements used by Calvert are proprietary, it would appear that the following items (disclosed by Salesforce) contribute to its success on the survey: at the governance level, Salesforce adheres to best practices consistent with ISS recommendations and applicable SEC and NYSE requirements; maintains a code of conduct and business conduct principles that address a variety of ESG-related issues; maintains a supplier diversity program to align the behaviors of its suppliers with the values of the company and a health safety program for its personnel; and discloses its political activities, including political action committees, lobbying, policy positions, and board oversight of such activities. With respect to customers, Salesforce notes that it is particularly cognizant of cybersecurity risk and employs a multilayered security system, including a platform that provides customers with real-time information on system performance and security.

---

39. L. Norton, *Barron's 100 Most Sustainable Companies*, BARRON'S (Feb. 3, 2018), https://www.barrons.com/articles/barrons-100-most-sustainable-companies-1517605530.

40. *100 Most Sustainable Companies*, CALVERT RESEARCH AND MANAGEMENT (Feb. 3, 2018), https://www.calvert.com/100-most-sustainable-companies.php.

41. *Id.*

42. *FY18 Stakeholder Impact Report Blazing a Trail toward a Better, More Equal World*, SALESFORCE (2018), https://www.salesforce.com/content/dam/web/en_us/www/documents/reports/sustainability-FY18-stakeholder-impact-report.pdf.

43. *Id.*

In addressing Calvert's planet stakeholder category, Salesforce notes that environmental sustainability is a core component of its business strategy: the company is a signatory to a number of environmental coalitions and in 2018 became a net-zero greenhouse gas emissions company. Salesforce also notes that it actively measures and discloses its annual emissions and energy consumption, including emissions arising from business travel and employee commuting. Meanwhile, with respect to the community aspect of Calvert's survey, Salesforce notes that it has integrated ESG concerns into its philanthropic activities, including with the introduction of an investment fund that aims to accelerate the growth of companies using the company's technology to address challenges in workforce development, equality, sustainability, and the social sector. Salesforce's annual stakeholder report reflects an effective integration of ESG concerns into a corporate mission and is an example of a company translating its messaging into concrete actions and goals whose performance and outcomes are regularly assessed and disclosed.

B. Peabody Energy and Exxon Mobil: The Disclosure of Material Climate Change Risks

Public filings have emerged as another battlefield for climate change activists and politicians. Litigation and activist pressures are forcing companies, especially in the fossil fuels sector, to disclose the material risks of climate change.

In 2010, the SEC issued interpretive guidance covering the potential inclusion of climate change risks within the existing disclosure regime.[44] The SEC highlighted the potential for climate change regulations, financial uncertainty, and operational considerations to affect existing markets, suppliers, and customers. However, the SEC sought to frame this discussion under the existing regulatory context. The current disclosure regime focuses on headings such as regulatory compliance, legal proceedings, risk factors, and management discussion and analysis. The SEC noted that these topics can reasonably include relevant climate risks.

Prior to the SEC's guidance, the New York Attorney General had already reached settlements with three energy companies over their emissions disclosures.[45] Since then, the New York Attorney General has continued to push forward on enforcement, while the SEC remains less active.

---

44. E. Murphy, *Secretary, Interpretation: Commission Guidance regarding Disclosure Related to Climate Change*, SECURITIES AND EXCHANGE COMMISSION (Feb. 2, 2018), https://www.sec.gov/rules/interp/2010/33-9106.pdf.

45. *Attorney General Cuomo, Joined by Vice President Gore, Announces Agreement with Major Energy Company, Dynegy Inc.*, NEW YORK STATE ATTORNEY GENERAL (2008), https://ag.ny.gov/press-release/attorney-general-cuomo-joined-vice-president-gore-announces-agreement-major-energy; *Attorney General Cuomo Announces Agreement with Aes to Disclose Climate Change Risks to Investors*, NEW YORK STATE ATTORNEY GENERAL (2009), https://ag.ny.gov/press-release/attorney-general-cuomo-announces-agreement-aes-disclose-climate-change-risks-investors.

A 2015 settlement between Peabody Energy and the New York Attorney General highlights emerging disclosure risks, particularly when companies' external messaging can be read to differ from internal business analysis. Peabody, one of the world's leading energy companies, had publicly denied that it had reliable methods to predict the impact of climate change regulations on its business. However, it had conducted analysis to quantify the impact of potential regulations on its business and specific assets.[46] In addition, the company cited optimistic assessments of the coal market by the International Energy Agency, while not at the same time citing other less optimistic internal assessments. The New York Attorney General charged that these statements and omissions violated New York law.[47] While the Attorney General's Office based its investigation on statutes focused on protecting shareholders, these efforts also had an intended policy impact. Then Attorney General Schneiderman announced: "I believe that full and fair disclosures by Peabody and other fossil fuel companies will lead investors to think long and hard about the damage these companies are doing to our planet."[48] Peabody ultimately settled and agreed to provide more robust climate-related disclosures.

While state-level agencies, like the New York Attorney General's Office, take the lead on investigating disclosure issues, the investment arms of state governments have taken action as shareholders.

In the case of Exxon Mobil, the New York State Comptroller, along with Walden Asset Management, had pushed the board to disclose additional climate risks.[49] After significant engagement, Exxon agreed to reverse its long-standing policy to enhance disclosures on "energy demand sensitivities, implications of two degree Celsius scenarios, and positioning for a lower-carbon future."[50] By agreeing in advance of a shareholder vote, the board was better able to shape its eventual disclosure report while also keeping up with regulatory and investor pressures.[51]

Exxon continues to face growing pressures from other major government shareholders. According to *Forbes*, the chief investment officer for the Seattle City Employees' Retirement System and two other pension funds "asked Exxon director

---

46. Press Release, *A.G. Schneiderman Secures Unprecedented Agreement with Peabody Energy to End Misleading Statements and Disclose Risks Arising from Climate Change* (November 2015), NEW YORK STATE ATTORNEY GENERAL, https://ag.ny.gov/press-release/ag-schneiderman-secures-unprecedented-agreement-peabody-energy-end-misleading; Assurance of Discontinuance, *Attorney General of the State of N.Y. Environmental and Investor Protection Bureaus* (Nov. 8, 2015), http://ag.ny.gov/pdfs/Peabody-Energy-Assurance-signed.pdf.

47. Martin Act (Article 23-A of General Business Law); S.8 63(12).

48. Press Release, *supra* note 46.

49. NYS Comptroller DiNapoli: ExxonMobil Agrees to Assess Impacts of Climate Change, Office of the New York State Comptroller (2017), https://www.osc.state.ny.us/press/releases/dec17/121217.htm.

50. Press Release, *Exxon Agreement Letter* (2017), New York State Comptroller, https://www.osc.state.ny.us/press/releases/dec17/exxon-agreement-letter.pdf.

51. Energy & Carbon Summary: Positioning for a Lower-Carbon Energy Future, ExxonMobil (2018), https://cdn.exxonmobil.com/~/media/global/files/energy-and-environment/2018-energy-and-carbon-summary.pdf.

Steven Reinemund to discuss governance reforms, such as changing pay programs and bringing in directors with 'climate-competent' perspectives."[52] Increased disclosure addresses some, but not all, of the increasing CSR pressure on the organization. Fulfilling regulatory obligations may not be enough—especially for socially aware institutional investors.

IX. SUMMARY AND TAKEAWAYS

As ESG becomes a key component of investor decision-making, boards will play an increasingly important role in the oversight of ESG risks. Boards should recognize that there is no one-size-fits-all approach to dealing with ESG concerns. Instead, boards should work closely with management to identify core ESG issues that relate to the company, develop a business strategy that accounts for ESG risks and opportunities, actively communicate the company's ESG initiatives both internally and externally, and remain prepared to engage with investors and community stakeholders. The ESG environment continues to evolve rapidly. As such, boards should ensure information is communicated on a timely basis and that the company has adequate processes in place to disclose its ESG performance. Boards should also review and adopt best practices from peer companies and remain responsive to the shifting priorities of major institutional shareholders.

X. PRACTITIONER'S RESOURCES LIBRARY

A. Articles

M. Lipton, S. Rosenblum, S. Niles, S. Lewis, and K. Watanabe, "The New Paradigm: A Roadmap for an Implicit Corporate Governance Partnership between Corporations and Investors to Achieve Sustainable Long-Term Investment and Growth," *World Economic Forum* (September 2, 2016).

D. Silk, D. Katz, S. Niles, and C. Lu, "ESG and Sustainability: The Board's Role" (June 29, 2018).

D. Silk, S. Niles, A. McCarthy, and C. Lu, "Department of Labor Sounds Cautionary Tone on ESG-Related Activities" (May 2, 2018).

A. Edgecliffe-Johnson, "Beyond the Bottom Line: Should Business Put Purpose before Profit?" *Financial Times* (January 3, 2018).

"ESG, Strategy, and the Long View: A Framework for Board Oversight," KPMG (2017).

---

52. D. Blackmon, *Public Pension Funds' Anti-Fossil Fuel Activism Raises Risks for Beneficiaries*, FORBES (2017), https://www.forbes.com/sites/davidblackmon/2017/12/05/public-pension-funds-anti-fossil-fuel-activism-raises-risks-for-beneficiaries/#553c48005fbb.

J. Bailey, B. Klempner, and J. Zoffer, "Sustaining Sustainability: What Institutional Investors Should Do Next on ESG" (Summer 2016).

"Sustainable Investing Is Moving Mainstream," J.P. Morgan Global Research Report on ESG (April 20, 2018).

"Sustainable Signals, Asset Owners Embrace Sustainability," Morgan Stanley (June 2018).

"ESG & Corporate Financial Performance: Mapping the Global Landscape," Deutsche Asset & Wealth Management (December 2015).

"Sustainable Reality: Understanding the Performance of Sustainable Investment Strategies," Morgan Stanley Institute for Sustainable Investing (March 2015).

M. Orsagh, "CFA Institute Survey: How Do ESG Issues Factor into Investment Decisions?" CFA Institute (August 17, 2015).

"21st Century Engagement: Investor Strategies for Incorporating ESG Considerations into Corporate Interactions," BlackRock (March 31, 2015).

"Exploring ESG: A Practitioner's Perspective," BlackRock (June 2016).

"Governance Challenges 2017: Board Oversight of ESG," National Association of Corporate Directors (March 27, 2017).

Investment Governance and the Integration of Environmental, Social and Governance Factors, OECD (2017).

B. Books and White Papers

J. Elkington, Cannibals with Forks: The Triple Bottom Line of 21st Century Business (1997).

G. Friede, T. Busch, and A. Bassen, "ESG and Financial Performance," *Journal of Sustainable Finance & Investment* (December 15, 2015).

G. Clark, A. Feiner, and M. Viehs, "How Sustainability Can Drive Financial Outperformance," Arabesque Partners and Oxford University (March 2015).

Recommendations of the Task Force on Climate-Related Financial Disclosures, Financial Stability Board (December 14, 2016).

C. Reporting and Disclosure Standards

Commission Legislative Proposals on Sustainable Finance, European Commission (May 24, 2018).

Recommendation regarding Disclosure of Board Diversity, SEC Advisory Committee on Small and Emerging Companies (December 2016).

Elizabeth M. Murphy, Secretary, Commission Guidance regarding Disclosure Related to Climate Change, Securities and Exchange Commission (February 2, 2018).

UN Principles for Responsible Investment.

SASB Standards (November 2018).

SEC Proxy Disclosure Enhancements, Securities and Exchange Commission (December 16, 2009).

SEC Interpretative Release on Disclosure Related to Business or Legal Developments regarding Climate Change, Securities and Exchange Commission (February 8, 2010).

EU Directive 2014/95—Disclosure of Non-Financial and Diversity Information by Certain Large Undertakings and Groups, European Parliament and Council (October 22, 2014).

Department of Labor Field Assistance Bulletin No. 2018-01 Relating to Interpretive Bulletins 2016-01 and 2015-01, Department of Labor (April 23, 2018).

Concept Release on Business and Financial Disclosure Required by Regulation S-K, U.S. Securities and Exchange Commission (April 13, 2016).

Chapter 3

Stakeholder Engagement

Keith T. Vernon, Michael B. Runnels,
Nicholas J.C. Santos, and Richard Duda

I. INTRODUCTION

This chapter sets out to provide the reader with an understanding of what a stakeholder engagement is in the context of corporate social responsibility (CSR) and offers best practices for how to professionally engage in a stakeholder engagement.[1] The topics covered include (1) why and how stakeholder resolutions are filed, (2) discerning the best course of action once shareholders express their intent to file a resolution, (3) general best practices in stakeholder engagements, (4) specific preparation needed to effectively dialogue in stakeholder engagements and techniques to gauge dialogue progress, and (5) resolving impasses and when to know it's time to conclude the stakeholder engagement and measure what was gained.

While Rule 14a-8 of the Securities and Exchange Act of 1934 provides a set of rules addressing who can bring a shareholder resolution along with a list of technical requirements for how and when the resolution can be brought, no definitive rules for stakeholder engagement procedure and practice control the stakeholder engagement process.[2] Professionals involved in a stakeholder engagement often enter the engagement with widely different ideas, practices, and expectations, both practical and philosophical—including reasons they agreed to enter into a stakeholder engagement with shareholders and how to communicate and manage the engagement. Without

---

1. While the primary focus of this chapter addresses stakeholder engagement in the context of a shareholder resolution, the principles covered have application, generally, to all CSR engagements.
2. *See* Rule 14a-8 of the Securities and Exchange Act of 1934.

the benefit and certainty that a procedural set of rules for conducting a stakeholder engagement can provide, professionals must rely on their best legal and business judgment, negotiation skills, problem-solving skills, and professional ethics as they seek to employ best practices. This chapter sets out to identify and explore best practices for both decision-making and operating actions in a stakeholder engagement. Recognizing that a stakeholder engagement between shareholders and the corporate professionals representing the company is an opportunity for the company to get better is perhaps the best way to begin a stakeholder engagement. Why? A stakeholder engagement, when done well, is an opportunity for a corporation to carefully listen and learn about concerns shareholders of the company have with some facet of the business. Through dialogue, the company may (often does) discover an issue of which it was unaware, an idea it had not thought of, or even perhaps a solution to a critical issue it never knew existed. The list of potential upsides is long. Employing best practices discussed in this chapter can help professionals in a stakeholder engagement increase the likelihood for positive outcomes, where all parties benefit.

II. LEGAL AND REGULATORY REQUIREMENTS

The authority to bring a shareholder resolution arises from Rule 14a-8. The Rule gives qualified shareholders the right to bring a resolution, articulate concerns about a corporation's operations, and bring the issues and "hoped for action" to vote by all shareholders. Often, the resolution centers on environmental concerns, sustainability concerns, or governance concerns—the three areas are commonly referenced as "ESG" concerns.[3] The resolution gives shareholders an opportunity to bring their concerns to the attention of the corporation and to all shareholders with the hope that some corrective action or change in operations/reporting will strengthen the corporation.

The proponents bringing the shareholder resolutions are "shareholders" of the corporation's stock. Only people or entities that own the stock and meet the requirements set forth in Rule 14a-8 can bring a shareholder resolution. Some of the professionals that often bring shareholder resolutions are faith-based groups, asset investment firms, foundations, and nonprofits focused on human rights and environmental issues. Often, the proponents who bring the shareholder resolutions are skilled in drafting the resolutions—and do so with the hope of having the resolution move into a stakeholder engagement so that the issues of concern can be discussed carefully and fully in a stakeholder engagement.

For the proponents wanting to bring a shareholder resolution, the starting point is to gather all the facts and information relevant to the issue while working to ensure all technical requirements of Rule 14a-8 are satisfied. While a full enumeration of all the

---

3. *See* Wikipedia "ESG" definition: "environmental, social and governance (ESG) refers to the three central factors in measuring the sustainability and ethical impact of an investment in a company or business. These criteria help to better determine the future financial performance of companies (return and risk)."

requirements exist in the Rule and should be consulted, shareholders should seek to confirm they have the requisite amount of the stock held (currently it is $2,000 in share value) in order to have standing to bring the resolution, have held it for a period of time per the Rule (currently one year), and make sure the resolution content does not exceed the word limitation set by the Rule (currently 500 words). While the Rule specifics may change over time, reference to Rule 14a-8 to ensure all requirements are complied with is essential to avoid technical exclusion.

A. Discerning the Best Course of Action

Once the shareholder group has expressed intent on filing a shareholder resolution, the company has several options that it can consider. For instance, it could allow the resolution to be filed or it could push back against the resolution and seek permission from the Securities and Exchange Commission (SEC) to exclude it from the proxy statement. It could also fight at the proxy level with reasons against the resolution seeking a "no" vote. Alternatively, recognizing that the stakeholder group bringing the resolution might have some perspective to offer the company, it could agree to engage in dialogue with the stakeholder group. We elaborate on each of these options below.

1. Allow the Resolution to Be Filed

If the requirements of Rule 14a-8 have been met and the resolution passes the relevancy test, namely, the issue that the resolution addresses relates to at least 5 percent of the company's total assets and at least 5 percent of its net earnings and gross sales for the most current fiscal year, then the company can choose to have the resolution listed on the proxy for the upcoming annual shareholder meeting. Allowing the resolution to be listed on the proxy statement assumes that the shareholder proposal does not recommend action that violates any state, federal, or foreign law.

2. Push Back and Seek SEC Exclusion

Instead of listing the shareholder proposal on the proxy statement, the company can push back and ask the SEC for permission to exclude the proposal. There are various grounds for seeking such SEC permission. For instance, the company can argue that the proposal does not conform to all the requirements of a shareholder proposal or that the proposal calls for action that violates a particular state, federal, or foreign law. It can also seek permission to exclude the proposal if it holds that the proposal is calling for action that the company has no power or authority to implement. Further, permission to exclude the proposal can be sought on grounds that the proposal conflicts with a resolution by another shareholder on the same subject or that the company's management holds that the company has already substantially implemented the proposal. Shareholders filing the resolution that is being challenged have a right to appeal the company's challenge to the SEC. Thus, this option might involve a legal battle and the company might have to discern whether it is in the company's best interest to engage in such a legal tussle.

3. Fight at the Proxy Level with Reasons against the Resolution

The company can choose to have the proposal listed on the proxy statement but give reasons as to why the management recommends *not* voting in favor of the resolution. Unless the company has strong grounds for seeking a *no* vote, this is a risky option because it signals the company's reluctance to deal with the CSR issue being raised. Further, SEC rules require a fairly low threshold for a proposal to be resubmitted a second and third year. According to these rules, a resolution must get at least 3 percent of the vote in its first year, 6 percent in the second year, and 10 percent in the third year and thereafter to be eligible to remain on the ballot. This allows the shareholders filing the resolution to build momentum and garner support for the resolution in subsequent years.

4. Offer to Engage in Dialogue

The company can acknowledge the issue that the shareholder proposal addresses but instead of filing it on the proxy statement for the shareholder meeting it can offer to engage the shareholder(s) filing the proposal in a dialogue. Such an approach recognizes that the shareholders wishing to file a resolution have some grievance about the company's operations but that they do bring a perspective that can help the company get a better idea of the impact of its operations on society or the environment. In the current competitive landscape, where negative news about the company's operations can spread quickly through social media, engaging the aggrieved shareholders through dialogue can help the company mitigate some of the perceived negative impacts of its operations.

B. Which Course of Action Is Best?

When a shareholder or a group of shareholders bring a proposal to the company, the company is obligated to act and to choose one of the four options listed above. In order to decide which course of action to take, the company needs to engage in a careful and strategic discernment. We outline a few steps of this discernment process below.

1. Gather as Much Information as Possible about the Issue Raised

The first step is to understand the issue that the shareholder group is raising in their proposal. Is this something that the company is already aware of? Is this something that the company has already begun addressing? If the concern is legitimate and the company is aware of it and has already begun addressing it, it does make sense to enter into dialogue with the stakeholder group or to let the resolution be filed on the proxy statement. Allowing the resolution to be filed on the proxy and recommending a "yes" vote does have the advantage of giving company management a sense about how other shareholders feel about the issue being raised. If the issue is something that the company has not really been aware of but still thinks that it is a legitimate issue, entering into dialogue with the shareholder group might be helpful. If the proposal is calling for action that the company has no control over, or is in violation of state or federal laws, the company could challenge the proposal at the SEC. If the company feels that the proposal is against the long-term interests of the company, it could file the proposal on the proxy and recommend a "no" vote.

2. Gather as Much Information about the Shareholder Group Bringing the Proposal

It is important to find out who the shareholder group is that is seeking to file the resolution. What is their history of filing resolutions? Are they an activist group seeking control of the board? Have they a vested interest in some of the company's operations? Are they genuinely concerned about the impact of the company on the host community or the environment? The more information that the company can gather on the shareholder group, the better it is for deciding about whether to engage the shareholder group or not. If the shareholder group has its own interests at heart and not that of the company, the best option might be to either challenge the resolution if it is in violation of any provision of Rule 14a-8 or allow the resolution to be filed and recommend a "no" vote. But if the shareholder group is trustworthy, then entering dialogue with them might be helpful. It is likely that they can help the company be a better company.

3. Assessing Ability to Enter into Dialogue

After establishing the legitimacy of the resolution and also the credibility of the shareholder group, the next step is to approach some key individuals in the company. What do they think about the issue? Would they be willing to engage in dialogue with the shareholder group? The latter question is important because unless there is an internal group that is willing to engage in dialogue, this option is not viable. Key people could include the head of investor relations or public relations, the chief financial officer, and the head of CSR. The tone for this team should not be adversarial but one that is open. It is important to determine whether the team will be willing to listen instead of just arguing their position. As a dialogue should be treated as a negotiation, it is also important to assess the company's ability to negotiate and to convey trustworthiness to the shareholder group before it decides to enter into dialogue engagement.

4. Being Mindful of Regulation Fair Disclosure

If the company does determine that it might be best to enter into dialogue, it still needs to be aware of SEC's Regulation Fair Disclosure (Reg FD) provisions that require a public company to make public disclosure of any material nonpublic information disclosed to certain individuals, including shareholders, who may trade on the basis of that information. The dialogue team must carefully review in advance any information that will be provided to the shareholder group, adhering to all requirements, including asking the two critical questions for purposes of Reg FD compliance: (1) Is the information material? and (2) Is the information nonpublic? Counsel on the dialogue team must be responsible for carefully guiding the team regarding what may and may not be disclosed.

Once the legitimacy of the claim that the shareholder group makes in the proposed resolution has been established and the credibility of the group verified, and despite some of the risks involved, it is often the case that stakeholder engagement is the best course of action. One such risk is that the engagement can break down and that the shareholder group will seek to file the resolution anyway. This risk is there for any negotiation and can be mitigated by transparency and goodwill communication between the parties. The other major risk is that of Reg FD. As long as the company is guided by a careful counsel who avoids disclosing any nonpublic material information, this risk can also be mitigated. Entering into stakeholder engagement, after careful assessment, could be considered a good practice for a company that is faced with a shareholder proposal. Indeed, in this age of social media, there is a risk that a story about a refusal to engage that appears arbitrary or evasive can gain traction and affect the company's reputation negatively.

III. GENERAL BEST PRACTICES IN STAKEHOLDER ENGAGEMENT

With the decision to enter into a stakeholder engagement now agreed upon by all parties, how do the parties best proceed? Many issues need to be considered, discussed, and incorporated into a plan to manage the stakeholder engagement setting forth expectations and dialogue practices. A well-documented plan will serve to keep the management and pace of the dialogue on track, facilitate sharing of information, and avoid any opportunities for perceptions of stonewalling.

What professionals should comprise the dialogue team? This question is one which is appropriate to ask at the beginning of a shareholder engagement, as well as continue to ask as needs and issues evolve in dialogue. For the shareholders bringing the resolution, dialogue teams should include professionals who are learned in the practice of stakeholder engagement. It is imperative that these professionals become very familiar with the specific facts of their stakeholder resolution as well as the business operations and environment in which the corporation operates. Understanding the challenges that exist for the business in addressing the concerns articulated in the shareholder resolution is critical. Without such an understanding, meaningful dialogue will be very difficult to achieve. For the corporate dialogue team, team selection is even more complicated and requires careful discernment. A legal professional, often from the general counsel's office, needs to be involved, perhaps leading the dialogue communications. Depending on the subject matter, a corporate representative with knowledge of the issues raised in the stakeholder resolution should be a member of the team—in some cases, behind the scenes, and in other cases, serving as a direct dialogue professional coming to meetings and engaging on the issues in dialogue. In this case, communication skills for this professional are essential so that meaningful sharing of information can be conveyed effectively and accurately in dialogue. Counsel involvement at all stages is needed to ensure legal issues are properly identified and managed. Communications and CSR professionals serving on the team will add great value by managing the outward business impacts the issues in dialogue often include. There are times, especially in high-profile stakeholder engagements, that having the CEO present for some portion of a dialogue can make sense, as well as potentially a board member with particular focus on the subject matter of the stakeholder resolution.

A. Setting Goals

Both parties to a dialogue are well served when they set both short- and long-term goals for how they hope the dialogue develops. While the stakeholder resolution often seeks a particular action, setting goals for how the issues can develop in the dialogue, the pace at which they can reasonably develop, and the realistic responses and action a corporation can take will help greatly in effectively navigating the dialogue. The corporation is likewise well served to have the practice in place to listen and comprehend the details and motivations of the stakeholders, carefully communicating—and sharing information where possible—to develop conversations that can lead to productive ways to respond to shareholders' concerns. Often, the corporation can learn about issues, learn about perspectives not considered, and even learn about ways to move forward and become stronger that were not previously considered. Setting goals will lead to a dialogue that is structured and capable of conversation from both sides that can lead to both parties getting what they seek. Being flexible in both the approach and delivery and taking the time to understand each party will increase the opportunity for a successful dialogue.

The written content of the shareholder resolution is the starting point for which shareholder goals are set forth—(hopefully) with clarity and factual support. For the corporation, it is the starting point for understanding the shareholders' concerns and hoped-for action. For the shareholders bringing the resolution, it is the first chance to make clear the positions and actions sought. Shareholders should take great care to draft the resolution with precision and seek action that is well articulated—and capable of being accomplished. While shareholders may not always know what the specific action is that can address a certain concern, articulating with precision in the resolution with supporting facts and actions sought is critical. Often, the action sought is the disclosure of information, data, or reporting that is not currently being provided or at least not at the level sought by shareholders. The identification of areas of change needed in an "ask" often results in the need for some internal evaluation to determine if the concern exist, followed by identification of how best to eliminate or mitigate down the concern. This often results in the drafting of a corporation policy designed to address the concerns. This process can be an excellent way, in dialogue, to collaborate on the very best practices to address the concern. This process can allow for direct dialogue discussion on a policy, drafting of the policy, and steps forward including training and implementation of the policy. There may be times when reporting on the policy impact is also appropriate for some time.

All parties to a dialogue need to have in place a set of expectations and goals for what can be gained through the dialogue process. While goals can be specific, flexibility and willingness to modify goals and outcomes are critical. Often a dialogue produces conversation that is unexpected, allowing for ideas and paths that were not originally on the agenda. Key is to have agreed-upon goals within your dialogue team and prepare and execute in dialogue on those goals. Equally critical is a willingness to modify goals to account for new dialogue facts, information, and ideas—doing so will strengthen the opportunity for a strong dialogue outcome.

B. Stay Engaged

Staying engaged in the context of a stakeholder engagement means keeping one another informed of progress on the subject matter being discussed and aware of new information or positions that impact the topics being discussed. Stakeholders typically hope for progress at speeds that exceed the corporation's pace, so having communications between dialogues is key to keeping reasonable expectations for pace in the dialogue and all parties engaged. In a dialogue where the parties have agreed to meet, either in person or telephonically, twice a year, a six-month gap in between dialogue day is a long time if there is little to no communication during this period. Work to prevent long gaps in communication. Set in place protocols that allow for regular updates on progress taking place on issues in dialogue. Consider setting a regular call, perhaps monthly, or consistent with some item that lines up with your subject matter, perhaps compliance or reporting requirements of internal or external events that impact the issues in dialogue. Doing this will help keep the engagement front and center, engaged, and at a pace that allows for an opportunity for the best results. The idea is to create communication bridges that keep the parties connected in between regular scheduled dialogues.

Inevitably, issues reported in either the media or other outlets will arise that impact the topics in dialogue. When such an event occurs, communicate as soon as reasonably possible on the issues. Allow the issues to help continue the dialogue in a productive way. For instance, if engaged in a human rights dialogue, and a human rights violation/allegation involving the corporation is reported in the media, utilize this incident as an opportunity to engage with one another. Recognize there may be limitations to the depth that the conversation can allow for, especially legal considerations that may prevent full discussion of all information—allow this to be an opportunity to build further trust and continued engagement toward solutions. Doing so will expand the opportunity for positive outcomes. Remember, it's a negotiation, stay connected, seek solutions, create trust.

C. It's a Long Road

Pace is critical. All parties need to be aware that the speed in which action can move will vary. Expectations are key. Identifying a process, shared with all parties, will keep things on track. Often, shareholders want fast actions, and the corporation wants to proceed at the pace they are most comfortable with, consistent with how they conduct normal business operations. Shareholders strengthen their odds of success by recognizing and understanding the pace in which a corporation can discern and act. Information flow and decision-making in corporations require essential folks be involved and multiple levels of discernment take place—sometimes involving C-suite and board level involvement, all of which can take significant time. Remembering that a dialogue is a long road, often taking years, will help all parties be mindful of what their goals are, the work it will take to meet the goals, and willingness to modify goals. Doing so increases the likelihood of a strong outcome for all parties.

D. General Guidelines for Expectations and Logistics

Stakeholder engagements benefit from guidelines in place to create structure, expectations, and reasonable parameters for the dialogue. Many guidelines can and should be set forth at the very early stages of a stakeholder engagement that relate to sharing of information, communication leads, dialogue day specific guidelines, and pre-dialogue logistic guidelines. Parties should discuss what expectations exist for confidentiality and sharing of information in dialogue. Counsel will need to be mindful of the legal implications of sharing information with shareholders.

General dialogue guidelines include setting forth communication leads to communicate respective parties' positions, exchange information when needed, communicate on any new issues that arise, and set up the dialogue day logistics. Important in that is working toward an agenda for the dialogue day, setting both the date and venue for the dialogue, and approving an agreed-upon agenda. An agenda that is created by both parties, with working draft exchanges to final agenda that ensures both parties' team members have influence on creating the topics for dialogue day, is critical. The agenda creating process will also identify if any information is needed to be shared in advance, and if any professionals with specialized subject matter knowledge are needed to join the dialogue day to ensure the best conversation can be had. Dialogue days often include many parties involved on both sides, so having a central figure coordinate and lead the dialogue teams is critical. Preparation for dialogue day presentation and assignment of team participation for issues and workload is similarly critical. All parties on a dialogue should know their role in dialogue day. Dialogue team leads should work to ensure dialogue days stay on track in both time and substance consistent with the agreed-upon agenda.

The steps leading to a dialogue, and in between dialogues, set the stage for a trusted dialogue, where all parties converge with a set agenda, in a professional venue, with a schedule and expectation of how the agenda will proceed in an effective manner—affording all parties the opportunity to be present and communicate positions. Doing this in a professional and organized way will help the parties create a trusted atmosphere allowing for "listening" and discussion centered around points and facts in the hope of facilitating conversation that produces ideas that prove beneficial to both parties.

IV. SPECIFIC PREPARATION NEEDED TO EFFECTIVELY DIALOGUE AND TECHNIQUES TO GAUGE PROGRESS AND RESOLVE IMPASSES

There is always an element of learning on the job in any stakeholder engagement process. Indeed, this process can best be understood as a learning cycle, as both the corporation and its stakeholders learn more about each other's motivations, working methodologies, and spheres of influence. This does not mean, however, that the process should not be planned in the same manner that other critical business activities are planned. Without proper planning, a stakeholder engagement process is unlikely to deliver for any party to the dialogue. Indeed, it may end in disappointment, recriminations, and damaged relationships with the very people who are critical to the corporation's success.

Before attending your first stakeholder engagement dialogue, it is essential to know the corporation's status on all material issues in question. To wit, how are the issues currently managed within the corporation? What policies and systems does the corporation already have in place to address these issues? For each party to the dialogue, they must know what is it that you can and want to do about these issues. Each party to the dialogue should also formulate simple, yet specific, objectives of that dialogue. For example: (1) to ensure that they are well informed of our approach to "x;" (2) to be aware of their actions regarding "x;" (3) to convince them to "x;" (4) to ensure that the corporate policy in question is responsive to the dialogue; and (5) to share responsibility with them for "x." Finally, each party to the dialogue must consider the worst and best-case scenarios resulting from the stakeholder engagement dialogue. This information not only provides the practical basis for building a more robust and responsive stakeholder engagement dialogue but also forms the basis upon which to assess the corporation's current practice against the objectives of the dialogue.[4]

As stakeholders have the ability to impact corporate success, a critical objective of any corporate stakeholder engagement is to cultivate the kinds of relationships with stakeholders that allow the corporation to develop a better understanding of their perspectives and concerns on key issues and, where appropriate, to integrate those perspectives and concerns into corporate strategy. Key to the cultivation of this relationship is trust. In this regard, the most important consideration is to simply tell the truth, full stop. This means getting the facts right and being consistent, and if the facts do change, informing stakeholders before they learn about the change from other parties. The corporation should provide relevant information that is calculated to meet the informational needs of the stakeholder team and articulate its corporate vision and strategy in a manner that is clear, understandable, and intersects with the articulated concerns of those stakeholders. Disseminating information in this regard results in enhanced trust, credibility, and ultimately creates value for all stakeholders.

A. Subject Matter Experts Add Value to and Help Cultivate Trust in the Stakeholder Engagement Dialogue

It is always valuable to know what others are doing in relation to similar issues underlying a stakeholder engagement. For example, what challenges have they faced and how have they achieved success? Is there evidence of positive outcomes from a stakeholder engagement on similar issues? Are there ongoing partnership initiatives or associations addressing this issue where working together would be beneficial? In many cases, it may turn out that the issues identified as material are not exhaustive and other issues arise during the dialogue. In this way, stakeholder engagement involves a cycle of

---

4. *See* Thomas Krick et al., *The Stakeholder Engagement Manual* (Accountability, the United Nations Environment Programme, and Stakeholder Research Associates, 2005), 63.

learning and innovation. This cycle of learning is accelerated when companies can learn from the mistakes and best practice of others.

Stakeholder engagement is a process likely to involve a broad variety of people with different levels of expertise and experience in the subject matter. For the corporation, this means efforts to develop stakeholder engagement-related skills should focus not only on CSR managers or stakeholder engagement specialists but also on general managers across the corporation. There is no generic stakeholder engagement skill set, per se, as different expertise and experience may be needed to engage with any range of stakeholders. However, a basic range of skills and characteristics can be identified. Sometimes it may be practical to develop these skills with people who are dealing directly with stakeholders, but are not engagement specialists. In other cases, it may be more suitable to draw on the expertise of practitioners from established professions such as lobbying, public relations, and/or marketing research.

In any successful stakeholder dialogue, it is vital that each party consider what internal skills are required. Certainly, in order to engage successfully, being knowledgeable on the subject matter is key. Another key contributor to successful engagement is perceived credibility. For example, successfully securing the trust of stakeholders may in part depend upon how well those corporate representatives relate to and are perceived by those stakeholders. This means that the corporation must ensure that its dialogue team has a good understanding of the stakeholders involved. In general, recruitment from local communities, which ensures equal opportunity regardless of demographic, will help ensure that corporate employees reflect the diversity of their stakeholders.[5]

B. Cultivating Trust on Dialogue Day: Behavioral Ground Rules

To cultivate the trust that is prerequisite to a successful stakeholder engagement dialogue, what are the procedural and behavioral ground rules for each party? What are your commitments to them? Each party to the dialogue must agree with, and then provide, a clear overview to their team members about the ground rules and what is expected of them. Some general ground rules for engagement can be: (1) adopt a solutions-oriented approach; (2) stay focused on the issues that are the subject matter of the dialogue; (3) avoid assigning intentions, beliefs, or motives to others; (4) ask others questions rather than stating uninformed assumptions about them; (5) respect each party's right to pass on a question if they are not ready, or willing, to speak; (6) allow others to express their opinions completely and without interruption; (7) demonstrate respectful and attentive body language throughout the dialogue—especially when listening to opinions with which you heartily disagree; and (8) ensure that opportunities for input are evenly distributed.[6]

---

5. *Id.* at 56.
6. *Id.* at 113.

C. Cultivating Trust on Dialogue Day: Role of the Team Leader

To facilitate a credible dialogue that is informed by mutual trust and respect, each team must have one leader to lead their respective dialogue teams to a productive outcome. The hallmarks of a competent team leader are several. Specifically, a team leader (1) helps their team define the intended outputs and how they will be used, (2) designs a tailor-made interaction that suits the requirements of all participants, (3) creates a suitable atmosphere for professional collaboration by demonstrating the same respect of the other team as you would for a work colleague, (4) checks that the participants are supportive and involved in the process, (5) holds clarity throughout the meeting, (6) encourages meaningful interaction, and (7) manages the engagement interaction as a learning opportunity.

D. Cultivating Trust on Dialogue Day: Corporate Representatives Must Be Flexible

The corporate dialogue team should consider any other issues that stakeholders may have, in advance if possible. In any given stakeholder engagement, stakeholders may raise issues that may be outside of the scope of the engagement. While it is important to be clear about this scope and to ensure that the dialogue is not derailed by less material issues, it is also critical that corporate representatives not casually dismiss, out of hand, any new issues that may arise. Indeed, some unanticipated issues may turn out to be more important than the subject matter of the engagement. As meaningful engagement will be difficult if stakeholders feel that any new issue(s) that they may raise are casually dismissed, corporate representatives must stay flexible and willing to reconsider approaches and priorities during the engagement dialogue. However, it may still be necessary to bracket the new issue(s) so as to not derail the dialogue. Stakeholders are likely to agree to this course of action if corporate representatives are prepared to make a clear and timed commitment to when and how these issues will be addressed.

E. Conclude Each Dialogue Day with an Action Plan

At the end of each dialogue day, each team should consider their strategic objectives and what outcomes were achieved. Specifically, each team should (1) identify the operational and strategic implications of any agreement, and assign responsibilities for follow-up on the resulting output; (2) identify next steps and decide when these are to be delivered; (3) identify any remaining questions or resulting issues that need to be addressed in any subsequent engagement dialogue, and assign responsibility for follow-up; (4) assign responsibilities for implementing and monitoring the follow-up activities; (5) ensure that information that could be of value to other dialogue participants are communicated to them as soon as possible; and (6) communicate back to the other dialogue team, where appropriate. In this way, each dialogue team is able to hold themselves, and each other, accountable for the successful conclusion of the stakeholder engagement.

V. RESOLVING IMPASSES

Corporate actors must be aware that they can only engage stakeholders on a meaningful strategic level if their companies are willing and able to reconsider its objectives and strategies. All parties to the dialogue should understand it as a potential opportunity, as the alignment of corporate objectives and strategy with material stakeholder interests is a key attribute of any successful stakeholder engagement. In addition to being knowledgeable on key issues, certain personality traits are crucial in the ability to successfully engage a broad diverse range of parties, such as integrity, a solutions-oriented attitude, motivation, and creativity. Despite strict adherence to the "behavioral ground rules" noted above and the best-intentioned actions by all dialogue participants, you may reach an impassioned disagreement. For example, participants may get locked into defending combative positions or individuals. Before "dialogue day," each party should formulate a contingency plan to deal with the most likely or damaging disagreements—and consider the negative impacts of the stakeholder engagement falling apart. For an emerging dialogue in progress to fall back into a resolution, while at times unavoidable, is generally not the best course of action for all parties. Indeed, despite the occasional impassioned disagreement on an issue, each party to the dialogue must understand that there is far more to learn from each other than whatever is gained by giving in to the distraction caused by the occasional slight.

Effective and strategically aligned stakeholder engagement (1) builds trust between the corporation and their stakeholders; (2) leads to more equitable and sustainable social environment by giving those who have a right to be heard the opportunity to be considered in the decision-making processes of the corporation; (3) prompts a more responsive management of corporate risk and reputation; (4) allows for the pooling of resources, such as subject matter experts, to solve problems and reach objectives that cannot be reached by any single actor; (5) facilitates understanding of a dynamic business environment, including market developments and identification of new strategic opportunities; (6) facilitates corporate learning from their stakeholders, which can result in both product and strategy improvements; and (7) informs, educates, and influences both the corporation and their stakeholders as they seek to improve the decision-making and actions that directly impact the company and the broader society. Despite the obvious challenges of stakeholder engagement, the outcomes of a well-considered process that informs the stakeholder engagement clearly justify the necessary efforts. Successful stakeholder engagement not only helps corporations secure leadership in an increasingly complex and dynamic global business environment, but it will also help galvanize change toward sustainable business development, a key desire for many CSR advocates. For these reasons, whenever impassioned disputes arise that may derail the dialogue and force the issue back to a possible resolution and proxy vote, focus on the objectives of that dialogue and move forward, together.

VI. WHEN TO KNOW IT'S TIME TO CONCLUDE THE DIALOGUE: YOU WILL KNOW

New learning, insights, and agreements must be translated into decisions, policies, and action plans, and from there into improved corporate practices. The trusting relationships that have been developed throughout the engagement process must be secured. This requires timely feedback about planned courses of action and further engagement, if necessary. As noted above, at the end of each dialogue day, each team should formulate an action plan that (1) identifies the operational implications of any agreement(s), (2) identifies next steps and when they are to be delivered, (3) identifies remaining questions that need to be addressed in any subsequent dialogue, (4) assigns responsibilities for implementing and monitoring follow-up activities, (5) shares valuable information with dialogue participants in a timely manner, and (6) maintains appropriate professional contact with the other dialogue team until all issues that underlie the stakeholder engagement are resolved. Moreover, corporations should consider assessing their stakeholder's experience with the engagement. Corporate dialogue participants should consider asking the following questions to identify their stakeholders' perspectives and measurements of success. Note that some of these questions may be incorporated into each dialogue day's "action plan": How was it for you? Was it safe, accessible, transparent, clear, trust-building, informed, involved, relevant, participative? Did we achieve the purpose of the engagement? How could we improve the engagement? How can we move forward to ensure attainment of the objective? How will you judge that we have listened, learned, and acted? What would make these evident for you? Would you like to continue the engagement process? How would you like to move on?[7] The further engagement of stakeholders on these questions not only reinforces trust between the corporation and their stakeholders but also identifies possible future improvements in any subsequent stakeholder dialogue. If both parties adhere to such an action plan and stakeholder assessment process, when it is time to conclude the dialogue, you will know.

VII. SUMMARY AND TAKEAWAYS

"Do well by doing good" is a phrase attributed, perhaps apocryphally, to Benjamin Franklin. It goes to the essence of responsible corporate citizenship. It seems beyond dispute that today's boards and executives not only should but must be aware of the impact of their businesses on society, their stakeholders, and the environment. To that end, engagement in dialogue with activist stakeholders is inevitable and beneficial.

The spirit of the phrase is also deeply embedded in the DNA of the legal profession. Lawyers are expected to both "do well" and "do good." Indeed, a corporation's in-house legal counsel, the lawyers whom are most often involved in a stakeholder engagement

---

7. *Id.* at 115.

on the company side, has been called "the guardian of the corporate integrity."[8] This responsibility goes hand in hand with the in-house lawyer's role of principal legal advisor to the CEO and board, actively "overseeing and guiding the design, direction, and monitoring of the corporation's business strategy, risk assessment, compliance, and operations."[9]

In what context is the confluence of these responsibilities more apparent than in a CSR stakeholder engagement? It requires the lawyer to soberly evaluate the legal implications of the stakeholder group's proposition and understand it in both the internal context (the corporation's resources and strategy) and the external context (the business and cultural environment in which the corporation operates). The lawyer must then effectively communicate those legal implications to the corporation's senior leaders in light of the internal and external contexts, advise them on the appropriate course of action (whether that is to agree, invite dialog, seek exclusion, fight at the proxy level, etc.), and perhaps persuade them to follow that path. Only then does he or she get down to the business of either dialogue and negotiation with the stakeholder group or fighting its resolution, as the case may be.

If the latter, so be it. Not every stakeholder proposition is in the shareholders' best interest, and it is the lawyer's duty to resist those that aren't. If the former, then congratulations! By the end you will have engaged in what might be one of the most interesting engagements of your career. Perhaps you will have gotten deep into a conversation about a topic outside the normal purview of a corporate lawyer. You might have taken risks, challenged the other side, and been challenged yourself. You may have had an opportunity to engage with the company's management team at a strategic level previously unknown to you. You may have had a hand in leading the company into a new and fascinating area of endeavor. You may even have helped educate the shareholder group on the larger context the company operates in—on the board's need to deploy limited resources to address the legitimate interests of a range of stakeholders. In any case, your perspective will be broader. You will have had new experiences. You will have new ideas and insights to incorporate into your professional life and into the way your company does business. Without a doubt, you will have "done well" and "done good."

VIII. PRACTITIONER'S RESOURCES LIBRARY

A. Articles

L. Lord and H. Matthews, "Stakeholder Engagement in Environmentally Sensitive Economic Development Projects," 66 *South Carolina Law Review*, 625 (2015).

---

8. *See* E. Norman Veasey, C. T., Indispensable Counsel—The Chief Legal Officer in the New Reality (Oxford University Press, 2013), 4.
9. *Id.* at 3.

B. Books and White Papers

E. Norman Veasey, C. T., *Indispensable Counsel—The Chief Legal Officer in the New Reality* (Oxford University Press), 4.

C. Instruments and Standards

Thomas Krick et al., *The Stakeholder Engagement Manual* (Accountability, the United Nations Environment Programme, and Stakeholder Research Associates), 63 (2005).

D. Reporting

Rule 14a-8 of the Securities and Exchange Act of 1934.

Chapter 4

Reporting and Disclosure

Michael R. Littenberg

I. INTRODUCTION

Corporate social responsibility (CSR) disclosure has gone from a "nice to have" to a "must have" for a significant number of companies. CSR disclosure requirements have been adopted across many jurisdictions. In addition, voluntary CSR disclosures, and the pressures to make these disclosures, have exponentially increased and new disclosure frameworks, standards, and guidance have been developed to bring more structure to voluntary CSR reporting.

This chapter provides a framework for thinking about CSR disclosure and discusses CSR disclosure regulations and voluntary instruments broadly applicable to U.S.-based companies, including from their activities abroad. It also discusses other foreign CSR disclosure instruments that, although not generally applicable to U.S.-based companies, are contributing to increased U.S. company disclosure and compliance expectations and industry practices.

II. A FRAMEWORK FOR THINKING ABOUT CSR DISCLOSURE

A. Types of CSR Disclosures

CSR disclosures fall into two broad categories, voluntary and mandatory disclosures. The legislation, frameworks, standards, and guidance highlighted in this section are discussed in more detail in the sections that follow.

Note that, for simplicity, in this chapter, "CSR" is used synonymously with "ESG," which stands for environmental, social, and governance, and sustainability. The terms are used interchangeably with alignment to the particular instruments that are discussed or to the extent more commonly used in a particular context.

1. Voluntary Disclosures

Most CSR disclosures are voluntary. Companies have discretion in what they say and where and how frequently they say it. As a result, not surprisingly, disclosures and disclosure philosophies vary significantly among companies, even among companies in the same industry and of a similar size.

Most CSR and sustainability reports and CSR-related website disclosures made by companies are voluntary. Although there is significant variation in these disclosures, the topics voluntarily covered in CSR and sustainability reports and on corporate websites often include the following:

- *An overview of the business*, including a discussion of strategy, products, and services, locations, customers, and material and salient CSR areas, all of which provide context to the company's approach to CSR and its CSR disclosures.
- *Human capital management*, including employee engagement, diversity and inclusion, training and development, compensation and benefits, health and wellness, and workplace safety.
- *Community involvement*, including charitable giving and volunteerism.
- *Environmental responsibility*, including energy management, energy usage, emissions, waste, water consumption, sustainable product design, and recycling.
- *Governance and compliance*, including leadership and oversight, ethics, regulatory compliance, human rights policies and programs, anti-bribery/anticorruption compliance, government relations and political contributions, customer privacy, and stakeholder engagement.
- *Supply chain*, including supplier codes of conduct, conflict minerals policies, modern slavery disclosures, commodity-specific disclosures (such as relating to chemical use, cotton, cobalt, palm oil, and timber), supplier expectations, and supplier audit results.

Many companies report CSR metrics and targets, especially relating to environmental and human capital matters. For example, many companies report historical data on greenhouse gas emissions, energy and water use, and diversity. Increasingly, companies also are reporting targets in these areas, as well as other CSR goals.

In the environmental area, investors are asking for, and more companies are setting and reporting, science-based/2°C scenario targets for greenhouse gas emissions reductions. Science-based targets align corporate greenhouse gas emissions with global 2°C scenario targets and enable investors to better evaluate emissions management strategies. This enhances credibility with investors that long-term strategy is aligned with business practices, regulatory considerations, and other risks of transitioning to a low carbon economy.

Another developing trend is aligning corporate strategies, initiatives, and long-term goals to the UN's Sustainable Development Goals (SDGs).[1] The SDGs, which were adopted in late 2015, include 17 economic, social, and environmental goals with 169 associated targets. The SDGs are intended to be universal goals that meet urgent environmental, political, and economic challenges facing the world.

At present, a minority of companies obtain external assurance of their CSR disclosures. Those that do obtain limited assurance, usually relating to greenhouse gas emissions data.

Although there is significant variation in the level of detail of voluntary CSR disclosures and the way in which topics are discussed, these disclosures do not entirely lack structure. Standards and frameworks have been developed to provide investors and other stakeholders with decision-useful information to enable them to better assess CSR risks, performance, and strategy. These standards and frameworks include, among others, those developed by the Global Reporting Initiative (GRI) and the Sustainability Accounting Standards Board (SASB).

2. Mandatory Disclosures

For U.S.-based companies, mandatory CSR disclosures primarily arise under Securities and Exchange Commission (SEC) rules, regulations, and guidance applicable to public companies and stand-alone, subject-specific disclosure legislation, in particular pertaining to modern slavery. As discussed below, there are two principal variants of disclosure-based CSR legislation applicable to U.S.-based companies.

Disclosure-only CSR legislation requires companies to put out disclosure on a specified topic, but it does not require them to adopt or implement compliance policies and procedures or take other remedial measures. The philosophy behind most disclosure-only CSR legislation is that shining a light on business practices focuses companies on the issues addressed by the legislation, encouraging a race to the top. Most disclosure-based CSR legislation, in particular current modern slavery legislation, falls into this category.

The second principal variant is legislation that not only requires disclosure relating to a particular issue but also requires companies to trace portions of their supply chains. The U.S. Conflict Minerals Rule is in this category.

Although not currently as relevant to U.S.-based companies, there is a third variant of disclosure-based CSR legislation that goes even further. In addition to requiring companies to trace portions of their supply chains and put out disclosure, this legislation requires companies to remediate identified human rights issues. The French Duty of Vigilance Law and proposed Dutch child labor legislation are in this category.

---

1. UN Sustainable Development Goals main page: https://sustainabledevelopment.un.org/sdgs.

B. Disclosure Drivers

Many factors are driving CSR programs and contributing to the rise in CSR disclosure by U.S.-based companies. Some of these factors are further discussed below.

1. Investors

Over the next few years, the single most significant CSR disclosure driver for U.S.-based companies is likely to be the continuing integration by mainstream institutional investors of ESG factors into investment decisions, ongoing portfolio monitoring, and engagement. Investors assess companies on ESG matters based on what they disclose. Therefore, if companies do not disclose it, they do not receive credit for it.

A principal driver of ESG integration by institutional investors is the growing body of research indicating that companies that are stronger on ESG tend to perform better over time and present less investment risk. The inflow of money to index funds also is driving investor engagement on ESG issues that are material to long-term performance, such as climate change. An index investor is required to maintain its investment in a company for as long as the company is in the index, which could be decades.

Large institutional investors are leading the call for decision-useful ESG information. These investors are looking for concrete ESG data that is material to investment decisions and long-term business sustainability, rather than boilerplate or general aspirational statements. In particular, institutional investors are seeking standardization of quantitative data to be able to more easily compare companies on key ESG metrics.

Disclosure topics of particular interest to at least some investors, as reflected by shareholder proposals submitted to U.S. public companies in connection with annual meetings, include the following:

- sustainability reporting
- climate change, in particular greenhouse gas emissions and science-based emissions reduction targets, energy efficiency goals, and risks relating to and strategies for managing a low carbon economy/2°C scenario
- workplace diversity and pay equity
- political contributions and lobbying.

2. The Growing Role of Third-Party ESG Data Providers

ESG integration by mainstream institutional investors has fueled investor demand for ESG data. By some estimates, there are now more than 150 ESG data providers, from solutions that focus on ESG broadly to narrow issue-specific solutions. The data providers pull data from CSR and sustainability reports, websites, other voluntary disclosures, and regulatory filings. In addition to preparing reports for their clients that describe companies' ESG policies, practices, oversight, deficiencies, risks, and controversies, ESG data providers score companies using proprietary scoring methodology and benchmark companies against their peers and competitors. These reports and the related scores are driving disclosure enhancements at many companies.

Well-known institutional investor-focused firms in this space include MSCI, Glass Lewis, and ISS, which introduced its Environmental & Social Disclosure QualityScore in 2018. Glass Lewis has partnered with Sustainalytics, another well-known firm in this space that also provides its analyses on a stand-alone basis. In late 2018, Glass Lewis announced that it will be integrating the SASB standards into its proxy research and vote management platform. These standards are discussed later in this chapter.

3. Regulation

The consensus is that additional broadly applicable disclosure-based CSR legislation is unlikely to be adopted in the United States over at least the next couple of years. However, both new and existing regulations in other parts of the world will continue to drive disclosure by U.S.-based companies.

As discussed later in this chapter, new regulations requiring additional CSR disclosures by many U.S.-based multinationals will take effect. These regulations include federal and state modern slavery acts in Australia and, to a lesser extent, the European Union's conflict minerals regulation. Companies also will continue to make incremental enhancements to disclosures made under existing regulations, such as the UK Modern Slavery Act, in response to guidance from regulators and NGOs, third-party rankings, and surveys, and to keep pace with peers and competitors.

Required CSR disclosures by companies outside of the United States also will indirectly impact voluntary CSR disclosures and related compliance practices by

U.S.-based companies. For example, enhancements to CSR disclosures by non-U.S. companies pursuant to the EU Non-financial Reporting Directive and various foreign stock exchange regulations over time will put pressure on leading U.S.-based companies to provide a similar level of disclosure.

4. Other Drivers

CSR disclosures also will continue to be influenced by traditional drivers, i.e., NGO pressures and customer and brand considerations. Over the last few years, there has been a significant increase in NGO benchmarking studies evaluating and ranking CSR disclosures and compliance practices. Not surprisingly, the increase in CSR disclosure has fueled, and continues to fuel, the increase in studies. These studies have resulted in disclosure enhancements by many companies. Customer and brand considerations are particularly important disclosure drivers at lifestyle brands and companies that promote socially responsible and sustainable business models.

Disclosure enhancements also are being driven by human capital considerations, which is a fairly new CSR disclosure driver at most companies. Anecdotal evidence indicates that employees, especially younger, more skilled employees, want to work for companies that share their values. CSR disclosures are therefore increasingly being viewed as part of employee recruitment, morale, and retention programs.

III. INSTRUMENTS, FRAMEWORKS, STANDARDS, GUIDANCE, AND REGULATIONS

Some of the key instruments, frameworks, standards, guidance, and regulations (for brevity, generally referred to in this chapter as instruments) relevant to both voluntary and mandatory CSR disclosures by U.S.-based companies are discussed below. Broadly applicable instruments are discussed first. A discussion of issue-specific instruments follows. Finally, this section discusses some of the more significant foreign instruments that are indirectly applicable to U.S.-based companies and proposed regulations of which U.S.-based companies should be aware.

A. Broad-Based Multilateral "Soft Law" Instruments

1. UN Guiding Principles on Business and Human Rights (2011)[2]

The Guiding Principles implement the United Nation's "Protect, Respect and Remedy" framework. They cover all internationally recognized human rights abuses and contain recommendations for states and businesses to mitigate adverse human rights impacts linked to business activity. The Guiding Principles provide a framework for both mandatory and voluntary CSR disclosures by both states and companies.

---

2. https://www.ohchr.org/Documents/Publications/GuidingPrinciplesBusinessHR_EN.pdf.

The State Duty to Protect Human Rights. The Guiding Principles indicate that in meeting their duty to protect human rights, states should encourage, and where appropriate require, business enterprises to communicate how they address their human rights impacts. The related commentary expands on this principle, indicating that:

- communication by business enterprises on how they address human rights impacts can range from informal engagement with affected stakeholders to formal public reporting;
- state encouragement of, or where appropriate requirements for, such communication is important in fostering respect for human rights by business enterprises. Incentives to communicate adequate information could include provisions to give weight to self-reporting in the event of a judicial or administrative proceeding. A requirement to communicate can be particularly appropriate where the nature of business operations or operating contexts poses a significant risk to human rights;
- policies or laws in this area can usefully clarify what and how businesses should communicate, helping to ensure both the accessibility and accuracy of communications;
- any stipulation of what would constitute adequate communication should take into account risks that the communication may pose to the safety and security of individuals and facilities, legitimate requirements of commercial confidentiality, and variations in enterprises' sizes and structures; and
- financial reporting requirements should clarify that human rights impacts in some instances may be material or significant to the economic performance of the business enterprise.

The Corporate Responsibility to Respect Human Rights. The Guiding Principles indicate that in order to account for how business enterprises address their human rights impacts, they should be prepared to communicate this externally, particularly when concerns are raised by or on behalf of affected stakeholders. Business enterprises whose operations or operating contexts pose risks of severe human rights impacts should report formally on how they address them.

According to the Guiding Principles, in all instances, communications should:

- be of a form and frequency that reflect an enterprise's human rights impacts and that are accessible to its intended audiences;
- provide information that is sufficient to evaluate the adequacy of an enterprise's response to the particular human rights impact involved; and
- not pose risks to affected stakeholders, personnel, or to legitimate requirements of commercial confidentiality.

The commentary to this principle indicates that the responsibility to respect human rights requires that business enterprises have in place policies and processes through which they can both know and show that they respect human rights in practice. Showing involves communication, providing a measure of transparency and accountability to individuals or groups who may be impacted and to other relevant stakeholders, including investors. The commentary notes that communication can take a variety of forms, including in-person meetings, online dialogues, consultation with affected stakeholders, and formal public reports.

Consistent with this principle as described above, the commentary further notes that formal reporting by enterprises is expected where risks of severe human rights impacts exist, whether this is due to the nature of the business operations or operating contexts. According to the commentary, the reporting should cover topics and indicators concerning how enterprises identify and address adverse impacts on human rights, independent verification of human rights reporting can strengthen the content and its credibility, and sector-specific indicators can provide helpful additional detail.

2. OECD Guidelines for Multinational Enterprises (Fifth Edition, 2011)[3]

The OECD Guidelines for Multinational Enterprises are nonbinding principles and standards for responsible business conduct in a global context. The MNE Guidelines are the only multilaterally agreed and comprehensive code of responsible business conduct that governments have committed to promote.

Disclosure is one of the topics covered in the MNE Guidelines. The disclosure recommendations in the MNE Guidelines, which apply broadly beyond just CSR, provide a useful framework for thinking about CSR disclosures. The commentary to the MNE Guidelines explicitly indicates that the MNE Guidelines encourage disclosure or communication practices relating to social and environmental reporting. The commentary specifically mentions greenhouse gas emissions and biodiversity as examples.

According to the MNE Guidelines, enterprises should ensure that timely and accurate information is disclosed on all material matters regarding their activities, structure, financial situation, performance, ownership, and governance. This information should be disclosed for the enterprise as a whole and, where appropriate, along business lines or geographic areas. The commentary to the MNE Guidelines indicates that clear and complete information on enterprises is important to a variety of users, ranging from shareholders and the financial community to other constituencies such as workers, local communities, special-interest groups, governments, and society at large; and to improve public understanding of enterprises and their interaction with society and the environment, enterprises should be transparent in their operations and responsive to the public's increasingly sophisticated demands for information.

The MNE Guidelines indicate that disclosure policies of enterprises should be tailored to the nature, size, and location of the enterprise, with due regard taken of costs, business confidentiality, and other competitive concerns. However, in addition to other enumerated items, disclosure policies of enterprises should include, but not be limited to, material information on the following items that may relate to CSR:

- enterprise objectives
- foreseeable risk factors

---

3. http://www.oecd.org/daf/inv/mne/48004323.pdf.

- issues regarding workers and other stakeholders
- governance structures and policies, in particular, the content of any corporate governance code or policy and its implementation process.

The MNE Guidelines encourage enterprises to communicate additional information, which could include the following:

- value statements or statements of business conduct intended for public disclosure, including, depending on its relevance for the enterprise's activities, information on the enterprise's policies relating to matters covered by the MNE Guidelines
- policies and other codes of conduct to which the enterprise subscribes, their date of adoption, and the countries and entities to which such statements apply
- the enterprise's performance in relation to these statements and codes
- information on internal audit, risk management, and legal compliance systems
- information on relationships with workers and other stakeholders.

Finally, the MNE Guidelines indicate that enterprises should apply high quality standards for nonfinancial disclosure, including environmental and social reporting.

3. OECD Due Diligence Guidance for Responsible Business Conduct (2018)[4]

The objective of the RBC Guidance is to provide practical support to enterprises on the implementation of the MNE Guidelines to help enterprises avoid and address adverse impacts related to workers, human rights, the environment, bribery, consumers, and corporate governance that may be associated with their operations, supply chains, and other business relationships.

The RBC Guidance indicates that enterprises should communicate externally relevant information on due diligence policies, processes, and activities conducted to identify and address actual or potential adverse impacts, including the findings and outcomes of those activities. Specific recommended actions include publicly reporting relevant information on due diligence processes, with due regard for commercial confidentiality, and other competitive or security concerns, such as through the enterprise's annual, sustainability, or corporate responsibility reports or other appropriate forms of disclosure.

The information reported should include:

- policies;
- measures taken to embed responsible business conduct into policies and management systems;
- the enterprise's identified areas of significant risks;
- the significant adverse impacts or risks identified, prioritized, and assessed, as well as the prioritization criteria;

---

4. http://mneguidelines.oecd.org/OECD-Due-Diligence-Guidance-for-Responsible-Business-Conduct.pdf.

- the actions taken to prevent or mitigate those risks, including where possible estimated time lines and benchmarks for improvement and their outcomes;
- measures to track implementation and results; and
- the enterprise's provision of or cooperation in any remediation.

The RBC Guidance indicates that this information should be sufficient to demonstrate the adequacy of an enterprise's response to the particular human rights impact involved and in turn not pose risks to affected stakeholders, personnel, or to legitimate requirements of commercial confidentiality.

The RBC Guidance further recommends that enterprises publish the foregoing information in a way that is easily accessible and appropriate, such as on the enterprise's website, at the enterprise's premises, and in local languages. The RBC Guidance notes that accessibility of information means that it is not only physically accessible but also understandable and disclosed at a time and in a format, language, and location that will best ensure those for whom it is intended will notice it and be able to use it effectively.

According to the RBC Guidance, for human rights impacts that the enterprise causes or contributes to, it should be prepared to communicate with impacted or potentially impacted rightsholders, in a timely, culturally sensitive, and accessible manner, the information described above that is specifically relevant to them, in particular when relevant concerns are raised by the rightsholders or on their behalf. Examples cited in the RBC Guidance include in-person meetings, online dialogues, consultation with impacted or potentially impacted rightsholders, formal public reports, the sharing of audit or assessment findings with trade unions, and through an appropriate intermediary.

B. Broad-Based Voluntary Disclosure Frameworks and Standards

Various voluntary disclosure frameworks and standards of broad applicability have been developed to promote usefulness, consistency, and comparability of CSR disclosures. These frameworks and standards are generally complementary, and there are initiatives under way to further harmonize them.

1. The Global Reporting Initiative Standards[5]

The GRI Standards are a voluntary framework for reporting on economic, environmental, and social impacts to a wide variety of global stakeholders, ranging from civil society to investors. The GRI Standards can be used for comprehensive sustainability reporting or more narrowly for issue-specific disclosures. The GRI Standards are in wide use. According to information published by GRI, approximately 76 percent of the world's 250 largest corporations report on their sustainability performance using the GRI Standards.

The Standards take a modular approach, consisting of three universal standards—Foundation (101), General Disclosures (102), and Management Approach (103)—and 33 topic-specific standards organized into Economic (200), Environmental (300), and Social (400) topics, as follows:

---

5. GRI Standards main page: https://www.globalreporting.org/standards/.

Economic	Environmental	Social
Economic Performance (201)	Materials (301)	Employment (401)
Market Presence (202)	Energy (302)	Labor/Management Relations (402)
Indirect Economic Impacts (203)	Water (303)	Occupational Health and Safety (403)
Procurement Practices (204)	Biodiversity (304)	Training and Education (404)
Anticorruption (205)	Emissions (305)	Diversity and Equal Opportunity (405)
Anti-competitive Behavior (206)	Effluents and Waste (306)	Non-discrimination (406)
	Environmental Compliance (307)	Freedom of Association and Collective Bargaining (407)
	Supplier Environmental Assessment (308)	Child Labor (408)
		Forced or Compulsory Labor (409)
		Security Practices (410)
		Rights of Indigenous Peoples (411)
		Human Rights Assessment (412)
		Local Communities (413)
		Supplier Social Assessment (414)
		Public Policy (415)
		Customer Health and Safety (416)
		Marketing and Labeling (417)
		Customer Privacy (418)
		Socioeconomic Compliance (419)

2. **The Sustainability Accounting Standards Board Standards**[6]

SASB's articulated mission is to help businesses identify, manage, and report on the sustainability topics that matter most to their investors. Codified in November 2018, the SASB standards are the newest set of broad-based voluntary disclosure standards.

---

6. SASB home page: https://www.sasb.org/.

SASB has designated 26 sustainability-related business issues as likely to affect the financial condition or operating performance of companies, although materiality will differ by industry:

Environment	Social Capital	Human Capital	Business Model and Innovation	Leadership and Governance
GHG Emissions	Human Rights & Community Relations	Labor Practices	Product Design & Lifecycle Management	Business Ethics
Air Quality	Customer Privacy	Employee Health & Safety	Business Model Resilience	Competitive Behavior
Energy Management	Data Security	Employee Engagement, Diversity & Inclusion	Supply Chain Management	Management of the Legal & Regulatory Environment
Water & Wastewater Management	Access & Affordability		Materials Sourcing & Efficiency	Critical Incident Risk Management
Waste & Hazardous Materials Management	Product Quality & Safety		Physical Impacts of Climate Change	Systemic Risk Management
Ecological Impacts	Customer Welfare			
	Selling Practices & Product Labeling			

At a more granular level, SASB has developed standards for 77 industries that take the foregoing issues into account. The standards contain an average of six disclosure topics and thirteen associated metrics.

3. UN Global Compact[7]

Founded by the United Nations, the UN Global Compact is involved with a variety of sustainability issues. Over 9,500 companies participate in the UN Global Compact. Other participating constituencies include civil society, labor, and the United Nations.

Participating companies are required to express a commitment to:

- the UN Global Compact and its ten principles, which address human rights, labor, the environment, and corruption;
- take action in support of UN goals; and
- preparing the annual Communication on Progress submission.

---

7. UN Global Compact home page: https://www.unglobalcompact.org/.

The Communication on Progress describes the practical actions taken or planned by UN Global Compact members to embed the ten principles into their strategies and operations. The format of the Communication on Progress is flexible. However, it must include the following:

- a statement of the participating company's chief executive officer expressing continued support for the UN Global Compact and renewing the company's ongoing commitment to the initiative;
- a description of practical actions taken or planned to implement the ten principles in each of the four areas indicated above; and
- a measurement of outcomes.

Based on a self-assessment, Communication on Progress falls into one of three levels:

- *GC Learner:* the Communication on Progress does not meet one or more minimum requirements
- *GC Active:* the Communication on Progress meets the minimum requirements or
- *GC Advanced:* in addition to qualifying as GC Active, the Communication on Progress covers implementation of advanced criteria and best practices.

The Communication on Progress can be a stand-alone document, part of a sustainability or CSR report, or part of an annual financial report. A Communication on Progress is made publicly available on the UN Global Compact website when submitted.

4. Delaware Certificate of Adoption of Transparency and Sustainability Standards (2018)[8]

The Delaware Certification of Adoption of Transparency and Sustainability Standards Act took effect on October 1, 2018. Under that Act, entities organized under Delaware law can request the Delaware Secretary of State to issue a Certificate of Adoption of Transparency and Sustainability Standards. The Certificate can be used by companies to help demonstrate a commitment to sustainability.

Compliance with the Act is voluntary. Companies are not required to obtain a Certificate. A company seeking a Certificate must file a standards statement with the Delaware Secretary of State that indicates the following:

- the company has adopted resolutions setting forth sustainability standards based on third-party criteria and related performance assessment measures;
- the website address for information on the standards and assessment measures; and

---

8. http://delcode.delaware.gov/title6/c050e/index.shtml.

- a commitment to (a) use the assessment measures to assess performance in meeting the standards, (b) review and assess the standards and assessment measures from time to time and modify them as necessary or advisable in furtherance of meeting the standards, and (c) prepare and make public a report within 90 days after each annual reporting period.

The publicly available annual report must include information on the following for the applicable reporting period:

- the standards and assessment measures in effect
- actions taken to meet the standards
- objective and factual information on performance in meeting the standards
- if the standards have not been met, any additional efforts to be undertaken to improve performance
- the identity of any third party assisting in measuring, managing, or reporting the impact of the entity's business and operations in light of its standards
- any changes to the standards, assessment measures, or reporting period
- a summary of any new actions for the next reporting period.

C. Issue-Specific CSR Disclosures

In addition to the broad-based instruments discussed above, there are voluntary and mandatory instruments pertaining to specific CSR issues. Some of these issue-specific instruments are discussed below.

1. Environmental Disclosures

a. U.S. Securities and Exchange Commission Guidance (2010)[9]

To the extent material to an investment decision, CSR matters are covered by the SEC's general disclosure framework. Among other topics, the SEC also has published guidance that discusses the relevance of existing SEC public company disclosure requirements to climate change.

The Guidance identifies four items in Regulation S-K that may require disclosures relating to climate change:

- *Item 1.01, Description of Business*, requires a description of the registrant's business, including its principal products and services, and the principal markets in which it operates. This item expressly requires disclosure of the material effects of complying with environmental laws upon the capital expenditures, earnings and competitive position of the registrant and its subsidiaries.
- *Item 1.03, Legal Proceedings*, requires a registrant to include information about certain material pending legal proceedings, including, in certain circumstances, those arising under any federal, state or local provisions that have been enacted

---

9. https://www.sec.gov/rules/interp/2010/33-9106.pdf.

or adopted regulating the discharge of materials into the environment or primarily for the purpose of protecting the environment.
- *Item 5.03(c), Risk Factors*, requires registrants to discuss the most significant factors that make investment in the registrant speculative or risky.
- *Item 3.03, Management's Discussion and Analysis of Financial Condition and Results of Operations*, requires registrants to identify and disclose known trends, events, demands, commitments and uncertainties that are reasonably likely to have a material effect on their financial condition or operating performance.

The Guidance also indicates climate change-related matters that may trigger disclosure:

- *Legislation and regulation:* pending or existing regulations or legislation related to climate change at all levels of government. For example, registrants could face costs to improve facilities and equipment to reduce emissions to comply with regulatory limits or to purchase or profit from the sale of allowances or credits under a "cap and trade" system.
- *International accords:* treaties or international accords relating to climate change.
- *Indirect consequences of regulation or business trends:* new opportunities or risks created by legal, technological, political, or scientific developments related to climate change. For example, registrants may face decreased demand for goods that produce significant greenhouse gas emissions and may face potential adverse consequences to their business operations or financial condition from the public's perception of publicly available data about their greenhouse gas emissions.
- *Physical impacts:* significant physical effects of climate change such as severity of storms, sea levels, and water availability. For example, severe weather could cause property damage and disruptions to operations for registrants with operations concentrated on coastlines. It could also cause indirect financial and operational impacts by disrupting the operations of major customers or suppliers.

b. TCFD Recommendations (2017)[10]

In mid-2017, the Financial Stability Board's Task Force on Climate-related Financial Disclosures published recommendations on climate-related financial disclosures. The objective of the recommendations is to encourage companies to evaluate and disclose, as part of their financial filing preparation and reporting processes, the material climate-related risks and opportunities pertinent to their business activities. This disclosure is intended to help investors and other financial market participants, such as lenders and insurance underwriters, to assess and price climate-related risks and opportunities.

---

10. https://www.fsb-tcfd.org/wp-content/uploads/2017/06/FINAL-2017-TCFD-Report-11052018.pdf.

The TCFD's high-level recommendations for all sectors center around four elements:

- governance
- strategy
- risk management
- metrics and targets.

The TCFD recommendations also include supplemental guidance[11] for the financial sector (banks, insurance companies, asset owners, and asset managers) and nonfinancial groups (energy; transportation; materials and buildings; and agriculture, food, and forest products). The supplemental guidance includes suggested metrics.

c. CDP[12]

CDP, formerly known as the Carbon Disclosure Project, focuses on climate, water, and forest impact disclosures. Among other things, CDP solicits information from companies on behalf of investors, via annual questionnaires. Companies also can join to gather information on their supply chains. Questionnaires request qualitative and quantitative information regarding, among other things, strategy, targets, performance, methodology, resource usage, and emissions data. Questionnaire responses can be public or private, although many companies elect to make their responses public.

d. Climate Disclosure Standards Board Framework[13]

CDSB is an international consortium of business and environmental NGOs. It works to provide decision-useful environmental information to markets via mainstream corporate reports, such as an annual report or SEC Form 10-K. CDSB has developed a framework for reporting environmental information, natural capital, and climate change-related information in these reports.

2. Modern Slavery

The focus on modern slavery has increased substantially over the last few years, in part due to new disclosure-only legislation. Although all of the disclosure-only regulations in this area are broadly similar, each new regulation seeks to address perceived deficiencies in those that came before it.

a. California Transparency in Supply Chains Act (2010)[14]

The California Transparency in Supply Chains Act, adopted in 2010, was the first modern slavery disclosure-only legislation. The California Act requires retail sellers

---

11. https://www.fsb-tcfd.org/wp-content/uploads/2017/12/FINAL-TCFD-Annex-Amended-121517.pdf.
12. CDP home page: https://www.cdp.net/en.
13. CDSB home page: https://www.cdsb.net/.
14. https://oag.ca.gov/sites/all/files/agweb/pdfs/cybersafety/sb_657_bill_ch556.pdf.

and manufacturers doing business in California with annual worldwide gross receipts exceeding $100 million to disclose on their websites information regarding their efforts to eradicate slavery and human trafficking from their direct supply chains for tangible goods offered for sale.

Statements are required to address the following topics:

- verification of product supply chains
- supplier audits
- supplier certifications
- internal accountability
- training.

b. UK Modern Slavery Act (2015)[15]

The UK Modern Slavery Act requires "commercial organizations" that supply goods or services do business in the United Kingdom and have annual turnover of at least £36 million annually to prepare a statement indicating the steps taken to ensure that modern slavery is not occurring in their supply chains or businesses.

Suggested disclosure topics include

- organizational structure, business model, and supply chain relationships;
- applicable policies;
- due diligence and auditing process;
- human trafficking risks and steps taken to assess and mitigate risk;
- compliance effectiveness and key performance indicators; and
- training.

At the time of the writing of this chapter (December 2018), signs are pointing to an increased focus by the UK Home Office on companies' compliance with the letter and spirit of the UK Act's transparency provisions. In mid-October 2018, the Home Office sent letters to more than 17,000 companies that it believes are required to publish an annual statement under the UK Act, including subsidiaries doing business in the United Kingdom of a significant number of U.S.-based multinationals, many of which had not previously published a modern slavery statement under the UK Act. Among other things, the letters requested companies to register on a Modern Slavery Contact Database established by the Home Office, publish up-to-date modern slavery statements by March 31, 2019, and submit their statements to the transparency database maintained by Transparency in Supply Chains and the Modern Slavery Registry.

During July 2018, the Home Office announced an independent review of the UK Act. The aim of the review is to report on the operation and effectiveness and potential improvements to provisions of the UK Act, including the UK Act's transparency provisions. The review will aim to report to the Home Secretary before the end of March 2019. As of this writing, it is premature to speculate whether, how, and when

---

15. http://www.legislation.gov.uk/ukpga/2015/30/pdfs/ukpga_20150030_en.pdf.

the transparency provisions of the UK Act may be modified through either guidance or legislative action. However, the review merits continued monitoring by companies given its potential impact on disclosure.

c. Australian Federal Modern Slavery Act (Proposed 2018)[16]

A bill to adopt an Australian federal Modern Slavery Act was introduced to the Australian Parliament in June 2018. This summary describes the bill, as introduced to the Parliament. An Australian Act is expected to be adopted shortly after the writing of this chapter. Based on the legislative input to date, the final Australian Act is expected to track the bill in most respects. However, an amendment has been proposed that would add a monetary penalty if a subject entity fails to publish a modern slavery statement.

As proposed, the Australian Act will apply to Australia-based entities and other entities that carry on business in Australia and that have at least A$100 million in annual consolidated revenue. Subject entities will be required to report each year on their actions to address modern slavery in both their operations and supply chains. Statements will be required to include information on the following:

- the structure, operations, and supply chains of the reporting entity
- modern slavery risks in the operations and supply chains of the reporting entity and any controlled entities
- actions taken to assess and address modern slavery risks, including due diligence, and remediation processes
- how the reporting entity assesses the effectiveness of the above actions
- the process of consultation with any controlled entities and, in the case of joint statements, between each reporting entity and the entity preparing the joint statement
- details of statement approval
- any other information that is considered relevant.

Statements will be required to be approved by the principal governing body of the reporting entity, which is the body or group of persons with primary responsibility for the governance of the entity. The statement also will be required to be signed by a responsible member of the reporting entity, which generally must be a member of the principal governing body.

Reporting entities will be required to submit statements to the Minister of Home Affairs for publication within six months after the applicable fiscal year-end. Statements will be published by the minister in an online Modern Slavery Statements Register.

Entities will be permitted to voluntarily submit modern slavery statements. As proposed, entities that wish to do so will be required to give written notice to the minister before the end of the reporting period. Once an entity volunteers to report, it will be

---

16. https://parlinfo.aph.gov.au/parlInfo/download/legislation/bills/r6148_first-reps/toc_pdf/18134b01.pdf;fileType=application/pdf.

required to comply with all of the Australian Act's reporting requirements, including discussion of the mandatory criteria and the due date. An entity that has volunteered to report will be able to opt out of future reporting by notifying the minister before the next reporting period begins.

d. New South Wales Modern Slavery Act (2018)[17]

The day before the Australian Act was introduced to the Australian Parliament, New South Wales adopted its own modern slavery legislation.

Under the New South Wales Act, an entity must prepare an annual modern slavery statement if it

- has employees in New South Wales;
- supplies goods and services for profit or gain; and
- has total turnover for the applicable fiscal year of at least A$50 million or such other amount as may be prescribed by regulation.

In contemplation of the Australian Act, the transparency provisions of the New South Wales Act do not apply to entities that are required to report under a law of the Commonwealth or another state or a territory prescribed as a corresponding law. Since the compliance threshold under the New South Wales Act is lower than under the Australian Act, some U.S.-based multinationals that are not subject to the Australian Act will be required to prepare a statement pursuant to the New South Wales Act.

Modern slavery statements will be required to contain information pertaining to the steps taken by the subject entity during the applicable fiscal year to ensure that its goods and services are not a product of supply chains in which modern slavery is taking place. The statement requirements will be specified in subsequent regulations. However, the New South Wales Act provides visibility on likely content. The New South Wales Act provides that the regulations may, without limitation, require a modern slavery statement to include information about

- the subject entity's structure, business, and supply chains;
- its due diligence processes in relation to modern slavery in its business and supply chains;
- the parts of its business and supply chains where there is a risk of modern slavery taking place, and the steps it has taken to assess and manage that risk; and
- the training about modern slavery available to its employees.

At the time of this writing, the commencement date for reporting had not yet been set. Following commencement, annual statements will be due and required to be made public as provided for in subsequent regulations.

---

17. https://www.legislation.nsw.gov.au/#/view/act/2018/30/whole.

A person who provides information in a statement that the person knows, or ought reasonably to know, is false or misleading in a material particular may be fined up to 10,000 penalty units, or A$1.1 million (a penalty unit currently is A$110). This is in addition to potential liability under the Crimes Act 1900 for false and misleading information. The maximum penalty for failing to publish a statement in accordance with that Act also is 10,000 penalty units.

e. Welsh Code of Practice for Ethical Employment in Supply Chains (2016)[18]

The Code of Practice covers procurement, supplier selection, tendering, and contract and supplier management. It is intended to ensure that workers in Welsh public sector supply chains are employed ethically and in compliance with both the letter and the spirit of UK and international laws. Although not binding legislation, the Welsh government has indicated that it expects businesses involved in Welsh public sector supply chains, including multinationals based outside of Wales, to adhere to the Code of Practice.

When signing up to the Code of Practice, an organization agrees to comply with twelve specified commitments. One of the commitments is that the organization produce an annual written statement outlining the steps taken during the financial year and plans for future actions to ensure that slavery and human trafficking are not taking place in any part of the organization or its supply chains. The statement must be signed off at the senior management/board level and published on the organization's website. Organizations also are encouraged to publish their statements on the Transparency in Supply Chains register. In exchange for preparing an annual statement and complying with the Code of Practice, an organization may make use of the Wales antislavery logo.

If an organization is subject to the UK Act, its statement prepared pursuant to that Act will satisfy the statement requirement of the Code of Practice.

3. Conflict Minerals (3TG: Tin, Tantalum, Tungsten, and Gold)

a. U.S. Conflict Minerals Rule (2012)[19]

The Conflict Minerals Rule applies to U.S. public companies. As a commercial matter, tens of thousands of companies of all sizes across the world that are not subject to the Conflict Minerals Rule must make the supply chain inquiries contemplated by the Conflict Minerals Rule to satisfy customer requests.

The Conflict Minerals Rule applies to tin, tantalum, tungsten, and gold, which often are referred to as "3TG." If 3TG are necessary to the functionality or production of a product manufactured or contracted to be manufactured by a public company, it must conduct a "reasonable country of origin inquiry" (RCOI) to determine whether the necessary 3TG in the product originated in the Democratic Republic of the Congo

---

18. https://gov.wales/docs/dpsp/publications/valuewales/170502-ethical-en.pdf.
19. https://www.sec.gov/files/formsd.pdf.

(DRC) or one of the nine adjoining countries. If the necessary 3TG originated outside of the DRC region or are from recycled or scrap sources, or the public company has no reason to believe that the necessary 3TG may have originated in the DRC region or it reasonably believes that the 3TG came from recycled or scrap sources, it must disclose on SEC Form SD its determination and briefly describe its reasonable country of origin inquiry and the related results. Form SD is an annual filing requirement and these filings are publicly available on the SEC's EDGAR website. Companies also are required to disclose the information required by the Conflict Minerals Rule on their own websites.

If the public company knows or has reason to believe that necessary 3TG are from the DRC region and are not from recycled or scrap sources, it must conduct enhanced due diligence and file a separate Conflict Minerals Report (CMR) exhibit to its Form SD. The CMR must describe the measures that the company has taken to exercise due diligence on the source and chain of custody of the 3TG. The CMR generally also must include a description of the products, the processing facilities, and country of origin of the necessary 3TG and the efforts to determine the mine or location of origin.

The Conflict Minerals Rule contains a requirement to obtain a mandatory independent private sector audit, or IPSA, relating to some of the disclosures in the report. In addition, the Conflict Minerals Rule requires companies to provide a description in their CMR of any products that have not been found to be "DRC conflict free." The IPSA requirement and the use of the foregoing label in the CMR were generally stayed by the SEC[20] following a court decision which held that the requirement to indicate that products "have not been found to be 'DRC conflict free'" is compelled speech that violates the First Amendment of the U.S. Constitution. However, a company is still required to obtain an IPSA to the extent it voluntarily elects to describe products as "DRC conflict free" in its CMR.

The SEC subsequently issued another statement indicating that the staff will not recommend enforcement action to the Commission if companies that otherwise are required to file a CMR exhibit only file a Form SD.[21] However, for various reasons, very few companies have scaled back their disclosure in reliance on this statement.

There have been various proposals in Congress to repeal the Conflict Minerals Rule, none of which have gained traction. There also has been speculation that the president would seek to revise or temporarily waive the requirements of the Conflict Minerals Rule in the interest of national security, which is permitted under Section 1502 of the Dodd-Frank Act. However, as of this writing, the consensus is that is unlikely to occur. In addition, in early 2017, the then acting chair of the SEC solicited comments on the Conflict Minerals Rule. Thus far, that process has not led the SEC to propose or make further changes to the Conflict Minerals Rule.

---

20. https://www.sec.gov/news/public-statement/2014-spch042914kfh.
21. https://www.sec.gov/news/public-statement/corpfin-updated-statement-court-decision-conflict-minerals-rule.

b. EU Conflict Minerals Regulation (2017)[22]

The EU Conflict Minerals Regulation requires importers of 3TG into the European Union to conduct due diligence and make disclosures concerning the 3TG that they import. Importers must make available to their immediate downstream purchasers information gained and maintained pursuant to supply chain due diligence. They also must publicly report annually on their supply chain due diligence policies and practices for responsible sourcing. The regulation takes effect on January 1, 2021.

Only a small number of U.S.-based companies are expected to have mandatory due diligence and disclosure obligations under the EU Conflict Minerals Regulation, since most U.S.-based companies will be downstream of the reporting obligation. However, well in advance of the effective date of the regulation, the European Commission will be launching a transparency database to provide a single location for downstream companies to voluntarily report on their due diligence practices. It is expected that, over time, many U.S.-based companies will elect to voluntarily report through the transparency database.

4. Pay Equity

Pay equity disclosure rules are intended to create more equitable pay practices over time.

a. U.S. Pay Ratio Rule (2015)[23]

Covered SEC registrants are required to disclose in their proxy statements the median of the annual total compensation of all employees (other than the chief executive officer) and the ratio of the median to the chief executive officer's annual total compensation.

b. UK Gender Pay Gap Information Regulations (2017)[24]

UK employers with 250 or more employees are required to publish annually gender pay gap information on their websites.

5. Other Foreign CSR Disclosure Instruments

U.S.-based companies are increasingly being held to a global disclosure standard by investors, NGOs, and other stakeholders. U.S.-based companies therefore also should be familiar with other foreign CSR instruments, in addition to those already discussed in this chapter, that are influencing U.S. company disclosure, compliance expectations, and practices. A detailed discussion of all of these instruments is beyond the scope of this chapter, but some of the more significant instruments are briefly described below.

---

22. https://eur-lex.europa.eu/legal-content/EN/TXT/PDF/?uri=CELEX:32017R0821&from=EN.
23. https://www.sec.gov/rules/final/2015/33-9877.pdf.
24. https://www.legislation.gov.uk/ukdsi/2017/9780111152010/contents.

a. EU Non-financial Reporting Directive (2014; Subsequently Implemented into National Legislation in EU Member States)[25]

The EU Non-financial Reporting Directive requires subject EU companies to disclose in their management reports material information relating to environmental matters, social and employee matters, respect for human rights, anticorruption and bribery matters, and diversity. Disclosure topics include

- business model;
- relevant policies, including due diligence processes implemented;
- outcomes of policies;
- principal risks, where relevant and proportionate, including business relationships, products, or services which are likely to cause adverse impacts and how the risks are managed; and
- nonfinancial key performance indicators.

b. French Duty of Vigilance Law (2017)[26]

The French Duty of Vigilance Law addresses serious violations of human rights and fundamental freedoms, as outlined in the UN Guiding Principles on Business and Human Rights, the health and safety of people, and the environment. The law requires large French companies to establish vigilance plans to identify and prevent severe human rights violations in their businesses and at certain subcontractors and suppliers. The vigilance plan and a report on its implementation must be made public and included in the subject company's annual report.

c. Stock Exchange Guidance

i. The Hong Kong Stock Exchange Environmental, Social and Governance Reporting Guide (2015)[27]

The Guide consists of both mandatory "comply or explain" provisions and recommended disclosures relating to environmental and social matters. For each of the subject areas, the Guide contains general disclosures and key performance indicators for issuers to report on to demonstrate how they have performed.

ii. Nasdaq ESG Reporting Guide (Nordic and Baltic Markets) (2017)[28]

The Guide presents Nasdaq's view regarding the long-term value of measuring, managing, and reporting environmental, social, and corporate governance data. It is intended as a support tool for listed companies in the relevant markets. The Guide focuses on both

---

25. https://eur-lex.europa.eu/legal-content/EN/TXT/PDF/?uri=CELEX:32014L0095&from=EN.
26. Unofficial translation by the Respect Initiative: http://www.respect.international/wp-content/uploads/2017/10/ngo-translation-french-corporate-duty-of-vigilance-law.pdf.
27. Main page: https://www.hkex.com.hk/Listing/Rules-and-Guidance/Other-Resources/Listed-Issuers/Environmental-Social-and-Governance/ESG-Reporting-Guide-and-FAQs?sc_lang=en.
28. https://business.nasdaq.com/media/ESG-Reporting-Guide_tcm5044-41395.pdf.

broad economic principles and specific performance measurements, 33 of which are discussed in the Guide. The Guide relies heavily upon other prevalent sustainability reporting frameworks—chiefly GRI—as well as emerging ESG disclosure regulations, such as the EU Non-financial Reporting Directive.

iii. London Stock Exchange Group ESG Reporting Guidance (2018)[29]

The LSE Group has published recommendations for ESG reporting for listed issuers. The guidance builds on the TCFD recommendations and the UN's SDGs.

d. International Integrated Reporting Council Framework[30]

The IIRC is a global coalition of regulators, investors, companies, standard setters, the accounting profession, and NGOs that seeks to promote integrated reporting. The IIRC has published a principles-based Framework that establishes guiding principles and content elements for integrated reporting.

e. Resource Extraction

i. EU Accounting and Transparency Directives (2013)[31]

The Directives require listed and large non-listed extractive and logging companies to annually publicly report, at a project level, payments of more than €100,000 that they make to governments.

ii. Canadian Extractive Sector Transparency Measures Act (2014)[32]

The ESTMA requires extractive entities engaged in the commercial development of oil, gas, or minerals to disclose publicly, on an annual basis, specific payments made to governments in Canada and abroad to the extent totaling at least C$100,000. The ESTMA applies to entities listed on a Canadian stock exchange or, if not listed on a Canadian stock exchange, that have a place of business in Canada, do business in Canada, or have assets in Canada and meet specified financial thresholds.

iii. Extractive Industries Transparency Initiative[33]

The EITI is a voluntary initiative with the objective of improving transparency and accountability in countries rich in oil, gas, and mineral resources. Once a host country endorses the initiative, the EITI process is mandatory for all extractive industry operators (including those that are state-owned) operating within that country. Among

---

29. https://www.lseg.com/sites/default/files/content/images/Green_Finance/ESG/2018/February/LSEG_ESG_report_January_2018.pdf.
30. IIRC home page: http://integratedreporting.org/resource/international-ir-framework/.
31. https://eur-lex.europa.eu/legal-content/EN/TXT/PDF/?uri=CELEX:32013L0050&from=EN.
32. https://laws-lois.justice.gc.ca/PDF/E-22.7.pdf.
33. EITI home page: https://eiti.org/.

other things, the EITI Standard contemplates public reporting of resource extraction-related payments.

iv. IPIECA[34]

IPIECA is a global oil and gas industry association for environmental and social issues. IPIECA has published industry guidance on voluntary sustainability reporting that addresses both the structure and content of sustainability reporting.

f. Proposed Legislation

All signs point to more mandatory CSR disclosures over time. Due to space constraints, this chapter does not discuss all of the proposed CSR disclosure legislation. These instruments, some of which are more likely to be adopted than others, span a number of jurisdictions and issues. Examples of proposed legislation that would require additional CSR disclosures include the following:

- *Canada:* modern slavery
- *Hong Kong:* modern slavery
- *Netherlands:* child labor
- *Switzerland:* human rights and environmental
- *United States:* environmental, modern slavery, resource extraction, and ESG broadly.

IV. THE EVOLVING LITIGATION AND ENFORCEMENT LANDSCAPE

Over the last few years, there has been a significant increase in CSR-related litigation and government investigations. Increasingly, claims in this area are based on companies' disclosures.

For example, energy companies have been targeted by states' attorneys general in Massachusetts and New York over alleged inaccuracies in climate change-related disclosures. Several claims also have been filed over the last few years relating to modern slavery disclosures. Class-action lawsuits have been filed in California and Massachusetts under state consumer protection laws in connection with alleged false and misleading statements in modern slavery disclosures. In addition, NGOs have filed a lawsuit in France against a foreign global electronics company alleging misleading advertising practices, arguing that the ethical commitments published by the company are not consistent with its labor practices.

Disclosure-based claims are widely expected to increase further. To mitigate risk in this area, CSR disclosures should be supportable and adequately vetted, explained, and, where appropriate, caveated.

---

34. IPIECA home page: http://www.ipieca.org/.

V. PARTING THOUGHTS—KEEPING THE BIG PICTURE IN MIND

As discussed in this chapter, voluntary and mandatory CSR disclosures have increased at a rapid pace, and all signs point to even more disclosure in the coming years.

Notwithstanding all of the focus on disclosure, it is important to keep in mind that disclosure is just one element of the CSR program, albeit an important one. What ultimately matters, for both stakeholders and internally, is how a company addresses CSR risks and opportunities, from policies to longer-term sustainability issues such as climate change. Managing CSR risks and opportunities is an even more complex and rapidly evolving topic than disclosure and one for another day.

Chapter 5

Environment

Margaret Richardson and Julie Kendig-Schrader

I. INTRODUCTION

Businesses large and small have taken on a variety of issues associated with the environment. Large global companies have created sustainability goals that ultimately will resonate throughout businesses including the legal and compliance departments. Understanding the basic framework of the global, federal, state, and local regulations will be critical. This chapter attempts to identify the critical pieces of the framework, identify regulations both binding and advisory, provide guidance on where to search for information that is specific to a geographical region, and highlight some past and ongoing litigation that may impact your clients and future regulatory regimes. This chapter includes regulations, guidance, and issues that span the international, federal, state, and local levels. As a practitioner, it is important to be aware that environmental issues may be regulated and/or considered at each level of governmental authority. This chapter also highlights voluntary environmental standards and recent trends in environmental litigation.

II. GLOBAL LEGAL AND REGULATORY ISSUES

The United States participates in multiple international agreements and initiatives involving environmental regulation. Several of the key initiatives are described in more detail in this section; however, this chapter is not intended to be a complete review of all global environmental regulations that impact businesses. The State Department maintains a list of all international agreements at www.state.gov/s/l/treaty/tif/index.htm for your information.

A. The London Convention

The Convention on the Prevention of Marine Pollution by Dumping of Wastes and Other Matter 1972, also known as the London Convention, is one of the first global conventions to protect the marine environment from human activities. The stated objective of the London Convention is to promote the effective control of all sources of marine pollution and to take all practicable steps to prevent pollution of the sea by the dumping of wastes and other matter.[1] The United States is a party to the London Convention and has implemented the London Convention through the Ocean Dumping Act or the Marine Protection, Research, and Sanctuaries Act (MPRSA).[2] In 1996, the London Protocol was set forth to further modernize the London Convention and, eventually, to replace it. Under the Protocol all dumping is prohibited, except for possibly acceptable wastes on the reverse list. The reverse list establishes exceptions and assessment protocol. While the United States has not yet ratified the London Protocol, it has adopted regulations that implement many of the points of the London Protocol. If the placement of materials in the ocean, from land or sea, is relevant to your business, it is advised that you familiarize yourself with the London Protocol annex 1 and annex 2 to understand the assessment process, so you may advise your client appropriately.

B. The Montreal Protocol

The second relevant global regulation is the 1987 Montreal Protocol on Substances that Deplete the Ozone Layer. This was the first treaty in the history of the United Nations to be ratified by all 197 countries. As part of the implementation of the Montreal Protocol, the Clean Air Act was amended to add provisions under Title VI for protecting the ozone layer.[3]

C. The Paris Accord

The 21st Session of the Conference of the Parties (COP 21) to the UN Framework Convention on Climate Change (UNFCCC) was held from November 30 to December 15, 2015, in Paris, France. The goal of COP 21 was to produce an agreement that will take force in 2020, binding on all countries, with its objective to keep global warming

---

1. http://www.imo.org/en/OurWork/Environment/LCLP/Pages/default.aspx.
2. https://www.epa.gov/ocean-dumping/ocean-dumping-international-treaties.
3. https://www.epa.gov/ozone-layer-protection/addressing-ozone-layer-depletion.

below 2 degrees centigrade compared to preindustrial times. COP 21 resulted in the adoption of the Paris Accord, which the United States agreed to participate in under the Obama administration. On June 1, 2017, President Trump announced that the United States would withdraw from the Paris Accord.[4]

The U.S. Environmental Protection Agency was processing several rules at the time of and after the Paris Accord, which would have assisted the United States in meeting the goals of the Paris Accord. It is unclear how the withdrawal (and accompanying administrative priority changes) will impact the processing of the previously begun rule changes, many of which are the subject of active litigation. Additionally, in response to the withdrawal, there have been state and local regulatory initiatives adopted which may require businesses to more closely monitor climate change and air issues at the state and local levels. The State Department maintains a list of international agreements at www.state.gov/s/l/treaty/tif/index.htm.

The announcement of the pending withdrawal from the Paris Accord is reflective of a change in policy priorities at the executive level but is only one example of these changes. As described in Law360, October 12, 2018:

> The Trump administration has pushed an energy strategy that it often describes as "energy dominance." In March 2017, President Donald Trump signed a broad executive order that incentivized developing fossil fuel resources and demanded that agencies act to roll back major parts of former President Barack Obama's regulations on energy and the environment. Since then, the U.S. Environmental Protection Agency has rescinded or delayed significant Obama-era regulations aimed at reducing climate change-causing emissions from power plants and reducing methane emissions on tribal and federal lands, among other actions. The Trump administration also has pushed to bring the coal industry back and proposed significant cuts in the EPA's budget.[5]

III. U.S. FEDERAL LEGAL AND REGULATORY REQUIREMENTS

This section will focus on key federal regulations of the United States and how those regulations may impact your activities as in-house counsel. As in-house counsel, you are not expected to be an expert on each regulation; rather, to spot issues and raise concerns appropriately to help reduce risks to your client. The majority of the federal regulations

---

4. https://www.whitehouse.gov/articles/president-trump-announces-u-s-withdrawal-paris-climate-accord/.
5. https://www.law360.com/articles/1073774/energy-dept-promises-9m-for-tribal-energy-projects.

broadly fall within EPA's Emergency Management Program and include the Clean Air Act (CAA), the Clean Water Act (CWA), the Oil Pollution Act (OPA), the Comprehensive Environmental Response, Compensation, and Liability Act (CERCLA), Superfund Amendments and Reauthorization Act, the Emergency Planning and Community Right-to-Know Act (EPCRA), and the Chemical Safety Information, Site Security and Fuels Regulatory Relief Act (CSISSFRRA). A majority of these are reviewed in this chapter.

A. Clean Air Act

The first key legislation that will be addressed is the Clean Air Act (CAA). Prior to the 1970s, most environmental policy was managed at a state or local level; however, because of key environmental disasters (e.g., Love Canal) the federal government stepped in and began shaping environmental policy. The Clean Air Act[6] regulates air quality and emissions from both stationary and mobile sources (e.g., vehicles). Although the CAA is generally enforced via the Environmental Protection Agency (EPA), a significant portion of the day-to-day operations of the legislation is managed at state and local levels.

The CAA requires that the EPA set the National Ambient Air Quality Standards (NAAQS) for six common air pollutants but the state and local agencies implement the standards via permitting and audit procedures. The six relevant air pollutants covered by the CAA are

- particulate matter (coarse and fine) e.g., dust;
- ozone;
- sulfur dioxide;
- nitrogen dioxide;
- carbon monoxide; and
- lead.

The CAA also allows the EPA to regulate emissions of listed hazardous air pollutants (known as HAPs and identified in §112(b) of the CAA) which are periodically updated and allows state and local agencies to regulate the level of acceptable HAP emissions via state implementation plans (SIPs) negotiated between the state and federal government. (California has negotiated stricter SIPs than required by the federal government via the CAA.)

As an attorney supporting a business the key legal issues to consider are related to permitting, self-auditing, reporting, and violations.

First, the CAA or the associated SIPs at the state and local levels require that all new or modified sources of air pollutants receive pre-construction approval. This approval process is generally managed at the state, county, or local level and often requires support of local counsel that understands the relevant agencies and approval processes.

---

6. 42 U.S.C. §7401 et seq. (1970) and amended in 1977 and 1990.

As in-house counsel, a key component of your business support may be framing an adequate amount of time to allow for this pre-construction approval process (e.g., the process typically requires 6–9 months).

Second, as in-house counsel, consider partnering with the internal subject matter experts to understand some of the science behind the proposed emissions and particularly identify not only whether this is a potential CAA concern but also if additional occupational safety measures need to be taken (e.g., significant fine dust would require respirators or full-face masks for the safety of employees).

Third, be clear during the negotiation process on a construction contract about how liability and/or responsibility will be allocated between your client and the construction and/or design-engineer related to the proposed pollution control equipment. It will also be critical to establish a compliance testing protocol following substantial completion that establishes sufficient data to confirm that the proposed pollution control equipment is working as planned and that if the equipment does not meet the testing protocol the contractor and/or design-engineer is responsible to correct the error and retest. Ultimately, your client will be responsible if there is a violation but establishing a baseline that proves the pollution control equipment works is recommended in managing any type of fine or damage calculation.

Fourth, during the negotiation process for the final permit, try to work directly with the operations and Environmental, Health, and Safety (EHS) teams to ensure that the requirements for monitoring and auditing the air quality are not significantly onerous to the business. The business can spend a significant amount of time and resources meeting difficult monitoring and auditing requirements that may not be necessary.

Fifth, make every effort to ensure that appropriate documentation is created and maintained within the business to identify air quality issues internally and further ensure that the appropriate lines of communication are established to raise internal concerns, if necessary.

Sixth, if the business becomes aware of a failure to comply, consider discussing a protocol for reaching out to local and/or state agencies and how best to communicate the information before the agency reaches out to your client. It is important to work with competent expert counsel and determine if a voluntary self-disclosure is in the best interest of your client and also if the business decides to perform an investigation ensuring that the information and investigation are subject to work product privilege.

Seventh, try to include reviews of permits and legislative changes as part of the organization's risk-management review process. This is especially important with regard to air quality permits, because, in general, a business can assert the affirmative defense of being in compliance with the permit and not be held liable for operations subject to the issued permit.

Eighth, consider purchasing insurance for environmental third-party claims particularly if your client is a heavy emitter or has air quality permit with very tight ranges. Finally, it is wise to create a formal review process to ensure the accuracy of the information submitted on all reports since many require a formal certification under oath and can therefore create a basis for claims against corporate officers who sign the certifications.

B. Clean Water Act

The second relevant federal legislation is the Clean Water Act (CWA),[7] which establishes the basic structure for regulating discharges of pollutants into the Waters of the United States (WOUS)[8] and regulating quality standards for surface waters. The EPA or various delegated state, county, and local agencies manage the point-source discharge into water, and the U.S. Army Corps of Engineers issues wetlands permits, subject to oversight by the EPA. Under the CWA, EPA has implemented pollution control programs such as setting wastewater standards for the wastewater treatment industry and also developed national water-quality criteria recommendations for pollutants in surface waters. Pursuant to the water-quality criteria, businesses and individuals are prohibited from polluting into the WOUS (rivers, oceans, lakes, etc.) unless the party has received a permit pursuant to the National Pollutant Discharge Elimination Systems (NPDES) that was created as part of the 1972 CWA.

If your client will discharge from a point source into the WOUS, you will likely need an NPDES permit. If your client discharges pollutants into a municipal sanitary sewer system, you probably won't need an NPDES permit, but the business will likely require a permit from the local, state, or county wastewater treatment authority. If the business discharges pollutants into a municipal storm sewer system, you may need a permit depending on what you discharge. Regardless of whether your client will require a NPDES permit or a local discharge permit, the process is generally managed at the state and/or local level with only four states (Idaho, New Mexico, New Hampshire, and Massachusetts) and the District of Columbia not having full or partial authority over the permitting process. Requirements vary by locality for permits but generally a discharge application will include the following elements:

- a summary of proposed activities
- identification of chemicals or by-products and the relevant levels in the discharge
- identification of any potential adverse consequences (environmental and health)
- disclosure of actions to limit or mitigate the discharge
- an open comment period, in many jurisdictions, the public has the right to comment.

As in-house counsel, several of the key legal issues discussed with regard to the CAA also apply to the CWA with a few key differences. First, many jurisdictions allow for public comment and therefore you may want to work with senior management on how to answer questions and be prepared to manage public inquiries and ensure that those responsible for answering incoming calls know how to appropriately route all questions.

---

7. 33 U.S.C. §1251 et seq. (1972).
8. 40 CFR 230.3(s).

Second, local discharge permits are heavily reliant on a third party, namely the local wastewater treatment plant; therefore, it is absolutely critical that your subject matter experts understand the ability and tolerances of the local wastewater treatment facilities.

Third, water discharge is often influenced by weather and therefore any system design must include worst-case scenarios for unusually heavy rainfall, hurricanes, etc. This information is also important for the business to develop its risk-management plan related to climate change. Again, ensuring that your design-engineers are under a contract that provides for indemnification protection for your client will be very important.

Fourth, under the NPDES, major and minor permittees are randomly selected on an annual basis to participate in the annual Discharge Monitoring Report—Quality Assurance (DMR-QA) study program. DMR-QA evaluates the analytical ability of the laboratories that perform self-monitoring analyses required by their NPDES permit. As in-house counsel, it will be very important to work with your quality-control team to ensure that the appropriate third-party laboratory is selected, the laboratory reps and warrants to its current state of certification, and the future state of certification is referenced in the testing agreement that exists between your client and the laboratory. A good place to start with regard to selecting a third-party laboratory is on the EPA website. The site lists accredited providers (see http://nelac-institute.org/content/NEPTP/ptproviders.php).

A fifth important element to be aware of under the CWA is that private citizens may seek redress against your client for alleged violations. Therefore, creating a strong internal compliance program that includes self-audits and regularly scheduled third-party audits that are commissioned by your client to identify potential issues will be important as part of the overall strategy to mitigate risk, provide documented due diligence records, and ensure that your client has the ability to defend against any alleged violations.

Finally, helping your clients to ensure that they have created a culture that encourages employees to speak up and identify issues early will be important to the overall success of your organization's ability to meet any and all of its various environmental commitments. Just a quick review of recent fines and penalties highlights that the cost to the business increases because of the cover-up rather than the initial violation.

C. Safe Drinking Water Act

The third federal legislation of note is the Safe Drinking Water Act (SDWA),[9] which is managed by a specific subagency within the EPA, the Office of Water (OW). The focus of the OW is ensuring that drinking water is safe. The EPA sets standards for drinking water quality that are implemented via a variety of state, local, and county agencies. The SDWA was originally passed in 1974 and was later amended in 1986 and 1996. The SDWA does not regulate private wells that serve less than 25 homes. The SDWA is different from the two previous acts discussed in that it protects water from both naturally occurring pollutants and man-made pollutants. As a business, the focus will

---

9. 42 U.S.C. §300f.

be on monitoring potential contaminants that might be discharged into the wastewater system. The EPA has a list of contaminants that is updated every five years.[10] It will be important that your client is aware of the current list and also monitors for changes in the list of potential contaminants. The EPA publishes a Federal Register Notice prior to modifying the list and as in-house counsel consider conducting a review of proposed changes on a five-year cycle as part of your risk mitigation plan.

The SDWA also regulates the construction, operation, permitting, and closure of injection wells used to place fluids underground for storage or disposal. Therefore, if your clients utilize this type of technology (common in oil and gas industry) you may want to help them understand the process of storage and also create a detailed monitoring program to identify any leaks or unusual movement of the stored fluids.

The previous recommendations for the CWA apply to compliance with the SDWA and more importantly the issue of litigation and establishment of detailed documentation to ensure that your client can prove compliance will be a critical part of any defense strategy associated with litigation. As in-house counsel, you may find that this particular statute can lead to significant public citizen criticism and litigation. However, you and your client will likely have the ability to mitigate any alleged violation since any citizen who alleges an adverse impact must give 60 days' notice of the alleged violation to your client, the state, and the EPA prior to filing suit.[11] Therefore, competent expert counsel should be engaged immediately to begin to help develop a risk mitigation plan and work with the subject matter experts to determine if a violation is taking place and a remediation plan (short- and long term) is required. It is very important that this information is appropriately communicated to the relevant potential plaintiffs. The goal of the notice period is intended to allow your client an opportunity to correct the violation and to give the EPA or state an opportunity to enforce compliance through their administrative process rather than via litigation. As in-house counsel, a few key suggestions to consider making to your clients are noted below and are relevant regardless of the specific regulatory issue:

- Develop a strong relationship with local environmental counsel before an issue arises. You want your local counsel to know and understand your business before a crisis arises. This will be time and money well spent.
- Develop a strong relationship with the local regulatory agencies. Invite the relevant parties to your site, welcome questions and dialogue. This will prove valuable, if your client ever has an allegation raised because the local agency will know who to call within your organization.
- Finally, ensure that your business has a strong Environment, Health, and Safety team. The ability for this team to monitor compliance, identify issues and solutions, and work cooperatively across your organization will be critical to meeting every type of regulation discussed in this chapter.

---

10. https://www.epa.gov/ccl/contaminant-candidate-list-4-ccl-4-0.
11. 40 CFR Part 135, Subpart B.

D. Resource Conservation and Recovery Act

The next set of relevant federal statutes impacts waste storage, generation, and transport. The first statute of relevance with regard to waste is the Resource Conservation and Recovery Act (RCRA). The RCRA allows the EPA to control and monitor solid waste pollution, although in many cases the relevant operational authority has been granted to state and local authorities. The RCRA[12] was enacted in 1976 and has been amended several times. The RCRA defines solid waste as "any garbage, refuse, sludge ... and other discarded material"[13] and includes "hazardous waste." As a result of the broad definition of hazardous waste under the RCRA, many manufacturers and other businesses qualify as hazardous waste generators. In addition, many states have broader definitions of hazardous waste. Therefore, it is crucial that as in-house counsel, you understand all types of waste that your client generates and subsequently stores or disposes, essentially cradle to grave management of the solid waste.

The RCRA has four codified (via case law and various EPA regulatory decisions) core legitimacy factors associated with whether waste as defined under the RCRA is essentially excluded because it is being recycled.[14] It will be very important to understand your client's waste stream based on the four legitimacy factors identified below:

- Factor 1: Materials must provide a *useful contribution* to the recycling process or to a product or intermediate.[15]
- Factor 2: Recycling must *produce a valuable product* or intermediate.[16]
- Factor 3: Materials must *be managed as valuable commodities*.[17]
- Factor 4: Products of recycling must be *comparable to legitimate products* or intermediates.[18]

Under the RCRA, your client will be responsible for storage, transport, and disposal of waste; therefore, the first step to assessing the risk of the business under the RCRA is clearly understanding all the types of waste that are generated while considering the four aforementioned factors. Identification will require outreach within the organization including operations and EHS. Waste may be deemed hazardous if it appears on one of four lists published by the EPA or demonstrates the characteristics of ignitability, corrosiveness, reactivity, or toxicity, as defined in the RCRA regulations.[19]

A second consideration is understanding how the Department of Transportation (DoT) regulations overlap with the RCRA and ensuring that any third-party logistics provider that your client engages has a process for remaining up to date on the regulations,

---

12. 40 CFR Parts 239–282.
13. 40 CFR Part 260.
14. at 40 CFR 260.43.
15. 40 CFR 260.43(a)(1).
16. 40 CFR 260.43(a)(2).
17. 40 CFR 260.43(a)(3).
18. 40 CFR 260.43(a)(4).
19. 40 CFR Part 261 subpart C.

because failure to properly transport waste will ultimately create liability for your client regardless of the third-party relationship. As in-house counsel, it will also be critical to partner internally and help ensure that you are managing employee risk appropriately and providing the correct personal protective equipment and monitoring the risk profile of any hazardous waste for changes in required protection for employees and the public.

A third issue to carefully monitor is the type of insurance that is available to your client and the limits. Liability under the RCRA can survive sale of property to third parties. It will be critical that you have coverage that has a relatively long lifecycle. An additional consideration regarding liability is cost associated with cleanup activities, and the fact that even if your client followed all the regulations under the RCRA during the relevant time period, if later an issue is discovered your client could be held responsible for cleanup costs under the Comprehensive Environmental Response, Compensation, and Liability Act. This is discussed in more detail later in this chapter.

As in-house counsel, the legal department is often viewed as an expense; however, the RCRA provides an opportunity for the legal department to be considered an OPEX reducer via significant cost savings if the business is able to recycle and reclassify hazardous secondary materials as recycled material that is not defined and therefore not regulated under the RCRA. This particular area of the law continues to be heavily litigated and therefore seeking expert counsel with an expertise in the RCRA can be very beneficial to your client.

An often overlooked but key consideration associated with the RCRA is the point at which materials become waste under RCRA. For some types of materials, such as merchandise returned by customers or expired inventory, it may not be obvious when material changed from being a product to a waste. While it is a product, RCRA does not apply, but once it becomes a waste, a determination has to be made as to whether it is hazardous waste, and penalties can be assessed for failure to handle it in accordance with the applicable requirements.

To determine when something becomes waste in your client's supply chain, consider partnering across the business and creating a risk assessment checklist that is updated at least annually to ensure compliance. Finally, once you have completed your assessment you may want to seek a permit and determine how much hazardous waste is generated and stored in each calendar month. Companies are required to count all hazardous waste generated or stored on a calendar-month-by-calendar-month basis. There are three categories of generators:

1. Conditionally Exempt Small Quantity Generators (CESQGs)

CESQGs are exempt from hazardous waste management regulations provided they identify all hazardous waste that they generate; generate no more than the following quantities of waste in a calendar month—100 kilograms (220 lbs.) of nonacute hazardous waste, 100 kilograms (220 lbs.) of acute spill cleanup residue, and/or 1 kilogram (2.2 lbs.) of other acute hazardous wastes; store no more than 1,000 kilograms (2,200 lbs.) of nonacute hazardous waste, no more than 100 kilograms (220 lbs.) of acute hazardous waste spill cleanup residue, and no more than 1 kilogram (2.2 lbs.) of other acute hazardous wastes on site at any time; and ensure that the hazardous waste they produce is sent to an appropriate offsite treatment or disposal facility.

2. Small Quantity Generators (SQGs)

SQGs are excused from some waste management requirements provided they generate no more than 1,000 kilograms (2,200 lbs.) of hazardous waste in a calendar month.

3. Large Quantity Generators (LQGs)

The full spectrum of hazardous waste requirements apply when the generator produces more than 1,000 kilograms (2,200 lbs.) of nonacute hazardous waste or 1 kilogram (2.2 lbs.) of acute hazardous waste in a calendar month.

Driving the above review as in-house counsel provides an excellent opportunity for you to be seen as a contributor to the bottom line of the business and a partner across the entire organization.

E. Comprehensive Environmental Response, Compensation, and Liability Act

The second statute related to waste is the Comprehensive Environmental Response, Compensation, and Liability Act (CERCLA or "superfund" sites). 42 USC §9601 addresses legacy disposal sites, liability, clean-up, and reporting requirements. The CERCLA was enacted on December 11, 1980, in response to several catastrophic environmental sites, including the Love Canal in New York,[20] and was later amended in 1986. The CERCLA is primarily utilized to enforce strict liability jointly and severely on potentially responsible parties including current or former owners or operators and transporters who disposed of and/or stored hazardous substances. Remember that when considering risk associated with environmental harm, the CERCLA is a strict liability statute meaning your client may be responsible to fund clean-up of contaminated property regardless of whether the activity was permitted. Although the allocation of damages between the various potentially responsible parties will take into consideration whether the activity was performed under a valid permit and costs will be proportioned accordingly when multiple parties are subject to CERCLA liability.

If you are supporting a client who actively purchases/resells real estate, ensuring that adequate environmental due diligence (phase I or phase II) is completed prior to each purchase can be essential to limiting damages under CERCLA. You will not be able to provide 100 percent defense to a CERCLA action but you may have the ability to mitigate the damage allocation among all the relevant parties. In addition, understanding the associated risk of potential contamination to adjacent landholders is

---

20. "Superfund: 20th Anniversary Report: A Series of Firsts." Washington, DC: U.S. Environmental Protection Agency (EPA). Archived from the original on Sept. 9, 2010. Retrieved July 18, 2010.

also very important, since your client can be held liable under CERCLA even if the contamination took place prior to your client purchasing the property in question. A few key recommendations associated with due diligence before concluding the purchase of real estate are identified below:

- Check the regulatory status of the property. Hire a subject matter expert and request copies of all reports, permits, and any documents associated with the land and facility in question. You should also try to ensure that any subject matter expert has adequate malpractice or general liability insurance.
- Conduct a Phase II study as defined in the 2002 Brownfields Amendment to the CERCLA utilizing an experienced environmental engineer.
- Try to ensure that the environmental engineer provides the cost of potential remediation and potential liabilities associated with current and historical generation of waste and use of the real estate.

In general, the seller of commercial real estate does not have an obligation to disclose environmental issues; therefore, it will be critical to complete thorough due diligence prior to closing on any commercial real estate, and in-house counsel should allocate sufficient time and resources to this task.

The CERCLA is unique from the previously reviewed statutes because it requires that the state participate in any remedial action. The EPA must enter into an agreement with the state that addresses issues such as treatment, storage, and disposal and the state must also provide 10 percent of the funding. An additional unique element to CERCLA is the petroleum exclusion. The definition under CERCLA of "pollutant or contaminant" specifically excludes "petroleum including crude oil or any fraction thereof, natural gas, liquefied natural gas, or synthetic gas." This particular exclusion has been heavily litigated and supported by case law.[21]

As in-house counsel, one of the key definitions to be aware of within the CERCLA is the difference between removal action and remedial action. Generally, a removal action is short term to prevent imminent harm and absent special circumstances are required to end after $2 million in expenditures or 12 months have elapsed.[22] By contrast, remedial action is long term and requires a permanent solution. In addition, the EPA must complete several steps before implementing remedial action including a formal environmental investigation and feasibility study regarding the proposed permanent solution. Unfortunately, the case law indicates that this bright-line distinction is often blurred. The distinction between the two is critical with regard to several important issues, including statute of limitations, different procedural postures, and costs. As an example, the statute of limitations for recovery of response costs associated with a remedial action is "6 years after initiation of physical on-site construction of the remedial action,"[23] whereas the statute of limitations for a removal action is "3 years after completion of

---

21. S.Pac. Trans. Co. v. Cal. Dep't of Transp, 790 F. Supp. 983 (C.D. Cal 1991) and Carriddi v. Consol. Aluminum Corp., 478 F. Supp. 2d 150 (D. Mass. 2007).
22. 42 USC §9604(c)(1).
23. CERCLA §113(g)(2)(B).

the removal action."[24] Therefore, it is absolutely critical that a careful review is made of any information request received from the EPA and that appropriate experts are engaged to craft a response. Failure to respond can result in substantial penalties including up to $37,500 per day of noncompliance.[25]

The business should also be aware of and ensure that any EPA Notice Letters received are routed appropriately internally to avoid delay in responding. Regardless of whether your client receives an information request or a Notice Letter, in-house counsel may want to consider the following:

- Appoint an expert local outside counsel for document collection and to maintain attorney-client privilege and work product protection.
- Identify and interview relevant personnel in some cases that may include contractors such as waste disposal transportation services.
- Review all documentation related to shipment and storage of waste.
- Identify all relevant insurance policies and consider providing notice under the relevant policies.

A final key risk factor under the CERCLA is a cause of action by consumers for alleged violations. Therefore, as in-house counsel, you could be facing not only action by the EPA but also private class-action lawsuits and further the ability for the government to assess damages to natural resources up to $50 million for each release.

A final waste-related statute is the Oil Pollution Act (OPA), which was passed in 1990[26] to prevent and respond to catastrophic oil spills. The OPA is also an example of a strict liability statute that provides a private right of action to recover costs associated with clean-up of oil spills. The OPA provides oversight of not only natural resources such as water and land but also vessels that carry oil. The U.S. Coast Guard is responsible for all the vessel requirements under the OPA including, for example, the requirement of a double hull design and also ensuring that each vessel owner carries sufficient insurance.

The OPA has a unique definition of "responsible party" since it is tied to the owner of the vessel, not to the owner of the oil cargo. Therefore, if your client is active in the oil and gas industry utilizing contract carriers, then ensuring that the contract carrier has sufficient insurance and resources to respond in the event of spill is critical to managing risk.

A second interesting aspect of OPA that does not exist with previously discussed statutes is the ability to recover damages such as loss profits or impairment of earning capacity due to injury of natural resources. As you may recall, the plaintiff's bar was very active following the BP oil spill with litigation focused on loss profits and impairment of earnings.[27]

---

24. CERCLA §113(g)(2)(A).
25. https://www.epa.gov/enforcement/superfund-compliance-and-penalties.
26. 33 U.S.C. §2701 et seq.
27. See the discussion contained in *In re*: Deepwater Horizon, 739 F.3d790 (5th Cir.), reh'g en banc denied, 756 F.3d 320 (5th Cir. 2014), cert.denied, 2014 WL 3841261.

The final two statutes focus on chemicals including the use, transportation, and sales of chemicals. These statutes are important because most companies use chemicals at some point in daily operation (e.g., cleaning) and therefore the reach of these statutes is broad.

F. The Toxic Substances Control Act

The first statute related to chemicals that your client should be aware of is the Toxic Substances Control Act (TSCA).[28] The TSCA regulates new and existing chemicals and products that contain chemicals identified specifically in the TSCA. The TSCA includes reporting, record-keeping, and other requirements that may apply to manufacturers (including importers), processors, distributors, and users of chemical substances. It is very likely that your client may be impacted by the TSCA even if the client does not actively manufacture chemicals because the TSCA also includes record-keeping requirements for the use, import, and export of certain chemicals. If your client does actively manufacture, the TSCA will be critical to understand and ensure that the business has a process to actively manage, inventory, store, and audit chemicals whether used in the manufacture process or as an end product. It is also important to understand that certain substances are generally excluded from TSCA, including, among others, food, drugs, cosmetics, and pesticides, because they are regulated by other government agencies.

The EPA is tasked with enforcing the TSCA. In general, the TSCA requires that all new chemical substances are registered and reviewed by the EPA and that the EPA makes an affirmative finding that the chemical is not likely to present an unreasonable risk or that the manufacture may be subject to a compliance order imposing restrictions on the new chemical. Because of the reach of the TSCA, in-house counsel should actively engage with operations, logistics, EHS, and procurement to understand how the client manages chemical inventories, import of chemicals, and use. The EPA maintains the TSCA inventory that currently contains listings of over 83,000 chemicals and as new chemicals are manufactured those are added to the list (https://www.epa.gov/tsca-inventory/how-access-tsca-inventory). The inventory list is publicly available and should be reviewed to identify any special requirements for handling or special record-keeping of certain chemicals. These requirements are identified via a flag system that the EPA utilizes. In-house counsel should help ensure that a process for reviewing the TSCA inventory is included in the risk management process including for importation to avoid liability associated with the TSCA.

It is also important to be aware that several steps should be followed to ascertain the TSCA Inventory/Significant New Use Rule status of a chemical substance. Information on nonconfidential chemical substances can be found in the TSCA Chemical Substance Inventory. Because the chemical identities of the chemical substances can be claimed to be Confidential Business Information (CBI) by the submitters, EPA maintains a CBI

---

28. 15 USC §2601 et seq.

version of the TSCA Inventory. If an intended manufacturer submits a Pre-Manufacturing Notice (PMN) or a Notice of Bona Fide Intent to Manufacture (pursuant to the procedures at 40 CFR Section 720.25 or 721.11) a substance that has a listing on the Confidential Inventory, the agency will notify the submitter of the existence of the Significant New Use Rule (SNUR).

Pursuant to the TSCA, the EPA also requires warning labels and instructions. This is another critical area of input for in-house counsel. A strong recommendation for any client that routinely manufactures chemicals is to create an advertising/labeling committee that includes subject matter experts, medical experts, statistician, and in-house counsel to review any proposed labeling and advertising to ensure compliance with the TSCA and also reduce potential product liability. The EPA has also been granted the right to inspect any facilities subject to the TSCA; therefore, a process for managing an EPA audit is critical to create prior to the agency arriving.

The TSCA has been amended over time and also covers issues such as asbestos, radon, and lead, which impact businesses that are involved with real estate and construction. Therefore, if you support a client that works in real estate and construction, it will also be important to understand the key elements of the TSCA that are specific to your industry.

The most recent amendment took place on June 22, 2016 (Lautenberg Chemical Safety Act 15 USC Ch. 53) and included express language that the Act does not preclude private rights of action for personal injury, wrongful death, property damage, or other injury based on negligence, strict liability, products liability, failure to warn, or any other legal theory of liability. Nor can EPA's safety reviews be used as "dispositive" evidence in such a case. This additional language may remove doubt with regard to whether your client might be subject to liability via class-action or private citizen suits.

An additional new potential area of liability under the TSCA is reliance on the False Claims Act for failure to make required disclosures under the TSCA, although a few recent cases[29] indicate the government does not favor this approach; it will likely continue to be a strategy utilized by plaintiff's counsel. Accordingly, businesses subject to TSCA should consider False Claims Act liability when assessing potential whistleblower actions by current or former employees.[30]

As a practice tip, it is important to be aware of numerous U.S. states requiring disclosure or reporting for chemicals in children's products and cleaning products (e.g., California Safe Drinking Water and Toxic Enforcement Act of 1986, also known as Proposition 65, New York Environmental Conservation Law (ECL), Article 35, and New York Code of Rules and Regulations (NYCRR) Part 659). It is also important to be aware of a recent expansion by the European Union related to mandatory chemical disclosure requirements for consumer products (REACH §33). If your client exports to Europe, you should start reaching out to the import brokers and suppliers that you work with and understand your compliance disclosure requirements.

---

29. Simoneaux v. E.I. du Pont de Nemours & Co., No 12-219-SDD-EWD, 2016 BL 14896 (M.D. La. January 20, 2016) and United States ex rel. Boise v. Cephalon, Inc., No. 08-287, 2015 BL 232385 (E.D. Pa. July 21, 2015).

30. Simoneaux v. E.I. du Pont de Nemours & Co., see the final decision U.S. Court of Appeals, Fifth Circuit, No. 16-30141, December 13, 2016.

The two final federal statutes that will be reviewed are more specific to certain industries such as logistics and construction; however, it is always important to be aware of potential legal issues that may ultimately impact a client's business through its supply chain or contracted third parties.

G. Hazardous Materials Transportation Act

The Hazardous Materials Transportation Act (HMTA) was enacted in 1976[31] and its purpose is to regulate transportation of hazardous materials as defined by the EPA. You are probably most familiar with HMTA through its labeling requirements that are visible on any vehicle that is transporting hazardous material. The day-to-day enforcement of HMTA is primarily via the DoT. Another unique feature of the HMTA is that it effectively preempts any state or local statutes, thereby making the review and enforcement process by in-house counsel simpler.

The HMTA is an example of a statute that is likely to create liability for your client via a subcontract or carrier agreement. Therefore, you should have standard language in your agreements with carriers that place the burden of compliance on the HMTA on the carrier including specific provisions that the carrier will be responsible for any criminal or civil penalties. Any agreements should also contain indemnification for your client on the part of the carrier to reduce the out-of-pocket expenses that your client may incur as a result of a violation. Partnering with your client's logistics department, in-house counsel should help to create a checklist that must be reviewed prior to loading/leaving a distribution center that ensures the carrier has the following before leaving with any hazardous waste:

- The shipping papers (bill of lading) should contain the following elements: proper shipping name, hazard class, identification number, and packaging group. The class names, IMO class and division numbers, or subsidiary hazard classes may be entered in parentheses. Entries are required for number and type packaging and weight (net or gross).
- All materials loaded should be properly labeled with approved placards and that the outside of the vehicle also has the appropriate labels both pursuant to 49 CFR 172(E).
- Confirm that the carrier has a safety plan and a communication plan in case of a spill or accident.

The HMTA has very stringent training and record-keeping requirements. As a result, it is important to work with your EHS and logistics teams to ensure that all employees are properly trained and that records are current. One important practical tip to help with all relevant environmental statutes is to create an internal audit plan within your client's risk management plan. This will allow you to flag opportunities for improvement. You

---

31. 49 USC §5101–5127.

should consider hiring a third party for the audit under attorney-client privilege, if you have received a whistleblower complaint or you have been made aware of potential violations under any statute so that you can decide how best to proceed.

As in-house counsel, it will also be important to work with your EHS and logistics team to establish a process for ensuring that all material being shipped is properly identified pursuant to the Hazardous Materials Table (see 49 CFR 172.101) or have a documented procedure for evaluating the material against all of the recognized Hazard classes (see 49 CFR 173.2). Generally speaking, your client should have created safety data sheets (SDSs) for every product it manufactures and should require that any material that is brought into a location has an SDS provided and that every material that your client ships includes an SDS with the shipping documents. The SDS is a required document that provides critical safety information in case of accidental exposure.

If your client is a logistics provider, the HMTA should be at the top of your list of federal statutes to understand and you should develop a relationship with outside counsel who is an expert in this area of law. Several elements of the HMTA that are relevant to in-house counsel at a logistics provider and are not covered in detail in this chapter are:

- routing requirements;
- right-to-know laws;
- hazardous material driver license requirements; and
- state permits/fees.

H. The Endangered Species Act

The final statute has broader implications for the environment and how your business impacts its geographical footprint. The Endangered Species Act (ESA) was enacted in 1973 and has been amended several times.[32] The goal of the act is to protect imperiled species from extinction as a "consequence of economic growth and development untempered by adequate concern and conservation."[33] The two main federal agencies tasked with implementation and enforcement of the ESA are the U.S. Fish and Wildlife Service (USFWS) and the National Marine Fisheries Service.

The ESA grants the state and federal government concurrent powers. From a practical perspective this means the federal agencies maintain a list of endangered or threatened animals that are subject to protection and the states can develop their own list of animals; as a result, the federal list is the floor and the state can designate additional animals. This means that in some states (e.g., California,[34] Florida[35]) it will be critical to understand both the state and federal lists particularly if your client is involved in land development or land use.

---

32. 16 U.S.C. §1531 et seq.
33. Tennessee Valley Authority v. Hill 437 US 153 (1978).
34. Fish and Game Code, chapter 1.5, sections 2050–2115.5.
35. http://www.myfwc.com/media/1515251/threatened-endangered-species.pdf.

A secondary aspect of the ESA is the right of the federal government to protect critical habitat. The ESA was formally amended to require protection of critical habitat in 1978. Although the policy with regard to maintaining critical habitat largely impacts management of land owned by the government, it could also impact your client if your client is involved in mining, the timber industry, or real estate development. As in-house counsel, it will be critical to help your client understand and document whether federal and/or state protected species will be impacted by development activities. This includes both animal and plant species and further if a species is potentially impacted you work closely with the subject matter expert as documentation is created and submitted to the relevant state agency and/or appropriate field office of the USFWS.

Each state has a USFWS field office, and one important practical tip is to develop a strong working relationship with the relevant field office. It is likely that no two field offices take the same approach to interpreting the ESA and therefore understanding the key drivers of concern to the relevant field office will help create predictability with regard to potential restrictions associated with land development and land use. Examples of potential restrictions include, but are not limited to, clearing, grading, mowing, and even chemical applications. An important working tip is that the states often have higher standards than the federal agencies and therefore may require additional biological surveys on the identified land prior to any commercial development. Under Section 10 of the ESA, if a planned activity by your client may threaten or possibly threaten an endangered species, your client will be required to file a Habitat Conservation Plan (HCP) and secure an Incidental Taking Permit. Failure to secure an Incidental Taking Permit could result in liability for your client associated with a "taking" under the ESA.

The process for creating the HCP is complex and varies greatly and therefore identifying local counsel with experience in the specific geographical location will be critical. As in-house counsel tasked with oversight, it will be important to consider the following issues:

- include all relevant internal stakeholders;
- prepare and train on how to manage public comments;
- allocate adequate time to gather all necessary data; and
- help ensure that your client understands the requirements for monitoring and that an internal audit process is established to ensure compliance.

Most recently, the USFWS and the National Marine Fisheries Service proposed major reforms to the ESA (see Federal Register published on July 25, 2018). The proposed changes will likely have a significant impact on businesses subject to the ESA including most importantly the inclusion of economic impacts in the decision to place a species on the endangered species list. Although this type of change may not have an immediate impact, it certainly will have a longer term impact on the overall total number of listed species and by inference decrease the likelihood that a particular piece of land is subject to scrutiny under the ESA.

IV. STATE AND LOCAL LEGAL AND REGULATORY REQUIREMENTS

This section does not necessarily describe specific state laws, but rather points out several areas regarding which states may have adopted their own statutory or regulatory requirements or where states participate in the federal regulatory regimes outlined previously.

A. State Participation in CERCLA

As previously discussed, the CERCLA requires that states participate in any on-site remedial actions. The state participation is generally memorialized in a document entitled Applicable or Relevant and Appropriate Requirements (ARARs) (Section 121(d) of CERCLA).

CERCLA requires that on-site remedial actions attain or waive federal environmental ARARs or more stringent state environmental ARARs. OLEM Directive 9200.2-187, October 2017, established a pilot process for meeting the CERCLA requirement to identify and determine state and federal ARARs when selecting remedial cleanup actions. EPA has created a manual called CERCLA Compliance with Other Laws that covers potential ARARs for laws including RCRA, CAA, CWA, and other environmental statutes.[36] The goal of this Directive and pilot program is to determine best practices and thereby drive appropriate state involvement. As in-house counsel, it will be very important to understand the current thinking by your state agencies and expectations of working with the EPA to control costs, time, and the overall scope of the proposed remedial action.

B. Electronic Waste

A second area that the states have created legislation is around the issue of electronic waste. According to the National Conference of State Legislators, as of March 2018, 25 states and the District of Columbia have enacted statutes regulating the disposal of electronic waste, or e-waste.[37] The number of electronics which Americans own has been increasing greatly, and it is now estimated that the average American household owns 24 electronic products. Some of these products contain parts, the disposal of which may already be regulated by other applicable hazardous waste laws. It is important to be aware of the potential for the disposal or recycling of e-waste and whether the disposal would be subject to specific state regulations, some of which require the recycling of specific e-wastes. For instance, the state of California adopted the Electronic Waste Recycling Act of 2003[38] that requires manufacturers of covered electronic devices to

---

36. https://www.epa.gov/superfund/applicable-or-relevant-and-appropriate-requirements-arars.
37. http://www.ncsl.org/research/environment-and-natural-resources/e-waste-recycling-legislation.aspx.
38. https://www.calrecycle.ca.gov/Electronics/RegInfo/.

report annually to the state on a wide variety of items related to recycling. As in-house counsel, you should develop a process to stay current as new state legislation is adopted that may impact your client. A suggestion is to monitor new and pending legislation via an online service such as StateScape (http://statescape.com/) and to also be an active member and participate in conferences that are specific to your client's industry.

C. Air Quality/Emissions

A third area that states are particularly active in is control of air emissions.

State roles under the CAA vary based upon the type of pollution at issue. For common pollutants, EPA sets the applicable air quality standard and the states develop enforceable SIPs to meet the standards. For toxic pollutants, states have the option to adopt a program that allows for a partial or complete delegation of federal authority but state programs can be no less stringent than the federal requirements. In most areas, state or local governments issue permits for stationary sources.[39] Therefore, it may be important to develop a relationship with the relevant state agency that has oversight of your client. This is another example of an area where local guidance will be helpful, can save your client's time and money, and may help ensure that your client is compliant. The practical pointers provided under the aforementioned CAA discussion are also relevant to addressing state and local regulation of air quality. In addition to roles that exist within the structure of the CAA, local governments may also have programs regulating air quality issues or incentivizing actions to reduce air emissions.[40]

D. Wetlands Permitting

As with all regulatory requirements certain issues are very specific to a geography, for example, wetlands permitting (e.g., Florida). At the federal level, the primary regulatory authority regarding the protection of wetlands is the CWA. Under the CWA, States can enact their own regulations regarding wetlands and can adopt more stringent limitations than those imposed by the federal program.[41] It is important to be aware that the regulation, and even the definition, of wetlands or state waters can vary between jurisdictions and between the federal, state, and local levels. Experienced local environmental counsel can be important as your client considers entering new locations and geographies.

E. Local Legal and Regulatory Requirements

Local requirements are too numerous to outline; however, as in-house counsel it is always important to recognize that local governments may have their own regulatory regimes and requirements or incentives with respect to environmental issues. This

---

39. https://www.epa.gov/clean-air-act-overview/government-partnerships-reduce-air-pollution.
40. http://blogs.lse.ac.uk/usappblog/2017/03/23/local-governments-are-hidden-but-important-partners-in-air-quality-management/.
41. https://www.eli.org/sites/default/files/eli-pubs/d17_17.pdf.

is particularly true in larger jurisdictions. Often, local jurisdictions have their own environmental regulatory agencies or regulate environmental issues through their zoning code. A resource to research some local governmental codes and regulations can be found at https://www.municode.com/.

V. VOLUNTARY ENVIRONMENTAL STANDARDS FOR BUSINESSES

Many businesses have decided it is in the best interest of their organizations to take on certain environmental and/or sustainability standards. As in-house counsel, you will want to provide guidance to your client with regard to the potential liability by adopting voluntary standards and how those standards may ultimately be used against your client during litigation. The voluntary standards are being formulated by a variety of different organizations (see, e.g., International Institute for Sustainable Development (iisd.org) and the Principles for Responsible Investing (UNPRI.org)):

- Covalence Ethical Quote;
- GRI Sustainability Reporting Guidelines;
- United Nations Global Compact Initiative; and
- World Business Council of Sustainable Development.

Additional risks that your client may take on upon adopting a voluntary standard include alleged false or misleading statements (financial statement risks and also litigation risks), shareholder action, and consumer protection lawsuits for overstatement or false advertising.

As in-house counsel, you will need to work across the business to help ensure that you can balance risks by reviewing all statements (regardless of where or how made) and see that the statements can be fully substantiated, that all statements are consistent and adjustments/updates are made as new information is learned, and that the appropriate internal and external subject matter experts have been consulted.

Establishing a formal sustainability committee within the organization that the legal department chairs or is a member of can also be very effective to help ensure that any statements made are accurate and can withstand litigation scrutiny. It will also be very important as in-house counsel to help develop an expertise generally on the different voluntary standards and create a formal monitoring system related to upcoming/proposed changes. In addition, for public companies that face additional scrutiny around financial disclosure, proxy statements, etc., it will be important to include an annual review process within the Audit Committee annual schedule that allows the Committee to highlight any potential high-risk standards and statements.

It should be noted that the SEC sought comments in 2016 on a proposed Concept Release that would include information about a public company's sustainability goals and efforts. In contrast the EU imposed a Directive on Non-Financing Reporting related to environmental, social, and labor matters. It is likely that some of the voluntary standards will eventually be adopted as legal or regulatory obligations; therefore, in-house counsel should be focused on creating dialogue with various internal stakeholders to ensure that their client is ready when standards change from voluntary to mandatory.

VI. RECENT ENVIRONMENTAL LITIGATION TRENDS

As in-house counsel, one key area to pay close attention to is litigation trends. Over time, the plaintiff's bar will develop new cause of actions or theories of liability, and it will be important for you to be aware of these trends so that you are considering issues, risks, and potential liabilities. One of the more recent trends is related to director and officer liability. As discussed previously, a majority of the relevant statutes are strict liability and in many cases directors and officers were not separately identified in litigation; however, that trend may be changing. For example, on August 3, 2018, in an alarming and unprecedented move, Arkema North America, its CEO, and plant manager were indicted by a local grand jury in Harris County, Texas, for an alleged reckless emission of an air contaminant under Texas Water Code §7.182 as a result of Hurricane Harvey.

Director and officer liability is a risk that in-house counsel must manage as it relates to a variety of environmental statutes. Recent cases include United States v. Mexico Feed & Seed Co.,[42] and Riverside Market Development Corp. v. International Building Products, Inc.,[43] where the courts have been willing to "pierce the corporate veil" and ask if a particular officer and/or director had "authority to control" a particular decision or environmental issue.

In-house counsel should consider the following:

- Develop an environmental policy focused on internal disclosure and provide a reward to employees who highlight potential issues.
- Help ensure the policy is understood and enforced at the highest levels of management.
- Perform regular internal environmental audits and do not rely solely on internal staff. Occasionally hire outside experts to complete the audit. Consider whether the outside audit should be subject to attorney-client privilege.
- Work with the supply chain and engineering teams to seek alternative technologies with a lower risk profile and that does not qualify as hazardous waste.
- Keep good records. Ensure that you have a documented environmental risk mitigation plan and that you document all the efforts that the company takes. This will mitigate findings by the government during an investigation and also lower any damage assessment.
- Ensure that you promptly report any violations of permits or spills.
- Seek and secure high-quality environmental insurance with a long lifecycle. This is especially important for businesses that provide contract services to

---

42. 764 F. Supp. 565 (E.D. MO 1991).
43. 931 F.2d 327 (5th Cir. 1991, cert. denied 112 S. Ct. 636 (1991)).

the building or construction space. Recent cases have demonstrated that even peripheral participants are being exposed to significant litigation including HVAC installers in mold cases and engineering consultants in water contamination cases (see Centex-Rooney Construction Co., Inc. v. Martin County, 706 So.2d 20 (Fla. Ct. App. 1997) and Mays, et al. v. City of Flint, et al., Genesee County Circuit Court).

It is also important to be aware as in-house counsel that the DOJ and the EPA have both adopted a very aggressive approach to parent and successor corporate liability under CERCLA. The EPA Liability Memo[44] indicates that the EPA should disregard corporate form and states that the statutory language may impose liability on shareholders directly. Although you can control liability under the Bona Fide Purchase process, it is a rigorous process and requires a significant amount of record-keeping, auditing, and reinforces the need to take the risk mitigation steps identified above.

A second developing trend with regard to litigation is related to false advertising claims and a cause of action known as "Greenwashing." Three relevant cases are Kamala D. Harris v. Enso Plastics, LLC, Kamala D. Harris v. Aquamantra, Inc., and Kamala D. Harris v. Balance Water Company LLC. Beyond litigation by the states, the Federal Trade Commission (FTC) has published the "Green Guide" (updated in 2012),[45] which provides information to marketers with regard to making claims related to sustainability and/or the environment. It will be very important for in-house counsel to review the Green Guide when considering claims by your client because failure to meet the guideline could result in fees being imposed by the FTC for deceptive trade practices. (A $450,000 penalty was awarded against AJM Packaging Corporation for deceptive trade practice for biodegradable plastics claim.)[46]

A second example of the FTC enforcing the Green Guide is highlighted by the recent case involving the Kauai Coffee Company. Pursuant to Section 260.7 of the Green Guide, you can only call a product compostable if (a) it will break down in a safe and timely manner in a home compost pile or (b) it is accompanied by qualifying language explaining that the product cannot be composted at home and that the appropriate composting facilities are not available in most places where the item is sold. Kauai Coffee included the appropriate qualifying language on its product right next to the word "compostable," where Kauai disclosed that the product is only "Compostable in industrial facilities. Check locally, as these do not exist in many communities. Not suitable for backyard composting."

However, that disclaimer was absent or not prominent in some of Kauai's online promotions and in an AARP Magazine advertisement. These ads were challenged by

---

44. Courtney M. Price., Assistant Administrator for Enforcement and Compliance Monitoring, EPA Memorandum "Liability of Corporate Shareholders and Successor Corporations for Abandoned Sites under CERCLA," June 13, 1984.

45. https://www.ftc.gov/news-events/press-releases/2012/10/ftc-issues-revised-green-guides.

46. https://www.ftc.gov/news-events/press-releases/2013/10/ftc-cracks-down-misleading-unsubstantiated-environmental.

NAD, which found that the use of the word "compostable" without any qualifying disclaimer language could create the false implication that the product was also safely compostable at home. NAD recommended that Kauai discontinue or modify these claims, and Kauai agreed.[47]

An additional potential cause of action that you may need to consider depending on your client's business is nuisance cases. The most recent example of a cause of action related to nuisance was in the recent decisions related to Smithfield Foods and its hog operations (on August 3, 2018, a jury awarded the plaintiffs $473.5 million—the largest to date).

Nuisance as a common law remedy for an alleged environmental contamination case derives from seventeenth-century nuisance and trespass case law. As a result, the type and amount of liabilities that a business may face tend to be difficult to predict.[48] The difficulty in predicting liability is caused by many factors. First, many of the cases require the balancing of competing property owners' interest. Second, plaintiffs and judges often confuse nuisance and trespass which leads to confusion as to the proper standard to be applied, negligence versus strict liability. Third, it is difficult to identify when a cause of action first arises and therefore what is the appropriate statute of limitations. Finally, the calculation of damages is dependent on whether the cause of action ultimately results in a finding of nuisance or trespass and whether the alleged action is permanent or continuing. Because the cases are so fact-specific, it is difficult for any business to predict the potential dollar damages. One mitigating factor is that several of the previously identified federal statutes (Clean Air Act, Clean Water Act, Toxic Substances Act, and Resource Conservation and Recovery Act) provided some level of statutory recovery associated with alleged wrongful/negligent acts.

The pleading of public versus private nuisance is predicated on whether a nuisance "affects at the same time an entire community or neighborhood ...."[49] A public nuisance does not necessarily create a private nuisance and therefore could be seen as a limitation on potential damages; however, given the overall lack of clarity in case law with regard to pleading and specificity of cause of action, in a practical sense a business be prepared for additional litigation regarding individual harm alleged via a private nuisance claim.

VII. SUMMARY AND TAKEAWAYS

The goal of this chapter is to provide some specific actions that in-house counsel can take to reduce their clients' risk as it relates to environmental issues. Although, no in-house counsel can be an expert on every law, you can be prepared to raise issues

---

47. *In re* Kauai Coffee Company, LLC, Case No. 6078 (NAD May 5, 2017).
48. Nuisance and Trespass Claims in Environmental Litigation: Legislative Inaction and Common Law Confusion, Santa Clara Law Review, Volume 36, Number 1, G. Nelson Smith III.
49. Cal. Civ. Code §3480 (West 1993 and Supp. 1995); Mangini, v. Aerojet-General Corp. 281 Cal. Rptr. At 832.

and work across the business to create solutions. The five key takeaway messages are as follows:

1. Develop strong working relationships with expert outside legal counsel. That will reduce the time that will be needed to provide feedback and advice to your client and ensure familiarity with the business unique needs and risks.
2. Develop strong internal working relationships across the entire business. Although you are in-house counsel you must also understand the business at every level and seek to know who can answer questions within the business.
3. Build a strong business culture related to compliance and record-keeping. This will be a benefit to the business regardless of the issue.
4. Create a formal risk management review process within the business and ensure that all relevant departments have a voice.
5. Create an informal network of other in-house attorneys that you can reach out to with questions and for advice.

Chapter 6

Labor and Supply Chain Practices

E. Christopher Johnson, Jr., Susan A. Maslow, Emily C. Brown,
Ed Broecker, and Fernanda Beraldi

I. INTRODUCTION

One of the most significant ways a corporation can meet its social responsibility obligations is to develop socially responsible labor and employment practices. Employees are a significant stakeholder in an organization's social responsibility framework. However, as this chapter will discuss, they are not the only stakeholders in a corporation's social responsibility when it comes to labor and employment practices. Laws, regulations, standards, and litigation in the area of employment and labor practices have evolved significantly over the years and across the globe exposing corporations that fail to adhere to applicable employment laws and regulations susceptible to government investigation and prosecution but also to consumer boycott and shareholder actions. Further, as recent developments, such as the emergence of the #MeToo movement, have demonstrated, a corporation that fails to act responsibly in its labor and employment practices may face significant reputational damage that may ultimately impact its value and the quality of its human capital.

This chapter will provide an overview of the laws, regulations, and global standards that an organization must consider when developing and improving socially responsible labor and employment practices, including working conditions, labor-management relations, occupational health and safety, diversity and equal opportunity; affirmative action and freedom of association; child labor and "forced" or compulsory labor. The chapter also addresses issues regarding labor exploitation in supply chains, which has seen significant evolution in the laws and regulations that mandate vigilance to avoid labor exploitation and therefore have driven both mandatory and voluntary corporate social responsibility (CSR) initiatives.

For corporations operating in a global environment, developing and establishing CSR initiatives in labor and employment relationships is not only a legal imperative but also the hallmark of a good corporate citizen. This chapter will provide best practices in developing compliance practices for assuring a robust CSR program that honors its employees and that complies with the law.

II.   LEGAL AND REGULATORY REQUIREMENTS

A.   U.S. Labor and Employment Laws

According to its website, as of the beginning of 2019, the U.S. Department of Labor (DOL) was administering and enforcing more than 180 federal laws and accompanying regulations that covered many workplace activities for about 10 million employers and 125 million workers. The following are the subjects covered by these laws and regulations[1]:

- Wages and Hours
- Workplace Safety and Health
- Workers' Compensation
- Employee Benefits
- Unions and Their Members
- Employee Protection
- Uniformed Services Employment and Reemployment Rights Act
- Employee Polygraph Protection Act
- Garnishment of Wages
- The Family and Medical Leave Act
- Veterans' Preference
- Migrant and Seasonal Agricultural Workers
- Mine Safety and Health
- Construction
- Transportation
- Plant Closings and Layoffs
- Posters

Besides the DOL, statutes that ensure nondiscrimination in employment are generally enforced by the Equal Employment Opportunity Commission (EEOC), and the Taft-Hartley Act regulates a wide range of employer-employee conduct and is administered by the National Labor Relations Board (NLRB).

---

1. For summaries of major laws and regulations enforced by the DOL, see https://www.dol.gov/general/aboutdol/majorlaws.

1. Wage and Benefits Laws: The Fair Labor Standards Act

The U.S. federal government and most states regulate wages and benefits. Generally, both U.S. federal laws and the state laws follow the same legal construction and have similar mandates when it comes to regulating wages and benefits. At the federal level, the Fair Labor Standards Act (FLSA) establishes legal requirements for paying minimum wage and for overtime pay for certain classes of workers. It also provides standards for using workers under the age of 16, whether they work a full or part-time schedule. It mandates that employers maintain certain records on their employment practices such as the number of employees, the hours that employees work, the hourly rate of compensation, and any deductions from compensation. The DOL's Wage and Hour Division administers and enforces the FLSA with respect to private employment, state and local government employment, and federal employees.

2. Equal Employment: Title VII of the Civil Rights Act of 1964

Title VII of the Civil Rights Act of 1964 and subsequent legislation which supplemented the Civil Rights Act[2] prohibit covered employers from discriminating against job candidates or employees based on race, color, religion, sex, pregnancy, age, disability, gender identity, transgender status, or national origin. The U.S. Supreme Court has held that Title VII sexual discrimination includes sexual harassment.[3] Additionally, some states and local governments have enacted laws that also prohibit discrimination based on such traits as height, weight, marital status, and sexual preference. Employers are covered under Title VII if they have 15 or more employees each working day in 20 or more calendar weeks in the current or preceding calendar year. In limited circumstances, if an employer can establish that a protected status is reasonably necessary to its normal business; the ability to perform the duties of the job; and there are no less restrictive alternatives the situation may permit an exception to the equal employment requirements.

The EEOC enforces Title VII; and state governments, as well as local governments, have authority to enforce Title VII as well as to enforce their own local statutes that prohibit discrimination. The EEOC also enforces a number of other laws that are focused on specific types of discriminatory practices including the Pregnancy Discrimination Act, which amended Title VII to make it illegal to discriminate against a woman because of pregnancy, childbirth, or a medical condition related to pregnancy or childbirth; the Equal Pay Act of 1963, which makes it illegal to pay different wages to men and women if they perform equal work in the same workplace; the Age Discrimination in Employment Act of 1967, which protects people who are 40 or older from discrimination because of age; and Title I of the Americans with Disabilities Act of 1990, which makes it illegal to discriminate against a qualified person with a disability in the private sector and in state and local governments.[4]

---

2. Pregnancy Discrimination Act of 1978, Age Discrimination in Employment Act, Americans with Disabilities Act.
3. Meritor Savings Bank v. Vinson, 477 U.S. 57 (1986).
4. https://www.eeoc.gov/laws/statutes/index.cfm.

3. Occupational Safety and Health Administration Act

The DOL enforces the Occupational Safety and Health Administration Act (OSHA), which establishes workplace safety and health standards. OSHA not only requires that employers maintain certain health and safety standards in the workplace, but it also mandates that employers provide training and assistance to their employees on workplace health and safety issues. With these mandates come certain rights for employees such as the following:

- training in a language the employee understands
- use of safe machinery
- to be provided adequate safety gear
- to be protected from toxic chemicals
- the right to speak to OSHA inspectors
- to report injuries or illness
- to get copies of medical records
- to view or get copies of workplace injury/illness logs
- to view or get copies of test results for workplace hazard checks.

An employer's violation is either categorized as being "willful," "serious," or "other than serious." Willful and serious violations generally result in a monetary fine and must be promptly remedied. "Other than serious" violations must be promptly abated, but there are generally no monetary fines. OSHA covers most private sector employers and their employees.

4. Workers' Compensation Laws

States have established laws that provide compensation to workers who suffer workplace injuries and that protect employers' liability from employee workplace torts. Generally, these laws provide employees with the only legal remedy for damages against the employer. So, employees may not sue their employer in court for damages related to pain, suffering, and emotional distress. If an employer commits an intentional tort, the employee may sue the employer and recover additional damages such as pain and suffering. Employees may still recover damages from third parties for work-related injuries. The law mandates that employees provide benefits to workers injured on the job. Most employers execute this legal mandate by purchasing private insurance, by joining self-insured business groups, or by self-insuring. Payable benefits include lost wages, payment of reasonable and necessary medical expenses, and payment of vocational rehabilitation expenses for up to two years. Employees are entitled to weekly wage loss benefits if the employee sustains the injury or develops the disease at work—"arises out of or in the course of employment"—and a disability results.

5. Labor-Management Relations

The Taft-Hartley Act of 1947 is a group of amendments to the National Labor Relations Act (NLRA) and together is referred to as the Labor Management Relations Act

(LMRA).[5] Together, these labor laws provide protections both to employees and to management. The NLRB is an independent federal agency that enforces the NLRA; the NLRB conducts union elections, decides or facilitates resolution of labor-management disputes, enforces orders, and investigates violations. The NLRA includes the right to seek injunctive relief for violations of the law. Most private sector employers and employees are subject to the NLRA. Exceptions include those employed by federal, state, or local government, those employed as independent contractors, those employed in domestic services, and agricultural laborers, among others. Employees, union representatives, and employers may file charges with their region's NLRB office if they feel their rights under the NLRA have been violated.

Among the provisions in the NLRA relating to employee rights are the following:

- States may pass laws prohibiting mandatory membership in a union or mandating employees pay union dues.[6]
- Employees may not be terminated for union-related reasons.[7]
- Employees' rights to form, join, or assist a union; select representatives to engage in collective bargaining with an employer; join together with other employees to benefit and protect themselves on issues related to matters such as wages and other workplace conditions.
- The right of two or more employees, or for one employee acting on behalf of other employees, to engage in "concerted activity" by joining together to take action for their mutual aid or benefit regarding the terms and conditions of their employment.
- In the event there is a union, the LMRA mandates that unions have a duty to fairly represent union members.
- The right to refrain from engaging in union activities, yet permits employees to join together to improve their working conditions even without a union.
- Prohibits employers from only hiring labor union members.

Among the employer protections in the NLRA are the following:

- Prohibits secondary boycotts—employees of one company may not picket an employer of another company.[8]
- Employers may sue unions for failing to comply with the terms of a collective bargaining agreement.[9]
- The duty for the union and management to bargain in good faith.
- Unions must give advance notice of a strike.
- Prohibits strikes by workers not involved in the labor dispute (sympathy strikes).
- Prohibits strikes by workers over a labor dispute between an employer and another union (jurisdictional strikes).

---

5. https://thebusinessprofessor.com/knowledge-base/labor-management-relations-act-taft-hartley-act/.
6. Taft Hartley Act, 14(b).
7. Id. at 8(b)(2).
8. Id. at 8(b)(7).
9. Section 301.

B. Human Trafficking and Labor Exploitation Laws and Regulations

As discussed below, forced labor, human trafficking, and child labor (all generally referred to herein as "forced labor") are illegal in most countries. Despite this, according to the International Labour Organisation (ILO), some 24.9 million people are trapped in human trafficking with profits of $150 billion. While most of those profits are from human sex trafficking ($99 billion), most are victims of forced labor and not sex trafficking.[10] Trafficking is a criminal enterprise and can be found in a wide range of economic activities including agriculture, construction, domestic work, and manufacturing.

Forced labor occurs in the supply chains of products in our everyday lives. A fact sheet distributed by the State Department's Office to Monitor and Combat Trafficking in Persons has shown that from the time one gets out of bed until the moment one goes to sleep, trafficking may be responsible for producing common products such as clothes, smartphones, computers, electronics, coffee, food, bricks, tires, and even cotton sheets. These products or their ingredients are among the hundreds of goods from dozens of countries on the DOL's *List of Goods Produced by Child Labor or Forced Labor* (DOL List), which is a list of goods and their source countries that involve a significant incidence of child labor or forced labor.

The exploitation usually occurs halfway around the world but starts right here with consumer demand for low prices. In order to meet this demand, businesses have increased the importance of supply chain management, which can increase value, savings, and drive innovation. Unfortunately, however, it can also lead to exploitation when unscrupulous labor brokers and others take advantage of workers. Considering this, as well as the reputational and legal damage an organization may suffer for failing to avoid using forced labor or having forced labor in its supply chain, it is vital that companies develop CSR protocols to mitigate the risk of noncompliance and to assure stakeholders it treats its employees with respect and in compliance with applicable laws.

The U.S. Trafficking Victims Protection Act of 2000 and its amendments prohibit forced labor and also provide the U.S. government with the authority to pursue criminal charges; provides victims a private cause of action; and mandates efforts the U.S. government must take to combat forced labor. The Act established the U.S. State Department's Office to Monitor and Combat Trafficking in Persons and the President's Interagency Task Force to Monitor and Combat Trafficking in Persons to coordinate U.S. government's work to combat forced labor (see U.S. Department of State website, U.S. Laws on Trafficking in Persons, https://www.state.gov/j/tip/laws/).

Although most nations prohibit forced labor, nations differ on the legal definition of "forced labor." U.S. statutes and regulations provide that forced labor means providing or obtaining labor based on threats of harm or physical restraint against the employee or using or threatening to use the legal process to restrain an employee, often the use

---

10. *See* E. Christopher Johnson, Jr., *Business Lawyers Are in a Unique Position to Help Their Clients Identify Supply-Chain Risks Involving Labor Trafficking and Child Labor*, 70 BUS. LAWYER 1083 1086–1087 (2015); See Definition of "Labor Trafficking" in the ABA Model Policies on Labor Trafficking and Child Labor.

of legal process itself may be an abuse of law. Forced labor also includes requiring a worker to pledge their labor or labor of others as security for debt, particularly when the value of the labor is not applied toward the debt or the nature of the work is not defined. It also includes exchanging sex acts for anything of value.[11] A subset of forced labor, "child labor" is defined as using children for labor that is mentally, physically, socially, or morally dangerous and harmful to children or that interferes with their schooling. The statutorily defined age for the type of work children may do varies by jurisdiction, as well as by the nature of the work the child will perform.[12]

In the United States and abroad, actions such as destroying, concealing, confiscating, or otherwise denying employees' access to their identity or immigration documents, such as passports or drivers' licenses, are also considered a form of forced labor.[13] Likewise, using misleading or fraudulent practices to recruit employees or when offering employment also often leads to forced labor (e.g., actions such as failing to disclose basic information about employment, in a format and language accessible to the worker; making material misrepresentations when recruiting employees regarding conditions of employment, including wages and benefits, work location, living conditions, housing and associated costs, any significant costs to be charged to the employee, and, if applicable, the hazardous nature of the work; and/or using recruiters who do not comply with local labor laws where the recruiting takes place).[14] Some regulations also consider failing to provide adequate and safe housing for employees or to provide or pay for return transportation for an employee when employment has ended, when the employee is not a national of the country where the work took place, and who was brought into that country to work to be forced labor.[15]

As awareness around forced labor has increased, strategic litigation by human rights organizations and others[16] to hold those engaged in forced labor accountable has become more prevalent. Although to date, U.S. businesses facing suits alleging they have engaged in forced labor in their supply chain have not succeeded, responsible corporations need to be alert to the legal theories used to pursue these cases because it will aid in assessing the risk of a forced labor situation in its supply chain and to prospectively develop controls to mitigate the risk of having forced labor. Plaintiffs have used a variety of legal theories to advance cases alleging forced labor: civil causes of action for engaging in forced labor; tort case for injuries or other damages; breach of contract, administrative actions such as labor complaints or lost wages; shareholder suits and consumer class action for deceptive or false advertising. To date, litigation relating to mistreatment of foreign workers in the supply chain outside of the United States has met

---

11. *See, e.g.*, 22 USC 7104b; 48 CFR 52.222-50(e), DFAR 252.222-7007.
12. *See* ILO Minimum Age Convention (No. 138); See Johnson, *supra* BUS. LAWYER at 1089.
13. *Id.*
14. *Id.*
15. *Id.*
16. *See Ending Impunity Securing Justice*, THE HUMAN TRAFFICKING PRO BONO LEGAL CENTER AND THE FREEDOM FUND (Dec. 15, 2015), http://www.htprobono.org/wp-content/uploads/2015/12/FF_SL_AW02_WEB.pdf; Daniel Werner & Kathleen Kim, *Civil Litigation on Behalf of Victims of Human Trafficking* (2008), https://www.splcenter.org/20081130/civil-litigation-behalf-victims-human-trafficking.

with no success in American courts. Historically, such litigation falls into four general categories: (i) negligence cases alleging a duty based on the domestic purchaser's knowledge of foreseeable harm; (ii) deceptive advertising claims based on the failure to disclose human trafficking in the supply chain and/or misleading website statements in breach of state consumer protection laws; (iii) claims based on the Alien Tort Statute; and (iv) claims made under the Trafficking Victims Protection Act of 2000. By contrast, litigation based on breach of domestic worker labor laws has proven more successful.

The United States and other nations also use trade laws, financial regulations, and other means to regulate and identify those who may fail to identify forced labor in their supply chain or who engage in forced labor. There is a dichotomy or fissure in the rule of law that separates protection of U.S. workers and foreign workers in the same supply chains. To fill this gap, regulators have or are in the process of enacting several laws in both the United States and abroad. For example, the UK passed its Modern Slavery Act, another disclosure law which requires commercial organizations operating on UK territory with turnover (revenue) exceeding £36 million to publish reports (approved by a senior officer, e.g., directors or partners) on steps taken during the prior financial year to ensure that slavery and trafficking are not taking place in the business or its supply chains. France requires French corporations and outsourcing companies with 5,000 or more employees, and multinational enterprises operating in France with 10,000 or more employees, to adopt and publish plans of vigilance that cover a wide variety of risks: human rights, fundamental freedoms, physical harm, environment, health, safety, and corruption. As it requires a plan to be adopted it goes a step further than other disclosure laws. This bill will also create civil liability in the event of human rights violations overseas. Various interested parties are empowered to initiate court actions and judges are authorized to enforce the duty of vigilance through injunction, damages/fines, etc.

Many of the laws in this area are not being fully enforced or have yet to be fully developed. Moreover, the majority of existing supply chain laws require public disclosure of efforts taken to address labor trafficking and/or child labor but do not require specific action taken toward that end. These laws are designed to provide consumers and the court of public opinion with information on the progress of corporations to address slavery issues in supply chains and appropriately reward or punish business enterprises based on their progress or lack thereof in doing so. Nonetheless, inattentiveness to forced labor issues can result in significant liability for businesses that requires the attention of boards of directors from multiple perspectives because they affect reporting, due diligence, and pricing in merger and acquisitions transactions, labor and employment issues, securities offerings, and other forms of financing and reputational issues.

C. Global Labor and Employment Laws and Regulations

Just as the United States has seen an increase in laws and regulations as well as litigation around employment practices, so too have other countries.[17] The foundation

---

17. The discussion of global labor and employment laws and regulations in this section is adapted from A. GUTTERMAN, GOING GLOBAL: A GUIDE TO BUILDING AN INTERNATIONAL BUSINESS (Eagan, MN: Thomson Reuters, 2018) §15:18.

for employment law in a particular country depends on the relevant legal tradition. For example, in common law countries, such as Canada and the United Kingdom, employment law principles are taken from the common law of contracts and torts. In civil law countries, such as France and Germany, greater reliance is placed on codes and statutes. However, regardless of legal traditions in a local jurisdiction, U.S. companies operating in foreign countries must be mindful of an increasing wave of government intervention into regulation of the workplace. As such, it is now typical to find numerous legislative acts covering all aspects of employment and the activities of trade unions and other associations representing the interests of employees.

In common law countries, such as the United Kingdom, employers can expect to be held accountable for paying remuneration to employees; indemnifying employees against all expenses and losses incurred in the course of employment; taking care of each employee's health and safety, including supplying safe machinery and a safe system of work and supervision; and selecting fit and competent fellow-employees. In turn, employees in those countries have common law duties with respect to rendering personal service, obeying reasonable and lawful instructions, exercising reasonable skill and care in performing duties and in looking after the employer's property, observing good faith, taking reasonable care for their own health and safety and that of other employees, and performing any specific terms in their contract of employment, including reasonable post-termination covenants that are not in restraint of trade.

As to statutory regulation of the employment relationship, it is obviously necessary to review the applicable laws of each foreign country. In general, countries have adopted one or more statutes that broadly address all aspects of the employment relationship and the individual rights of employees and then supplement those statutes with other legislative initiatives covering special aspects of the employment relationship, including collective bargaining arrangements, immigration, discrimination, working conditions (e.g., minimum wage; time off work; working time and holidays; and pregnancy, maternity, and parental rights), and dispute resolution. In addition, countries will generally have separate and complex regulatory schemes covering insurance and taxes.

III. VOLUNTARY STANDARDS, NORMS, AND GUIDELINES

National laws relating to labor and employment are heavily influenced by the international labor standards developed through the consultative processes administered by the ILO. The ILO is continuously involved in drawing up conventions and recommendations in collaboration with representatives of governments, employers, and workers. The ILO's Governing Body has identified eight conventions as "fundamental," covering subjects that are considered as fundamental principles and rights at work: freedom of association and the effective recognition of the right to collective bargaining; the elimination of all forms of forced or compulsory labor; the effective abolition of child labor; and the elimination of discrimination in respect of employment and occupation. The eight fundamental conventions are as follows:

1. Freedom of Association and Protection of the Right to Organise Convention, 1948 (No. 87)
2. Right to Organise and Collective Bargaining Convention, 1949 (No. 98)
3. Forced Labour Convention, 1930 (No. 29)
4. Abolition of Forced Labour Convention, 1957 (No. 105)
5. Minimum Age Convention, 1973 (No. 138)
6. Worst Forms of Child Labour Convention, 1999 (No. 182)
7. Equal Remuneration Convention, 1951 (No. 100)
8. Discrimination (Employment and Occupation) Convention, 1958 (No. 111).

The relevant provisions of the OECD Guidelines for Multinational Enterprises relating to employment and industrial relations provide that enterprises should (within the framework of applicable law, regulations, and prevailing labor relations and employment practices)

- respect the right of their employees to be represented by trade unions and other bona fide representatives of employees, and engage in constructive negotiations, either individually or through employers' associations, with such representatives with a view to reaching agreements on employment conditions;
- contribute to the effective abolition of child labor and the elimination of all forms of forced or compulsory labor;
- not discriminate against their employees with respect to employment or occupation on such grounds as race, color, sex, religion, political opinion, national extraction, or social origin, unless selectivity concerning employee characteristics furthers established governmental policies which specifically promote greater equality of employment opportunity or relates to the inherent requirements of a job;
- provide facilities to employee representatives as may be necessary to assist in the development of effective collective agreements;
- provide information to employee representatives which is needed for meaningful negotiations on conditions of employment;
- promote consultation and cooperation between employers and employees and their representatives on matters of mutual concern;
- provide information to employees and their representatives which enables them to obtain a true and fair view of the performance of the entity or, where appropriate, the enterprise as a whole;
- observe standards of employment and industrial relations not less favorable than those observed by comparable employers in the host country;
- take adequate steps to ensure occupational health and safety in their operations;
- in their operations, to the greatest extent practicable, employ local personnel and provide training with a view to improving skill levels, in cooperation with employee representatives and, where appropriate, relevant governmental authorities;
- in considering changes in their operations which would have major effects upon the livelihood of their employees, in particular in the case of the closure of an entity involving collective layoffs or dismissals, provide reasonable notice of

such changes to representatives of their employees, and, where appropriate, to the relevant governmental authorities, and cooperate with the employee representatives and appropriate governmental authorities so as to mitigate adverse effects to the maximum extent practicable;
- in the context of bona fide negotiations with representatives of employees on conditions of employment, or while employees are exercising a right to organize, not threaten to transfer the whole or part of an operating unit from the country concerned nor transfer employees from the enterprises' component entities in other countries in order to influence unfairly those negotiations or to hinder the exercise of a right to organize; and
- enable authorized representatives of their employees to negotiate on collective bargaining or labor-management relations issues and allow the parties to consult on matters of mutual concern with representatives of management who are authorized to take decisions on these matters.

IV. COMPLIANCE

A. Employment Laws and Practices

Even when we look at the highly developed labor and employment laws in the United States, we see that there are numerous best practices that can and should be implemented in this area to not only help a business avoid liability but also continue to protect its reputation and brand.

1. Recruiting and Advertising

A number of legal and regulatory issues must be considered with respect to recruiting and hiring. For example, discrimination laws prohibit hiring practices that unfairly limit employment opportunities for protected individuals. Additionally, companies may be restricted from obtaining certain types of information, such as medical histories, and from running certain tests, such as lie-detector tests. Moreover, companies need to comply with requirements imposed under specific federal laws, including Title VII of the Civil Rights Act and the Age Discrimination in Employment Act. Besides avoiding illegal discrimination, companies must also comply with other laws regulating their right to gather certain types of information on applicants. For instance, companies must follow special rules to obtain an applicant's credit report, personal background report, fingerprints and photograph, and medical information and test results. Finally, the impact of any collective bargaining agreements and regulations imposed at the state and local levels may impact your hiring procedures.

2. Employment Agreements

An employment agreement is a contract between an employer and employee that sets out the respective duties and obligations of the parties. A contract of employment does not have to be in writing. If there is no written contract, the employer-employee relationship is entered orally and the employee is hired for a specified salary but without a specified term of employment. In most situations, however, there should be some form of written employment agreement. The parties often find it helpful to formalize the terms of the relationship in an employment contract when the company wants to retain the services of the employee for a specified length of time or when the company seeks to protect trade secrets, inventions, or sales territories. For closely held companies, employment agreements may also be used to define the terms of employment of shareholder-employees for tax-planning purposes. Although the language and provisions of employment contracts will vary widely, certain essential provisions run through all such contracts. A general employment agreement will describe the duties to be performed by the employee, the employee's compensation and benefits, the duration of employment, and any special rules relating to termination of employment.

3. Compensation and Benefits

The FLSA requires that most employees in the United States be paid at least the federal minimum wage for all hours worked and overtime pay at time and one-half the regular rate of pay for all hours worked over 40 hours in a workweek. Computation of the regular rate of pay requires consideration of a variety of factors, particularly in cases where an employee is not compensated on a straight salary basis. Time does not permit a detailed discussion of computing the regular rate of pay and you need to be extremely careful when employees are being by the hour or pursuant to a "piece rate" arrangement.

Employee compensation may take a variety of forms and the type and terms of compensation should be described in detail in the employment agreement. Compensation can be divided into four categories: regular, including base compensation such as salaries and commissions; incentive compensation, such as year-end bonuses, percentage compensation based on net profits or gross sales, and compensation plans tied to changes in the value of the business; deferred compensation plans, which provide the employee with the right to receive cash in the future for current services; and fringe benefits. Companies will also be obligated to reimburse the employee for reasonable business expenses. The scope and extent of this obligation will vary depending on the employee's duties and it is common to condition reimbursement on satisfaction of various conditions including, in many instances, pre-approval by an officer of the company.

Incentive compensation includes all forms of compensation for which the amount of compensation earned by an employee is tied to attaining certain performance goals. Incentive compensation can take a variety of forms. Cash bonus and profit-sharing plans can be used to provide financial incentives to employees based on attainment of specified performance targets. Equity-based arrangements include phantom stock plans, stock option plans, and restricted stock purchase plans. While some agreements set out the terms of the specific incentive compensation arrangement, it is also common for the agreement to simply refer to the employee's eligibility to participate in applicable plans or arrangements that are described in separate documents and policies. Of course, the applicable plans may vary depending on the position and his means that an executive or senior manager would be folded into the particular plans that are offered to similarly situated employees.

Bonuses can be structured in several different ways including discretionary bonuses, profit-sharing bonuses, and target performance plans. Both profit-sharing bonuses and target performance plans tie incentive compensation directly to the profitability or performance of the company and hence may provide more of an incentive to employees than the traditional discretionary bonus. The parties may also choose to design an individual bonus plan or formula that is specific to the employee and his or her activities. If this option is selected, the parties must carefully consider if bonus payments will be guaranteed or whether the bonus will be conditioned on satisfaction of certain performance standards. In addition, the agreement should clearly state when bonus payments will be made, if earned.

4. Noncompetition and Non-Solicitation Agreements

Employee confidentiality and assignment of innovations agreements are generally effective to protect a company's rights with respect to its intellectual property and are treated with favor by the courts. However, a company can best protect its confidential information and business relationships with agreements from employees restricting their ability to engage in specified competitive activities. One device is a noncompetition agreement. This is a contractual agreement between an employer and employee pursuant to which the employee agrees not to engage in certain activities which compete with the business of the employer and is effective both during employment and following the termination of employment.

Another strategy is to use a non-solicitation covenant. This agreement prohibits employees from contacting or soliciting customers of the employer except on behalf of the employer or from soliciting employees of the employer to leave the employment of the employer. Each type of agreement has its specific advantages and use. Restrictive covenants are easier to monitor than confidentiality agreements since all that is necessary for there to be a violation is for the employee to engage in specified competitive activities; however, there are often serious issues regarding the enforceability of these types of agreements since many courts and jurisdictions oppose them on grounds that they constitute unfair oppression of employees and unreasonable restraints on trade.

5. Payment and Scheduling Practices

Pay employees on pay date/take care when mailing checks so that they arrive to the employee by payday—employees rely on a living wage. If paycheck does not arrive by mail by the pay date, then the employee may bring a lawsuit to recover back wages. Be attentive when scheduling and managing minor employees—numerous regulations must be filed for minors' well-being. Provide rest periods and premium pay for holiday work even though not required by law—boosts employee morale and productivity. Avoid further litigation by providing these rest periods—i.e., avoid injuries at work due to fatigue/lack of energy. Define overtime—explain which employees are entitled to it and provide a precise definition (i.e., "hourly employee will be paid time and a half for all time worked over 40 hours in a single work week"). Finally, maintain communication between management and employees—inform employees when they will be paid, how often, mode of payment, and the protocol when payday falls on an odd day such as a weekend or holiday.

6. Diversity

Foster a culture of inclusion. Juries sympathize the most with plaintiffs who claim they have been discriminated based on age as all jurors can relate to this type of situation as everyone ages (as opposed to all employees being of one race/gender/etc.)—especially important to base hiring/firing decisions on specific/articulable facts when individuals are older. In addition, create and support diversity groups, reports, and forums to facilitate a fair and respectful environment. Diversity has become a core CSR topic and should be addressed by employers in their own workplaces and throughout their supply chains. A range of corporations have clearly gone on the record regarding diversity not only on their websites but in briefs filed at the Supreme Court of the United States. Among them are General Motors ("economic and business success in today's market requires cross-cultural understanding and the ability to view and resolve problems from multiple perspectives"), American Express, Deloitte LLP, eBay, Johnson & Johnson, Marriott International, Inc., Microsoft, PepsiCo Inc., Shell Oil, Sprint, and Starbucks.

7. Performance Reviews and Assessments

Document employee poor performance over time as evidence of specific reasons for termination that are not based on discriminatory practices. Acknowledging the accomplishments of all employees—document successes as well as problem areas—provides encouragement and also justification for retaining certain employees over others based on nondiscriminatory reasons. Complete full investigations before making termination decisions—it is important to know all of the facts and circumstances and hinders pretext arguments.

8. Employment-Related Decision-Making Processes

Carefully evaluate an applicant/employees' qualifications and how they correspond with the particular position's requirements by documenting the decision-making process and consulting with others. It is easy to let unconscious biases influence decisions; management may not realize the effect their subconscious has on hiring/termination decisions. By taking the time to analyze the facts and circumstances of a particular employment situation and discussing the reasoning behind a decision with colleagues, it is less likely one's unconscious bias will influence hiring/firing decisions. However, it is important to be aware of groupthink—at times one's viewpoints can influence others if others are afraid to speak up or challenge the other's authority.

9. Union Matters

Train supervisors regarding union formation—teach them how to respond to and manage union organization; educate them on the distinction between acceptable and non-acceptable practices so they are prepared and do not make rash decisions that lead to NLRA violations; explain to management why employees join unions to foster understanding and respect. Encourage a culture of communication so problems are resolved in an efficient manner rather than simply discussed behind closed doors. Reinforce key messages and policies via repetition—for example, reiterate company's open door policy in numerous communications. Be mindful of the current composition of the NLRB—the Board is always changing as the members are appointed by the president for five-year terms; as the Board changes, so do acceptable practices.

10. Worker Health and Safety

Create and foster a safe workplace/encourage observation of safety standards—it is possible to curb injuries with proper education and training; expend resources on properly training employees to save money and time later. Implement a comprehensive written safety and health program—reduces the incidents of occupational injuries and illnesses and increases awareness and cautiousness; qualifies the employer for reductions in assessed monetary fines for injury/illness. Actively encourage the reporting of health and safety violations—employees may not be retaliated against in any way (disciplined, discharged, discriminated against, etc.) for reporting violations or filing a safety complaint; it is important to maintain a safe workplace and to discover any issues or concerns promptly. List safety rules in a conspicuous area to increase awareness and vigilance. Finally, explain the complaint/reporting procedure to all employees when they begin work to avoid confusion and a lack of reporting simply due to a failure to communicate.

Make an effort to place injured employee in a position that corresponds with his training and qualifications—avoids having to dip into insurance policy and helps injured employee provide for himself and/or his family. Assert that all injuries/illnesses/other violations should be reported no matter how minor—important to assess all injuries so employers can remedy minor situations before they become major or serious. OSHA makes it very easy to report complaints—employees can file complaints online, via fax/mail, or by telephone; make this information known to employees. Workers do not have to *know* whether a specific OSHA standard has been violated—they may file a complaint as long as they *believe* there is a serious workplace hazard or that an OSHA standard has been violated. Citations may be issued only for current violations and those that existed within the past 6 months, so it is important to report immediately after noticing a potential violation.

11. Training and Education

Specific types of training and education are seldom required by law, but it is important for employers to train and educate new employees on its policies and practices early on; employees are more likely to retain information presented to them at the beginning of their employment as opposed to later when they are under the stress of the job. Labor law compliance involves training, but specific training programs are not "required" by law. All employees must simply know the laws and understand their roles and responsibilities and the Human Resources department is generally tasked with ensuring employees have this information. Examples of useful training programs include sexual harassment and diversity training, training on various labor and employment laws (FLSA, NLRA, FMLA, ADEA, etc.), OSHA training, wages and benefits training, and training on general company standards and expectations. Certain professions require continuing education classes; although not required by all professions, employers may benefit from providing similar type courses that educate employees on the intricacies and difficulties of their profession.

12. Employee Handbooks

In 2017, the NLRB issued a decision changing the way the NLRB reviews employee handbooks. Before the decision, handbooks were reviewed every time there was an alleged NLRA violation and each policy within a handbook was reviewed under intense scrutiny. Any policy that could be construed to inhibit protected concerted activity or any other rights under Section 7 of the Act was considered unlawful no matter the justification. With the decision, the NLRB developed a new standard for determining whether a policy within a handbook is unlawful. The board must consider the effect a policy may have on protected concerted activity, but may also consider the employer's justifications for the policy and extent of the interference with the employees' rights. Policies that used to be automatically deemed unlawful may now be considered appropriate under this new balancing test.

Despite the new, laxer standard, employers should not draft overly restrictive employee handbooks. Allowing employees to discuss workplace issues is important for a business's growth, success, and productivity. Allowing employees the freedom to engage in protected concerted activity boosts employee morale, fosters the sharing of diverse views and ideas, and encourages the employer to address issues and facilitate positive change rather than ignore problems. Employers commonly restrict the use of social media platforms in their employee handbooks, but employers should keep in mind that although these restrictions would likely be deemed lawful by the NLRB, social media can create buzz about a company's accomplishments and facilitate positive discussion when properly used. Allow social media usage, but also monitor these platforms. Employee handbook acknowledgment should be a stand-alone document and not included within the handbook itself or its table of contents; require employees to sign the acknowledgment.

13. Retaliation

Avoid retaliation. Employees who have filed complaints or provided information cannot be discriminated against or discharged on account of such activity; or if an employer retaliates, then the employee may file suit for relief on various claims including reinstatement to his or her job, payment of lost wages, and damages.

14. Termination

While it is sometimes difficult to think about the end of the employment relationship before the employee has even started working, it is important for the parties to take the time to consider what should happen in the event of a "divorce" somewhere down the road and negotiate termination provisions that identify the various events that might lead to the end of the relationship and define the rights and obligations should attach to each party if those events occur.

At-will employment is the most common form of employment relationship for employees who are not executives or senior managers. While, by definition, at-will employment allows the parties to end the employment agreement at any time, it is not uncommon for the agreement to include a requirement that a party wishing to terminate the agreement without cause must provide the other party with a specified minimum amount of advance notice, which might run anywhere from two weeks to 90 days. While at-will employment is the default rule in many jurisdictions, it is still recommended that companies include specific language in their employment agreements that makes it clear that the employee acknowledges that his or her employment relationship is at-will and can be terminated by the company at any time and for any reason (or no reason).

When the parties have agreed to a fixed term for the duration of the employment relationship, it is customary to include a variety of provisions that address the possibility that the agreement will need to be terminated prior to the end of the term such as a description of the grounds for termination "for cause" and the procedures for early termination of the agreement without cause, including the possibility of death, disability, or incapacity of the employee. A particularly challenging issue is the payment of severance if the company initiates an early termination without cause. The employment agreement should also outline the post-termination rights and duties of both parties, including ongoing obligations of the employee under other agreements above.

15. Sexual Harassment

Sexual harassment in the workplace is an issue that can cause morale in a company to decrease significantly and rapidly. Unhappy employees result in lower productivity and tense working conditions. Moreover, sexual harassment claims can adversely affect a company's reputation, resulting in lost profits and market share.[18] Corporations benefit from strong preventative due diligence to protect employees from harassment by promoting a zero-tolerance policy as a part of a larger CSR agenda. Social impact programs targeting the elimination of workplace harassment can have long-term advantages for a company. Companies can start by taking a look at the changing laws and legal requirements relating to harassment in the workplace. In light of the #MeToo movement, business negotiation tactics and laws are evolving with a focus on increasing diversity and protecting employees from harassment, and corporations should take these developments into serious consideration.

In 2017, the #MeToo movement exploded across the United States. Following the accusations against Hollywood producer Harvey Weinstein, protests and awareness campaigns erupted demanding an end to sexual harassment and violence, especially

---

18. Serena Does et al., *Research: How Sexual Harassment Affects a Company's Public Image* (June 11, 2018), https://hbr.org/2018/06/research-how-sexual-harassment-affects-a-companys-public-image.

in the workplace.[19] In 2018, the Equal Employment Opportunity Commission reported an increase of 13.6 percent in charges filed alleging sexual harassment.[20] Legislators and companies are responding to the #MeToo movement and the increase in sexual harassment claims in various ways.

On Wall Street, companies are now incorporating what is referred to as "Weinstein clauses" into merger and acquisition agreements.[21] A Weinstein clause could require a seller to put money in escrow if a social scandal were to arise or highlights the right of a buyer to take back some of the money paid if there are any revelations of inappropriate behavior that damage the business.[22]

From a legislative perspective, some states are considering new laws that would force corporations to remove arbitration clauses for claims related to sexual harassment. Mandatory arbitration clauses are prohibited in New York pursuant to the 2019 budget, which also imposed several other requirements on corporations related to sexual harassment in the workplace.[23] Also in California, a law prohibiting mandatory arbitration for sexual harassment claims was proposed and passed through the Assembly and Senate; however, it was ultimately vetoed by the governor.[24] Moreover, similar legislation is currently working its way through the state legislator in New Jersey.[25] There are also trends to prohibit the use of secret settlements for claims related to sexual misconduct, such as laws which have passed in California[26] and New York.[27]

The #MeToo movement has propelled not only the conversation about sexual harassment in the work place but also the need to increase diversity. California passed a bill, SB 826, which requires publicly held corporations with a headquarters in California to have a "representative" number of women on its board of directors.[28] Specifically, all corporations must have at least one female board member by the end of 2019. If the

---

19. Samantha Schmidt, *#MeToo: Harvey Weinstein Case Moves Thousands to Tell Their Own Stories of Abuse, Break Silence* (Oct. 16, 2017), https://www.washingtonpost.com/news/morning-mix/wp/2017/10/16/me-too-alyssa-milano-urged-assault-victims-to-tweet-in-solidarity-the-response-was-massive/?utm_term=.1fbc2d7f0d40.

20. https://www.eeoc.gov/eeoc/newsroom/wysk/preventing-workplace-harassment.cfm.

21. Nabila Ahmed, *Wall Street Is Adding a New "Weinstein Clause" before Making Deals* (Aug. 1, 2018), https://www.bloomberg.com/news/articles/2018-08-01/-weinstein-clause-creeps-into-deals-as-wary-buyers-seek-cover.

22. *Id.*

23. Lindsay Colvin Stone, *Update: New York State Passes Budget, Creates New Sexual Harassment Obligations for Employers* (Apr. 18, 2018), https://www.laboremploymentlawblog.com/2018/04/articles/sexual-harassment/ny-passes-budget/.

24. California AB 3080, *Employment Discrimination: Enforcement*, http://leginfo.legislature.ca.gov/faces/billTextClient.xhtml?bill_id=201720180AB3080.

25. New Jersey S121, Bars provisions in employment contracts that waive rights or remedies; bars agreements that conceal details relating to discrimination claims, https://legiscan.com/NJ/text/S121/id/1752556.

26. California Senate Bill No. 820, Chapter 953 Settlement agreements: confidentiality, https://leginfo.legislature.ca.gov/faces/billNavClient.xhtml?bill_id=201720180SB820.

27. Ahmed, *supra* note 17.

28. California Senate Bill No. 826, Chapter 954 Corporations: boards of directors, https://leginfo.legislature.ca.gov/faces/billTextClient.xhtml?bill_id=201720180SB826.

corporation has five directors, the law requires that two of the directors are female. Or, if a corporation has six directors on its board of directors, three are required to be women. The aim is to increase women at the leadership level, with the hopes that increased female participation will also decrease the occurrences of sexual harassment. When signing California Senate Bill 826, Governor Edmund Brown stated:

> There may have been numerous objections to this bill and serious legal concerns have been raised. I don't minimize the potential flaws that indeed may prove fatal to its ultimate implementation. Nevertheless, recent events in Washington, DC—and beyond—make it crystal clear that many are not getting the message.[29]

It is prudent for companies to reassess current sexual harassment policies as a means of strengthening CSR and accountability to its employees. It could improve company culture and protect against untold reputational damage and associated losses. With social media and the power that the #MeToo movement has demonstrated, constituents are holding companies accountable more than ever to have a workplace free of harassment and that promotes equality.

B. Forced Labor

Recent regulatory and statutory mandates to identify and mitigate the risk of forced labor in the United States and other nations have included requirements for developing compliance programs designed to mitigate the risk of forced labor. Again, although each nation has taken its own particular approach, for practical purposes when developing a CSR program to manage the risk of forced labor, a holistic view of these requirements provides the needed direction. Generally, a forced labor mitigation compliance plan should be designed based on the size and complexity of the organization as well as the nature and scope of the organization's activities, including the nature of the workforce and the risk that the organization's operations are susceptible to forced labor. The compliance plan should include policies and procedures designed to monitor, prevent, detect, and terminate any employees, agents, subcontracts, or subcontractor employees that have engaged in activities of forced labor, which likely is a violation of laws and regulations which prohibit forced labor.[30]

1. Training and Communications

Employees and agents shall be advised through training and communications on the U.S. laws and regulations that prohibit human trafficking and the actions that will be taken in the event of a violation, including but not limited to removal from the contract, reduction in benefits, or termination of employment or the contract. The relevant contents of the compliance plan must be posted, no later than when the contract performance starts, at

---

29. Governor Brown signing message to SB 826, https://www.gov.ca.gov/wp-content/uploads/2018/09/SB-826-signing-message.pdf.
30. 48 CFR 52.222-50(h).

the workplace and on the contractor/subcontractor's website. If posting at the workplace or on the website is impracticable, the relevant contents of the compliance plan shall be provided to each worker in writing.

2. Reporting

The compliance plan must include processes for employees or agents to report, without fear of retaliation, any activity inconsistent with the laws and regulations that prohibit human trafficking, including information on reporting concerns to government agencies.

3. Recruiting and Hiring

Organizations should develop recruiting and wage policies and procedures that define when and how the organization will use recruiting companies with trained employees; that prohibit charging employees a recruitment fees; and that ensure wages meet applicable host-country legal requirements or any variance must be explained. If housing employees, policies and procedures must ensure housing meets host-country housing and safety standards.[31]

4. Contracting

Organizations should develop appropriate due diligence procedures to identify responsible business partners who do not engage in forced labor. Once engaged, business partners should be required to have compliance plans for identifying and mitigating the risk of forced labor and must regularly certify compliance with labor laws. As described below, companies should adopt the Model Clauses and integrate the UN Guiding Principles, ABA Model Policies on Labor Trafficking and Child Labor, OECD Guidelines, or similar human rights protections into their supply agreements, lest tragedies like a factory fire or the building collapse in Bangladesh cause the public and shareholders to view the business as contributing to conditions that result in the loss of life.

5. Risk Assessment

As an initial matter, regardless of the laws and regulations that apply to an organization, it should conduct a risk assessment for its potential exposure to forced labor issues. It should consider the nature of its workforce, the type of work that is performed, its use of third parties for work, its supply chain, and where it has operations and where it sources globally. In fact, France's forced labor law requires companies to have procedures to identify and analyze the risks of human rights violation in connection with the company's operations. Risk assessment procedures need to regularly assess risks associated with not only the organization itself but also its subsidiaries, subcontractors, and suppliers with which the company has a commercial relationship. Further, once the risk assessment

---

31. *See, e.g.*, 48 CFR 52.222-50(i).

is completed, organizations should define a process to mitigate identified risks and to execute those mitigation plans. In addition, organizations should not only regularly conduct risk assessment but should also, based on its risk profile, identify methods to alert the company on an ongoing basis about its exposure for the risk of forced labor.

6. Monitoring and Auditing

In addition to having internal controls to mitigate the risk of forced labor, organizations also need to develop actionable plans to measure the effectiveness of the controls and of its risk identification procedures. Companies should also develop plans to audit its third parties, to include those in its supply chain to determine compliance with forced labor laws.

7. Disclosure Requirements

In parallel with laws and regulations that mandate an organization have compliance program to mitigate risks of forced labor, many laws and regulations require organizations to disclose, publicly, its practices for managing the risk of forced labor in its operations or in its supply chain, including disclosing if no action is being taken. For jurisdictions that require disclosures, the information that must be disclosed should be posted on the organization's website, included in its financial reports, or disclosed to regulatory authorities. Some nations, the European Union for example, require companies to include in their management reports material information on their forced labor policies and risks exposure.[32] The information that must be disclosed informs the responsible organization on controls and actions it should take to mitigate the risk of forced labor, as well as to comply with disclosure and other laws and regulations that prohibit forced labor. Many of these reporting and disclosure laws require companies to report or disclose information such as the following:

- its structure and governance to manage forced labor issues
- the structure of its supply chain operations
- any actions the company is taking to identify, manage, and mitigate the risk of forced labor in its supply chain, to include identifying whether the organization uses a third party to execute this analysis
- its procedures for auditing third parties it works with for compliance with forced labor laws and regulations including whether audits are independent and announced
- the due diligence the organization undertakes to identify forced labor
- the efforts made to identify geographic locations where the entity has operations that are particularly prone to forced labor and efforts it has undertaken to mitigate these risks

---

32. UK Human Trafficking—2015 Modern Slavery Act, Part 6; Australia Modern Slavery Bill 2018; *Transparency in Supply Chain; European Commission Memorandum, Disclosure of Non-Financial and Diversity Information by Large Companies and Groups—Frequently Asked Questions* (Apr. 5, 2014), http://europa.eu/rapid/press-release_MEMO-14-301_en.htm.

- an assessment of the effectiveness of its controls that were designed to detect and prevent human trafficking
- whether the organization requires third parties to certify compliance with forced labor laws and regulation in their contracts
- any internal controls the organization has to assess whether employees and third parties comply with forced labor laws, regulations, or corporate policies
- the entity's policies and procedures designed to prevent and detect human trafficking
- whether training is developed and delivered in the organization, to include identifying the employees who must take the training, topics covered, and the frequency of training.

Many of the laws and regulations that mandate these disclosures require the company to certify to the disclosures. False certifications may expose an organization to legal liability or reputational damage.

8. Reporting to the Government and Cooperating with the Government

Some regulatory regimes require organizations to have policies and procedures in place to enable the organization to identify, investigate, and disclose instances of possible forced labor violations to the government. The U.S. federal acquisition regulations are a typical example of these requirements that guide an organization subject to disclosure requirements to create the necessary controls to comply with these requirements. Under the U.S. federal acquisition regulations, organizations with U.S. federal government contracts must[33]

- immediately inform the appropriate U.S. government agency of any credible information it receives from any source (including host country law enforcement) that alleges an employee, subcontractor, subcontractor employee, or their agent has engaged in conduct that violates forced labor laws and regulations;
- disclose information sufficient to identify the nature and extent of an offense and the individuals responsible for the conduct;
- describe the organization's mitigation actions it has taken or will take against the offending employee or their agent;
- fully cooperate with any U.S. federal agency undertaking an audit, investigation, or corrective action relating to trafficking; and
- protect all employees suspected of being victims of or witnesses to prohibited activities and must not prevent or hinder the ability of these employees from cooperating fully with government authorities.

---

33. 48 CFR 52.222-50(d, g); 22 U.S.C. 7104(b-c).

V. LABOR ISSUES IN THE SUPPLY CHAIN

Identification, management, and mitigation of human rights and labor issues in the supply chain has been identified above as an important element of an organization's social responsibility duties and activities.[34] The ISO 26000 Guidance on Social Responsibility developed by the International Organization for Standardization (ISO), ISO 26000, which is a voluntary standard for which certification is not available, provides that, at a minimum, organizations should avoid passively accepting or actively participating in the infringement of the human rights of others, a duty that can only be discharged by undertaking due diligence to identify, prevent, and address actual or potential human rights impacts resulting from their activities or the activities of those with which they have relationships (e.g., suppliers and other value chain partners). Specifically, Section 6.3.3.2 of ISO 26000 requires organizations to design and implement a due diligence process that is appropriate to the organization's size and circumstances and which includes a human rights policy for the organization that gives meaningful guidance to those within the organization and those closely linked to the organization; a means of assessing how existing and proposed activities may affect human rights; a means of integrating the human rights policy throughout the organization; a means of tracking performance over time, to be able to make necessary adjustments in priorities and approach; and actions to address the negative impacts of its decisions and activities.[35]

In addition to ISO 26000, many of the universal guidelines for responsible business operations, most of which are focused primarily on multinationals that have expansive global operations, refer to responsibilities with respect to supply chains. For example, Principle 13 of the UN Guiding Principles on Business and Human Rights states that the responsibility to respect human rights requires that business enterprises seek to prevent or mitigate adverse human rights impacts that are directly linked to their operations, products, or services by their business relationships, even if they have not contributed to those impacts; and the OECD Guidelines for Multinational Enterprises require enterprises to seek to prevent or mitigate an adverse impact, even where they have not contributed to that impact, when that impact is directly linked to their operations, products, or services by a business relationship.[36] Organizations adopting the Business Social Compliance Initiative's Code of Conduct are expected to require supply chain partners to have a social responsibility policy and management system to ensure that the requirements of the Code are understood and satisfied including operating procedures to prevent corruption and bribery and additional procedures addressing freedom of association and collective bargaining; discrimination; fair compensation; reasonable working hours, breaks, and

---

34. Portions of the discussion in this section are adapted with permission from A. GUTTERMAN, CORPORATE SOCIAL RESPONSIBILITY: A GUIDE FOR SUSTAINABLE ENTREPRENEURS (Oakland, CA: Sustainable Entrepreneurship Project, 2019). For further information, see www.seproject.org.
35. ISO 26000 GUIDANCE ON SOCIAL RESPONSIBILITY (Geneva: International Organization for Standardization, 2010), 26.
36. Handbook on Corporate Social Responsibility (CSR) for Employers' Organizations (European Union CSR for All Project, Apr. 2014), 9.

time off; occupational health and safety; ban on child labor and special protections for young employees; no bonded labor and protection of the environment.[37]

One way that organizations can exercise influence over the human and labor rights practices of their supply chain partners is through the use of contractual provisions or incentives. In that regard, notice should be taken of the work of the Working Group to Draft Human Rights Protections in International Supply Contracts within the American Bar Association Business Law Section. The Working Group released a report and model contract clauses in 2018 with the aim of helping companies control their suppliers and supply chains and meet growing compliance obligations; protecting workers in international supply chains; and minimizing companies' litigation and other liability risks. The goal is to make supply chain control and worker protection both legally effective and operationally likely. Frequently companies have no shortage of policies; they often appear on the company website, and they may be incorporated by reference into supply contracts (frequently as a "Code of Conduct"). The issues are more complicated than can be handled easily by a simple incorporation clause, however, and the model clauses developed by the Working Group (the "Model Clauses") attempt to address those complexities.

The Model Clauses fully recognize that companies have different policies and practices with respect to supply chain management; the Working Group is keenly aware that there is no broad consensus on the standards to be applied or the operational methods to implement them. The Model Clauses are agnostic as to particular standards and operational methods; each company can use its own. The policies may relate to antitrafficking, worker safety, conflict minerals, antidiscrimination, sustainability, or other issues. Companies that do not already have such policies can use the ABA Model Business and Supplier Principles on Labor Trafficking and Child Labor (https://www.americanbar.org/groups/business_law/initiatives_awards/child_labor/principles/) or the work of the UN, the OECD, or other projects.

In addition to the measures discussed above, an organization that has identified as part of its third-party risk management profile a significant global supply chain that poses the risk of exposing its supply chain to instances of forced labor should develop recruiting and hiring policies and procedures to manage the risk of forced labor. Depending on an organization's risk footprint includes unsophisticated or vulnerable workers such as agricultural or factory workers, for example, the organization should have policies directly addressing these risks.

First, policies and procedures should require that any recruiting agencies that the organization uses or that its suppliers use should be undergo risk-based due diligence to identify the recruiting agency's risk of engaging in abusive recruiting and hiring practices that may indicate its complicity in forced labor or human trafficking. Beyond policies and procedures that define appropriate due diligence methods, the organization should also have policies and procedures that define the terms and conditions that must be included in contracts with recruiting agencies that the organization and its suppliers use.[38] Recruiting agencies then need to be regularly evaluated for their commitment to

---

37. BSCI Code of Conduct (Version 1/2014) (Brussels: Foreign Trade Association, 2014).
38. See Chapter on Risk Management, Ethics, and Compliance for best practices for contracts with third parties.

the organization's policies and procedures for legal and socially responsible recruiting and hiring but also for the actual ability to comply with contractual terms and conditions that are in the organization's contract with the recruiting company that mandate compliance with applicable laws, regulations, standards, and an organization's policies.[39] Additionally, organizations should consider insisting that their suppliers require the same for the recruiters they use.[40]

Policies should prohibit workers in the supply chain for paying for a job, direct how recruitment costs should be paid, and direct how employment documents should be gathered and ensure adequate record-keeping for these practices.[41] Policies and procedures should also assure that its suppliers have concrete methods to demonstrate it has complied with these requirements and that any workers the recruiting agency has recruited and hired have been informed of the organization's commitment to their human and worker rights.[42]

Finally, as discussed relating to reporting, companies must be prepared to report to regulators and other stakeholders regarding their policies and procedures relating to supply chain management. For example, the California Transparency in Supply Chains Act, which was adopted in 2010, was the first modern slavery disclosure-only legislation and requires retail sellers and manufacturers doing business in California with annual worldwide gross receipts exceeding $100 million to disclose on their websites information regarding their efforts to eradicate slavery and human trafficking from their direct supply chains for tangible goods offered for sale. Statements are required to address verification of product supply chains, supplier audits, supplier certifications, internal accountability, and training.[43] Other reporting frameworks around the world suggest more extensive reporting including disclosures relating to organizational structure, business model, and supply chain relationships; applicable policies; due diligence and auditing process; human trafficking risks and steps taken to assess and mitigate risk; compliance effectiveness and key performance indicators; and training.[44]

---

39. https://knowthechain.org/wp-content/uploads/KTC_FB_2018.pdf, 37–39.
40. *Id.*
41. *Id.*
42. *Id.*
43. https://oag.ca.gov/sites/all/files/agweb/pdfs/cybersafety/sb_657_bill_ch556.pdf.
44. *See* UK Modern Slavery Act (2015): http://www.legislation.gov.uk/ukpga/2015/30/pdfs/ukpga_20150030_en.pdf.

Chapter 7

Product and Customer Responsibility

Randal M. Shaheen and W. Stanford Smith

I. INTRODUCTION

Product responsibility and customer care are core issues when discussing corporate social responsibility (CSR). Good corporate citizens must acknowledge, understand, and incorporate appropriate compliance on issues related to a company's main business purpose—to sell goods or services to customers. That means that for companies that sell products, those products must be safe and must inform and sometimes warn customers of any potential issues with such products. Additionally, marketing and advertising for goods and services should also reflect the overall CSR policies of a corporate entity including truthfulness and fairness of such materials. Finally, companies should also plan for and acknowledge potential or possible privacy issues when it comes to their customers' data.

This chapter is divided into the three subsections: customer health and safety; marketing and labeling; customer privacy. Each subsection will include information on the statutory regime, relevant U.S. government agencies, best practices, and international considerations.

One pleasure in writing this chapter was the opportunity to work with old and new friends, and valued colleagues. The authors would like to gratefully acknowledge the contributions to this work of Heather Capell Bramble, Senior Corporate Counsel with Amazon.com, and Stephen K. Gallagher, a partner with Venable, LLP.

In addition to the material set forth in this chapter concerning customer privacy, the reader may also refer to chapters 13 and 14 concerning CSR and cybersecurity for additional information on privacy issues.

II. LEGAL AND REGULATORY REQUIREMENTS—CUSTOMER HEALTH AND SAFETY

A. Consumer Product Safety Commission (CPSC)[1]

Congress created the Consumer Product Safety Commission (CPSC) to promote the safety of consumer products by developing safety standards to educate manufacturers, conducting research for product-related injuries, and authorizing recalls. The CPSC is an independent agency, reporting to neither any department nor agency of the federal government.

1. Relevant Statutes[2]

Consumer Product Safety Act (CPSA): The Consumer Product Safety Act established the CPSC and authorized the agency to develop standards and bans for consumer product safety. Specifically, under CPSA Section 15, manufacturers, importers, distributors, and retailers have a duty to notify CPSC immediately about product information that: (1) fails to comply with a safety rule or voluntary standard; (2) fails to comply with any other rule, regulation, standard, or ban under the CPSA; (3) contains a defect which could create a substantial product hazard; or (4) creates an unreasonable risk of serious injury or death.[3] The only exception to the reporting requirement is if there is "actual knowledge that the Commission has been adequately informed" of any defect, failure to comply, or risk.[4]

The CPSA defines a "substantial product hazard" as a product defect that "creates a substantial risk of injury to the public." The Act identifies factors in assessing whether there is a "substantial risk of injury," including a pattern of defect, number of defective products distributed in commerce, severity of the risk, or other considerations.[5]

The CPSA defines "consumer product" as any article produced or distributed (i) for sale to a consumer or (ii) for the personal use, consumption, or enjoyment of a consumer. Both definitions of consumer products include their use in or around a home, a school, in recreation, or otherwise. The CPSA excludes consumer products like motor vehicles, food, drugs, tobacco, cosmetics, and medical devices—the safety of these products is regulated by other agencies like the FDA and NHTSA which will be later discussed.

---

1. www.cpsc.gov.
2. https://www.cpsc.gov/Regulations-Laws–Standards/Statutes.
3. 15 U.S.C. §2064(b).
4. 15 U.S.C. §2064(b).
5. *See* 16 C.F.R. §1115.12(g)(1).

In one case, an administrative law judge (ALJ) expanded CPSC's authority by finding the agency's jurisdiction over allegedly defective fire sprinklers even though they were installed in commercial and industrial buildings and marketed primarily to professional contractors. The ALJ found that a consumer product need not be available at the retail level or used in consumer homes to qualify, but rather the "focus of the Act is directed towards consumers' exposure to hazards associated with products."[6]

Consumer Product Safety Improvement Act (CPSIA)[7]: The Consumer Product Safety Improvement Act (CPSIA) amended CPSA in 2008 to provide CPSC with new enforcement tools. The law increased the CPSC budget, increased the number of authorized CPSC commissioners from three to five, and enhanced maximum civil penalties. The CPSIA addresses different provisions including lead, phthalates, toy safety, tracking labels, third-party testing and certification, imports, and civil and criminal penalties. Under CPSIA, CPSC was required to create SaferProducts.gov, a publicly searchable database of consumer product incident reports. The CPSIA requires that children's products comply with children's product safety rules, be tested by a CPSC-accepted accredited laboratory, include a Children's Product Certificate as proof of compliance, and have permanent tracking information on the product and its packaging.

Other relevant statutes: The breadth of the CPSC's mission is further reflected in the variety of other laws for which it is responsible, including the following:

- The Children's Gasoline Burn Prevention Act (CGCPA) requires domestic manufacturers to include closures on portable gasoline containers in conformity with safety requirements for child-resistant packaging. Under the CGCPA, "portable gasoline container" means any portable containers intended for consumer use.
- The Federal Hazardous Substances Act (FHSA) requires that all consumer household products have warning labels and authorizes the CPSC to ban or regulate hazardous products. Regulated products under the FHSA include electrically operated toys, cribs, rattles, pacifiers, bicycles, and children's bunk beds.
- The Flammable Fabrics Act (FFA) regulates the manufacture of highly flammable clothing and interior furnishings. Pursuant to FFA, CPSC has established standards for clothing textiles, vinyl plastic film used in clothes, carpets, and rugs, children's sleepwear, mattresses, and mattress pads.
- The Refrigerator Safety Act requires refrigerators to have a mechanism (e.g., magnet latch) that enables the refrigerator door to be opened from the inside in case of accidental entrapment.
- Poison Protection Packaging Act requires many household substances to be packaged in child-resistant packaging.

---

6. *In re* Central Sprinkler Corp., CPSC Docket No. 98-2 (Apr. 6, 1998).
7. https://www.cpsc.gov/Regulations-Laws–Standards/Statutes/The-Consumer-Product-Safety-Improvement-Act.

2. Relevant Voluntary Standards/Reference Resources

The following three organizations handle over 90 percent of the voluntary safety standards on which the CPSC staff works: (1) American National Standards Institute (ANSI); (2) ASTM International; and (3) Underwriters Laboratories (UL).[8] The ANSI standardization process requires consensus among representatives from affected and interested parties, undergoes public review, and requires an appeals process.[9] Examples of voluntary standards developed by the ANSI include all-terrain vehicles, furnaces, gas appliances, and turkey fryers. ASTM International provides technical standards for materials, products, and services.[10] The organization develops voluntary standards for children's products, bunk beds, playground equipment, toys, and other products. UL develops standards addressing the following types of equipment: electrical products and appliances, batteries, smoke alarms, and fire protection equipment. UL also has an online certifications directory to verify UL listed product use and product safety standards.[11] The CPSC website states that the voluntary standards are not endorsed by the CPSC but failure to comply with the standards may lead to a CPSC finding of a substantial product hazard and result in a recall. However, following the voluntary standards does not exempt companies from abiding with the Section 15 reporting requirements.

CPSC has also incorporated voluntary consensus standards from different organizations into its regulations. Some of these organizations include the American Association of Textile Chemists (AATCC), the Window Covering Manufacturers Association (WCMA), the International Organization for Standardization (ISO), the National Electrical Manufacturers Association (NEMA), and the National Fire Protection Association (NFPA).[12] For example, a voluntary standard developed by WCMA provides requirements for window covering products to address strangulation hazards associated with cords.[13] In a CPSC guide for apparel and household textile requirements, the standard is considered voluntary, yet the CPSC can and has requested a recall for products that may be a strangulation hazard.

The Regulated Products Handbook outlines the best practices for manufacturers, importers, retailers, and others to comply with CPSC statutes and regulations. The Handbook covers basic requirements like product certification, sanctions under various CPSC statutes, and evidence that a product is not a violation of CPSC laws. It also provides guidance on preparing for a product recall and recommended procedures for establishing internal recall plans within a company. The Regulated Products Handbook covers reporting requirements and confidential treatment of information. It is a practical guide for those regulated by the CPSC to understand what procedures and actions to take in case of product violations.[14]

---

8. https://www.cpsc.gov/Regulations-Laws–Standards/Voluntary-Standards/Search-for-Voluntary-Standards.
9. https://www.ansi.org/.
10. https://www.astm.org/.
11. https://ulstandards.ul.com/.
12. https://www.standardsportal.org/usa_en/USG/cpsc.aspx.
13. https://www.cpsc.gov/s3fs-public/Guide-to-US-Apparel-and-Household-Textiles.pdf?Uy5dQwgi41YbPckmAjj265aT8iK31MCK.
14. https://www.cpsc.gov/s3fs-public/RegulatedProductsHandbook.pdf.

3. Enforcement Mechanisms

The CPSA has civil penalties for manufacturers who "knowingly" fail to notify CPSC of product hazards. Effective August 14, 2009, the maximum civil penalty increased from $8,000 per violation and $1.825 million for related series of violations to $100,000 per violation and $15 million for related series of violations. As of 2018, the maximum civil penalty is $110,000 per violation and $16.025 million for any related series of violations.[15] CPSC considers a multitude of statutory factors to determine the amount of a civil penalty including the nature, circumstances, extent and gravity of the violation, the nature of the product defect, the occurrence or absence of injury, the number of defective products distributed, and the severity of the risk of injury. Additionally, CPSC has identified non-statutory factors that may be considered in calculating civil penalties on a case-by-case basis including safety and compliance programs, history of noncompliance, economic gain from noncompliance, and failure to respond in a timely and complete manner to the CPSC's requests for information or remedial action.[16] Under egregious circumstances, government can seek criminal sanctions against companies for late reporting violations or against corporations or its agents who "knowingly and willfully" engage in violations under the CPSA.[17] A five-year statute of limitations applies to actions for failure to timely report to CPSC under Section 15(b).[18]

CPSC has two common routes to a consumer product safety recall: (1) a preliminary determination; and (2) the Fast Track recall program. Under the preliminary determination process, CPSC classifies risks as Class A, B, or C hazards varying on the likelihood of serious injury or illness. After receiving a preliminary determination letter, the company may conduct a voluntary recall. Absent a voluntary recall, CPSC may initiate administrative litigation to require a recall. The CPSC may also seek a preliminary injunction in a federal district court to restrain the distribution of the product pending completion of the proceeding. Following discovery and the opportunity for a hearing, the ALJ files an initial decision with the CPSC. The decision becomes final 40 days after issuance absent appeal to the CPSC or issuance of an order by the CPSC to review the initial decision.[19] In lieu of the administrative route, CPSC has authority to proceed directly to a federal district court under Section 12 of the CPSA to seek "temporary or permanent relief as may be necessary to protect the public" with respect to products that serve an imminent hazard.[20]

According to the CPSC Recall Handbook, companies agree to publicly announce a corrective action plan within 20 business days after notifying CPSC under the Fast Track program. The program benefits reporting companies by avoiding receipt of a preliminary determination letter, which plaintiffs would seek to use in subsequent consumer

---

15. Eric Rubel et al., *How CPSC Late Reporting Penalty Trends Are Evolving* (Apr. 17, 2018), https://www.arnoldporter.com/en/perspectives/publications/2018/04/how-cpsc-late-reporting-penalty.
16. *See* 16 C.F.R. §1119.4.
17. *See* 16 C.F.R. §1115.22.
18. 28 U.S.C. §2462.
19. 16 C.F.R. §1025.54.
20. 15 U.S.C. §2061(b)(1).

protection litigation. The Fast Track program is an efficient method for both the CPSC and the company to work together on an action plan rather than expending resources and time to investigate reported defects.[21] With expanding Section 15 reporting obligations and risk of civil and criminal penalties, companies should focus on internal mechanisms to ensure compliance with their duty to notify CPSC.

B. Food and Drug Administration (FDA)[22]

The Food and Drug Administration (FDA) regulates the safety of foods, drugs, medical devices, cosmetics, biological products, and tobacco products. The FDA is an agency within the U.S. Department of Health and Human Services. The Federal Food, Drug, and Cosmetic Act (FD&C Act) is a federal law which establishes the legal framework within which FDA operates. FDA develops regulations based on the FD&C Act and follows procedural notice and comment rulemaking prior to finalizing regulations. FDA follows the "Good Guidance Practice" regulation to issue FDA guidance documents.

1. Relevant Statutes

Federal Food, Drug, and Cosmetic Act (FD&C Act)[23]: The FD&C Act, codified in Title 21 of the U.S. Code, authorized the FDA to demand evidence for the safety of new drugs, medical devices, and cosmetics, issue standards for food, and conduct factory inspections. The FD&C Act has been amended many times to expand and strengthen the FDA's regulatory power. The principal amendments include the 21st Century Cures Act, the Food and Drug Administration Modernization Act (FDAMA) of 1997, the FDA Food Safety Modernization Act (FSMA), the Prescription Drug Marketing Act (PDMA) of 1987, and the Food and Drug Administration Safety and Innovation Act (FDASIA). Other amendments include the Kefauver-Harris Amendments of 1962 which strengthened the rules for drug safety and the Medical Device Amendments of 1976 which applied safety and effectiveness rules to new medical devices.

21st Century Cures Act (Cures Act)[24]: The Cures Act is designed to accelerate medical product development and bring treatments to the market faster. The Act modified the FDA drug approval process and eased the requirements for drug companies by allowing companies to provide data summaries and real world evidence such as observational studies, patient input, and anecdotal evidence rather than full clinical trial results. The Act established expedited product development programs including the Regenerative Medicine Advanced Therapy (RMAT) for eligible biologics and the Breakthrough Devices Program for new medical devices. The Cures Act aims to modernize clinical trial design to increase access to drugs and treatments and incorporate patient feedback in the drug development and review process.

---

21. https://www.cpsc.gov/s3fs-public/8002.pdf.
22. https://www.fda.gov/.
23. https://www.fda.gov/RegulatoryInformation/LawsEnforcedbyFDA/SignificantAmendmentstotheFDCAct/default.htm.
24. Pub. L. No. 114–255, 130 Stat. 1033 (2016).

Food and Drug Administration Modernization Act (FDAMA)[25]: The FDAMA amended the FDCA relating to the regulation of food, drugs, medical devices, and biological products. The Act reauthorized the Prescription Drug User Fee Act of 1992 (PDUFA), which allows the FDA to collect fees from drug manufacturers to fund the new drug approval process. FDAMA provides an expanded database on clinical trials which will be accessible to patients. Under this law, patients will receive advance notice when a manufacturer plans to discontinue a drug on which they depend on for their serious or debilitating conditions.

Food Safety Modernization Act (FSMA): The FSMA directs FDA to establish standards for foods grown, harvested, and processed. Under the FSMA, food facilities are required to implement a written Hazard Analysis and Risk-based Preventive Controls (HARPC) plan. This allows facilities to: (1) identify and evaluate foreseeable food safety hazards; (2) specify preventative steps, or controls, that will be put in place to prevent the hazards; (3) identify how the facility will monitor the controls; (4) maintain routine records of monitoring; and (5) specify the actions the facility will undertake to correct problems that arise.[26]

Under FSMA, the FDA has implemented rules and programs to ensure imported products meet U.S. standards and are safe for consumers. For example, the rule on Accredited Third-Party Certification establishes a voluntary program through which third parties can certify that foreign food facilities comply with U.S. food safety standards to facilitate an entry of imports.[27] Another program, the Voluntary Qualified Importer Program (VQIP), is a voluntary fee-based program that provides expedited review and import entry of human and animal foods into the United States.[28] Both consumers and importers benefit from this program. FSMA also gives FDA mandatory recall authority and overall aims to better oversee the food industry, strengthen the global food safety system, and improve public health mainly by reducing the risk of foodborne illnesses.

Food and Drug Administration Safety and Innovation Act (FDASIA)[29]: FDASIA expands FDA's authority by: (1) giving the authority to collect user fees from industry to fund innovator drugs and other products; (2) promoting innovation for faster patient access; (3) increasing stakeholder involvement in FDA processes; and (4) enhancing the safety of the drug supply chain. The FDA has developed a three-year implementation plan and provides monthly updates toward accomplishing requirements under FDASIA. FDASIA includes the fifth authorization of the Prescription Drug User Fee Act, initially passed in 1992, and the third authorization of the Medical Device User Fee Act (MDUFA). Both PDUFA and MDUFA ensure that FDA will continue to receive stable and consistent funding to allow the agency to bring to the market new drugs.

---

25. https://www.fda.gov/RegulatoryInformation/LawsEnforcedbyFDA/SignificantAmendmentstothe FDCAct/FDAMA/ucm089179.htm.
26. https://www.harpc.com/harpc-requirements/.
27. https://www.fda.gov/food/guidanceregulation/fsma/ucm361903.htm.
28. https://www.fda.gov/Food/GuidanceRegulation/ImportsExports/Importing/ucm490823.htm.
29. https://www.fda.gov/RegulatoryInformation/LawsEnforcedbyFDA/SignificantAmendmentstothe FDCAct/FDASIA/default.htm.

2. Relevant Voluntary Standards

FDA Guidance: FDA guidance documents provide FDA's current thinking on a particular topic. The documents are nonbinding for the FDA and the public. The guidance documents describe the FDA's interpretation of a regulatory issue and discuss specific issues or products including the design, product, labeling, manufacturing, and testing of regulated products. The public is afforded an opportunity to provide comments to FDA on draft documents. FDA guidance documents are easily accessible by topic, date issued, document type, and other features on the FDA website. (See the Practitioner's Resource Library at Section VII of this chapter for references to this and other resources.)

Manufactured Food Regulatory Program Standards (MFRPS)[30]: The MFRPS seeks to implement a nationally recognized, risk-based, food safety system that focuses on protecting customer health. The MFRPS establishes a uniform and consistent way to measure and improve the prevention, intervention, and response activities of manufactured food regulatory programs across the United States. The development of standards is intended to help federal and state programs direct regulatory resources toward reducing foodborne illnesses. Similarly, the FDA and the Association of American Feed Control Officials (AAFCO) helped develop the Animal Feed Regulatory Program Standards (AFRPS). The feed standards establish uniformity for state programs in regulating animal feed.

Center for Devices and Radiological Health (CDRH) Standards Program[31]: The CDRH Standards Program was established under FDAMA, promoting consumer health and safety through the development and recognition of voluntary consensus standards for medical devices, radiation-emitting products, and emerging technologies. Medical device manufacturers, consumers, patients, and providers have access to the CDRH database to learn more about national and international medical device consensus standards.

3. Enforcement Mechanisms

Under the FDA, recalls are mostly voluntary and only in rare cases will FDA request a recall. Often, companies will recall a product on its own and FDA remains in an oversight role to monitor and assess the adequacy of the recall. FDA may hear about product defects through different avenues including when: (1) a company discovers a problem and contacts FDA; (2) FDA inspects a facility and determines the possibility of a recall; (3) FDA receives reports of health issues through reporting systems; and (4) the Centers for Disease Control and Prevention (CDC) informs FDA about public health risks. Even though not all recalls are publicly announced, they are compiled into FDA's weekly Enforcement Report according to classifications. There are three recall classifications: (1) Class I recalls for dangerous or defective products that could cause serious health problems or death; (2) Class II recalls for products that may cause a temporary health

---

30. https://www.fda.gov/ForFederalStateandLocalOfficials/ProgramsInitiatives/RegulatoryPrgmStnds/default.htm.

31. https://www.fda.gov/AboutFDA/CentersOffices/OfficeofMedicalProductsandTobacco/CDRH/.

problem; and (3) Class III products that are unlikely to cause adverse health issues but that violate FDA labeling laws.[32] In addition to administrative recall authority, FDA has statutory authority to initiate judicial enforcement actions including injunctions, seizures, and criminal prosecutions.[33]

Separate from FDA's recall classification process, FDA works with different industries to publish press releases and public notices to inform consumers about significant or serious risks from the use of the product. The FDA website maintains a Recall and Safety Alerts Archive for press releases issued more than 60 days ago. FDA also maintains recall and withdrawal pages specific to different product areas including drugs, animal health, biologics, medical devices, and cosmetics. For example, FDA's MedWatch[34] page includes safety information and holds the Adverse Event Reporting System (AERS) information regarding adverse events, medication errors, and product problems post-approval of drugs. On the MedWatch page, FDA encourages voluntary and mandatory reporting of consumers and health problems through different online reporting forms for medical products, food products, and dietary supplements.[35]

C. The National Highway Traffic Safety Administration (NHTSA)[36]

The National Highway Traffic Safety Administration (NHTSA) aims to save lives, prevent injuries, and reduce economic costs related to traffic accident through education, research, safety standards, and enforcement authority. The Highway Safety Act of 1970 created NHTSA to enforce consumer safety laws regarding motor vehicles. The National Traffic and Motor Vehicle Safety Act was enacted in 1966 to allow the federal government to administer new safety standards for motor vehicles and traffic safety. The Act established mandatory federal safety standards for vehicles.[37]

NHTSA has a legislative mandate under Title 49 of the U.S. Code to issue Federal Motor Vehicle Safety Standards (FFMVSS) and Regulations to which manufacturers of motor vehicles must conform and certify compliance. FFMVSS specify design, construction, and performance requirements for motor vehicles and related equipment.

1. Relevant Statutes

Moving Ahead for Progress in the 21st Century Act (MAP-21)[38]: MAP-21 funded surface transportation programs at over $105 billion for the 2013 and 2014 fiscal years.[39] MAP-21 aims to improve safety, maintain infrastructure, reduce traffic congestion, improve

---

32. https://www.fda.gov/forconsumers/consumerupdates/ucm049070.htm.
33. EMILY M. LANZA, CONG. RESEARCH SERV., R43927, FOOD SAFETY ISSUES: FDA JUDICIAL ENFORCEMENT ACTIONS (2002).
34. https://www.fda.gov/safety/medwatch/default.htm.
35. https://www.fda.gov/Safety/Recalls/default.htm.
36. https://www.nhtsa.gov/.
37. Pub. L. No. 89–563, 80 Stat. 718 (1966).
38. https://www.fhwa.dot.gov/map21/summaryinfo.cfm.
39. https://www.fhwa.dot.gov/map21/.

efficiency of the system and freight movement, and reduce delays in project delivery. The Act reforms the environmental review process for efficient project development, reduces and consolidates bicycle and pedestrian transportation into the Transportation Alternatives program, mandates development of a national freight policy, and reforms tolling on federal highways. The law includes provisions that will benefit the Federal Motor Carrier Safety Administration (FMCSA) in its mission to reduce crashes and fatalities involving commercial motor vehicles.

Fixing America's Surface Transportation Act (FAST): In December 2015, the FAST Act was enacted to provide long-term funding for surface transportation infrastructure planning and investment. The Act authorizes $305 billion until 2020 for highway and motor vehicle safety, public transportation, motor carrier safety, hazardous materials safety, and research and technology programs. The law aims to improve mobility on highways by easing congestion and facilitating the movement of freight, creating jobs, and accelerating project delivery and promoting innovation.

Transportation Recall Enhancement, Accountability, and Documentation Act (TREAD): The TREAD Act intends to increase consumer safety through mandates assigned to NHTSA. Under the Act, there are three major provisions. First, it requires vehicle and equipment manufacturers to report to NHTSA when it conducts a recall or safety campaign in a foreign country. Second, manufacturers are obligated to report information relating to safety defects and product-related injury or death incidents. Third, there is criminal liability if a manufacturer intentionally violates the reporting requirement and provides misleading information about defects that have caused serious injuries or death. The TREAD Act was drafted and enacted in response to the Firestone tire recalls and its resulting fatalities and injuries.[40]

2. Relevant Voluntary Standards

For product design considerations, NHTSA encourages importers and manufacturers to check standard-setting organizations including UL, ANSI, the American Welding Society (AWS), ASTM International, and the Society of the Automotive Engineers, International.[41]

In September 2017, NHTSA through the Automated Driving Systems (ADS): A Vision for Safety 2.0 offered voluntary guidance for manufacturers, designers, suppliers, and other entities involved in implementing automated driving systems (ADSs). The guidance applies to the design aspects of motor vehicles, including low-speed vehicles, motorcycles, passenger vehicles, and commercial motor vehicles. The purpose of the guidance is to offer recommendations and suggestions as the industry develops best practices in the design, development, testing, and deployment of ADSs, with no compliance requirement or enforcement mechanism. The guidance includes different

---

40. https://one.nhtsa.gov/nhtsa/announce/testimony/tread.html.
41. *Recommended Best Practices for Importers of Motor Vehicles and Motor Vehicle Equipment*, https://www.nhtsa.gov/DOT/NHTSA/Traffic%20Injury%20Control/ … /BestPractices.pdf.

safety design element considerations including vehicle cybersecurity, human-machine interface, crashworthiness, and consumer education and training. NHTSA encourages entities engaged in testing to publicly disclose Voluntary Safety Self-Assessments of their system to show their different approaches to achieving safety.

3. Enforcement Mechanisms[42]

NHTSA can learn about possible safety-related defects in various ways. Through Safercar.gov and the Department of Transportation Vehicle Safety Hotline, consumers can report safety defects with vehicles and related equipment. NHTSA may also discover defects through its own vehicle testing or from manufacturers that are statutorily obligated to report defects. After a preliminary evaluation, NHTSA officials either decide to close the investigation or conduct an engineering analysis. During the analysis, NHTSA gathers information about the alleged defect and sometimes conducts tests or surveys. Following the engineering analysis, the investigation may be closed without further action or the agency may send a "Recall Request Letter" to the manufacturer. If the manufacturer does not comply, then a NHTSA administrator may issue a final decision that a safety defect exists and order a recall. NHTSA has the authority to go to court to compel a manufacturer to comply with the order, and manufacturers can challenge the recall order in the federal district court. Like those regulated by the CPSC or the FDA, manufacturers subject to the NHTSA's jurisdictions undertake voluntary recalls often to avoid or minimize product liability claims and adverse publicity.

NHTSA on its webpage encourages reporting problems regarding safety-related defects. These complaints are shared publicly. The next phase includes screening, analysis of any petitions, and investigation. For the recall phase, NHTSA provides a vehicle identification number (VIN) lookup tool to access recall information provided by the manufacturer conducting the recall.[43]

D. The Federal Communications Commission (FCC)[44]

The Federal Communications Commission (FCC) regulates interstate communications by radio, television, wire, satellite, and cable in all 50 states, the District of Columbia, and U.S. territories. The FCC is responsible for the following tasks: to develop and implement regulatory programs; process applications for licenses and other filings; encourage the development of innovative services; maintain public safety and homeland security; and conduct investigations and respond to consumer complaints. Under the Federal Advisory Committee Act (FACA), advisory committees provide their expertise and advice to the FCC on a broad range of issues impacting policies and programs. Some current advisory committees established under FACA include the Broadband Deployment

---

42. https://www.nhtsa.gov/sites/nhtsa.dot.gov/files/810552.pdf.
43. https://www.nhtsa.gov/recalls.
44. https://www.fcc.gov/.

Advisory Committee, the Communications Security, Reliability and Interoperability Council, the Consumer Advisory Committee, and the Technological Advisory Council.

1. Relevant Statutes

21st Century Communications and Video Accessibility Act (CVAA)[45]: In October 2010, the CVAA was signed into law to increase accessibility of persons with disabilities to emerging communications including new digital, broadband, and mobile innovations. In 2009, an FCC study revealed that people with disabilities are less likely to use Internet-based communication technologies: 65 percent of Americans have broadband at home, but only 42 percent of Americans with disabilities have the services. Title I of CVAA addresses communications access to make products and service using Broadband accessible to people with disabilities. For example, CVAA requires that smartphones be usable by visually impaired individuals and that there is reliable access to next generation 911 services. Title II focuses on expanding the video programming platform for people with disabilities. The title requires video programming distributors and providers to convey emergency information that is accessible to people who are blind or visually impaired and requires programs shown on television with captioning to include captioning when they are reshown on the Internet.

Children's Internet Protection Act (CIPA)[46]: The CIPA was enacted in 2000 to address concerns about children's access to obscene or harmful information over the Internet. CIPA imposes requirements on schools and libraries that receive discounts through the E-rate program for Internet access to ensure protection measures are in place. Schools and libraries subject to CIPA have to comply with protection measures to prevent access to obscene, child pornography, or other harmful content to minors. Furthermore, organizations subject to CIPA have two additional certification requirements: (1) Internet safety policies which include monitoring the online activities of minors; and (2) pursuant to Protecting Children in the 21st Century Act, they must educate minors about appropriate online behavior. This includes showing students how to interact with others on social networking sites and in chat rooms, and informing them about cyberbullying and how to respond.

2. Relevant Voluntary Standards

The FCC, like other federal agencies, often issues guidance with reference to industry or other standards, since in certain cases there will be no applicable federally developed national standard. For example, there is no federally recognized national standard for safe levels of exposure to radiofrequency (RF) energy. The FCC's guidelines and rules regarding RF exposure are based upon standards developed by ANSI, the Institute of Electrical and Electronics Engineers (IEEE), and the National Council on Radiation Protection and Measurements (NCRP). The FCC also relies on input from other federal agencies including the Environmental Protection Agency (EPA), the FDA, the National

---

45. Pub. L. No. 111–260, 124 Stat. 2751 (2010).
46. https://www.fcc.gov/consumers/guides/childrens-internet-protection-act.

Institute for Occupational Safety and Health (NIOSH), and the Occupational Safety and Health Administration (OSHA) to formulate standards.

3. Enforcement Mechanism/Consumer Resources

The FCC's Enforcement Bureau (EB) is the primary unit responsible for enforcing compliance with the FTCA. The EB publishes Enforcement Advisories which are designed to educate companies on how to comply with the FCC rules. The Advisories include the FCC's thinking on consequences of noncompliant behavior and what is important to the general public.

The FCC has a Consumer Help Center[47] with consumer complaint data and consumer guides for different topics including telephone, privacy and security, broadcast, cable and satellite, and fraud-related issues. There is also a consumer complaint center where consumers can file a complaint about a telecom billing or service issue, which the FCC will serve upon the provider and require a response to the consumer within 30 days.

III. LEGAL AND REGULATORY REQUIREMENTS—MARKETING AND LABELING

A. Federal Trade Commission (FTC)[48]

Under the Federal Trade Commission Act (FTCA), advertising must be truthful, nondeceptive, and cannot be unfair. The FTC derives its law enforcement authority from Section 5 of the FTC Act which provides: "Unfair methods of competition in or affecting commerce, and unfair or deceptive acts or practices in or affecting commerce, are hereby declared unlawful."[49] Advertisers must have a reasonable basis for its claims which means objective evidence that supports the claim. The FTC views the advertisement from the reasonable consumer point of view when determining if an ad is deceptive. The FTC evaluates both express and implied claims. According to the FTC's Deception Policy Statement,[50] the FTC evaluates whether the claim would be material to the consumer's decision to buy or use the product. Examples of material claims include performance, feature, safety, price, or effectiveness claims.

1. Relevant Statutes

Fair Packaging and Labeling Act (FPLA)[51]: FPLA authorizes the FTC and the FDA to issue regulations requiring that "consumer commodities" be labeled appropriately to

---

47. https://www.fcc.gov/consumers.
48. https://www.ftc.gov/.
49. 15 U.S.C. §45.
50. https://www.ftc.gov/public-statements/1983/10/ftc-policy-statement-deception.
51. https://www.ftc.gov/enforcement/rules/rulemaking-regulatory-reform-proceedings/fair-packaging-labeling-act.

disclose net contents, identity of the commodity, and the name and place of business of the product's manufacturer or distributor.[52] FPLA authorizes additional regulations to prevent consumer deception with respect to ingredient descriptions, slack fill packages, or the technique of lower price labeling. The purpose of FPLA is to help consumers compare products and prevent deceptive packaging and labeling of household consumer products. The FDA administers FPLA with respect to food, drugs, cosmetics, and medical devices.

Children's Online Privacy Protection Act (COPPA)[53]: COPPA applies to the online collection of personal information from children under 13 years of age. COPPA includes requirements that a website operator must include in its privacy policy, when and how to seek consent from parents or guardians, and what responsibilities he or she has to protect children's privacy and safety online. Pursuant to COPPA, the FTC has authority to issue regulations and designate safe harbor provisions to encourage increased industry self-regulation. Under the provision, industry groups may submit for FTC approval self-regulatory guidelines to govern the participants' conduct and compliance. The FTC has approved the following seven safe harbor programs: Aristotle International Inc., Children's Advertising Review Unit (CARU), Entertainment Software Rating Board (ESRB), iKeepSafe, kidSAFE, Privacy Vaults Online, Inc., and TRUSTe.[54]

The Controlling the Assault of Non-Solicited Pornography and Marketing Act of 2003 (CAN-SPAM)[55]: The CAN-SPAM Act authorizes the FTC to establish national standards for sending commercial e-mails. The main requirements of CAN-SPAM include: (1) avoid use of false or misleading header information; (2) avoid use of deceptive subject lines; (3) identify messages as an ad; (4) inform recipients where the message is coming from; (5) inform recipients how to opt out of receiving future e-mails; (6) honor opt-out requests promptly; and (7) monitor activity of those sending messages on your behalf. Each separate e-mail in violation of the CAN-SPAM Act is subject to penalties up to $41,484. The Act covers all commercial messages, which is defined as "any electronic mail message the primary purpose of which is the commercial advertisement or promotion of a commercial product or service." The law does not exclude business-to-business e-mails.

2. Relevant Voluntary Standards/Resources

Better Business Bureau (BBB): The FTC focuses on national advertising, usually referring local advertising matters to state, county, or city agencies. Often, state or local consumer protection agencies or private groups like the BBB can resolve claim disputes involving local advertising. BBB includes tips on truthful advertising and advertisers can refer to the voluntary Code of Advertising to help ensure ethical advertising regarding different types of claims. For example, the BBB Code of Advertising has specific standards for comparative price and savings claims, "free" claims, price match guarantee claims, and many other claims.[56]

---

52. 16 C.F.R. §500.
53. 16 C.F.R. §312.
54. https://www.ftc.gov/safe-harbor-program.
55. Pub. L. No. 108–187, 117 Stat. 2699 (2003).
56. https://www.bbb.org/en/us/code-of-advertising/.

National Advertising Division (NAD)[57]: The FTC refers to the National Advertising Division of the Council of Better Business Bureaus, a self-regulatory body to provide recommendations to advertisers for alleged deceptive claims. Companies can file a complaint with the NAD challenging a competitor's claims and the NAD will investigate allegations of deceptive advertising practices. Some practical advantages of the NAD process include a timely decision, low procedural costs, and more predictability in the outcome of the decision, as the NAD publishes its case precedents and is staffed by experts who are familiar with advertising claims. NAD recommendations to modify or discontinue claims are not considered findings of wrongdoing nor are an advertiser's voluntary discontinuation construed as admission of impropriety.

Children's Advertising Review Unit (CARU)[58]: Similarly, the FTC works with the Review Unit of the Council of Better Business Bureaus to evaluate advertising claims aimed at children. Like the NAD, CARU is a private, self-regulatory group that publishes guides for children's advertising. In 2001, CARU was approved by the FTC as the first safe harbor program under COPPA. Advertisers who adhere to CARU's guidelines are deemed in compliance with the Act and essentially insulated from FTC enforcement. CARU provides guidance to children's advertisers, including on children's privacy issues that are unique to the Internet directed at children 12 and under. CARU's inquiries are recorded in the NAD/CARU Case Reports and are publicly available.

Advertiser Resources: Advertisers can search the FTC website for news, recent enforcement actions, speeches, and agency views related to advertising of specific products to better understand how to avoid deceptive advertising claims (see www.consumer.gov for consumer and business information from the FTC, FDA, and other federal agencies).

3. Enforcement Mechanisms

In the past, legally binding cease and desist orders have required companies to stop running deceptive advertisements, provide substantiation for claims in future ads, and to report periodically to FTC staff. Monetary remedies can include civil penalties and consumer redress whereby the advertiser sometimes agrees to give full or partial refunds to all consumers who bought the product. Informational remedies require advertisers to introduce new advertisements to correct misinformation conveyed in the original advertisement, notify purchasers about the deceptive claims, include disclosures in future advertisements, or provide other corrective information to consumers.[59]

Pursuant to a long-standing liaison agreement between the two agencies, the FTC and the FDA exercise concurrent jurisdiction over the labeling and marketing of foods, drugs, and other health-related products.[60] FTC exercises primary authority over advertising claims while the FDA exercises primary authority over product labeling.

---

57. https://bbbprograms.org/programs/nad/.
58. https://bbbprograms.org/programs/caru/.
59. https://www.ftc.gov/tips-advice/business-center/guidance/advertising-faqs-guide-small-business.
60. FTC-FDA Liaison Agreement, 4 Trade Reg. Rep. (CCH) ¶ 9851 (1971).

For example, the FDA handles most claims regarding the labeling of over-the-counter (OTC) drugs, while the FTC handles advertisement claims for OTC drugs. Similarly, the FDA handles most issues regarding food labels while the FTC handles claims regarding food advertisements. The FTC promulgated its *Enforcement Policy Statement on Food Advertising* to evaluate claims made in food advertisements and provide a consistent set of information on labels and advertisements for marketers who must follow both FDA labeling standards and FTC advertising standards.[61] As applied to dietary supplements, the FDA has primary responsibility for product labeling claims, including packaging, inserts, and other promotional materials distributed to consumers. The FTC has primary responsibility for claims in advertising, including print and broadcast advertisements, catalogs, and other marketing materials. The FTC provides guidance and guidelines for advertising for different types of products including foods, dietary supplements, environmentally friendly merchandise, and advertising credit on its website. For example, the FTC refers to its guidance *Dietary Supplements: An Advertising Guide for Industry* to evaluate claims regarding vitamins, dietary supplements, and similar products.[62]

B. Food and Drug Administration (FDA)[63]

1. Relevant Statutes

Prescription Drug Marketing Act (PDMA)[64]: PDMA was enacted to ensure consumer purchase of safe and effective drug products and reduce public health risks from the sale of counterfeit, adulterated, misbranded, subpotent, or expired prescription drugs. PDMA provides that drugs manufactured in the United States and exported can no longer be reimported unless by the product's manufacturer. The law places restrictions on the distribution of drug samples and bans certain resale of drugs by hospitals and other health care providers. This law was passed in response to the development of a whole submarket for prescription drugs.

Nutrition Labeling and Education Act of 1990 (NLEA)[65]: NLEA gives FDA authority to require nutrition labeling and nutrient content information for foods regulated under the agency. Under NLEA, all nutrient content claims like "fat free" and "low fat" and health claims should meet FDA regulations. An FDA inspection guide serves as reference material for investigators and other FDA personnel regarding NLEA requirements including information about the nutrition facts panel, the serving size, serving per container, and additional content.

Food and Drug Administration Modernization Act of 1997 (FDAMA): The FDAMA, amended the Federal Food, Drug, and Cosmetic Act, relates to the regulation of food,

---

61. https://www.ftc.gov/public-statements/1994/05/enforcement-policy-statement-food-advertising.
62. https://www.ftc.gov/tips-advice/business-center/guidance/dietary-supplements-advertising-guide-industry.
63. https://www.fda.gov/.
64. https://www.fda.gov/regulatoryinformation/lawsenforcedbyfda/significantamendmentstothefdcact/prescriptiondrugmarketingactof1987/default.htm.
65. https://www.fda.gov/iceci/inspections/inspectionguides/ucm074948.htm.

drugs, devices, and biological products.[66] With the passage of FDAMA, Congress enhanced FDA's mission in ways that recognized the agency would need to meet increasing technological, trade, and public health complexities. Under new procedures in the FDAMA, manufacturers may use nutrient content claims and health claims in food labeling based on an "authoritative statement" of a governmental scientific body if the manufacturer notifies FDA of the claim 120 days before marketing and FDA fails to object to the claim.

Dietary Supplement Health and Education Act (DSHEA)[67]: DSHEA regulates dietary supplements. DSHEA defines "dietary supplement" as a product intended to supplement a diet that contains one or more dietary ingredients like a vitamin, a mineral, an amino acid, or any other dietary substance. The Act requires that a dietary supplement be labeled as one and must not be represented as conventional food. DSHEA and other regulations require certain information on dietary supplement labels including quantity of contents, nutrition information like serving size, complete list of ingredients, and the name and place of the manufacturer's business. If a structure/function claim is made, the label should also include the disclaimer: "This statement has not been evaluated by the Food and Drug Administration. This product is not intended to diagnose, treat, cure, or prevent any disease."

Food Allergen Labeling and Consumer Protection Act (FALCPA)[68]: FALCPA amended the FDCA by requiring all food labels to list the eight most common food allergens or ingredients. These major food allergen groups account for about 90 percent of food allergies and are: (1) milk; (2) eggs; (3) fish (e.g., bass, flounder, or cod); (4) crustacean shellfish (e.g., crab, lobster, or shrimp); (5) tree nuts (e.g., almonds, pecans, or walnuts); (6) wheat; (7) peanuts; and (8) soybeans. Spices, colorings, or other additives that contain one of these allergens must also adhere to the labeling requirements.

Family Smoking Prevention and Tobacco Control Act (Tobacco Control Act)[69]: The Tobacco Control Act allows FDA to regulate the manufacture, distribution, and marketing of tobacco products. The Act prohibits tobacco marketing and sales to minors, requires smokeless tobacco product warning labels, requires that any "modified risk" claims have to be supported by scientific evidence, and requires disclosure of ingredients in tobacco products.[70] The restrictions on tobacco marketing include a prohibition on vending machine sales (except in adult-only facilities) and free giveaways of sample cigarettes. Under this Act, manufacturers of smokeless tobacco products are required to use conspicuous product warning labels, and tobacco company owners are required to register annually with the FDA and be subject to facility inspections.

---

66. https://www.fda.gov/regulatoryinformation/lawsenforcedbyfda/significantamendmentsto thefdcact/fdama/default.htm.
67. Pub. L. No. 103–417, 108 Stat. 4332 (1994).
68. Pub. L. No. 108–282, 118 Stat. 905 (2004).
69. Pub. L. No. 111–31, 123 Stat. 1776 (2009).
70. https://www.fda.gov/tobaccoproducts/labeling/rulesregulationsguidance/ucm246129.htm.

2. Relevant Voluntary Standards

The Food Labeling Guide[71] serves to answer common food labeling questions from manufacturers, distributors, and importers about the proper labeling of their food products. The guide has questions and answers as well as pictures and diagrams for reference on different topics including ingredient lists, nutrition labeling format and graphics, claims, and general food labeling requirements. The guidance summarizes requirements that must appear on food labels pursuant to laws and regulations. The guidance represents the FDA's current thinking on food labeling but is not legally binding on either the FDA or the public.

The Food Marketing Institute (FMI) works to help develop labeling standards. The Grocery Manufacturers Association (GMA) also provides its expertise on food labeling rules and food standards requirements. FMI provides standards for menu labeling, GMO labeling, and product code dating. GMA offers workshops and webinars to educate the industry on food labeling rules and beverage products regulated by the FDA. The FDA has shown willingness to work with both FMI and GMA to ensure that consumers receive reliable and standardized information to make healthy food choices. In 2011, both organizations requested FDA exercise enforcement discretion for certain aspects of Nutrition Keys, a voluntary labeling program. Products labeled with Nutrition Keys included four basic icons that provide information on the nutrition facts panel on calories, saturated fat, sodium, and total sugar content.

IV. LEGAL AND REGULATORY REQUIREMENTS—CUSTOMER PRIVACY

There are a number of federal laws and regulations concerning customer privacy. The federal legal and regulatory approach to privacy is similar in some respects to the federal legal and regulatory approaches to consumer health and safety, and marketing and labelling discussed in the preceding subsections of this chapter. However, in the privacy area, there are also some new developments of note on the international stage including, in particular, the EU's General Data Protection Regulation (GDPR). In addition, there are areas not currently governed by federal legislation, and in those areas, individual states are now becoming more active in the discussion about what should (and should not) be done in the area of privacy.

A. FTC and Current Federal Legal Approaches to Privacy

The Federal Trade Commission Act, passed in 1914, created and established the Federal Trade Commission (FTC).[72] The FTC describes its mission as "working to protect customer by preventing anticompetitive, deceptive and unfair business practices,

---

71. https://www.fda.gov/downloads/food/guidance%20complianceregulatoryinformation/%20guidancedocuments/foodlabelingnutrition/foodlabelingguide/ucm265446.pdf.

72. 15 U.S.C. §41 et seq.

enhancing informed consumer choice and public understanding of the competitive process, and accomplishing this without unduly burdening legitimate business activity."[73] In fact, the scope of the FTC's jurisdiction is dizzying, and it is the only federal agency with consumer protection and competition jurisdiction in broad sectors of the economy.[74]

The FTC's Bureau of Consumer Protection has several divisions, one of which—the Division of Privacy and Identity Protection (DPIP)—administers issues that relate to consumer privacy, credit reporting, identity theft, and information security.[75] In this area, the DPIP protects consumer privacy by enforcing data security laws, promotes identify fraud prevention and victim assistance, handles criminal law enforcement, and works to promote policies protecting consumer privacy.

The following is a summary of some of the current key federal privacy legislation which is overseen by the FTC.

1. Section 5 of the FTC Act[76]

Section 5(a) of the FTC Act is the principal consumer protection statute enforced by the FTC and specifically provides that "unfair or deceptive acts or practices in or affecting commerce" are unlawful. This includes statements and unfair practices involving the use or protection of personal information of consumers.[77]

2. Children's Online Privacy Protection Act (COPPA)

As mentioned in Section III.A.1 of this chapter, the Children's Online Privacy Protection Act of 1998[78] requires operators of website or online services directed to children under 13 years of age to adhere to certain requirements. COPPA also applies to operators of other websites or online services that have actual knowledge that they are collecting personal information online from a child under 13 years of age. COPPA is intended to protect individually identifiable information about an individual (under 13 years of age) which is collected online. This includes: a first and last name; a home or other physical address; an e-mail address or other online contact information (such as instant messaging user identifiers or screen name information); telephone number; social security number; persistent identifier, such as a customer number held in a cookie or a processor serial number; any combination of a last name or photograph with other information that permits physical or online contacting; and information about the child or the parents of that child which the website collects online from the child and combines with an identifier.

---

73. https://www.ftc.gov/about-ftc.
74. https://www.ftc.gov/about-ftc.
75. https://www.ftc.gov/about-ftc/bureaus-offices/bureau-consumer-protection/our-divisions/division-privacy-and-identity.
76. 15 U.S.C. Sec. 45(a).
77. https://www.ftc.gov/about-ftc/bureaus-offices/bureau-consumer-protection/our-divisions/division-privacy-and-identity (see fn. 4 above).
78. 15 U.S.C. 6501-6505. See also the Children's Online Privacy Protection Rule at 16 CFR Part 312.

In one notable recent example, electronic toy manufacturer VTech Electronics Limited and its U.S. subsidiary settled charges brought by the FTC that VTech violated COPPA by collecting personal information from children without providing direct notice and obtaining their parent's consent, and failing to take reasonable steps to secure the data it collected. VTech agreed to pay $650,000 as part of its settlement with the FTC. In a complaint filed by the Department of Justice on behalf of the FTC, the FTC alleged that the Kid Connect app used with some of VTech's electronic toys collected the personal information of hundreds of thousands of children, and that the company failed to provide direct notice to parents or obtain verifiable consent from parents concerning its information collection practices, as required under COPPA. The VTech case was FCT's first children's privacy case involving Internet-connected toys and hinged in part on FTC's allegations that VTech failed to use reasonable and appropriate data security measures to protect personal information it collected.

3. Fair Credit Reporting Act

The Fair Credit Reporting Act[79] was designed to give consumers the right to know what information credit bureaus and other consumer reporting agencies are distributing about them to creditors, insurance companies, and employers. The Fair Credit Reporting Act includes the "Red Flags Rule" which requires businesses and organizations to implement a written Theft Prevention Program which should be designed to detect the warning signs (or red flags) of identity theft in their day-to-day operations. The Fair Credit Reporting Act is also intended to ensure that credit bureaus and other consumer reporting agencies are keeping accurate information about consumers and, further, that the information they are keeping is kept private.

One example of the FTC's involvement on behalf of consumers came in the aftermath of the Equifax data breach, which compromised some of the personal information of approximately 143 million Equifax customers or data subjects. Equifax, one of three principal credit reporting agencies in the United States, had its data center operations hacked. The hackers accessed data of subjects' names, Social Security numbers, birth dates, addresses, and, in some instances, driver's license numbers. It is reported that hackers also stole credit card numbers for about 209,000 people and dispute documents with personal identifying information for about 182,000 people. The breach was not confined to the United States, as they stole personal information of people in the UK and Canada too.[80]

4. Gramm-Leach-Bliley Act

The Gramm-Leach-Bliley Act[81] obligates financial institutions to safeguard the security and confidentiality of customer information which they collect. Covered institutions

---

79. 15 U.S.C. §§1681–1681x.
80. https://www.consumer.ftc.gov/blog/2017/09/equifax-data-breach-what-do.
81. Pub. L. No. 106–102, 113 Stat. 1338, codified in relevant part primarily at 15 U.S.C. §§6801–6809, §§6821–6827.

must also provide notices to consumers about the institution's information gathering and security practices, and give consumer the opportunity to direct that their personal information is not be shared with certain third parties who are not affiliated with the institution.

5. Other Privacy Statutes Enforced or Administered by the FTC

The scope of FTC's sphere of activity is extremely broad. Some of the other statutes which FTC enforces in the privacy arena include Health Information Technology (HITECH) Provisions of American Recovery and Reinvestment Act of 2009, Title XIII, Subtitle D[82] (covering entities that obtain consumers' personal information but that are not subject to HIPAA[83]) and the Identity Theft Assumption and Deterrence Act of 1998 (making FTC a clearinghouse for identity theft complaints).

B. U.S. State Law Approaches

Not surprisingly, certain state legislatures have recently identified privacy as a key legislative initiative. Some of the more relevant state law approaches to the protection of consumer data privacy are highlighted in the following discussion.

1. California Consumer Privacy Act of 2018

California's new data privacy law, the California Consumer Privacy Act of 2018,[84] gives consumers more rights to know about the information companies are gathering about them, as well as the right to know why—and with whom—they are sharing it. It also includes a "right to be forgotten" (e.g., the ability to demand that a company delete an individual's information). The California law becomes effective January 1, 2020. One issue for multinational companies already dealing with the EU's GDPR is to try and decide whether to update their GDPR compliance program to comply with the California law or to try and have a bifurcated approach which deals with EU citizens one way and California citizens another. Because the California legislature has allowed for amendments to the law, the final framework of what California will require is still unknown as of the writing of this chapter. Nevertheless, a more practical approach to privacy compliance may dictate that a global program seeks to comply with the high water mark of privacy legislation, wherever that may be: the EU, California, or elsewhere.

2. Colorado

In June 2018, Colorado passed a new law, House Bill 18-1128,[85] "concerning strengthening protections for consumer data privacy." The new law took effect on

---
82. Pub. L. No. 111–5, 123 Stat. 115, codified in relevant part at 42 U.S.C. §17937 and 17953.
83. Pub. L. No. 104–191, 110 Stat. 1936.
84. https://leginfo.legislature.ca.gov/faces/billTextClient.xhtml?bill_id=201720180AB375.
85. https://www.cde.state.co.us/dataprivacyandsecurity/crs22-16-101.

September 1, 2018. Colorado already had a data breach notification law, but the new law includes enhanced notification requirements, along with data security requirements to be applied to businesses and third-party service providers. It also amends prior state law to address the proper disposal of personal information. This law continues the GDPR-like trend of establishing more detailed rules to be applied to businesses and third-party service providers who handle such personal information of individual consumers or customers, whether they be individuals or businesses in their own right.

3. Illinois Biometric Information Privacy Act

Illinois's Biometric Information Privacy Act (BIPA) is a relatively older law in this area, as it was passed in 2008. BIPA is designed to regulate the collection, use, safeguarding, handling, storage, retention, and destruction of biometric identifiers and information collected by corporations in Illinois.[86]

4. Other State and Local Privacy Legislation and Regulation

Other relevant legislation and regulatory activity at the state and local levels in the United States includes the following:

- New York State Department of Financial Services 23 NYCRR 500, Cybersecurity Requirements for Financial Services Companies[87]
- Chicago Personal Data Collection and Protection Ordinance,[88] introduced on April 18, 2018
- San Francisco Privacy First Policy, submitted as a ballot proposal to amend the Charter of the City and County of San Francisco, and approved by voters on November 6, 2018[89]
- South Carolina's Insurance Data Security Act,[90] which is modeled on a model law formulated by the National Association of Insurance Commissioners, the NAIC Insurance Data Security Model Law.[91]

C. European Union's General Data Protection Regulation[92]

Probably the most prominent data privacy legislation is the European Union's (EU) General Data Protection Regulation or GDPR. In 2016, the EU continued to enhance its

---

86. 740 ILCS 14; http://www.ilga.gov/legislation/ilcs/ilcs3.asp?ActID=3004&ChapterID=57.
87. https://www.dfs.ny.gov/legal/regulations/adoptions/dfsrf500txt.pdf.
88. https://chicago.legistar.com/LegislationDetail.aspx?ID=3480452&GUID=241F981B-94D6-43E8-AC73-D122DBECD413.
89. https://sfelections.sfgov.org/sites/default/files/Documents/BSC/2018%20Nov/4-Legislative_digest_0.pdf.
90. https://www.scstatehouse.gov/sess122_2017-2018/bills/4655.htm.
91. https://www.naic.org/store/free/MDL-668.pdf.
92. REGULATION (EU) 2016/679 OF THE EUROPEAN PARLIAMENT AND OF THE COUNCIL of April 27, 2016, on the protection of natural persons with regard to the processing of personal data and on the free movement of such data, and repealing Directive 95/46/EC (General Data Protection Regulation).

data protection laws by adopting the GDPR. The EU takes an enormous amount of pride in its data protection legislation. The European Data Protection Supervisor's official website refers to data protection laws which are a "gold standard" and the adoption of the GDPR as one of the EU's "greatest achievements in recent years."[93]

Whether GDPR or any legislative regime can live up to its billing remains to be seen. However, there is no question that the onset of GDPR—the EU mandated that the GDPR go into effect on May 25, 2018—was preceded by legal implementation efforts of a size and scale similar to the compliance efforts expended by companies in the years preceding January 1, 2000, attempting to ensure that they would not suffer problems as the result of the Y2K computer programming problem.

A lot of the attention generated by GDPR is the result of its penalties framework. Most companies and their counsel are by now well aware that fines for noncompliance with GDPR can be as high as €20,000,000 or 4 percent of a company's annual global turnover, whichever is higher.

The GDPR replaced the 1995 Data Protection Directive, which was adopted at a time when both the Internet and the businesses that would grow to exploit its benefits were still relatively immature. While generally attempting to strengthen the data protection regime which protects the private information of EU citizens, some of the specific enhancements include:

1. Appointment of a Data Protection Officer

Pursuant to Article 37 of the GDPR, some organizations are required to appoint a data protection officer to ensure they comply with the GDPR. Primarily, this obligation falls to companies whose core activities involve "regular and systematic monitoring of personal or sensitive data on a large scale," as well as public sector organizations.[94]

2. Right to Erasure ("Right to be Forgotten")

In addition to reinforcing a wide range of previously existing rights, Article 17 of the GDPR[95] actually established certain new rights for individuals, such as the right to erasure (dubbed the "right to be forgotten"), which allows an individual to request that an organization delete the personal data relating to that individual. An example would be where that individual's data is no longer necessary for the purposes for which it was originally collected or where the individual has subsequently withdrawn her consent.

---

93. https://edps.europa.eu/data-protection/data-protection/legislation/history-general-data-protection-regulation_en.
94. https://edps.europa.eu/data-protection/data-protection/legislation/history-general-data-protection-regulation_en and https://gdpr-info.eu/art-37-gdpr/.
95. https://gdpr-info.eu/art-17-gdpr/.

3. Right of Data Portability

Pursuant to Article 20 of the GDPR, individuals have the right to receive their personal data from an organization in a "commonly used form" so that individuals can easily share it with others.[96]

4. Right Not To Be Profiled

Unless is it necessary by law or by a contract, Article 22 of the GDPR makes it illegal in the EU for decisions to be made about individuals on the solitary basis of automated processing.[97]

5. Data Processing Agreements

One of the main compliance activities of many organizations subject to the GDPR has been and will be the completion of data processing agreements. Under the GDPR, controllers (an individual or entity that "determines the purposes and means of processing of personal data"[98]) can only work with data processors (an individual or entity that processes personal data on behalf of a controller[99]) that provide sufficient guarantees to implement appropriate technical and organizational measures in such a manner that processing will meet the requirements of GDPR. Under the GDPR, data controllers are obliged to enter into a written contract, or other binding or legal act under EU or Member State law, with each of its data processors.[100] The GDPR sets out very precise requirements for these agreements (sometimes called "data processing agreements" or DPAs).[101]

A question arises whether each and every controller must have a DPA. Most global companies would appear to come within the scope of GDPR to the extent that they gather information about EU individuals, whether they are individual customers or even the representatives of other entities, such as corporate customers, vendors, or partners. However, some entities may not, to the extent they truly do not process the personal and protected information of EU citizens. Further, some entities in possession of information concerning EU individuals are exempt from the GDPR's rules, such as law enforcement agencies when data are collected and processed for the prevention, investigation, detection, or prosecution of crimes. As a practice pointer, it may be better to assume—due to the increasing level of interconnectedness between businesses and consumers, and the onset of other U.S.-based laws (such as the new California law)—that entry into a data processing agreement is a prudent step for just about every company.

---

96. https://gdpr-info.eu/art-20-gdpr/.
97. https://gdpr-info.eu/art-22-gdpr/.
98. GDPR, Article 4 (7). Also: https://www.gdpreu.org/the-regulation/key-concepts/data-controllers-and-processors/.
99. GDPR, Article 4(8).
100. GDPR, Article 28.
101. This is a potentially confusing acronym, because you can also find references in the GDPR to Data Protection Authorities or Supervisory Authorities as per Article 51 of the GDPR.

D. Additional EU Privacy Frameworks

EU data protection rules are relevant in the European Economic Area (EEA), which includes the member countries of the EU and non-EU countries such as Iceland, Norway, and Switzerland. When personal data is transferred beyond the boundaries of the EEA, special protections are expected to be taken to help ensure that the protection resident in the EU "travels with" the data.[102] This framework has actually been in place since 1998, when the European Data Directive (Directive) was passed. The GDPR essentially mirrors the same framework set forth in the Directive when it comes to the handling of personal data being transferred outside of the EU.[103] With regard to transfers, for example, to the United States, both the Directive and the GDPR provide similar mechanisms.

1. Adequacy Decision by the European Commission

The GDPR has a hierarchy or preference for adequacy decisions. However, the process for an adequacy decision for a country outside the EU is quite involved and probably not a practical approach for practitioners in most cases.

2. EU Model Clauses

The EU can also decide if standard contractual clauses are sufficient to protect data transferred internationally. The European Commission has issued two sets of contractual clauses for data transfers from data controllers in the EU to data controllers outside the EU or EEA and one set of contractual clauses for controllers in the EU to processors outside the EU or EEA.[104] However, the model clauses are not likely to be a good fit for most larger, multinational companies and, further, a reliance on the adequacy of the model clauses—which are not as comprehensive in their coverage as GDPR and, consequently, not as good a protection from GDPR's hefty fine regime—could put such companies at greater risk of both violating the requirements of GDPR and being exposed to fines.

3. EU-US Privacy Shield

The EU-US and Swiss-US Privacy Shield Frameworks were designed by the U.S. Department of Commerce and the European Commission and Swiss Administration to establish a framework for companies to comply with data protection requirements when engaged or working together on the transfer of personal data from the EU (or

---

102. https://ec.europa.eu/info/law/law-topic/data-protection/data-transfers-outside-eu/rules-international-transfers-personal-data_en.

103. https://files.alston.com/files/docs/Roadmap-to-the-GDPR-International-Data-Transfers.pdf.

104. https://ec.europa.eu/info/law/law-topic/data-protection/data-transfers-outside-eu/model-contracts-transfer-personal-data-third-countries_en; EU controller to non-EU or EEA controller, see decision 2001/497/EC at: http://eur-lex.europa.eu/legal-content/en/ALL/?uri=CELEX:32001D0497 and decision 2004/915/EC at: http://eur-lex.europa.eu/legal-content/EN/TXT/?uri=CELEX%3A32004D0915, and for EU controller to non-EU or EEA processor, see decision 2010/87/EU at http://eur-lex.europa.eu/legal-content/en/TXT/?uri=CELEX%3A32010D0087.

Switzerland, as applicable) to the United States in support of transatlantic commerce.[105] The Privacy Shield is not negated or superseded by the GDPR, but while compliance with the Privacy Shield can help a company get up to speed on the proper safeguarding of data, it is not a guarantee of compliance with the more detailed and rigorous GDPR.

E. Other International Laws and Regulations

Currently, given the expansion of many companies into global markets, it is not unusual for many businesses to be faced with the reality of understanding and complying with international rules concerning the management of customers' private information and data. Some of the principal international privacy regimes are discussed in this section.

1. Canada

Canada has maintained a privacy protection regime at the federal level pursuant to the Privacy Act,[106] which is the law in Canada which governs the personal information handling practices for all Canadian federal government institutions. This is a slightly more comprehensive approach than the more limited approach in the United States which is focused on a batch of laws primarily overseen and enforced by the FTC. Canada's rules are similar to those of the EU's, although arguably not as comprehensive with the effectiveness of GDPR. The Office of the Privacy Commissioner of Canada (OPC) has responsibility for enforcement of two federal privacy laws[107]: the Privacy Act; and the Personal Information Protection and Electronic Documents Act (PIPEDA),[108] which deals with the practices of many businesses when handling personal information.

2. Brazil Data Protection Law

On July 10, 2018, Brazil's Federal Senate approved a new Data Protection Bill of Law,[109] which provides for personal data protection and seems clearly inspired by the EU's GDPR. Upon presidential sanction, the new law will come into effect 18 months from its publication, which, for example, is a shorter period of time for implementation than was provided by the EU. The new law addresses a wide range of issues related to the subject and will create a deep change in the way that Brazilian individuals, businesses, and the public authority handle and access personal data in connection with their daily activities and routines.[110]

---

105. https://www.privacyshield.gov/welcome.
106. https://www.priv.gc.ca/en/privacy-topics/privacy-laws-in-canada/the-privacy-act/.
107. https://www.priv.gc.ca/en/privacy-topics/privacy-laws-in-canada/.
108. https://www.priv.gc.ca/en/privacy-topics/privacy-laws-in-canada/the-personal-information-protection-and-electronic-documents-act-pipeda/.
109. *Lei Geral de Proteção de Dados*, PLC 53/2018.
110. The authors wish to recognize Ms. Cris Cortez of the law firm Cortez, Rizzi & Miranda in São Paulo for her contributions to understanding the new Brazilian legal framework.

F. Relevant Voluntary Standards

The lack of relevant voluntary or meaningful industry standards is one of the reasons that laws of the type described above have been passed in the United States at the state and local levels and internationally by the EU and other countries. In the United States, technology companies have lobbied Congress for a federal privacy law, but so far without a great deal of success.[111]

V. PRIVACY GOVERNANCE, COMPLIANCE, AND PRACTICE TOOLS

It remains to be seen if the privacy law and regulations discussed in this chapter actually set the stage for the proper handling of personal data on a global basis. In a global economy where more and more companies are operating across national borders, or where customers are able to reach out to companies across national borders, the early adoption of rules like those set out in the GDPR may end up setting the bar for how consumers and companies expect personal data to be handled.

In the aftermath of highly publicized privacy failures such as the Facebook/Cambridge Analytics 2016 presidential election manipulation scandal, clients would do well to consider the benefits of a proactive—instead of reactive—approach to data confidentiality and privacy.[112] Utilizing a proactive approach, a corporation may learn to appreciate the value of holding itself accountable for protection and security of customers' and employees' personal information while simultaneously reinforcing the value of customer choice and consent throughout an information lifecycle.[113]

The problem with a reactive approach is that in addition to the possibilities of exposure to significant fines like those set out in the GDPR framework, companies also lose control of the ability to study an issue, make informed decisions about data governance and, finally, have a say in the cost of preventive data governance measures. By contrast, in the event of a data breach which compromises customers' personal information, the impacted company will be forced to: expend great sums of money in responding to the breach by informing customers, suppliers, and vendors, as applicable; retain counsel and other experts to assist in managing the legal, public relations, and communications aspects of the breach; and obtain hardware, software, and consulting services necessary to build a more secure enterprise on a going forward basis.

Consider that a proactive approach is all the more critical following the SEC's issuance of a *Commission Statement and Guidance on Public Company Cybersecurity Disclosures*.[114] The SEC release emphasizes the importance of maintaining comprehensive

---

111. https://www.nytimes.com/2018/08/26/technology/tech-industry-federal-privacy-law.html.

112. For more on the Facebook/Cambridge Analytics scandal, and its impact on Facebook, see https://www.newyorker.com/magazine/2018/09/17/can-mark-zuckerberg-fix-facebook-before-it-breaks-democracy.

113. https://iapp.org/media/pdf/knowledge_center/Guide_to_Data_Governance_Part1_The_Case_for_Data_Governance_whitepaper.pdf.

114. 17 CFR Part 229 and 249, Release Nos. 33-10459; 34-82746, at https://www.sec.gov/rules/interp/2018/33-10459.pdf.

policies and procedures related to cybersecurity risks and incidents, including effective disclosure controls and procedures that enable companies to make accurate and timely disclosures of material events, which include those relating to cybersecurity.[115] There is also a compliance component relating to the duties of companies and their directors, officers, and other corporate insiders with regard to the applicable insider trading prohibitions under the general antifraud provisions of the federal securities laws, especially with regard to the obligation to refrain from making selective disclosures of material nonpublic information about cybersecurity risks or incidents.

VI. ADDITIONAL REPORTING CONSIDERATIONS

Most states, including the District of Columbia, Puerto Rico, and the U.S. Virgin Islands, have data breach notification laws which will cover any breaches with regard to customer, supplier, or employee personal information. Under these laws, companies may be required by law to notify (1) affected customers or employees, (2) state regulatory agencies or attorneys general, and, possibly even (3) credit reporting agencies.

In the EU, under GDPR,[116] and in Canada, under PIPEDA,[117] there will be mandatory reporting requirements in the event of a data breach.

Companies can audit or review their compliance by looking within to determine if there exist inside their organizations any common gaps in information security compliance. Common gaps include, but are not limited to, not having (or not complying with) internal policies for data governance; appointment of the wrong subject matter experts or failing to secure executive-level sponsorship of an internal policy or program; permitting unstructured collection and sharing of personal information inconsistent with internal policies or programs; and failing to update policies and processes to respond to ongoing developments in the law which apply to the company. There can also be gaps in connection with the collection, storage, and disposal practices, especially if the corporation and its privacy, IT and legal experts are not aligned relative to who/what/where/how/why questions relating to the data in the possession of the company. Self-assessment or audit is a readily available tool for internal experts to work with their colleagues and make a determination concerning the suitability of current policies and processes for the increasingly complex requirements of securing data which contains personally identifiable information. Self-assessment is also an opportunity to capitalize on CSR opportunities. Within certain limits, self-assessment findings may provide a framework to create transparency with constituencies like governments, customers, analysts, suppliers, and employees.

---

115. 17 CFR Part 229 and 249, Release Nos. 33-10459; 34-82746, at https://www.sec.gov/rules/interp/2018/33-10459.pdf.

116. GDPR, Article 33.

117. https://www.priv.gc.ca/en/privacy-topics/privacy-laws-in-canada/the-personal-information-protection-and-electronic-documents-act-pipeda/.

VII. SUMMARY AND TAKEAWAYS

Many of the laws and regulations discussed in this chapter were designed to provide protections for consumers and individuals when purchasing products like foods or medicines, or using services which might implicate their personal and private information. In a sense, the instincts behind many of these laws and regulations reflect a desire for the corporations which serve us to engage in, or exhibit more, corporate social responsibility. However, the fact that laws and regulations are necessary in certain cases where voluntary self-regulation or self-assessment is absent or has failed is a cautionary tale. Corporations which are willing to embrace a CSR outlook, and which are willing to view proactive efforts to enhance customer safety and privacy as opportunities for market differentiation and innovation, may find that they are able to benefit from investing to prevent problems, rather than waiting to find out the cost of solving or settling problems later if customer safety and privacy issues are not prioritized.

VIII. PRACTITIONER'S RESOURCE LIBRARY

This section will provide resources that readers should refer to in order to build their own library for practicing effectively in these areas:

A. Customer Health and Safety

- **CPSC**
  - Recall Handbook: https://www.cpsc.gov/s3fs-public/8002.pdf
  - The Regulated Products Handbook: https://www.cpsc.gov/s3fs-public/RegulatedProductsHandbook.pdf
  - CPSC Small Business Ombudsman: https://www.cpsc.gov/Business–Manufacturing/Small-Business-Resources
  - CPSC Regulatory Robot: https://www.cpsc.gov/Business–Manufacturing/Regulatory-Robot/Safer-Products-Start-Here/
  - ANSI: https://www.ansi.org/consumer_affairs/overview?menuid=5
  - UL: https://www.standardsportal.org/usa_en/sdo/ul.aspx
  - ASTM International: https://www.standardsportal.org/usa_en/sdo/astm.aspx
  - SaferProducts.gov: https://www.saferproducts.gov/
  - Recalls: www.Recalls.gov
- **FDA**
  - 21st Century Cures Act: https://www.fda.gov/RegulatoryInformation/LawsEnforcedbyFDA/SignificantAmendmentstotheFDCAct/21stCenturyCuresAct/default.htm
  - Recognized Consensus Standards: https://www.accessdata.fda.gov/scripts/cdrh/cfdocs/cfStandards/search.cfm
  - FDA Guidance Documents: https://www.fda.gov/RegulatoryInformation/Guidances/default.htm#about

- Recalls, Market Withdrawals, & Safety Alerts: https://www.fda.gov/safety/recalls/
- Recall and Safety Alerts Archive: https://www.fda.gov/Safety/Recalls/ArchiveRecalls/default.htm
- Food Recalls and Alerts: https://www.foodsafety.gov/
- CRS Report for Food Safety FDA Judicial Enforcement Actions: https://fas.org/sgp/crs/misc/R43927.pdf
- MedWatch for Drug Adverse Event Reporting: https://www.fda.gov/Safety/MedWatch/default.htm
- MedWatch Voluntary and Mandatory Reporting Forms: https://www.fda.gov/Safety/MedWatch/HowToReport/default.htm

- **NHTSA**
  - Safety Issues & Recalls: https://www.nhtsa.gov/recalls
  - FAST Act: https://www.fhwa.dot.gov/fastact/summary.cfm

- **FCC**
  - CVAA: https://www.fcc.gov/consumers/guides/21st-century-communications-and-video-accessibility-act-cvaa
  - CIPA: https://www.fcc.gov/consumers/guides/childrens-internet-protection-act
  - Enforcement Bureau's Enforcement Advisories: https://www.fcc.gov/general/enforcement-advisories

B. Marketing and Labeling

- **FTC**
  - FPLA: https://www.ftc.gov/enforcement/rules/rulemaking-regulatory-reform-proceedings/fair-packaging-labeling-act
  - NAD: https://bbbprograms.org/programs/nad/
  - CARU: https://bbbprograms.org/programs/caru/

- **FDA**
  - NLEA: https://www.fda.gov/iceci/inspections/inspectionguides/ucm074948.htm
  - Food Labeling Guide (Revised January 2013): https://www.fda.gov/food/guidanceregulation/guidancedocumentsregulatoryinformation/labelingnutrition/ucm2006828.htm
  - FMI: https://www.fmi.org/industry-topics/labeling
  - GMA: https://www.gmaonline.org/issues-policy/product-safety/food-and-product-safety/manufacturing-processing-and-regulatory-support/food-labeling-and-standards/

C. Customer Privacy

- **FTC**
  - Children's Privacy: https://www.ftc.gov/tips-advice/business-center/privacy-and-security/children%27s-privacy

- Consumer Privacy: https://www.ftc.gov/tips-advice/business-center/privacy-and-security/consumer-privacy
- Credit Reporting: https://www.ftc.gov/tips-advice/business-center/privacy-and-security/credit-reporting
- Data Security: https://www.ftc.gov/tips-advice/business-center/privacy-and-security/data-security
- Gramm-Leach-Bliley Act: https://www.ftc.gov/tips-advice/business-center/privacy-and-security/gramm-leach-bliley-act
- Red Flags Rule: https://www.ftc.gov/tips-advice/business-center/privacy-and-security/red-flags-rule
- Tech resources for companies involved in the design, development, or sale of mobile apps, smartphones, or other tech tools: https://www.ftc.gov/tips-advice/business-center/privacy-and-security/tech

- **European Union**
  - GDPR and data protection in the EU: https://ec.europa.eu/info/law/law-topic/data-protection/data-protection-eu_en
  - Data transfers outside the EU: https://ec.europa.eu/info/law/law-topic/data-protection/data-transfers-outside-eu_en
  - EU-US Privacy Shield: https://ec.europa.eu/info/law/law-topic/data-protection/data-transfers-outside-eu/eu-us-privacy-shield_en
  - Binding corporate rules: https://ec.europa.eu/info/law/law-topic/data-protection/data-transfers-outside-eu/binding-corporate-rules_en
  - International data transfers using model contracts: https://ec.europa.eu/info/law/law-topic/data-protection/data-transfers-outside-eu/model-contracts-transfer-personal-data-third-countries_en

- **State Laws**
  - Colorado's Consumer Data Protection Laws: Colorado Attorney General's FAQs for Businesses: https://coag.gov/resources/data-protection-laws
  - California Privacy Laws—California Attorney General resource page: https://oag.ca.gov/privacy/privacy-laws
  - Illinois Biometric Information Privacy Act: http://www.ilga.gov/legislation/ilcs/ilcs3.asp?ActID=3004&ChapterID=57

Chapter 8

Community Engagement and Investment

Alan S. Gutterman

I. INTRODUCTION

Sustainability is about the long-term well-being of society, an issue that encompasses a wide range of aspirational targets including the sustainable development goals (SDGs) of the 2030 Agenda for Sustainable Development adopted by world leaders that went into effect on January 1, 2016.[1] Among other things, the SDGs include ending poverty and hunger, ensuring healthy lives and promoting well-being for all, ensuring inclusive and equitable quality education and promoting lifelong learning opportunities for all, and promoting sustained, inclusive, and sustainable economic growth, full and productive employment, and decent work for all. The goals listed above are based on the recognition that society in general is vulnerable to a number of significant environmental and social risks including failure of climate-change mitigation and adaptation, major biodiversity loss and ecosystem collapse, man-made environmental planning and disasters (e.g., oil spills), failure of urban planning, food crises, rapid and massive spread of infectious diseases, and profound social instability.[2]

For further discussion of the topics covered in this chapter, see A. Gutterman, *Community Engagement and Investment* (Oakland, CA: Sustainable Entrepreneurship Project, 2019).
1. http://www.un.org/sustainabledevelopment/sustainable-development-goals/.
2. THE GLOBAL RISKS REPORT 2017 (Geneva: World Economic Forum, 12th ed. 2017), 61–62. The Report and an interactive data platform are available at http://wef.ch/risks2017.

Clearly the challenges described above are daunting and for most businesses it may be difficult for them to see how they can play a meaningful role in addressing them. While it is common for society to be identified as an organizational stakeholder, the reality is that one company cannot, acting on its own, achieve all the goals associated with societal well-being. However, every company, regardless of its size, can make a difference in some small, yet meaningful way in the communities in which they operate, and more and more attention is being focused on the impact that companies have within their communities.[3] Focusing on the community level allows an organization to set meaningful targets and implement programs that fit the scale of its operations and which can provide the most immediate value to the organization and its stakeholders. Societal well-being projects and initiatives must ensure that the organization does not compromise and instead improves the well-being of local communities through its value chain and in society at large.

While the community is often mentioned as one of the stakeholders of any organization, it would be a mistake to think of community as a monolithic concept. In reality, community for any organization is a complex network of multiple stakeholders, each of which must be considered and engaged including neighborhoods, community development groups, environmental organizations, development organizations, citizen associations, nongovernmental organizations, local nonprofit organizations, local regulators and governmental officials, other businesses in the community, indigenous peoples, and underrepresented groups in the community.[4] All of this makes community engagement and investment especially challenging since each of these community stakeholders has their own issues, concerns, and perspectives.

While the concept of community as a stakeholder typically focuses on the communities where the company is directly involved, it should not be forgotten that decisions that a company makes with regard to other stakeholders can also impact communities. The clearest illustration of this is the impact that outsourcing to foreign countries by larger retailers has had on the communities in which their former domestic suppliers were operating. As those suppliers, many of which were among the largest employers in their local communities, lost the business previously provided from the retailers, drastic measures were needed to keep their doors open. Many of them were forced to lay off workers, frequently people who had worked for the suppliers for many years and whose parents and grandparents had done the same. The economic and psychological impact on the communities where the suppliers were operating was often devastating and has led to a strong activist backlash against the retailers.

Suppliers are important stakeholders and companies have taken a great interest in the actions of their suppliers and the impact of the business activities of those suppliers on the local communities in which they operate. A number of U.S. companies have been

---

3. Communities have been described as individuals linked by issues (i.e., people concerned with the same issue); identity (i.e., people who share a set of beliefs, values, or experiences related to a specific issue such as the environment or public health); interaction (i.e., people who are linked by a set of social relationships); and geography (i.e., people who are in the same location). See ENGAGE YOUR COMMUNITY STAKEHOLDERS: AN INTRODUCTORY GUIDE FOR BUSINESSES (Network for Business Sustainability, 2012), 3.

4. ENGAGE YOUR COMMUNITY STAKEHOLDERS, *supra* note 3, 3.

embarrassed by disclosures regarding the poor treatment of local workers by their foreign suppliers and the adverse impacts that the manufacturing processes of those suppliers have had on the local ecosystems. In response, U.S. companies have implemented due diligence and inspection procedures for their foreign suppliers to ensure that those suppliers are acting as good citizens in their communities.

II. LEGAL AND REGULATORY REQUIREMENTS

The legal issues associated with the community engagement and investment activities of an organization will depend on the decisions made by the organization regarding the types of contributions that will be made (cash, in-kind, human resources, etc.), the nature of the projects and activities that will be supported, and the specific topical areas of interest. All businesses will need to determine the appropriate legal and organizational structures for their community-focused activities, and this often means that a decision will eventually need to be made about whether to form a separate legal entity, owned and controlled by the parent company, through which community investments will be funneled (i.e., a corporate foundation). Other common legal issues arise due to the nature of the business' involvement in the community and would include mitigating potential legal risks associated with employee volunteer programs, sponsoring and/or hosting community events, and entering into joint ventures and other types of alliance arrangements with local nonprofit organizations. Specialized legal guidance will be required when businesses get involved in complex and high-regulated areas such as helping to provide financial services for low-wealth and underserved communities, supporting public and private financing of community cultural facilities, participating in community-based efforts to preserve open space while expanding the availability of affordable housing, and assisting local courts looking to positively and proactively address juvenile delinquency by providing vocational training and job opportunities.

A. Structuring Corporate Philanthropy Initiatives

While there are a number of different ways that for-profit businesses can give back to their communities by making gifts of cash and other items to charities and other nonprofit organizations, it is important to understand three basic methods that are commonly used for philanthropic activities: direct-giving programs coordinated through an internal group; a company foundation formed and sponsored by the business, which can be a private foundation or a public charity; and a donor advised fund. Businesses are not limited to just one of these methods and may shift the focus of their philanthropic activities from one method to another as time goes by and the goals of the philanthropic program change. For example, smaller businesses will generally begin with a modest direct-giving program in order to conserve resources. As the business expands and revenues sufficient to support more ambitious philanthropy become available, it may be appropriate to establish a foundation while continuing direct giving for certain types of causes and programs. Regardless of whether a company creates an internal group or a separate entity, job descriptions and roles and responsibilities need to be prepared and defined for all team members, and appropriate connections need to be forged between the community engagement and development team and departments and groups within the company that can provide support such as budgeting, procurement, accounting, finance, administration, and information technology.

B. Charitable Contributions

When businesses engage in philanthropic activities in their communities, such as making cash and/or in-kind contributions to local charities or other nonprofit organizations, they need to establish compliance programs to ensure that their activities conform to applicable laws and regulations and that their contributions are being put to effective use. Due diligence with respect to potential donees has become particularly important as the size and scope of corporate philanthropy has expanded and many businesses, particularly larger ones, have taken on global issues such as disaster relief, humanitarian crises, health, and education and in doing so they have taken to giving to organizations working far away from the communities in which the companies are operating.[5] Compliance programs for charitable contributions need to incorporate consideration of all applicable laws and regulations pertaining to the initial transfer of funds and other resources to the charitable organization and the capacity of the recipient to effectively use the funds and resources free from financial abuse and mismanagement. Among the questions that should be asked and considered before any contribution is approved and completed are the following:

- Is the proposed recipient a duly organized nonprofit organization in good standing under the laws of its jurisdiction of organization based on certificates obtained from the authorized regulator (e.g., the secretary of state or the state attorney general for organizations formed in the United States)?
- Is the proposed recipient in compliance with all requirements for tax-exempt status under the regulations applicable to its specific types of activities (e.g., in the United States is the recipient a valid and current 501(c)(3) organization or equivalent)?
- Has the proposed recipient and its named directors, officers, and principal donors been screened against a comprehensive set of sanctions lists, both domestically and internationally?
- Does the proposed form of the contribution create any issues that might adversely impact the nonprofit/tax status of the entity of the business that will be making the contribution (e.g., foundation status of an affiliate of the main business established to engage in philanthropic activities)?

---

5. Portions of the discussion in this section are adapted from *Regulatory Compliance for Corporate Philanthropy: Why, What, How?*, (July 28, 2014), http://blog.cybergrants.com/regulatory-compliance-for-corporate-philanthropy-201407.html; and THE IMPORTANCE OF COMPLIANT GIVING PROGRAMS (CyberGrants, 2014).

- Has sufficient information regarding the proposed recipient been collected and analyzed to allow the business to properly report the contribution on tax and other reports?
- Have all internal policies regarding charitable contributions been complied with and has the company's database of established charitable organizations been updated to reflect all new information gathered during the due diligence process?
- If the business will be asking employees to consider donating to the proposed recipient, have steps been taken to ensure the recipient has in place adequate security procedures to protect the personal and financial information of donating employees?
- Has sufficient investigation been done of the controlling persons of the proposed recipient to ensure that there are no conflicts of interest involving directors and/or officers of the business?
- If the relationship involves volunteer activities by employees of the business that are endorsed by the business as opposed to cash donations, has consideration been given to relevant legal issues?

Establishing a compliance program for corporate philanthropy is not a one-time activity and provision must be made for ensuring that the group responsible for corporate philanthropy remains current with all relevant laws and regulations. When giving activities extend across foreign borders, attention needs to be paid to continuously changing sanctions screening and watch lists and evolving laws in foreign jurisdictions relating to money transfers, tax filings, and data privacy. Fortunately, the burden of carrying out the extensive screening has become more manageable through the availability of technology platforms that corporate philanthropy teams can access to receive reliable support in screening, verification, and other aspects of due diligence.

C. Corporate Volunteer Programs

There is a growing body of evidence that employees who engage in volunteer activities for causes that are important to them with the support of their employers are happier and more loyal; however, employers must bear the legal risks associated with employee volunteering in mind. Two major areas of concern for businesses sponsoring corporate volunteering programs in which their employees will have the opportunity to participate are compliance with federal and state labor laws, especially the federal Fair Labor Standards Act (FLSA), and liability for injuries or other damages to employees arising from their engagement in the volunteer activities. The key question under the FLSA is whether the employee's participation is truly voluntary, which goes to whether the employee gave up his or her nonwork time to engage in the volunteer activity without a reasonable expectation of compensation from his or her employer. If it turns out that an employee had no choice about whether he or she should participate, was required to engage in the activity during a period that was otherwise inconvenient, and was subject to directions from management personnel of his or her employer during the activity, rather than a supervisor from the party holding the volunteering event, failure to compensate the employee will likely expose the employer to liability for violations of minimum wage, overtime, and timekeeping requirements. Statutory liability is also a real risk for employers in situations where failure of an employee to participate in a volunteer activity as directed, or "strongly suggested," by the employer leads to some sort of adverse employment action against the employee.

In order to reduce potential problems under the FLSA businesses should implement clear formal policies regarding participation of employees in volunteer programs sponsored or others endorsed by the company. While businesses can, and often do, select specific volunteer activities to support, the policy should allow employees to select the programs and events that are best suited to their schedules and interests. Businesses should also allow the volunteering activities of their employees to be overseen by personnel from the outside charity or other organization conducting the event or activity. In addition, before the employee begins his or her work, he or she should sign a certificate that includes an acknowledgment that his or her participation is truly voluntary, the location and time of the activity is convenient for him or her, and that participation in the activity will not have any impact, favorable or unfavorable, on the employee. The certificate from employees described above should also be used as an opportunity to attempt to mitigate potential liability for injuries to the employee during the volunteering activity by including a waiver of liability against the employer for any such injuries. However, employers should not rely only on such releases for protection and should take other steps such as inspecting the locations where the volunteer activities will be occurring, seeking and obtaining indemnification from the party conducting the event or activity, and checking with insurance carriers to confirm that the company's general liability and workers' compensation insurance policies cover employees participating in corporate volunteer programs.

D. Events

As part of their initiatives relating to community involvement and development, it is likely that businesses will hold events to which community members will be invited. Each event must be considered separately; however, there are certain issues that are fairly commonplace such as governmental permitting and licensing requirements; contracting for venues and/or equipment to be used in connection with the event; intellectual property issues; insurance, safety, and security considerations; providing for access to events; sponsorships; and raising money and/or soliciting in-kind donations in connection with the event. In addition, businesses should consider the impact of the event on the surrounding neighborhoods in the community. For example, failure to consider how noise from the event and/or litter from persons walking to the event might impact the neighbors may trigger legal complaints from neighbors (and even if neighbors don't make formal complaints, upsetting neighbors by hosting events does nothing to improve the community citizen profile of the business).[6]

---

6. The list of issues in this section is adapted from several sources including LEGAL ISSUES TO CONSIDER WHEN HOLDING EVENTS (Melbourne: Justice Connect, October 2014).

E. Community Consultation Requirements

Before proceeding with any community investment program, particularly one that will involve development of new structures and/or impacts to the natural habitat in the community, consideration needs to be given to laws, regulations, and informal community expectations regarding engagement and consultation with members of the community.[7] Practices within communities vary so it will be important to seek advice from local experts familiar with any permitting or licensing requirements applicable to community development activities. In most cases even a small project such as making changes to the landscaping around the company's facility and/or adding more lighting to the parking lot used by customers and employees will require preparation and publication of an impact report and a minimum period of waiting before proceeding with the project during which community members can submit comments on, and raise objections to, the project. Evidence that the company has completed these preliminary steps will need to be presented to the regulatory body responsible for issuing permits or licenses. When a proposed community investment/development project is reasonably anticipated to have an impact on indigenous peoples, notice must be taken of the procedures that may have been established by local governments to comply with the letter and spirit of the United Nations Declaration on the Rights of Indigenous Peoples (UNDRIP), which identifies, describes, and affirms certain rights believed to be essential for the preservation of indigenous peoples' identity and culture including meaningful participation in decision-making following consultation and dialogue.[8]

F. Fair Labor Standards

Many community investment and development activities focus on training and skills development for community members, including students, to improve their opportunities in the local job market, and businesses interested in that area need to be mindful of applicable provisions of the FLSA, which has been introduced and discussed above. The FLSA includes extensive requirements between parties in an "employment relationship" relating to minimum wage, overtime pay, record-keeping (i.e., personal employee information, wages, hours), and child labor, and businesses need to consider whether or not students receiving vocational training in work settings will be considered employees under the FLSA and thus be entitled to the benefits and rights of employee status under the FLSA. Recognizing that businesses may be reluctant to launch training and internship programs, the federal Departments of Labor and Education developed guidelines that

---

7. COMMUNITY ENGAGEMENT TOOLKIT FOR PLANNING (The State of Queensland Australia: Department of Infrastructure, Local Government and Planning, Aug. 2017), 3. For further discussion of the methods that can be used for community engagement, see Chapter 3, "Stakeholder Engagement," in this volume.

8. http://www.un.org/esa/socdev/unpfii/documents/faq_drips_en.pdf. For further discussion, see C. Lewis, CORPORATE RESPONSIBILITY TO RESPECT THE RIGHTS OF MINORITIES AND INDIGENOUS PEOPLES (Minority Rights Group International, 2012); and IMPLEMENTING THE UN DECLARATION ON THE RIGHTS OF INDIGENOUS PEOPLE (Inter-Parliamentary Union, 2014).

can be followed to properly structure the programs so that participants have access to the protections of the FLSA and businesses have proper and clear guidance as to how the programs should be designed and executed (see, for example, the Statement of Principle relating to vocational exploration, assessment, and training programs for students with physical and/or mental disabilities).

III. VOLUNTARY STANDARDS, NORMS, AND GUIDELINES

Businesses have long been called upon to comply with a range of formal laws and regulations in various areas related to sustainability-related responsibilities including laws and regulations pertaining to the environmental impact of their operations, the employment relationship, working conditions, and health and safety standards. However, apart from satisfying the requirements of local governments with respect to permits and licenses necessary for engaging in certain activities in the community, businesses generally are not heavily constrained by legal guidelines with respect to their community involvement and development activities. This is an area in which voluntary standards have played an important role in providing business with ideas for objectives for their community involvement.

Since the late 1990s, there has been a proliferation of transnational, voluntary standards for what constitutes CSR, including standards that have been developed by states; public/private partnerships; multistakeholder negotiation processes; industries and companies; institutional investors; functional groups such as accountancy firms and social assurance consulting groups; NGOs; and nonfinancial ratings agencies.[9] While voluntary standards focusing specifically on the relationship of businesses and the communities in which they operate are still evolving, lessons can be drawn from many widely recognized normative frameworks, principles, and guidelines such as the United Nations Sustainable Development Goals, the United Nations Global Compact, the OECD Guidelines for Multinational Enterprises (http://mneguidelines.oecd.org/) ("OECD Guidelines"), the United Nations Guiding Principles on Business and Human Rights, and the Future-Fit Business Framework.[10] Specialized standards can be used as reference points for support of sustainability-related initiatives in local communities, such as requiring that recipients of grants and other investments for sustainable sourcing and agricultural activities adhere to the guidance developed by the Sustainable Agriculture Initiative Platform (http://www.saiplatform.org/).

Additional guidance comes from guidelines established for companies engaged in extractive activities where the potential for adverse impact on local communities

---

9. C. Williams, *Corporate Social Responsibility and Corporate Governance, in* OXFORD HANDBOOK OF CORPORATE LAW AND GOVERNANCE (J. Gordon & G. Ringe eds., Oxford: Oxford University Press, 2016), 7, http://digitalcommons.osgoode.yorku.ca/scholarly_works/1784.

10. *Id.* at 8–9.

is especially high. For example, Equitable Origin (https://www.equitableorigin.org/) is an independent nonprofit organization dedicated to promoting socially and environmentally responsible energy development. Equitable Origin claims to be the world's first stakeholder-led, independent, voluntary standards system designed to enable high social and environmental performance, transparency, and accountability in energy development. Equitable Origin has developed EO100 Standards for Responsibility Energy, Conventional Onshore Oil and Gas, and Shale Oil and Gas Operations, each of which are based on six basic principles addressing corporate governance, accountability, and ethics; human rights, social impacts, and community development; fair labor and working conditions; indigenous peoples' rights; climate change, biodiversity and environment; and project lifecycle management. The Equitable Origin website contains references to technical information, tools, guidelines, and best practices for topics covered by each of the principles including engagement and participation, resettlement, grievance mechanisms, community health, community investment, and cultural impacts.

While many of the standards and guidelines discussed herein can reasonably be characterized as aspirational, the International Organization for Standardization (ISO) (www.iso.org) seeks to provide organizations with easy access to international state-of-the-art models that they can follow in implementing their management systems. ISO has developed and distributed ISO 26000 Guidance on Social Responsibility which, although not a management system standard, is a useful guide for improvement of organizational practices with respect to social responsibility. ISO 26000 identifies and explains various core subjects such as organizational governance, human rights, labor practices, the environment, fair operating practices, and consumer issues and, notably for purposes of this discussion, also explicitly includes community involvement and development among its core subjects.[11] The issues for businesses relating to community involvement and development identified in ISO 26000 include community involvement and respecting the laws and practices of the community; social investment (i.e., building infrastructure and improving social aspects of community life); employment creation (i.e., making decisions to maximize local employment opportunities); technology development (i.e., engaging in partnerships with local organizations and facilitating diffusion of technology into the community to contribute to economic development); wealth and income (i.e., using natural resources in a sustainable way that helps to alleviate poverty, giving preference to local suppliers, and fulfilling tax responsibilities); education and culture (i.e., supporting education at all levels and promoting cultural activities); health (i.e., promoting good health, raising awareness about diseases, and providing access to essential health care services); and responsible investment (i.e., incorporating economic, social, environmental, and governance dimensions into investment decisions along with traditional financial dimensions).[12]

---

11. See International Organization for Standardization, ISO 26000 GUIDANCE ON SOCIAL RESPONSIBILITY: DISCOVERING ISO 26000 (2014) and Handbook for Implementers of ISO 26000, GLOBAL GUIDANCE STANDARD ON SOCIAL RESPONSIBILITY BY SMALL AND MEDIUM SIZED BUSINESSES (Middlebury, VT: Ecologia, 2011).

12. Handbook for Implementers of ISO 26000, *supra* note 11, 32–33.

In addition to the various standards mentioned above, businesses and other organizations will also be impacted by relevant standards on their key stakeholders, particularly investors. For example, large institutional investors around the world have been moving quickly to embrace "responsible investment," a concept that has been defined in the Principles for Responsible Investment (www.unpri.org) as an approach to investing that aims to incorporate environmental, social, and governance (ESG) factors into investment decisions to better manage risk and generate sustainable, long-term returns. Not surprisingly, one of the social factors is local communities, including indigenous communities, and businesses with investors that are signatories to the Principles can expect that those investors will take their community involvement activities into account in making investment decisions and require appropriate disclosures regarding their impact on the development and well-being of the local communities in which they operate. Investments from the International Finance Corporation (IFC) also come with requirements that clients adhere to the IFC's Performance Standards on Environmental and Social Sustainability, which relate to assessment and management of environmental and social risks and impacts in local communities; community health, safety, and security; indigenous peoples and cultural heritage.[13]

IV. GOVERNANCE AND COMPLIANCE

Community engagement and investment is a multifaceted activity that requires formal management and planning. Working with and in the community is part of the broader CSR activities of the company and this means that management should begin at the top of the hierarchy with the board of directors or, in most cases, the committee of the board that has been delegated responsibility for overseeing CSR activities on behalf of all of the directors.[14] The CSR committee, working in collaboration with senior management of the company and specialists working specifically on community-related matters, should be tasked with developing strategies and policies relating to community engagement and investment; deciding on the optimal organizational structure for community-related activities, including perhaps the formation of an affiliated corporate foundation; ensuring that procedures are in place for conducting due diligence on prospective recipients of grants and other resources from the company and potential partners in community development projects; developing and approving of projects; overseeing the implementation of projects, including preparing definitive agreements with community partners, monitoring progress, and measuring impact; and compiling and analyzing relevant information regarding community activities for presentation in the company's sustainability reporting.

---

13. See International Finance Corporation Performance Standard 1—Assessment and Management of Environmental and Social Risks and Impacts—and IFC Performance Standard 4—Community Health, Safety, and Security.

14. For further discussion of the role of the board of directors in CSR, see Chapter 2, "ESG, Sustainability, and CSR: Governance and the Role of the Board," in this volume.

A. Strategies and Policies

The first step in the process of designing, implementing, and managing the company's community engagement and investment should be developing appropriate strategies and policies. If the company's activities are limited to occasional actions that fall into the realm of traditional philanthropy (i.e., small grants to local nonprofits and/or annual volunteering days), it may actually be that it has no specific strategy, which may be fine for a short period of time when the company is just launching and has scarce planning resources that need to be focused on other issues. However, as companies take on more ambitious plans with respect to involvement with communities and tackle issues that cannot be solved with one act, such as addressing poor education and poverty in the community, long-term strategies that go out three to five years are appropriate since the company's resources will need to be committed to the issue over an extended period of time. Strategies should describe what the company expects to achieve over the planning period in relation to its vision, mission, and goals with respect to community development and how it plans to achieve those goals in terms of organizing and committing its available resources.

The development of a strategy is the time for the CSR committee, and the company as a whole, to focus on three fundamental questions. First, the company should decide on the group within its community that will be the primary target of the activities. For example, many companies prefer to be involved in programs for young people in their communities, such as improving primary education and/or providing recreational spaces. Other groups that might be targeted include older people, community members with disabilities, and groups that have been marginalized and/or discriminated against due to gender or ethnicity. The next thing that needs to be done is to determine whether activities should be focused on specific parts of the community, such as a particular neighborhood, or can and should be scaled to have an impact throughout the entire geographic area. For most companies, the answer, at least initially, should be to concentrate on the areas surrounding the company's facilities. Finally, in order to have a strategy the company needs to decide on the sector and related issues on which the community-related activities will concentrate. Sector refers to the broader community development area, such as education, health, the environment, and job creation, on which the company's community-related activities will concentrate. Issues are specific aspects of the selected sector, such as early childhood education in the education sector, encouraging regular medical screenings and tests in the health sector, and entrepreneurship training in the job creation sector.

B. Community Engagement

Community engagement and dialogue—sharing information and listening to community members to provide them with a voice on matters that impact them—is the cornerstone of everything a company does vis-à-vis the community in which it operates.[15] Community

---

15. For further discussion of the methods that can be used for community engagement, see Chapter 3, "Stakeholder Engagement," in this volume.

engagement appears in many of the voluntary standards relating to sustainability and reporting on sustainability-related matters. For example, the OECD Guidelines call on enterprises to seek and consider the views of community members before making decisions regarding changes in operations that would have major effects on the livelihood of employees and their family members living in the community and the community as a whole (e.g., proposed closures of facilities), and take steps to mitigate adverse effects of such decisions on the community. The Sustainability Reporting Standards created by the Global Reporting Initiative (GRI), and discussed in more detail below, call for reporting organizations to discuss their management approach to local communities by describing the means by which stakeholders are identified and engaged with; which vulnerable groups have been identified; any collective or individual rights that have been identified that are of particular concern for the community in question; how it engages with stakeholder groups that are particular to the community (e.g., groups defined by age, indigenous background, ethnicity, or migration status); and the means by which its departments and other bodies address risks and impacts or support independent third parties to engage with stakeholders and address risks and impacts.[16]

Effective community engagement must be built on a sense of trust between the company and the members of the community, and engagement should be carried out in a manner that conforms to recognized standards of professionalism and ethical conduct. In fact, the International Association for Public Participation (IAP2) (https://www.iap2.org/) has developed a Code of Ethics for Public Participation Practitioners that is intended to serve as a guide to the duties of public participation practitioners and ensure the integrity of the public participation process. Among the guiding principles in the code are enhancing the public's participation in the decision-making process and assisting decision-makers in being responsive to the public's concerns and suggestions; building trust and credibility for the process among all the participants; carefully considering and accurately portraying the public's role in the decision-making process; encouraging the disclosure of all information relevant to the public's understanding and evaluation of a decision; ensuring that stakeholders have fair and equal access to the public participation process and the opportunity to influence decisions; and ensuring that all commitments made to the public, including those by the decision-maker, are made in good faith.[17]

C. Measurement and Assessment

Whenever a business is involved in a strategic planning exercise, provision must be made for regular and continuous measurement and assessment of performance against the goals and objectives that should have been established early in the planning process. Measurement and assessment of a company's performance with respect to community engagement and investment are not only important to the company but also to the employees for whom community engagement is a valuable motivator, the

---

16. GRI 413: LOCAL COMMUNITIES 2016 (Amsterdam: Global Sustainability Standards Board, 2016).
17. https://www.iap2.org/page/ethics.

communities in which the company operates, and, of course, the investors who provide a significant amount of the funding that ultimately is transformed into the resources that the company distributes in its community investment programs. Effective community investment also matters to customers and other business partners. Measurement and assessment is also an opportunity for further engagement with community groups and other stakeholders in that part of the assessment process should involve sitting down with partners to discuss how projects have gone and, hopefully, build further trust during those discussions.

D. Reporting

While more and more companies produce reports that emphasize the importance of being a good community citizen and effectively managing their relationships with community members and the community environment, those same reports often reflect difficulties in identifying and describing specific goals for community involvement and the impact that company activities are having on the community. As with all aspects of sustainability reporting, practices of companies regarding their disclosures relating to community engagement and investment have been evolving as time has passed and stakeholder interest in such activities has increased. Although mandatory reporting requirements have been slow to emerge, the need to keep communities informed has found its way into global standards such as the OECD Guidelines, which provide that enterprises are expected to ensure that timely, regular, reliable, and relevant information is disclosed to the community regarding the activities, structure, financial situation, and performance of the enterprise and relationships between the enterprise and its stakeholders; and communicate information to the community regarding the social, ethical, and environmental policies of the enterprise and other codes of conduct to which the enterprise subscribes (including voluntary standards relating to community involvement and development).

1. Global Reporting Initiative

The Sustainability Reporting Standards developed by the GRI (www.globalreporting.org) are the most widely used standards on sustainability reporting and disclosure around the world and include several types of disclosure categories that cover various aspects of community involvement, investment, and impact. The GRI reporting framework covers a wide range of performance indicators and disclosure standards in three categories: economic, environmental, and social. With respect to operations and other activities that might directly or indirectly have a material impact on their communities, organizations that have adopted the GRI framework are expected, among other things, to make disclosures regarding the impact that their investments and other support infrastructure and local services has had on their stakeholders and the economy; the indirect economic impacts their operations and activities have had on their communities; community investment activities; engagement with local communities; the actual and potential negative impacts of their actions on local communities and their managerial approach to community issues.

2. London Benchmarking Group

A framework for reporting promoted by the London Benchmarking Group (LBG) (http://www.lbg-online.net/), which is managed by Corporate Citizenship, a global corporate responsibility consultancy based in London with offices in Singapore and New York, is an effective tool for quantifying and organizing information about their corporate community investment activities and, most importantly, assessing and reporting on the impact of their relationships with communities and how to manage it.[18] LBG explained its framework as being "a simple input output model, enabling any [corporate community investment] activity to be assessed consistently in terms of the resources committed and the results achieved."[19] Applying the framework begins with inputs (i.e., what resources did the company provide to support a community activity), continues with outputs (i.e., what happened within the community and the company as a result of the activity and what additional resources were brought to bear on a particular issue as a result of the company's contributions and participation in the activity), and finishes with identifying and measuring the impacts achieved on various groups (i.e., the changes that occurred for people, organizations, and the environment within the community and for the involved employees and overall business of the company).

V. PRACTICING COMMUNITY INVOLVEMENT

A. Community Development

One of the most-cited aspirations for business organizations with respect to their communities is providing a positive impact on community development and improving the quality of life and levels of well-being among the members of the community.[20] Community development is not the sole responsibility of organizations operating in the community, but rather comes from community stakeholders working together out of a sense of shared responsibility. From that perspective, the goal for each organization is to find the best way for it to contribute, and the commentary in ISO 26000 suggests that organizations can contribute by[21]

- creating employment through expanding and diversifying economic activities and technological development;
- making social investments in wealth and income creation through local economic development initiatives both within and outside the organization's core operational activities;

---

18. From Inputs to Impact: Measuring Corporate Community Contributions through the LBG Framework—A Guidance Manual (London: Corporate Citizenship, 2014), 4.
19. *Id.* at 6.
20. International Organization for Standardization, ISO 26000: Guidance on Social Responsibility (Geneva, 2010), 61.
21. *Id.*

- expanding education and skills development programs;
- promoting and preserving culture and arts;
- providing and/or promoting community health services;
- facilitating and participating in institutional strengthening of the community, its groups and collective forums, cultural, social, and environmental programs, and local networks involving multiple institutions;
- supporting related public policies and engaging in partnerships with governmental agencies to pursue development priorities identified during the course of the community's own deliberative processes;
- engaging with a broad range of stakeholders with special emphasis on identifying and consulting with and, where possible, supporting vulnerable, marginalized, discriminated, or underrepresented groups; and
- engaging in socially responsible behavior.

ISO 26000 explains that some activities of an organization may be explicitly intended to contribute to community development, while others may aim at private purposes but indirectly promote general development. For example, programs focusing on preserving local culture and arts, which typically take the form of financial support and employee volunteerism, are generally unrelated to the core operational activities of the business but presumably provide value through enhancement of the reputation of the business and tighter integration with various segments of the community. On the other hand, investing in improvement to access roads and other aspects of the transportation infrastructure in the areas next to the facilities of the business provides not only direct operational benefits to the business but also indirect benefits to the community if the changes are well planned after consultation with impacted groups within the community. While each of the contributions listed above are important, businesses, regardless of size and like any other type of organization, do not have unlimited resources, nor do they necessarily have the expertise to make a significant impact, at least initially, in each of the areas. Every business has the capacity to continuously engage in socially responsible behavior; however, ISO 26000 notes that beyond that the most important contributions to community involvement and development will depend on the circumstances in the community itself, the unique knowledge, resources, and capacity each organization brings to the community, and the degree of alignment between the activity and the core operational activities of the business.

B. Community Investment

Most businesses, once they reach a certain size and level of resources, provide support for the activities of organizations in their communities that are dedicated to address social issues or needs in the community. The form of community contribution and engagement by a company can vary significantly, running from a one-time cash donation to a good cause to investment of cash, in-kind resources, and management time into the creation of long-term partnership with a community organization that works on a broader and deeper solution to a particular issue that has a material impact on the business and the community in which it operates. ISO 26000 notes that organizations generally choose from among a wide array of potential community social investments including projects related to education, training, culture, health care, income generation, infrastructure development, improving access to information, or any other activity likely to promote economic or social development; however, when creating its community social investment agenda an organization should purposefully seek to align its contribution with its core competencies and the needs and priorities of the communities in which it operates and take into account priorities set by local and national policymakers and the actions that are already being taken by other community stakeholders.

Corporate philanthropy (e.g., grants, volunteering, and donations) has a long tradition and companies have often been attempting various types of community investment. While these efforts are generally well meaning and have led to significant improvements in well-being in the communities in which the companies are operating, there are also signs that community investments fail to fulfill their full potential, for either the company or the community. Given that many investment projects involve significant amounts of resources, including time and goodwill, falling short on results means that employee morale may suffer and that community members lose faith and trust in the company. While companies could abandon community investments in order to obtain relief from the challenges described above, such an approach is no longer practical or advisable for firms looking to build a sustainable business. Community engagement and involvement, including community investment, is essential for attracting talent and satisfying the expectations of customers, investors, and other stakeholders. As such, companies need to apply the same discipline to community investing that they do to all other aspects of their business, and this means following a deliberative process to develop a comprehensive community investment strategy that effectively deploys the company's core competencies to support community-focused projects that deliver the strongest impact given the level of investment.

Tran, in an article prepared for the quarterly publication of Social Ventures Australia, argued that businesses should use a combination of social investment approaches as part of a well-managed portfolio in order to deliver greater impact, support the generation of social and business value in different ways, and engage different stakeholders.[22] The portfolio approach would include initiatives and activities from among four categories: traditional philanthropy, engaged philanthropy, catalytic philanthropy (i.e., catalyzing a campaign that achieves a measurable social impact), and "creating shared value."[23] According to Tran and others, adapting a range of approaches can provide a number of benefits and advantages to businesses including appealing to different sets of stakeholders; achieving a broader set of social and business outcomes; diversifying the risk in achieving the social and business objectives; making use of a wider range of skillsets across the organization; taking advantage of different available opportunities and forming nontraditional alliances; and designing complementary initiatives which increase the overall impact of the portfolio.

---

22. N. Tran, *A Portfolio Approach to Corporate Social Investment*, SVA QUARTERLY (Aug. 25, 2016), https://www.socialventures.com.au/sva-quarterly/a-portfolio-approach-to-corporate-social-investment/.

23. *Id.* (noting adaptation from M. Kramer, *Catalytic Philanthropy*, SSI R (Fall 2009) and M. Porter & M. Kramer, *Creating Shared Value*, HARV. BUS. REV. (Jan.–Feb. 2011)).

In most cases businesses make changes in their approaches incrementally. For example, a fairly common transition for businesses is shifting from almost total reliance on traditional philanthropy (e.g., community sponsorships, grants to local nonprofits, employee volunteering, and fundraising) to engaged philanthropy including multiyear partnerships with various community organizations to address a large and important social issue such as supporting local schools and creating meaningful job opportunities for teenagers in the community who have grown up in difficult conditions. As businesses become more involved in engaged philanthropy, often participating in multiple partnerships dealing with social issues that intersect with their core businesses and resource competencies (e.g., Toyota formed a community foundation to work with local nonprofit organizations on projects relating to road safety, education, and the environment), they may eventually decide to stretch for even greater impact through shared value, such as launching a community innovation fund to combine financial and human capital to invent new technical solutions to social and environmental issues.

While creating shared value is discussed as an extension of philanthropic approaches, it is somewhat unique in that it is essentially grounded in business strategy with the goal of addressing social problems at the same time that the company continues to pursue its traditional mission of creating economic benefit. Among the most vocal and visible proponents of shared value have been Porter and Kramer, who have pushed businesses to make a fundamental shift in their purposes away from short-term financial performance toward "creating economic value in a way that also creates value for society by addressing its needs and challenges."[24] According to Porter and Kramer, shared value can be pursued and created by businesses in three distinct ways: by reconceiving products and services to address societal needs and/or by opening new markets by redesigning products or adopting different distribution methods in order to serve unmet needs in underserved communities; by redefining productivity in the value chain; and by building strong and supportive industry clusters with capable local suppliers and institutions and a healthy business environment in the communities in which the company operates.[25]

C. Community Partnering

In addition to developing a comprehensive strategy for community investment, companies must master the nuances of effectively partnering with local nonprofit organizations, including community development corporations, in order to collaboratively address a social or environmental issue or cause that neither one of them can adequately address on their own and for which local government has also failed to find a solution. While partnerships between businesses and nonprofit organizations make sense, they can be challenging because they bring together organizations with different ideologies and ways of looking at problems, setting goals, and measuring outcomes. On the other

---

24. Porter & Kramer, *supra* note 24, 64.
25. *Id.* at 67.

hand, the so-called community business partnership is an excellent opportunity to bring together two or more organizations with common goals and complementary resources to leverage those resources, and the talents and experiences of their employees, to pursue and achieve goals that will benefit the businesses, the nonprofit organizations, and the community. Common elements of successful community business partnerships include a clearly articulated and shared mission; a commitment of time and funding; compatible strategy and values; continual measure and evaluation of programs, as well as the partnership itself; good governance and transparency; identity and integration of the partnership; open communications; and suitable programs that fit with the available resources and core competencies of the partners, organizational size, and location.[26]

D. Start-Ups and Small Businesses

While corporate philanthropy and social investment are commonly discussed with respect to larger businesses, there are significant and effective ways for start-ups and smaller firms to engage with their communities and have a positive impact that enhances their reputation and their morale of employees. Some of the ideas that should be considered by entrepreneurs and small business owners include sponsoring the activities and/or specific events of nonprofit organizations in the community; incorporating employee volunteering into the company's mission and personnel policies; designing a business model that gives back to the community (e.g., setting aside a portion of the profits from each sale for automatic investment toward a solution of a community social or environmental issue); contributing to the local economy by prioritizing hiring from within the community and selecting local vendors for procurement of necessary goods and services; and promoting local businesses to customers and other contacts through co-marketing efforts or referrals.[27]

VI. THE CASE FOR COMMUNITY ENGAGEMENT AND INVESTMENT

While the potential benefits of community engagement and investment for businesses are often framed as being readily apparent, it is useful to consider ideas about the specific aims and objectives of corporate community involvement. One comprehensive list included making people inside and outside the community aware of various

---

26. Adapted from ENDURING PARTNERSHIPS: RESILIENCE, INNOVATION, SUCCESS (Boston College Center for Corporate Citizenship, 2005); and J. Levine, ELEMENTS OF SUSTAINABLE PARTNERSHIPS (Boston College Center for Corporate Citizenship, 2004) (as cited and discussed in *Relationship Matters: Not-for-Profit Community Organizations and Corporate Community Investment* (Australian Government Department of Social Services, Oct. 2008), https://www.dss.gov.au/our-responsibilities/communities-and-vulnerable-people/publications-articles/relationship-matters-not-for-profit-community-organisations-and-corporate-community-investment?HTML#p4).

27. B. Berger, *5 Ways Entrepreneurs Can Enhance Local Communities*, ENTREPRENEUR (Aug. 24, 2016), https://www.entrepreneur.com/article/280501.

problems in the community; ensuring that investment and development efforts occur across all sectors of the community and in multiple areas including education, health, recreation, and employment; motivating members of the community to participate in community welfare programs; providing equal opportunities within the community for access to education, health, and other facilities necessary for better well-being; building confidence among community members to help themselves and others; generating new ideas and changing patterns of life within the community in positive ways that do not negatively interfere with traditions and culture; bringing social reforms into the community; promoting social justice; developing effective methods to solve community programs including better communications between community members and local governments; and creating interest in community welfare among community members and mobilizing those members to participate in the collective work for community development.[28]

The Conference Board reported on the collaboration between Points of Light and Bloomberg LP to identify the 50 most community-minded companies in the United States for 2014 and noted that companies included on the list were typically strong with respect to one or more of the following[29]:

- Employer-led community programs positively impacted employee engagement, meaning that employees who participated in community engagement initiatives with the support of the employers scored higher on measures of morale, engagement, pride, and productivity than employees who did not.
- Companies and communities found value in skills-based volunteering: skills-based volunteering strengthened employees' morale and workplace skills while providing five times greater value to the community than traditional volunteering.
- Companies raised their voice to advance social change by taking national leading positions on social issues related to their own operations, thus taking advantage of their ability to contribute lasting solutions.
- Purpose was aligned with profit, with most of the companies integrating their community engagement into at least one of three business areas: marketing, skill development, and diversity and inclusion.

VII. SUMMARY AND TAKEAWAYS

Surveys have shown that commitment to CSR and related activities, including community involvement, is an important driver of employee engagement, and employees care a great deal about how their employer is perceived with respect to

---

28. http://www.studylecturenotes.com/social-sciences/sociology/339-aims-and-objectives-of-community-development.

29. Y. Turner, *The Civic 50: Best Practices in Corporate Community Engagement*, GIVING THOUGHTS (The Conference Board, Mar. 2015).

social responsibility in the communities in which they operate. Community engagement and investment activities provide organizations with important opportunities to leverage the impact of their contributions given that businesses typically rely on their local communities as a source of talent for the employee base, for contractors, for services that the organization seeks to outsource, and, of course, as a market for the organization's products and services. By contributing to educational and health programs in the community, an organization can increase the skills base of potential workers, thereby reducing training costs when new employees are hired and lowering the risk of adverse impacts to productivity due to illnesses among its employees or their immediate family members, either of which can cause employees to miss time at work. Organizations can provide financial support, as well as licensed technology, to launch a local network of engineers, scientists, and/or software developers to generate innovations that not only benefits the organization but also provides new opportunities for other members of the community, thus improving overall community well-being. Finally, the proximity of local customers makes it easier for organizations to develop and communicate their marketing messages and seek and obtain feedback on the effectiveness of those messages and the quality and value of the product and services distributed by the organization. In fact, one of the compelling reasons for investing in community involvement at all levels is the relative ease of collecting and analyzing information relating to operational performance. Proximity to human, technical, and other resources that can be developed and nurtured through community engagement and investment also allows organizations to move more quickly to seize opportunities and obtain a competitive advantage.

Community engagement must be a permanent part of the strategy and operations of any organization, and this means identifying community stakeholders as soon as possible and moving quickly to establish communications and understand their needs and expectations regarding the organization and how it will operate within the community. Organizations need to understand the issues that concern community members, and the beliefs, values, and experiences that drive the actions of community members and how community groups interact with one another. Organizations also need to carefully select the best strategies for their relationships with their communities, typically choosing from among community investment, which is essentially a one-way process of providing information and resources to the community (information sessions, charitable donations, employee volunteering, etc.); community involvement, which involves two-way communications, such as consultation processes prior to launching a major project; and/or community integration, which involves sharing information and consultation in advance of launching collaborative projects that are jointly controlled with, and often led by, community groups.[30]

---

30. Network for Business Sustainability, *Engage Your Community Stakeholders: An Introductory Guide* (Sept. 14, 2012), https://nbs.net/p/engage-your-community-stakeholders-an-introductory-gui-615902ab-e363-47ff-a3fc-d87188938739.

VIII. PRACTITIONER'S RESOURCES LIBRARY

A. Articles

N. Tran, "A Portfolio Approach to Corporate Social Investment," *SVA Quarterly* (August 25, 2016).

M. Kramer, "Catalytic Philanthropy," *Stanford Social Innovation Review* (Fall 2009).

M. Porter and M. Kramer, "Creating Shared Value," *Harvard Business Review* (January–February 2011).

S. Petit, *A Basic Guide to Corporate Philanthropy* (Adler & Colvin, March 2010).

B. Berger, "5 Ways Entrepreneurs Can Enhance Local Communities," *Entrepreneur* (August 24, 2016).

Y. Turner, "The Civic 50: Best Practices in Corporate Community Engagement," *Giving Thoughts* (The Conference Board, March 2015).

M. Ismail, "Corporate Social Responsibility and Its Roles in Community Development: An International Perspective," *The Journal of International Social Research*, 2/9 (Fall 2009), 199.

B. Books and White Papers

Engage Your Community Stakeholders: An Introductory Guide for Businesses (Network for Business Sustainability, 2012).

Regulatory Compliance for Corporate Philanthropy: Why, What, How?, July 28, 2014.

Legal Issues to Consider When Holding Events (Melbourne: Justice Connect, October 2014).

Community Engagement Toolkit for Planning (The State of Queensland Australia: Department of Infrastructure, Local Government and Planning, August 2017).

C. Lewis, *Corporate Responsibility to Respect the Rights of Minorities and Indigenous Peoples* (Minority Rights Group International, 2012).

Implementing the UN Declaration on the Rights of Indigenous People (Inter-Parliamentary Union, 2014).

Enduring Partnerships: Resilience, Innovation, Success (Boston College Center for Corporate Citizenship, 2005).

J. Levine, *Elements of Sustainable Partnerships* (Boston College Center for Corporate Citizenship, 2004).

Relationship Matters: Not-for-Profit Community Organizations and Corporate Community Investment (Australian Government Department of Social Services, October 2008).

Developing Effective Community Involvement Strategies (Joseph Roundtree Foundation, March 1999).

C. Instruments and Standards

International Finance Corporation Performance Standard 4—Community Health, Safety and Security.

International Organization for Standardization, ISO 26000 Guidance on Social Responsibility: Discovering ISO 26000 (2014).

Handbook for Implementers of ISO 26000, Global Guidance Standard on Social Responsibility by Small and Medium Sized Businesses (Middlebury, VT: ECOLOGIA, 2011).

International Organization for Standardization, ISO 26000: Guidance on Social Responsibility (Geneva, 2010).

United Nations Declaration, "Universal Declaration of Human Rights" (1948).

United Nations Convention, "International Covenant on Civil and Political Rights" (1966).

United Nations Convention, "International Covenant on Economic, Social, and Cultural Rights" (1966).

United Nations Declaration, "Declaration on the Right to Development" (1986).

D. Reporting

GRI 203: Indirect Economic Impacts 2016 (Amsterdam: Global Sustainability Standards Board, 2016).

GRI 413: Local Communities 2016 (Amsterdam: Global Sustainability Standards Board, 2016).

Reporting on Community Impacts: A Survey Conducted by the Global Reporting Initiative, the University of Hong Kong and CSR Asia (Amsterdam: Stichting Global Reporting Initiative, 2008).

From Inputs to Impact: Measuring Corporate Community Contributions through the LBG Framework—A Guidance Manual (London: Corporate Citizenship, 2014).

Chapter 9

Corporate Social Responsibility and Indigenous Rights

Charlotte Teal, Sharon Singh, and Radha Curpen

I. INTRODUCTION

Indigenous rights are a central component of human rights and corporate social responsibility (CSR). When companies require the use of land, water, or other elements, Indigenous rights are, depending upon the region, often impacted. Indigenous peoples and their rights tend to be portrayed as risks to be managed; however, in many cases Indigenous peoples are either actual or potential rightsholders and present several opportunities for sustainable development, including as potential partners, service providers, and employees of the company.

This chapter considers CSR in the context of Indigenous rights, with a focus on Indigenous (Aboriginal) law in Canada. It is targeted toward companies in extractive or natural resources sectors. In Canada, protections for Aboriginal peoples are enshrined in the country's constitution and in common law. Aboriginal rights have been, and continue to be, subject to substantial litigation, which has resulted in a large body of case law interpreting Aboriginal rights and shaping the way both the government and companies interact with Aboriginal groups.

The authors acknowledge and thank Adam Shumka, Amy O'Connor, and Zoe Hutchinson for their contributions to this chapter.

While this chapter is written from a Canadian perspective, it offers an overview of key considerations that companies should consider when operating in jurisdictions where Indigenous rights are triggered and when developing and implementing CSR practices related to Indigenous peoples. This chapter will begin with an overview of Canadian Aboriginal law, which demonstrates how Indigenous or Aboriginal rights relate to and shape corporate practices. Next, it will provide a brief overview of three other jurisdictions—Australia, Chile, and Mexico—to demonstrate the differing situations of Indigenous rights abroad. It will then discuss the role of international law, customs, and norms in shaping corporate practice, and discuss key international instruments that companies should take into account when developing Indigenous rights policies. Finally, this chapter will discuss trends in corporate practice and will conclude with a checklist of best practices for companies whose activities have the potential to impact Indigenous rights.

II. LEGAL AND REGULATORY REQUIREMENTS—INDIGENOUS RIGHTS

A. Overview of Aboriginal Law in Canada

Indigenous peoples, or "Aboriginal peoples" as they are also referred to in Canada, are protected under Section 35 of Canada's Constitution Act, 1982.[1] The term "Aboriginal peoples" refers to three distinct cultural groups in Canada—Indians, Métis, and Inuit—each offered the same constitutional protection. Many First Nations prefer this term instead of "Indians"; however, the nomenclature depends upon the preference of each community. Métis are a distinct Aboriginal group, whose ancestors are a mix of European and Aboriginal peoples. The Inuit reside predominantly in regions of the Northwest Territories, Nunavut, Northern Quebec, and Northern Labrador.

There are three basic forms of Aboriginal rights entrenched in and protected by the Constitution Act, 1982: Aboriginal rights, Aboriginal title, and treaty rights.

1. Aboriginal Rights

Aboriginal rights are collective rights that derive from the continuous use or occupation of an area and relate to the activities, practices, customs, or traditions that, prior to contact with Europeans, were integral to the distinctive culture of an Aboriginal group.[2] These rights often include the right to hunt, trap, harvest, and fish on ancestral lands. Although constitutionally protected, the Crown may infringe on these rights in limited

---

1. Constitution Act, 1982, *c 11(U.K.),* reprinted in *R.S.C. 1985,* app II, no 44 (Can.).
2. R v. Van der Peet, [1996] 2 S.C.R. 507 (Can.) para. 46.

circumstances. However, such infringement must be justified and to do so the Crown must balance Aboriginal rights with other societal interests.[3]

2. Aboriginal Title

Aboriginal title is sui generis (unique) and entitles the Aboriginal group to the exclusive right to use, control, and benefit from the land.[4] Aboriginal title arises from Aboriginal occupation of land prior to British sovereignty. It is a collective right, and it cannot be alienated or encumbered to prevent future generations of the Aboriginal titleholders from using and enjoying it.[5] To establish a claim for Aboriginal title, the Aboriginal group asserting the title must show

1. that the land was occupied prior to British sovereignty in 1846;
2. if present occupation is relied on as proof of pre-sovereignty occupation, that there is continuity between present and pre-sovereignty occupation; and
3. at sovereignty, occupation was exclusive.[6]

Project development may not occur on Aboriginal title lands unless the Crown has obtained prior consent from the Aboriginal group or, alternatively, where the Crown can justify an infringement to Aboriginal title. To justify an infringement of Aboriginal title, the Crown must show that

1. it discharged its procedural duty to consult and accommodate;
2. its actions were backed by a compelling and substantial objective (which may include, for example, the development of agriculture, forestry, mining, and hydroelectric power); and
3. the governmental action is consistent with the Crown's fiduciary obligation to the group.[7]

3. Treaty Rights

Treaty rights refer to negotiated rights that are set out in either historic treaties or land claim agreements (modern treaties) between an Aboriginal group and the Crown. Treaties are often, but not exclusively, a surrender of Aboriginal title to lands in exchange for rights.[8] Examples of historic treaty rights include rights to reserve lands, farming equipment and animals, annual payments, ammunition, clothing, hunting, and fishing

---

3. Haida Nation v. British Columbia (Minister of Forests), [2004] 3 S.C.R. 511 (Can.).; R. v. Sparrow, [1990] 1 S.C.R. 1075 (Can.).
4. Tsilhqot'in Nation v. British Columbia, [2014] 2 S.C.R. 257, para. 70 (Can.); Delgamuukw v. British Columbia, [1997] 3 S.C.R. 1010, para. 117 (Can.).
5. *Tsilhqot'in Nation,* [2014] 2 S.C.R. 257, para. 74.
6. *Id.*, para. 30; *Delgamuukw*, [1997] 3 S.C.R 1010, para. 143.
7. *Tsilhqot'in Nation,* [2014] 2 S.C.R. 257, para. 77.
8. JACK WOODWARD, NATIVE LAW 5 §210 (2018), Thomson Reuters ProView eReference Library (last visited Sept. 18, 2018).

within a traditional territory. Modern treaty rights may be more comprehensive than those contained in historic treaties and may include surface and subsurface rights within the treaty area. More recently, incremental, limited scope (e.g., resource management) agreements, or agreements for a defined time period have also been negotiated.

4. The Duty to Consult

A principle referred to as the "honor of the Crown" requires the Crown to act honorably when dealing with Aboriginal peoples in order to reconcile its interests with preexisting Aboriginal rights. Due to the honor of the Crown, the Crown has a duty to consult with and, where appropriate, accommodate Aboriginal peoples any time that Crown conduct has the potential to affect Aboriginal rights.

A growing body of case law continues to refine the duty to consult and accommodate, and to create new norms related to Aboriginal rights. The Supreme Court of Canada's decision in *Haida Nation v. BC and Weyerhaeuser*[9] sets out the framework for the Crown's duty to consult and, where appropriate, accommodate. The duty to consult is triggered when the Crown has knowledge of asserted or actual Aboriginal rights and is contemplating conduct that might adversely affect those rights.[10] The depth of consultation required is proportionate to the strength of the claim and the potential harm.[11] It calls for meaningful engagement with the Aboriginal group on the proposed conduct and seeks to identify the potential adverse impacts on the asserted or actual right and to avoid or minimize the adverse impacts. Accordingly, the effect of good faith consultation reveals a duty to accommodate.[12]

While it is the Crown's duty to consult, companies operating in Canada should understand when the duty to consult arises, as well as the scope and content of the duty. In practice, the Crown often delegates the procedural elements of consultation to companies seeking Crown approvals. If there are Aboriginal claims or existing rights in an area and the duty to consult has been triggered, regulatory agencies cannot issue approvals until the duty has been satisfied. Whether the Crown's duty to consult has been met has significant implications for project proponents. Disputes related to the sufficiency of consultation can delay or stop a project. Inadequate consultation can lead to years of legal challenges, public controversy, and other delays (e.g., protests).

5. The Duty to Accommodate

The duty to accommodate arises where consultation exposes a potential impact on an asserted right.[13] Where necessary, accommodation may include avoiding, minimizing, and mitigating the adverse effects that arise from actions or decisions that may affect Aboriginal rights. The duty to accommodate does not impose a duty on the parties to

---

9. *Haida Nation* [2004] 3 S.C.R. 511 (Can.).
10. *Id.*, para. 35.
11. *Id.*, paras. 39 and 68.
12. *Id.*, para. 47.
13. *Id.*, para. 47.

agree, require a project proponent to obtain consent, or provide for an Aboriginal veto over governmental decision-making processes.[14] It requires meaningful consultation and the opportunity for meaningful dialogue carried out in good faith. Aboriginal peoples have reciprocal obligations to participate in consultation in good faith.

In Canada, to obtain and demonstrate a community's acceptance and/or support of a project, project proponents regularly enter into Impact Benefit Agreements (IBAs) with surrounding Aboriginal communities, as discussed further below.

6. United Nations Declaration on the Rights of Indigenous Peoples (UNDRIP): Developments in Canadian Law

UNDRIP is a United Nations instrument that addresses both the individual and collective rights of Indigenous peoples around the world, including rights to life, physical and mental integrity, liberty, and security of person.[15] It also addresses rights to self-determination, self-government, and freedom from discrimination, as well as rights to freely determine political status and freely pursue economic, social, and cultural development.[16]

In 2017, the federal government announced that it would support Bill C-262, the United Nations Declaration on the Rights of Indigenous Peoples Act,[17] which, if passed, would "implement" UNDRIP in Canada.[18] However, it is as yet unclear what implementation would entail. Bill C-262 affirms UNDRIP as a universal international human rights instrument with application in Canadian law. The bill also obligates the Canadian government to take all measures necessary to ensure that Canadian law is consistent with UNDRIP, and to develop and implement a national action plan to achieve the objectives of UNDRIP.[19] At the time of writing, Bill C-262 was passed in the House of Commons and had gone through first reading in the Senate.[20]

In 2018, the federal government began engaging the public to develop a Recognition and Implementation of Rights Framework (the "Framework"), which is intended to support Indigenous peoples' constitutional rights, align with the articles of UNDRIP, and be consistent with the federal government's "Principles Respecting the Government of

---

14. *Id.*, paras. 48–49.
15. G.A. Res 61/295, United Nations Declaration on the Rights of Indigenous Peoples, art. 7 (Oct. 2, 2007).
16. *Id.,* arts. 2, 3, 4.
17. An Act to ensure that the laws of Canada are in harmony with the United Nations Declaration on the Rights of Indigenous Peoples, 2016, H.O.C., Bill C-262, 1st Sess., 42nd Parl. (1st Reading Apr. 21, 2016) (Can.).
18. Government of Canada, *Overview of a Recognition and Implementation of Indigenous Rights Framework*, Canada.ca, https://www.rcaanc-cirnac.gc.ca/eng/1536350959665/1539959903708?wbdisable=true (last modified Sept. 10, 2018).
19. An Act to ensure that the laws of Canada are in harmony with the United Nations Declaration on the Rights of Indigenous Peoples, 2018, H.O.C., Bill C-262, 1st Sess., 42nd Parl. (3rd Reading May 30, 2018) (Can.)
20. Parliament of Canada, *Private Member's Bill C-262: An Act to ensure that the laws of Canada are in harmony with the United Nations Declaration on the Rights of Indigenous Peoples*, LEGISinfo, https://www.parl.ca/LegisInfo/BillDetails.aspx?Language=E&billId=8160636&View=6 (last modified Dec. 14, 2018).

Canada's Relationship with Indigenous Peoples."[21] According to the federal government, the Framework "will ensure that the Government of Canada recognizes, respects and implements Indigenous rights, including inherent and treaty rights, and provides mechanisms to support self-determination."[22]

The Framework would consist of both legislative and policy components. The legislative component would, further to Bill C-262, impose obligations on the government to "ensure that the recognition and implementation of rights is the basis of all relations between the federal crown and Indigenous peoples."[23] The policy component would follow and complement the legislation. It would assist federal officials in engaging with Indigenous peoples on issues of Indigenous self-government, self-determination, and treaty rights, and would facilitate the implementation and exercise of Indigenous rights. The policy component would also recognize Indigenous law-making power and Indigenous peoples' inherent right to land and, in some cases, title within traditional territories.[24] At the time of writing, the Framework had not yet been introduced to the House of Commons.

In addition, Bill C-69, "An Act to enact the Impact Assessment Act and the Canadian Energy Regulator Act, to amend the Navigation Protection Act and to make consequential amendments to other Acts" (which had gone through second reading in the Senate at the time of writing), incorporates the government's commitment to implementing UNDRIP as part of the preamble in both the proposed Impact Assessment Act and the Canadian Energy Regulation Act, and takes steps toward implementing the spirit of UNDRIP.[25] For example, the proposed Impact Assessment Act requires the body conducting an impact assessment for a "designated project" to consider several Indigenous-focused factors. These factors include, among other things, the impact that a designated project may have on any Indigenous group and their rights, Indigenous knowledge provided with respect to a project, and considerations related to Indigenous cultures raised with respect to the designated project. It also includes measures for Indigenous participation throughout the impact assessment process, cooperation with Indigenous governing bodies, the delegation of any part of an impact assessment to certain Indigenous governing bodies, or the

---

21. Government of Canada, *Principles respecting the Government of Canada's relationship with Indigenous peoples*, DEPARTMENT OF JUSTICE, https://www.justice.gc.ca/eng/csj-sjc/principles-principes.html (last modified February 14, 2018); Government of Canada, *National engagement on the recognition of Indigenous rights*, CANADA.CA, https://www.rcaanc-cirnac.gc.ca/eng/1512679042828/1539886236551 (last modified September 10, 2018).

22. Government of Canada, *supra* note 18.

23. Id.

24. Id.

25. Parliament of Canada, *House Government Bill C-69: An Act to enact the Impact Assessment and the Canadian Energy Regulator Act, to amend the Navigation Protection Act and to make consequential amendments to other Acts*, LEGISINFO, https://www.parl.ca/LegisInfo/BillDetails.aspx?Language=E&billId=9630600&View=0 (last modified Dec. 12, 2018).

substitution of another jurisdiction's assessment process (including certain Indigenous governing bodies) for the impact assessment process under the Impact Assessment Act.[26]

Provinces are also considering how to incorporate and implement UNDRIP. For example, in 2017, British Columbia Premier John Horgan tasked all government ministers with fully adopting and implementing UNDRIP. The BC Ministry of Indigenous Relations and Reconciliation is leading the effort to work collaboratively and respectfully with Indigenous peoples to establish a clear, cross-government vision of reconciliation, guided in part by UNDRIP.[27] The BC government introduced the Draft Principles that Guide the Province of British Columbia's Relationship with Indigenous Peoples (the "Draft Principles") to help guide the public service in implementing UNDRIP. The Draft Principles mirror the Principles Respecting the Government of Canada's Relationship with Indigenous Peoples that were published in 2017 by the federal government. Among other things, the Draft Principles recognize that all relations with Indigenous peoples need to be based on the recognition and implementation of their right to self-determination, including the inherent right to self-government.[28] However, the Draft Principles do not articulate how the BC government will implement UNDRIP.

The BC government has also started to legislate UNDRIP, for example in Bill 51: Environmental Assessment Act which received royal assent on November 27, 2018, but had not come into force as of the time of writing.[29] The enactment of Bill 51 will repeal the Environmental Assessment Act, S.B.C. 2002, c. 43. Section 2 of Bill 51 states that the purpose of the Environmental Assessment Office includes supporting reconciliation with Indigenous peoples in British Columbia by supporting the implementation of UNDRIP and collaborating with Indigenous nations in relation to reviewable projects, consistent with UNDRIP. The environmental assessment process prescribed in Bill 51 incorporates consent obligations and requires efforts to achieve consensus with Indigenous peoples at several points throughout the provincial environmental assessment process.[30]

---

26. An Act to enact the Impact Assessment Act and the Canadian Energy Regulator Act, to amend the Navigation Protection Act and to make consequential amendments to other Acts, 2018, H.O.C., Bill C-69, 1st Sess., 42nd Parl. (1st Reading Feb. 8, 2018). (Can.).

27. Government of British Columbia, *About the United Nations Declaration on the Rights of Indigenous Peoples*, https://www2.gov.bc.ca/gov/content/governments/indigenous-people/new-relationship/united-nations-declaration-on-the-rights-of-indigenous-peoples (last visited Dec. 17, 2018); Government of British Columbia, *Frequently Asked Questions: The United Nations Declaration on the Rights of Indigenous Peoples*, https://www2.gov.bc.ca/gov/content/governments/indigenous-people/new-relationship/frequently-asked-questions-the-united-nations-declaration-on-the-rights-of-indigenous-peoples (last visited Dec. 17, 2018); Government of British Columbia, *Draft Principles that Guide the Province of British Columbia's Relationship with Indigenous Peoples*, 2 (2018), https://news.gov.bc.ca/files/6118_Reconciliation_Ten_Principles_Final_Draft.pdf?platform=hootsuite (last visited Dec. 17, 2018).

28. Government of British Columbia, *supra* note 27.

29. Government of British Columbia, *Progress of Bills*, LEGISLATIVE ASSEMBLY OF BRITISH COLUMBIA, https://www.leg.bc.ca/parliamentary-business/legislation-debates-proceedings/41st-parliament/3rd-session/bills/progress-of-bills (last visited Dec. 17, 2018).

30. Environmental Assessment Act, 2018, Bill 51, 3rd Sess., 41st Parl. (3rd Reading Nov. 26, 2018) (B.C., Can.).

The extent to which the Framework and upcoming legislation will implement UNDRIP in practice remains to be seen. However, Canadian governments are increasingly consulting with Indigenous peoples on the drafting of legislation and policies on a government-to-government basis rather than as a stakeholder.

B. Indigenous Rights Abroad

In Canada, Aboriginal rights are protected based on their constitutional entrenchment, and there is a large body of case law interpreting these rights. While it remains a complex and developing area of law, there is guidance for industries operating in Canada, something that may not be available elsewhere in the world. When a company's operations may impact Indigenous rights or interests, it is critical for the company to understand the rights that are protected, the sources of protection (including common law, legislation, and international law and customs), and the legal nuances of the jurisdiction in which they are operating.

This section briefly discusses Indigenous rights in three jurisdictions—Australia, Mexico, and Chile. It does not offer guidance on these jurisdictions; rather, it provides a high-level comparison of differing situations of Indigenous rights abroad.

1. Australia

Unlike Canada, Australia does not offer constitutional protection of Indigenous rights at the federal level. The Australian government, however, has acknowledged the need for constitutional reform to recognize the Aboriginal and Torres Strait Islander peoples of Australia, protect their rights, and guarantee nondiscrimination. In 2013, the Aboriginal and Torres Strait Islander Peoples Recognition Act 2013[31] came into force. It recognized the Aboriginal and Torres Strait Islander peoples and obligated the minister to consider a referendum and proposals for constitutional recognition of Aboriginal and Torres Strait Islander peoples. While this Act had a sunset period of two years, the Aboriginal and Torres Strait Islander Peoples Recognition (Sunset Extension) Act 2015[32] extended it until March 2018.

Australia is comprised of six states and ten federal territories (which includes two mainland territories). Although there is no constitutional recognition at the federal level, Aboriginal peoples are recognized in all six state-level constitutions. Such recognition, however, may be merely symbolic.[33] Section 2 of the South Australian Constitution Act 1934, for example, acknowledges past injustices of Aboriginal peoples, recognizes their current status, and proposes a continuing role for them in South Australia, but expressly

---

31. *Aboriginal and Torres Strait Islander Peoples Recognition Act 2013* (Cth) (Austl.).
32. *Aboriginal and Torres Strait Islander Peoples Recognition (Sunset Extension) Act 2015* (Cth) (Austl.).
33. *See* Benjamen Franklen Gussen, *A Comparative Analysis of Constitutional Recognition of Aboriginal Peoples*, 40(3) MELB. U. L. REV. 868 (2017).

states that "Parliament does not intend this section to have any legal force or effect."[34] Similarly, New South Wales[35] and Victoria[36] both ensure that Aboriginal recognition does not create any legal rights or liabilities, give rise to any civil causes of action, or affect the interpretation of any laws.

Despite a lack of constitutional recognition, Australia recognizes Aboriginal rights through other common law and legislative means. In the landmark decision *Mabo v. Queensland (No. 2)*[37], the High Court of Australia held that the common law of Australia recognizes continuing Indigenous title to traditional lands in accordance with traditional Indigenous laws and customs. The Court also rejected the discriminatory doctrine of terra nullis (vacant land or land belonging to no one). While significant, the scope of this finding was limited, and the Court found that otherwise valid government statutes that are inconsistent with title rights extinguish those title rights.

The Native Title Act[38] was enacted one year after *Mabo*. Among other things, it recognizes and protects native title[39] and outlines a process for the determination of native title.[40] It also established the Native Title Tribunal to make decisions, conduct inquiries and reviews, and assist parties with native title applications and Indigenous Land Use Agreements (ILUAs).[41] ILUAs are voluntary agreements between native title holders and others regarding the use of native title matters, such as the consent to future acts, compensation, protection of significant sites and culture, as well as how native title rights and interests can be exercised alongside other interests.[42]

On an international stage, Australia endorsed UNDRIP in 2009. However, Australia has notably not ratified the International Labour Organization Convention No. 169, Indigenous and Tribal Peoples Convention ("ILO Convention No. 169"). Both UNDRIP and ILO Convention No. 169 are discussed in further detail below.

2. Mexico

Mexico, with one of the largest Indigenous populations in the world, offers constitutional recognition and protection of Indigenous rights.

---

34. Constitution Act 1934 (SA) §2 (Austl.).; *see also* Gussen, *supra* note 33, 10–11.
35. Constitution Act 1902 (NSW) §2(3) (Austl.).
36. Constitution Act 1975 (Vic) §1A(3) (Austl.).
37. Mabo v. Queensland [No. 2] (1992) 175 CLR 1 (Austl.).
38. Native Title Act 1993 (Cth) (Austl.)
39. *Id.*, §10.
40. *Id.*, §13.
41. *Id.*, pt. 6.
42. Native Title Tribunal, *About Indigenous Land Use Agreements (ILUAs)*, NATIONAL NATIVE TITLE TRIBUNAL (2014), http://www.nntt.gov.au/Information%20Publications/1.About%20Indigenous%20Land%20Use%20Agreements.pdf.

Article 2 of Mexico's Constitution recognizes the multicultural nature of Mexico, originating in its Indigenous peoples.[43] In particular, Article 2 recognizes and protects Indigenous peoples' right to self-determination, such that Indigenous peoples have the right to

- determine forms of internal coexistence and social, political, and cultural organizations;
- apply their own legal systems to regulate and solve internal conflicts (subject to principles in the constitution);
- elect representatives for self-governance;
- preserve and protect their languages;
- maintain and improve their lands;
- attain, with preferential use, the natural resources on the lands inhabited by Indigenous communities (except for certain resources defined in the constitution);
- vote and elect Indigenous representation in municipalities with Indigenous populations; and
- trial in their native language.[44]

Indigenous peoples are also recognized, to varying degrees, at state level. As of 2017, 28 out of 32 states explicitly recognized rights of Indigenous peoples, and many states had developed regulatory regimes for Indigenous rights.[45]

In addition, Mexico's Indigenous communities are protected by human rights legislation. Notably, Article 1 of Mexico's Constitution stipulates that constitutionally protected human rights are to be interpreted according to the Constitution and international treaties relating to human rights.[46] Mexico has ratified several international treaties protecting Indigenous rights; Mexico ratified ILO Convention No. 169 and, in 2007, Mexico voted in favor of UNDRIP. Several institutions are in place to assist in the protection of human rights and Indigenous peoples. This includes, for example, the National Indigenous Institute, which facilitates consultation with Indigenous communities, and the National Commission of Human Rights, which receives human rights complaints.

Despite these constitutional and human rights protections, Indigenous peoples in Mexico continue to face high levels of discrimination and are often subject to human rights violations. The extractive sector has a particularly bad reputation. In 2017, the United Nations special rapporteur on the rights of Indigenous peoples, Victoria

---

43. Constitución Política de los Estados Unidos Mexicano, art. 2, CP, Diario Oficial de la Federación [DOF] 05-02-1917, ultimas reformas DOF 27-08-2018 (Mex.).

44. *Id.*, art. 2A (i)–(vii).

45. Victoria Tauli Corpuz (UN Human Rights Council Special Rapporteur on Rights of Indigenous Peoples), *Report of the Special Rapporteur on the rights of indigenous peoples on her visit to Mexico*, 4, U.N. Doc. A/HRC/39/17 (Sept. 28, 2018).

46. Constitución Política de los Estados Unidos Mexicano, art. 1, CP, Diario Oficial de la Federación [DOF] 05-02-1917, ultimas reformas DOF 27-08-2018 (Mex.).

Tauli-Corpuz, visited Mexico and highlighted the harmful effects, flawed or lacking consultation and consent, rights violations, and an increased risk of violence toward or criminalization of Indigenous peoples that arise out of megaprojects.[47]

3. Chile

In Chile, Indigenous peoples and, consequently, Indigenous rights are not recognized or protected by Chile's Constitution of 1980[48]; however, there are ongoing calls for constitutional reform. In 2016, for example, Chile began a process to replace the Constitution under former president Michele Bachelet, which included an Indigenous consultation process; however, she was unable to bring a new constitution into force before her successor took office in 2018. Despite the lack of constitutional recognition, Indigenous rights are protected by other laws in Chile, including Law No. 19.253 of 1993.[49]

Law No. 19.253 acknowledges the existence of several distinct Indigenous groups. It also established a fund for the (re)distribution of Indigenous land and water and created the Corporación Nacional de Desarrollo Indígena (CONADI), which is a governmental organization focused on the economic, social, and cultural development of Indigenous peoples, with a mandate to ensure the implementation of Indigenous law. In addition, Chile signed UNDRIP in 2007 and ratified ILO Convention 169 in 2008. In 2014, Chile enacted Supreme Decree No. 66[50] (replacing Supreme Decree No. 124 of 2009[51]), which regulates Indigenous consultation procedures.

Since the creation of CONADI and the land and water fund, some lands have been returned to Indigenous communities, in particular to the Mapuche.[52] However, land rights continue to be an issue in Chile, particularly with regard to development projects. For example, Chile has seen a proliferation of investment in the extractive sector, including investment in mining, forestry, and hydroelectricity projects, many of which are carried out on lands and territories legally or historically belonging to Indigenous groups. These projects often take place without adequate consultation processes and without companies obtaining free, prior, and informed consent (FPIC).[53] In recent years, these projects have resulted in confrontations including protests and, in some cases, violent action on Indigenous territory.[54]

---

47. Tauli Corpuz, *supra* note 45, at 6–9, U.N. Doc. A/HRC/39/17 (Sept. 28, 2018).
48. Constitución Política de la República de Chile [C.P.].
49. Law No. 19.253, Septiembre 28, 1993, Diario Oficial [D.O.] (Chile).
50. Supreme Decree No. 66, 2014 (Chile).
51. Supreme Decree No. 124, implementing Article 34 of Act No. 19.235, Sept. 2009 (Chile).
52. Minority Rights Group International, *World Directory of Minorities and Indigenous Peoples – Chile*, UNHCR (last updated Sept. 2017), http://www.refworld.org/docid/4954ce4dc.html.
53. The International Work Group for Indigenous Affairs, The Indigenous World 2018 at 218 (Pamela Jacquelin-Anderson et al. eds., 2018), https://www.iwgia.org/images/documents/indigenous-world/indigenous-world-2018.pdf.
54. José Aylwin, *Intercultural Conflict and Peace Building: The Experience of Chile, in* INDIGENOUS PEOPLES' RIGHTS AND UNREPORTED STRUGGLES: CONFLICT AND PEACE 20–27 at 22 (Elsa Stamatopoulou, ed., 2017), https://academiccommons.columbia.edu/doi/10.7916/D82R5095.

III. NORMS, STANDARDS, AND GUIDELINES

A. General Considerations: Indigenous and Human Rights

Indigenous rights, while unique in that they apply only to Indigenous peoples, should not be viewed narrowly. When considering the implementation of corporate practices related to Indigenous rights, corporations must consider Indigenous rights within a broader human rights framework.

While a detailed discussion of human rights is beyond the scope of this chapter, corporations should consult the appropriate human rights instruments and guidelines. For example, corporations should consider: the International Bill of Human Rights[55]; OECD Guidelines for Multinational Enterprises (MNEs)[56]; United Nations Global Compact Principles[57]; United Nations Guiding Principles on Business and Human Rights[58]; Voluntary Principles on Security and Human Rights[59]; International Finance Corporation's (IFC) Performance Standards[60]; and the Global Reporting Initiative (GRI) Sustainability Standards.[61]

B. The Role of International Standards and Guidelines

Norms for corporate practices are established through several channels in both the business and legal realms. Competitor practices and the policies of influential transnational actors, such as the lending policies of multilateral banks, establish best practices in the corporate context, while national law establishes the regulatory framework within which corporations operate. Because of the concept of state sovereignty, states generally maintain the responsibility of regulating corporate practices. That said, international laws and customs (including nonlegal instruments, such as declarations) are relevant to corporate practices and should be carefully considered by companies when dealing with Indigenous rights; they shape the context within which nation-states regulate by imposing obligations on the nation itself.

---

55. G.A. Res. 217 (III), International Bill of Human Rights (Dec. 10, 1948).
56. Organisation for Economic Co-operation and Development [(OECD)], *Guidelines for Multinational Enterprises* (2011), http://dx.doi.org/10.1787/9789264115415-en.
57. United Nations Global Compact, *The Ten Principles* (last updated 2015), https://www.unglobalcompact.org/what-is-gc/mission/principles.
58. UN Office of the High Commissioner for Human Rights, Guiding Principles on Business and Human Rights: Implementing the United Nations "Protect, Respect and Remedy" Framework, U.N. Doc. [ST/]HR/PUB/11/4 (2011).
59. Voluntary Principles on Security and Human Rights, *Voluntary Principles* (2000), http://www.voluntaryprinciples.org/what-are-the-voluntary-principles/.
60. World Bank, *IFC Performance Standards on Environmental and Social Sustainability* (Jan. 1, 2012), http://documents.worldbank.org/curated/en/586771490864739740/IFC-performance-standards-on-environmental-and-social-sustainability.
61. Global Reporting Initiative [GRI], *Sustainability Standards*, https://www.globalreporting.org/standards/.

While international law typically applies to the state, there are some international instruments that address both states and corporations, and some suggest that there may be a shift toward the imposition of international obligations on corporations.[62] Regardless, international instruments, including voluntary and nonlegal initiatives, influence normative expectations for corporate behavior. For example, although it does not create any new legal obligations, the United Nations' Guiding Principles on Business and Human Rights "apply to all States and to all business enterprises"[63] and recognize a corporate responsibility to protect human rights.[64] In addition, the United Nations Global Compact, which is a voluntary initiative that asks corporations to embrace, support, and enact a set of ten principles, states that "businesses should support and respect the protection of internationally proclaimed human rights" (Principle 1) and "make sure they are not complicit in human rights abuses" (Principle 2).[65]

While many of the principles and obligations found in international instruments are directed at governments, companies should actively seek to avoid violations of human and Indigenous rights and should actively promote good practice in line with international standards. Ensuring that corporate practice meets obligations traditionally imposed on states can reduce the risk that a project is stalled or halted if the government fails to meet its international obligations. Moreover, transnational actors (e.g., the IFC) are incorporating standards and requirements found in international instruments and conventions, like ILO Convention No. 169 and UNDRIP (directed at state obligations), into their policies.

The remainder of this section will discuss several influential documents, both legally and nonlegally binding, that influence corporate norms and offer guidance on how to implement best practices in an international context.

1. ILO Convention No. 169, Indigenous and Tribal Peoples Convention, 1989

ILO Convention No. 169 is a legally binding instrument for ratifying governments that recognizes both individual and collective rights of Indigenous peoples and sets standards for economic, social, and political rights. It has been ratified primarily by Latin American governments, including both Mexico and Chile. Neither Canada nor Australia has ratified ILO Convention No. 169.

ILO Convention No. 169 recognizes several land rights that are noteworthy to companies operating in ratifying countries, particularly in extractive sectors. Article

---

62. Michael Kerr et al., CORPORATE SOCIAL RESPONSIBILITY: A LEGAL ANALYSIS 310 (Chip Pitts ed., 2009).

63. UN Office of the High Commissioner for Human Rights, Guiding Principles on Business and Human Rights: Implementing the United Nations "Protect, Respect and Remedy" Framework, at 1, U.N. Doc. [ST/]HR/PUB/11/4 (2011).

64. Un Office of the High Commissioner for Human Rights, Guiding Principles on Business and Human Rights: Implementing the United Nations "Protect, Respect and Remedy" Framework, at 13, U.N. Doc. [ST/]HR/PUB/11/4 (2011).

65. United Nations Global Compact, *supra* note 57.

14(1) requires that Indigenous peoples' ownership rights are recognized and that state measures are taken to protect their rights to use the lands to which they have traditionally had access for subsistence and traditional activities.[66] Article 15(1) protects Indigenous rights to natural resources pertaining to their lands, including the right to participate in the use, management, and conservation of these resources.[67] Article 15(2) imposes a duty on governments to consult with Indigenous peoples where the state retains ownership of minerals or resources before permitting exploration or exploitation of such resources. It stipulates that, where possible, Indigenous peoples shall participate in the benefits and receive compensation for any damages sustained due to such activities.[68]

Companies operating abroad should consider not only whether a country has ratified ILO Convention No. 169 but also how that ratification has been treated by the courts on a national, regional, and international level.

2. United Nations Declaration on the Rights of Indigenous Peoples

As noted above, UNDRIP[69] is an instrument adopted by the United Nations in 2007 that enshrines the minimum rights and protections for Indigenous peoples around the world and includes protections for both collective and individual rights. One of the most noteworthy (and also controversial) aspects of UNDRIP is the obligation imposed on states to obtain the FPIC of Indigenous peoples, including before

- removing and relocating Indigenous peoples[70];
- adopting and implementing legislative measures that may affect Indigenous peoples[71];
- the confiscation, taking, occupation, use, or damage of Indigenous peoples' lands or territories[72];
- storing or disposing of hazardous materials on Indigenous peoples' lands or territories[73]; and
- approving any project affecting Indigenous peoples' lands or resources.[74]

Essentially, obtaining FPIC requires the party seeking to obtain FPIC, in advance of any authorization to commence activities, to

- engage in good faith consultation;

---

66. International Labour Organization, Indigenous and Tribal Peoples Convention, C169 art. 14(1), Jun. 27, 1989, ILO C169.
67. *Id.*, art. 15(1).
68. *Id.*, art. 15(2)
69. G.A. Res 61/295, United Nations Declaration on the Rights of Indigenous Peoples (Oct. 2, 2007).
70. *Id*, art. 10.
71. *Id.*, art. 19.
72. Id., art. 28.
73. *Id.*, art. 29.
74. *Id.*, art. 32.

- provide information on various aspects of the project such as the nature, size, pace, reversibility, and scope of the project; and
- obtain the affected Indigenous groups' consent to the activity without coercion, intimidation, manipulation, undue influence, or pressure.[75]

UNDRIP is not legally binding in and of itself unless incorporated into national law, which may occur in some states. For example, as discussed above, Canada's federal and provincial governments have taken steps toward incorporating or implementing UNDRIP in Canadian law. Even unincorporated into law, however, UNDRIP can provide legal context for national, regional, or international courts in the interpretation of applicable laws. For example, UN Treaty Bodies and regional courts, including the Inter-American Court of Human Rights and the African Commission on Human and Peoples' Rights, have interpreted FPIC in accordance with UNDRIP.[76]

3. A Business Reference Guide: United Nations Declaration on the Rights of Indigenous Peoples

UNDRIP applies to governments and does not apply directly to corporations; however, companies still operate within the context of UNDRIP and should consider how to align their business practices accordingly. The United Nations Global Compact's *A Business Reference Guide: United Nations Declaration on the Rights of Indigenous Peoples*[77] offers guidance to companies for engaging with Indigenous peoples in the context of UNDRIP. It notes that businesses have a responsibility to avoid causing a negative impact on human rights, which includes the human rights of Indigenous peoples, as recognized by the UN Guiding Principles.[78]

The Business Reference Guide outlines key actions for businesses, including

- adopting and implementing a formal policy on Indigenous rights;
- conducting human rights due diligence on the potential adverse impacts on Indigenous peoples;
- consulting in good faith with Indigenous peoples;
- committing to obtaining FPIC for projects that may impact Indigenous rights;
- establishing legitimate processes to remediate adverse impacts on Indigenous peoples; and
- establishing an effective and culturally appropriate grievance mechanism.

---

75. See United Nations Global Compact, *A Business Reference Guide: United Nations Declaration on the Rights of Indigenous Peoples* 26–28 (2013), https://www.unglobalcompact.org/docs/issues_doc/human_rights/IndigenousPeoples/BusinessGuide.pdf.

76. Saramaka People v. Suriname, Judgment, Inter-Am. Ct. H.R. (ser. C) No. 172 (Nov. 28, 2007); United Nations Global Compact, *supra* note 75, at 25.

77. United Nations Global Compact, *supra* note 75.

78. *Id.,* at 6–7.

It also offers useful instructions on implementing these key actions and is a good source for companies to gain an understanding of best practices, including when to implement actions and what implementation may entail.

Companies may also wish to consult the United Nations' *Practical Supplement: Business Reference Guide to the UN Declaration on the Rights of Indigenous Peoples*,[79] which compiles case studies of businesses taking action to support the rights of Indigenous peoples.

Also noteworthy is Amy K. Lehr's *Indigenous Peoples' Rights and the Role of Free, Prior and Informed Consent: A Good Practice Note, Endorsed by the United Nations Global Compact Human Rights and Labour Working Group on 20 February 2014*.[80]

4. GRI 411: Rights of Indigenous Peoples, 2016

The GRI Sustainability Standards are broadly recognized international reporting standards that represent global best practices in sustainability reporting. GRI 411 is the standard for Indigenous rights.[81] It can be used by any organization that wants to report on its impacts relating to Indigenous rights. It includes both topic-specific disclosures (e.g., the number of identified incidents of violations of the rights of Indigenous peoples, reports on the status of such incidents, and actions taken) and disclosures on an organization's management approach (such as how an organization manages material topics, impacts, and the reasonable expectations of stakeholders).

5. IFC Performance Standard 7: Indigenous Peoples

The IFC's Sustainability Framework represents the IFC's commitment to sustainable development. The IFC requires its clients to apply the Performance Standards to manage social and environmental risks and impacts.

Key requirements in IFC Performance Standard 7[82] include that the IFC client must (i.e., the company)

- avoid adverse impacts and, where impacts are unavoidable, minimize, restore, and/or compensate for the impacts in a culturally appropriate manner, proportionate with the nature and scale of the impacts and the vulnerability of the impacted Indigenous community;

---

79. United Nations Global Compact, *Practical Supplement: Business Reference Guide to the Un Declaration on the Rights of Indigenous Peoples* (last updated 2015), https://www.unglobalcompact.org/docs/issues_doc/human_rights/IndigenousPeoples/Case_Examples.pdf.

80. United Nations Global *Compact, Indigenous Peoples' Rights and the Role of Free, Prior and Informed Consent* (2014), https://www.unglobalcompact.org/docs/issues_doc/human_rights/Human_Rights_Working_Group/FPIC_Indigenous_Peoples_GPN.pdf.

81. Global Reporting Initiative [GRI], *GRI Standard 411: Rights of Indigenous Peoples 2016* (July 1, 2018), https://www.globalreporting.org/standards/media/1026/gri-411-rights-of-indigenous-peoples-2016.pdf.

82. International Finance Corporation [IFC], *Performance Standard 7 Indigenous Peoples* (Jan. 1, 2012), https://www.ifc.org/wps/wcm/connect/1ee7038049a79139b845faa8c6a8312a/PS7_English_2012.pdf?MOD=AJPERES.

- undertake engagement processes with affected Indigenous communities and, in specified circumstances, obtain FPIC;
- identify mitigation measures and opportunities for culturally appropriate and sustainable development benefits; and
- collaborate with the responsible government agency where the government has a defined role in managing Indigenous peoples.

The specified circumstances where a client must obtain FPIC include

- where the company proposes to locate a project on or commercially develop natural resources on traditionally owned land or land under the customary use of Indigenous peoples and adverse impacts are anticipated;
- where Indigenous peoples are required to relocate from lands and natural resources subject to traditional ownership or customary use; or
- if a project may significantly impact critical cultural heritage.[83]

6. OECD Guidelines for Multinational Enterprises

The OECD Guidelines for Multinational Enterprises (OECD Guidelines)[84] are a set of nonbinding principles and standards, consistent with international standards, for businesses operating internationally. They offer recommendations to multinational enterprises that operate within, or are from, the 48 countries that have signed on. While observance of the OECD Guidelines is voluntary, national or international law may also regulate some of the issues they address.

C. International Standards in Canadian Policy: Industry Guidance in the Extractive Sector

Canada's CSR policies guide Canadian companies in the extractive sector and include CSR guidance related to Indigenous rights. Canada's CSR policy is focused on ensuring that Canadian companies are leaders in responsible development. The policies and guidance documents are based predominantly on international standards and may serve as a useful resource for extractive companies (both Canadian and non-Canadian) to understand standards for CSR in respect of both human and Indigenous rights, among other CSR practices.

Canada's CSR policy was developed when the global extractive industry as a whole increasingly became the subject of international critique, particularly with respect to human rights abuses. In 2009, Canada issued its first CSR policy, Building the Canadian Advantage: A Corporate Social Responsibility (CSR) Strategy for the Canadian International Extractive Sector (the "2009 Policy"). In 2014, it issued a new policy, Doing

---

83. *Id.*, at 3–5.
84. Organisation for Economic Co-operation and Development (OECD), *supra* note 56.

Business the Canadian Way: A Strategy to Advance Corporate Social Responsibility in Canada's Extractive Sector (the "2014 Policy"), addressing some of the shortcomings of the 2009 Policy.[85]

Canada's CSR policy is not legally binding. Instead, it is promotional in nature and imposes expectations for the conduct of Canadian extractive companies operating abroad. It expects companies to "integrate CSR throughout their management structures so that they operate abroad in an economic, social and environmentally sustainable manner," and to "respect human rights and all applicable laws, and to meet or exceed widely-recognized international standards for responsible business conduct."[86]

Following the implementation of its CSR policies, the government of Canada issued several tools and guidance documents, including the CSR Checklist for Canadian Mining Companies Working Abroad,[87] and the CSR Standards Navigation Tool for the Extractive Sector (the "CSR Navigation Tool").[88] The CSR Navigation Tool is useful for extractive companies; it is "designed to help Canadian companies, civil society organizations, communities, Corporate Social Responsibility (CSR) practitioners and host country governments more easily access the best practices and guidance outlined in the six international standards endorsed by the Government of Canada in the [2014 Policy]."[89] It includes a chapter on Indigenous peoples, which offers guidance on due diligence, practices, policies and procedures, monitoring and evaluation, and disclosure and transparency.

D. Additional Resources

In addition to the resources already referenced and discussed in this chapter, practitioners and project proponents may also look to national and international industry associations and organizations, which often provide updated guidance documents related to Indigenous engagement. For example, several national and international organizations in the mining industry offer useful resources, including the Mining Association of Canada (MAC), the Association for Mineral Exploration (AME), the International Council on Mining and Metals (ICMM), Prospectors & Developers Association of Canada (PDAC), and

---

85. Penelope Simons, *Canada's Enhanced CSR Strategy: Human Rights Due Diligence and Access to Justice for Victims of Extraterritorial Corporate Human Rights Abuses*, 56(2) THE CAN. BUS. L. J. 167, 172–173 (2015).

86. Global Affairs Canada, *Doing Business the Canadian Way*, at 3 (last modified 2018), http://www.international.gc.ca/trade-agreements-accords-commerciaux/topics-domaines/other-autre/csr-strat-rse.aspx?lang=eng.

87. Natural Resources Canada, *Corporate Social Responsibility: CSR Checklist for Canadian Mining Companies Working Abroad* (2015), https://www.nrcan.gc.ca/sites/www.nrcan.gc.ca/files/mineralsmetals/pdf/Corporate%20Social%20Responsibility%20Checklist_e.pdf.

88. Office of the Extractive Sector Corporate Social Responsibility Counsellor, *CSR Standards Navigation Tool for the Extractive Sector* (2015), http://www.international.gc.ca/csr_counsellor-conseiller_rse/assets/pdfs/csr-nav-en.pdf.

89. *Id.*

the Canadian Institute of Mining, Metallurgy and Petroleum. While these associations are industry-specific, the principles for Indigenous engagement and corporate social responsibility are generally applicable across sectors.

IV. TRENDS

Given the increasing awareness and recognition of Indigenous rights, industry is seeing a trend toward extensive consultation and is more frequently trying to obtain consent prior to operating. Companies are also making use of tools, such as Impact Benefit Agreements, which have become common practice in Canada, to ensure that Indigenous peoples are consulted and the impacts of the project on the community are discussed. In exchange for certain benefits offered under an IBA, Indigenous communities may agree to support a particular project. For example, an Indigenous group may agree to consent to a project or agree not to oppose a project as it moves through the regulatory process. Ideally, IBAs help ensure sustainable development by ensuring that Indigenous rights are minimally infringed and by providing benefits to affected communities.

In addition, IBAs can help establish a solid foundation for what may be a long-term working relationship between a company and Indigenous peoples. While IBAs are flexible and can be tailored to specific circumstances, they often address issues such as: education, training, and employment opportunities; economic development and business opportunities; social, cultural, and community support; environmental issues; and financial provisions (including compensation and revenue sharing).

Benefit sharing is an important component of a company's engagement with Indigenous peoples. In his 2010 report to the Human Rights Council,[90] Special Rapporteur James Anaya advised that benefit sharing should not be treated as an award to secure support for a project but should instead be seen as a means of complying with an Indigenous right. Further, the report critiqued the restrictive approach to benefits, which is often based solely on financial compensation. Instead, benefit-sharing should "genuinely strengthen the capacity of indigenous peoples to establish and follow up their development priorities and which help to make their own decision-making mechanisms and institutions more effective."[91] In Canada, IBAs have moved toward building long-term capacity not only by offering Indigenous groups equity ownership or the opportunity to share in revenue but also by moving toward a co-management model. For example, IBAs often set up environmental monitoring committees which include input and members from the Indigenous group. While the goal is to build long-term capacity, IBAs are often reviewed and renewed frequently to ensure that the parties' objectives remain aligned.

---

90. James S. Anaya (UN Human Rights Council Special Rapporteur on Rights of Indigenous Peoples), *Report of the Special Rapporteur on the Situation of Human Rights and Fundamental Freedoms of Indigenous People, James Anaya*, U.N. Doc. A/HRC/15/37 (July 19, 2010).
91. *Id.*, at 18.

V. BEST PRACTICES

When companies are engaged in activities that may impact Indigenous rights, they should ensure that they conduct due diligence and employ practices that respect Indigenous rights, both upfront (before engaging in any potentially rights-impacting activities) and on an ongoing basis throughout a project's lifecycle.

Best practices include

- Developing a policy for Indigenous rights that applies throughout the lifecycle of a project that
    - is based on and incorporates the objectives of the Indigenous community and the company;
    - considers guidance from international bodies, industry-specific guidance documents, and other key transnational actors (e.g., the IFC); and
    - meets or exceeds international standards.
- Ensuring that policies are flexible enough to be tailored to the specific context, the needs and interests of the particular Indigenous groups whose rights may be impacted, and the requirements and expectations of the jurisdiction in which the company is operating;
- Ensuring that not only management teams but all company employees are committed to corporate policies related to Indigenous peoples. While it may be a select few who engage with Indigenous nations one-on-one, all employees should understand the policies, abide by them, and find opportunities to meet those commitments;
- Setting up board committees responsible for monitoring Indigenous relations and ensuring that policies are followed and commitments made to Indigenous groups are met;
- Setting up and maintaining an efficient, functional, and user-friendly complaints register that records all complaints, and ensuring that complaints are monitored and followed up on;
- Conducting extensive due diligence prior to and throughout activities that may impact Indigenous rights, including with respect to
    - the applicable state law, including how national courts have applied law relating to Indigenous rights;
    - international law, including how it has been interpreted by national, regional, and international bodies, and to what extent international commitments have been incorporated into national law;
    - community and national extra-legal and normative expectations;
    - Indigenous communities in the area;
    - existing or potential Indigenous rights, title, or land claims;
    - governance structures in the Indigenous communities with which they are working;
    - relevant industry best practices; and
    - broader human rights due diligence.

- Consulting all potentially impacted Indigenous groups and while engaging in consultation
  o working with the appropriate government agencies, if any; and
  o considering FPIC in line with UNDRIP and its implementation in the jurisdiction.
- Assessing the potential adverse impacts of the proposed activities, including the nature, scale, and severity of the impacts (both the direct and indirect social, economic, and environmental impacts); and
- Where adverse impacts are unavoidable, accommodating the affected or potentially affected Indigenous groups in a way that
  o is collaborative with the impacted or potentially impacted Indigenous groups and takes into consideration their needs, interests, and expectations;
  o is culturally appropriate;
  o is commensurate with the nature, scale, and severity of the adverse impact;
  o seeks to minimize impacts and compensate in a culturally appropriate way; and
  o goes beyond solely financial compensation.

VI. SUMMARY AND TAKEAWAYS

Indigenous rights must be incorporated into CSR policies and practices where corporate activities have the potential to impact Indigenous peoples and their rights. Indigenous rights are often framed in the context of Indigenous-government relations; however, companies share in the responsibilities toward Indigenous groups and should work toward incorporating best practices. While Indigenous rights must be considered within a broader human rights framework and must be consistent with regulatory requirements, companies should recognize the distinction between legal requirements and socially responsible and sustainable practices that go above and beyond the bare-minimum legal framework.

To implement responsible and sustainable practices, companies interacting with Indigenous groups must have regard to the highly contextual nature of the potentially impacted groups' rights, history, culture, and expectations. Indigenous rights receive varying degrees of protection depending on the jurisdiction; however, policies based on best international practices and adapted to fit the local context and legal requirements, and that work to meet and exceed the expectations of Indigenous groups in a culturally appropriate manner, can guide companies and assist them in ensuring they surpass legal requirements and normative expectations.

Chapter 10

Building a CSR Program through an Ethics and Compliance Program

Margaret M. Cassidy, Renée Brooker, and Travis Miller

I. INTRODUCTION

The expectations and requirements for being a good corporate citizen have evolved.[1] Where once compliance with laws and making ethical business decisions were the bare minimum, new expectations have emerged. Corporations are responsible for not only increasing shareholder value and following the law while doing so but also meeting a more holistic set of obligations to a variety of stakeholders: regulators, prosecutors, shareholders, employees, business partners, customers, and the communities where they operate.

"Corporate social responsibility" (CSR) is a concept which increasingly informs an organization's ethics and compliance program. In the symbiotic relationship between ethical decision-making, compliance with laws, and acting as a socially responsible organization, an organization is able to not only foster legal compliance but also add shareholder value and deliver on the expectations of a socially responsible organization.[2]

---

1. Many of these requirements discussed in this chapter apply to all organizations—profit, non-profit, private and public. Thus, throughout this section the term "organization" or "corporation" includes all these entity forms.
2. Robert Reiss, *Top CEOs Place High Value on Corporate Ethics And Social Responsibility to Drive Business*, Forbes, (Sept. 11, 2017), https://www.forbes.com/sites/robertreiss/2017/09/11/top-ceos-place-high-value-on-corporate-ethics-and-social-responsibility-to-drive-business/#2152dabd4473.

This chapter will provide an overview of the legal and regulatory requirements as well as internationally accepted standards for a corporate compliance and ethics program as they relate to evolving mandates for organizations to be socially responsible, to include managing its third-party relationships.

The notion of a compliance and ethics program suggests that an organization will identify the unique compliance requirements it is subject to as an organization based on the nature of its operations. Since each chapter in this book discusses a substantive area of law and provides guidance on what an organization must do to comply with those legal requirements, this chapter will not discuss the laws each organization must comply with, but instead leaves that to the specific guidance and best practices of the substantive chapters. Rather, this chapter provides guidance on establishing methods to foster the mandated requirements of having an organization that makes legally compliant, socially responsible, value-based decisions.

Finally, to illuminate how a corporation may develop or enhance a culture of ethical decision-making, Uber will be used as a case study. Uber was facing systemic allegations of failing to comply with laws and regulations, as well as claims that it harassed and disrespected its employees and customers that resulted in not only reputation-damaging headlines but a number of criminal and civil lawsuits that threatened the organization's viability. In the aftermath of these allegations, Uber has made a titanic shift in its culture, and therefore is a solid model for any company looking to foster a culture of ethics and integrity that is a precursor to CSR.

II. SOURCES OF LEGAL REQUIREMENTS FOR CORPORATE ETHICS AND COMPLIANCE PROGRAMS

A. Overview of Legal Requirements: Consistent across Jurisdictions and across Standard-Setting Organizations

A number of countries, including the United States, as well as international standard-setting organizations such as the United Nations, have laws that either mandate or encourage having an ethics and compliance program or provide guidance to companies on developing one. Despite the vast array of laws, regulations, and guidance in this area, the basic requirements for an ethics and compliance program remain consistent.

- demonstrating leadership commitment to ethics and compliance
- assessing and mitigating the risks of not complying with laws
- developing and implementing policies and procedures to facilitate ethical choices and legally compliant behavior
- effectively managing third-party relationships to facilitate their ethical and compliant behavior
- training and communication on the ethics and compliance program, policies, and procedures
- monitoring and auditing program effectiveness and compliance with laws, policies, and procedures

- adapting methods for employees and others to raise concerns without fear of retaliation.[3]

Further, laws, regulations, and international standards make clear that an effective ethics and compliance program needs to be tailored to the organization. Thus, there are no specifications for how an ethics and compliance program must be designed and implemented beyond these core requirements.

Even so, large organizations are expected to have more formal compliance and ethics operations than small organizations and to have a greater resource commitment.[4] U.S. laws encourage large organizations that have business relationships with smaller organizations to collaborate with them to implement an ethics and compliance program.[5] From a practical perspective, this means for small organizations that supply to or partner with larger organizations, they too must implement ethics and compliance programs that meet the minimum standards imposed on the larger organization. In these situations, larger partners may be willing for the small organization's employees to attend the large business's training or have access to policies and reporting systems.

Small organizations' programs need not have the level of sophistication a large organization has for its program, and they may rely on existing processes and resources.[6] However, the small organization must still have the basic elements of a compliance and ethics program in place or both organizations could encounter liability.[7]

Recently, the U.S. Department of Justice (DOJ) made this clear when it issued guidance on how it will evaluate an ethics and compliance program.[8] Specifically, DOJ notes that each company needs to assess its own risk profile and develop a way to prioritize the risks it faces and ways to mitigate the risks of noncompliance and unethical behavior not only for itself but for its third parties as well.[9]

---

3. *See, e.g.,* U.S. Federal Sentencing Guidelines, §8B2.1; *Evaluation of Corporate Compliance Programs,* U.S. DEP'T OF JUST., CRIM. DIVISION, FRAUD SEC, https://www.justice.gov/criminal-fraud/page/file/937501/download (last visited Feb. 16, 2019); 48 C.F.R. 3.101, 9.1; USAM 9–28.000— *Principles of Federal Prosecution of Business Organization,* THE U.S. DEP'T OF JUSTICE, https://www.justice.gov/jm/jm-9-28000-principles-federal-prosecution-business-organizations; UK Bribery Act 2010; *Good Practice Guidance On Internal Guidance on Internal Controls,* OECD, https://www.oecd.org/daf/anti-bribery/44884389.pdfEthics And Compliance (last visited Feb. 16, 2019); *Compliance Program,* THE WORLD BANK GROUP, https://www.worldbank.org. (last visited Feb. 16, 2019); UN Global Compact, *Corporate Governance: The Foundation for Corporate Citizenship and Sustainable Businesses,* https://www.unglobalcompact.org/docs/issues_doc/Corporate_Governance/Corporate_Governance_IFC_UNGC.pdf (last visited Feb. 19, 2019); David Jaffe, *Europe Moves to Require Compliance Programs—Implications for Business in Europe, the U.S. and Beyond,* LEXOLOGY (Mar. 9, 2016), https://www.lexology.com/library/detail.aspx?g=cfcdad12-a15a-4450-a696-79824fa5db03; Jose Martin, *Mexico's Anticorruption Legislation: New Compliance Program Requirements,* LATIN AMERICA LEGAL (Apr. 26, 2018), https://www.latlegal.com/2018/04/mexicos-anticorruption-legislation-new-compliance-program-requirements-part-3/.
4. *See, e.g.*, U.S. Federal Sentencing Guidelines, §8B2.1.
5. *Id.*
6. *Id.*
7. *Id.*
8. *Evaluation of Corporate Compliance Programs, supra* note 3.
9. *Id.*

Beyond statutory and regulatory mandates, U.S. case law establishes that boards need to ensure that corporate information and reporting systems are adequate to identify and address the risks of noncompliance. Failing to do so exposes directors to personal liability for breaching their fiduciary obligations.[10]

Globally, some countries have very different interpretations regarding the ethics and compliance program. Accordingly, U.S. businesses must exercise increased caution and due diligence when dealing with third parties from different jurisdictions. Ethics and compliance obligations must also be spelled out in advance and throughout the relationship to ensure the U.S. company can mitigate potential noncompliance findings and penalties. Similarly, some countries do not have the legal construct to hold corporations liable, which means liability can rest exclusively on the U.S. business.

On the other hand, some countries' laws, such as the UK Bribery Act, afford an organization a defense against criminal liability for bribery offenses if it can establish that it had "adequate procedures" that were reasonably designed to prevent people associated with the organization from engaging in bribery.[11]

Some countries criminalize failing to prevent the third parties a business works with from engaging in criminal wrongdoing.[12] Recently, the British government has stated that it will consider extending the crime of a corporation's failure to prevent certain criminal offenses beyond bribery, to include crimes such as money laundering, accounting fraud, and other types of fraud.[13]

Standard-setting organizations, nonprofits, and international organizations also subscribe to these same essential elements of an effective ethics and compliance program, which dovetail with the tenets of CSR: transparency, accountability, and stakeholder engagement.[14] For example, in April 2016, the Ethics and Compliance Initiative (ECI) released the final version of its report, Principles & Practices of High-Quality Ethics & Compliance Programs. The report was prepared by a blue-ribbon panel of prominent ethics and compliance practitioners, academics, white collar and whistleblower attorneys,

---

10. *See, In re Caremark Int'l Inc.*, 698 A.2d 959 (Del. Ch. 1996).

11. UK Bribery Act 2010; UK Serious Fraud Office, *Bribery Act Guidance*, https://www.unglobalcompact.org/docs/issues_doc/Corporate_Governance/Corporate_Governance_IFC_UNGC.pdf (last visited Feb. 19, 2019).

12. *See, e.g.*, UK Bribery Act 2010 (failing to prevent bribery and failing to prevent a person associated with the company from tax evasion would be a criminal violation for the organization).

13. Jessica Elgot, *Management Could Be Prosecuted for Failure to Prevent Fraud by Staff*, THE GUARDIAN (Sept. 12, 2016), https://www.theguardian.com/uk-news/2016/sep/12/prosecution-failure-prevent-fraud-by-staff-white-collar-crime.

14. *High-Quality E&C Programs (HQP) Standards,* ETHICS AND COMPLIANCE INITIATIVE, https://www.ethics.org/resources/high-quality-ec-programs-hqp-standards/ (last visited Feb. 16, 2019); *See also* THE DEFENSE INDUSTRY INITIATIVE, https://www.dii.org/home (last visited Feb. 16, 2019); *Good Practice Guidance on Internal Guidance on Internal Controls supra* note 3; *Compliance Program,* THE WORLD BANK GROUP, https://www.worldbank.org. (last visited Feb. 16, 2019); UN Global Compact, *supra* note 3.

as well as former enforcement officials.[15] The report listed five core principles for the ethical and compliant corporation to embrace, which included

- having ethics and compliance as part of business strategy;
- identifying and mitigating ethics and compliance risks;
- demonstrating leadership commitment to a culture of integrity;
- adapting methods for employees to raise concerns; and
- taking accountability for wrongdoing that may occur.[16]

Essentially, whether a legal requirement or guidance, a compliant and socially responsible organization should have an ethics and compliance program that establishes measures to prevent and detect illegal and unethical conduct in the organization and by its third parties.[17] The program should "ensure that the values of the company are strongly supported by top management, that staff is trained and educated, that guidance exists for situations requiring judgment, that effective information and reporting within and by the company is granted."[18]

Failing to have an ethics and compliance program poses risks to the organization in several ways. First, if a company is subject to laws or regulations mandating that the entity have a corporate ethics and compliance program, and it does not, the company will suffer the ramifications. For example, U.S. organizations are required to establish compliance and ethics programs that are sufficient to "prevent, detect, deter and punish organizational criminal misconduct."[19] These requirements grew out of the mandate of 805(a)(5) of the Sarbanes-Oxley Act of 2002 that federal sentencing guidelines be crafted so that organizations that lack diligence in their efforts to prevent and detect criminal conduct are more harshly punished than those organizations that diligently and effectively establish compliance and ethics program to prevent and detect corporate wrongdoing.[20]

As result, if a company finds itself under criminal investigation or regulatory scrutiny not only in the United States but in many jurisdictions around the globe, the prosecuting entity will evaluate the effectiveness of the company's program for complying with laws and making ethical decisions. Failing to have an effective ethics and compliance program may result in additional liability for the company or will result in more significant penalties.

Although, again governments in most jurisdictions consider the same factors when determining the sanctions for corporate criminal acts, the U.S. government's approach exemplifies the factors governments consider:

---

15. *High-Quality E&C Programs (HQP) Standards*, *supra* note 14.
16. *Id.*
17. *See, e.g., Good Practice Guidance on Internal Guidance on Internal Controls supra* note 3.
18. *Id.*
19. U.S. Federal Sentencing Guidelines, §8B2.1.
20. 805(a)(5) of the Sarbanes-Oxley Act of 2002.

- the seriousness of the offense, to include who was harmed by the actions[21]
- whether the criminal behavior was pervasive and whether management was complicit[22]
- whether the organization has a history of similar conduct that resulted in previous civil, criminal, or administrative liability[23]
- whether the corporation voluntarily disclosed the wrongdoing in a timely manner[24]
- whether the corporation cooperated in the investigation[25]
- whether the corporation had an effective ethics and compliance program which included managing its third parties[26]
- what remedial actions the corporation took to address the situation and to prevent it from occurring again, to include terminating employees or business partners involved in the misdeeds, and improving processes and procedures[27]
- whether there are individuals who should be held liable for the corporation's wrongdoing.[28]

Second, U.S. DOJ takes the position that the company if engaged in illegality must identify the individuals responsible and disclose that information to DOJ to receive any cooperation credit.[29] Likewise, the UK Serious Fraud Office also advises that prosecuting a company is not a substitute for prosecuting individuals such as directors, officers, employees, or shareholders.[30] Governments take the position that prosecuting individuals "provides a strong deterrent against future corporate wrongdoing."[31]

Directors, officers, and employees who are not informed of the personal risk they face for violating the law in the course of performing their job may expose the organization to the risk of noncompliance. An ethics and compliance program mitigates this risk through training and communication on ethical and compliant expectations and requirements.

Additionally, from a CSR perspective, a company that is unable to assure its stakeholders that it has a thoughtful, effective way to comply with laws and to make

---

21. USAM 9-28.400—*Principles of Federal Prosecution of Business Organization*, THE U.S. DEP'T OF JUSTICE, https://www.justice.gov/jm/jm-9-28000-principles-federal-prosecution-business-organizations (last visited Feb. 16, 2019).
22. USAM 9-28.500.
23. USAM 9-28.600.
24. USAM 9-28.900.
25. USAM 9-28.700.
26. USAM 9-28.800.
27. USAM 9-28.1000.
28. USAM 9-28.1300; *Codes and Protocols, Bribery Act 2010, Joint Prosecution Guidance of the Director of the Serious Fraud Office and the Director of Public Prosecutions*, SERIOUS FRAUD OFFICE (Mar. 30, 2011), https://www.sfo.gov.uk/publications/guidance-policy-and-protocols/codes-and-protocols/.
29. USAM 9-28.000—*Principles of Federal Prosecution of Business Organization,* THE U.S. DEP'T OF JUSTICE, https://www.justice.gov/jm/jm-9-28000-principles-federal-prosecution-business-organizations.
30. *See, e.g., Codes and Protocols, Bribery Act 2010, supra* note 28.
31. *See id.*

ethical decisions risks not only legal exposure but reputational damage, damage to its overall value, and a loss of trust among its stakeholders. The Uber case study demonstrates this.

B. Sources of Laws Requiring Reporting, Encouraging Reporting, and Incentivizing Employees to Report

Select laws and regulations mandate that organizations report certain types of noncompliant behavior, and guidance from government agencies advises that organizations will obtain deferential treatment for self-reporting violations of law to government authorities.

1. Mandatory Reporting Obligations

Given the vast array of regulations and requirements of standard-setting or member-based organizations that may require mandatory reporting, organizations should familiarize themselves with the regulations, standards, and requirements of member organizations when it comes to disclosing noncompliance. Two examples, one a regulation and the other a member organization standard, demonstrate mandatory reporting schemes.

U.S. federal government contractors holding federal government contracts or subcontracts valued at more than $5 million and lasting longer than six months have a mandatory reporting obligation for certain offenses.[32] Specifically, a federal government contractor must report, in a timely manner, violations of certain criminal laws; violations of False Claims Act; or significant overpayment by the federal government.[33]

Member organizations may also require their members to make certain disclosures. For example, members of the New York Stock Exchange "must adopt and disclose a code of business conduct and ethics for directors, officers and employees, and promptly disclose any waivers of the code for directors or executive officers."[34]

2. Discretionary Reporting

For several substantive areas of law, governments have developed guidance directing companies to self-report violations of law, and in exchange for the self-disclosure, the corporation may receive credit against any sentence or punishment against the organization. Significantly, this includes not only a report to the government detailing the organization's wrongdoing but, often a requirement to report if a third party engaged in wrongdoing as an agent of the organization.[35] The belief is that by self-policing,

---

32. 48 CFR 52.203–13; 3.1004.
33. *Id.*
34. NYSE Listed Company Manual, §303A.10.
35. A Resource Guide to the U.S. Foreign Corrupt Practices Act, https://www.justice.gov/sites/default/files/criminal-fraud/legacy/2015/01/16/guide.pdf (last visited Feb. 17, 2019); *Codes and Protocols, Bribery Act 2010, supra* note 28.

self-reporting, and self-correcting noncompliant behavior, organizations and society benefit by avoiding protracted and costly government investigations. For example, in Britain, failing to report corporate criminal violations within reasonable time of when the behavior was known as well as failing to report the extent of any wrongdoing are factors prosecutors may consider when determining a corporation's punishment.[36]

In the United States, to motivate disclosure when an organization violates the Foreign Corrupt Practices Act (FCPA), the DOJ has offered to companies that self-disclose FCPA violations in a timely fashion; fully cooperate in the investigation; and remediate their violations, the possibility that DOJ may decline to prosecute the organization absent any aggravating circumstances or lesser penalties.[37] If a company is charged with an FCPA violation, a self-disclosure may result in up to 50 percent off any penalties, an opportunity to avoid having a compliance monitor assigned to the organization, which is usually a costly and time-consuming experience, as well as obtaining a deferred prosecution agreement with no penalty.[38]

Disclosure should be timely and the investigation into the wrongdoing should be thorough and objective. The organization must take remedial action to include identifying the executives, employees, and third parties involved in the wrongdoing and to otherwise remediate the issue.[39]

Likewise, the U.S. Department of Commerce's Bureau of Industry and Security (BIS) has also issued guidance that encourages companies to self-report violations of export regulations.[40] BIS keeps track of the reduction in penalty that companies who self-report certain U.S. Export Administration Regulations (EAR) violations related to the unauthorized export and re-export of certain U.S.-origin exports receive.[41]

In the United States and in multiple jurisdictions around the globe, governments have corporate and individual leniency programs providing, in some instances, complete amnesty for the first organization to report the violation and cooperate in the investigation.[42]

DOJ's antitrust reporting program is an example of how the process works. Individuals or corporations who are first to report an antitrust violation may, if no investigation is currently under way and certain other conditions are met, receive amnesty from any criminal prosecution.[43] This includes directors, officers, and employees who report and cooperate in the investigation.

---

36. *Codes and Protocols, Bribery Act 2010, supra* note 28.
37. 15 U.S.C. §78u-6(a)(6); A Resource Guide to the U.S. Foreign Corrupt Practices Act, *supra* note 35, 54–55.
38. A Resource Guide to the U.S. Foreign Corrupt Practices Act, *supra* note 35, 54–55.
39. *Id.*
40. *Voluntary Self-Disclosure*, BUREAU OF INDUSTRY AND SECURITY, U.S. DEP'T OF COM, https://www.bis.doc.gov/index.php/enforcement/oee/voluntary-self-disclosure (last visited Feb. 17, 2019).
41. *See, e.g., id.*
42. *Frequently Asked Questions about the Antitrust Division's Leniency Program and Model Leniency Letters,* DEP'T OF JUSTICE (Jan. 26, 2017), https://www.justice.gov/atr/page/file/926521/download.
43. *Id.*

3. Whistleblower Laws

In addition to the laws, regulations, and guidance that either mandate or encourage reporting, laws and regulations also provide monetary incentives for those who witness corporate wrongdoing to report the violations to the government. These laws and regulations also inform how a corporation should develop and execute its corporate ethics and compliance program not only to mitigate the risk of a whistleblower investigation but also to foster trust with employees and other stakeholders.

a. Federal False Claims Act

The federal False Claims Act, enacted by President Abraham Lincoln during the Civil War, is a federal law that imposes liability on individuals and companies that defraud governmental programs.[44] It is the federal government's primary enforcement tool for combating fraud that affects public funds. This law has unusual procedures that are unfamiliar to many lawyers. The federal False Claims Act allows private citizen whistleblowers (known as "relators") to file suit on behalf of the U.S. government in certain circumstances when the government has been defrauded. Cases filed by whistleblowers remain confidential under seal while the government investigates and decides whether to join in the case. As a reward, a private citizen who exposes the fraud can receive 15 percent to 30 percent of the money recovered. Defendants can be liable for three times the amount of damages ("treble damages") and penalties. Further, the Act protects individuals from retaliation for conduct protected under the statute.

b. State False Claims Acts

At least 31 states have passed their own False Claims Acts to protect public funds and to reward whistleblowers for helping promote integrity. Many of these state laws also provide whistleblower protections.

c. SEC Whistleblower Program, Sarbanes-Oxley and Dodd-Frank

The Sarbanes-Oxley Act of 2002 and the Dodd-Frank Act of 2010 both contain provisions affecting whistleblowers who report certain violations of law. Sarbanes-Oxley prohibits security issuers from retaliating against whistleblowers and provides that employees who are retaliated against for reporting possible securities law violations may file a complaint with the Department of Labor, for which they would be eligible to receive reinstatement, back pay, and other compensation.[45] Sarbanes-Oxley also prohibits retaliation against employee whistleblowers under the obstruction of justice statute.[46] The U.S. financial

---

44. 31 U.S.C. §§3729 et seq.
45. 18 U.S.C. §1514A(c).
46. 18 U.S.C. §1513(e).

crisis and the Bernie Madoff Ponzi scheme scandal prompted Congress to enact the Securities and Exchange (SEC) Whistleblower Program, as part of Section 922 of the Dodd-Frank Wall Street Reform and Consumer Protection Act of July 21, 2010 (Dodd-Frank).[47] This law also created a similar whistleblower program for the Commodity Futures Trading Commission.

The Dodd-Frank Act also expanded the protections for whistleblowers and broadened the prohibitions against retaliation. Following the passage of Dodd-Frank, the SEC implemented rules that enabled the SEC to take legal action against employers who have retaliated against whistleblowers. This generally means that employers may not discharge, demote, suspend, harass, or in any way discriminate against an employee in the terms and conditions of employment because the employee reported conduct that the employee reasonably believed violated the federal securities laws. Dodd-Frank also created a private right of action that gives whistleblowers the right to file a retaliation complaint in federal court.[48]

The SEC is authorized by Congress to provide monetary awards to eligible individuals who come forward with original information that leads to an SEC enforcement action.[49] The range for awards is between 10 percent and 30 percent of the amounts collected from any party. The Office of the Whistleblower administers the SEC's Whistleblower Program. The program's main goal is to incentivize the reporting of specific, timely, and credible information to the SEC. The Whistleblower Program allows the SEC to minimize the harm to investors, better preserve the integrity of the United States' capital markets, and more swiftly hold accountable those responsible for unlawful conduct. The SEC calls its program a powerful weapon in its law enforcement arsenal.

d. International Whistleblowers

Dodd-Frank also provides protections to whistleblowers who are foreign nationals and allows them to apply for monetary rewards based on reporting bribery prohibited under the FCPA.[50] The FCPA is a federal law that mandates accounting transparency and prohibits companies from paying bribes to foreign government officials and political figures for the purpose of obtaining business. It is the first American law that gives full protection to foreign nationals for reporting bribes and contains extraordinary procedures for their protection. The proposed whistleblowing law is part of a wider movement worldwide, notable in the EU proposals for class-action lawsuits to encourage individuals to take action against corporate wrongdoing.[51]

---

47. 15 U.S.C. §78u-6(a).
48. *Protections against Retaliation,* U.S. SECURITIES AND EXCHANGE COMMISSION, https://www.sec.gov/whistleblower/retaliation (last visited Feb. 17, 2019).
49. *Office of the Whistleblower,* U.S. SECURITIES AND EXCHANGE COMMISSION, https://www.sec.gov/whistleblower (last visited Feb. 17, 2019).
50. 15 U.S.C. §78u-6(a)(6).
51. *The EU's Whistleblowing Directive Proposal's Impact on Financial Services Firms,* Dentons (July 17, 2018), https://www.dentons.com/en/insights/articles/2018/july/17/the-eus-whistleblowing-directive-proposals-impact-on-financial-services-firms.

e. The IRS Whistleblower Program

Since December 2006, tax whistleblowers who report tax fraud, tax evasion, and other tax liability can receive awards of 15 percent to 30 percent of the amount recovered by the U.S. Internal Revenue Service[52]

f. CFTC Whistleblower Program

The U.S. Commodity Futures Trading's (CFTC) Whistleblower Program provides monetary incentives to individuals whose reports of possible violations of the Commodity Exchange Act lead to a successful enforcement action, as well as privacy, confidentiality, and anti-retaliation protections for whistleblowers.[53]

g. Confidential Declarations of Whistleblowers under FIRREA

Under 12 U.S.C. §4201(a), a whistleblower may file a private declaration with the U.S. Attorney General alleging facts that relate to a particular transaction or transactions that constitute a prima facie case of a violation that gives rise to an action for civil penalties under the Financial Institutions Reform, Recovery, and Enforcement Act of 1989 (FIRREA).[54] If an action brought by the U.S. Department of Justice is successful under this law, a whistleblower may receive a share of any recovery.

Under all these government programs, whistleblowers can help the government regulators identify possible fraud and other violations much earlier than might otherwise have been possible through their knowledge of the allegations and individuals involved.

III. DEVELOPING AND IMPLEMENTING AN ETHICS AND COMPLIANCE PROGRAM

A detailed discussion on the elements of an effective corporate ethics and compliance program, informed by laws, regulations, and standards, provides a framework and best practices for a company as it implements and manages the program. However, abstract notions of what governments demand of an organization's ethics and compliance program often do not provide the practical, actionable steps an organization may take. For these reasons, a case study of Uber's journey from an organization seemingly without any ethics and compliance systems to one that is changing its culture and systems to facilitate ethical and compliant practices informs the concrete steps an organization may take. The Uber case study follows this discussion on establishing a program.

---

52. *Whistleblower—Informant Award*, IRS, https://www.irs.gov/compliance/whistleblower-informant-award (last visited Feb. 18, 2019).

53. *Whistleblower Protections*, U.S. COMMODITIES FUTURES TRADING COMM'N, https://www.whistleblower.gov/protections/ (last visited Feb. 18, 2019).

54. 12 U.S.C. §1833a.

The U.S. government, UK government, and many standard-setting organizations have provided guidance on developing an ethics and compliance program.[55] While the U.S. Department of Justice does not use any rigid formula to assess the effectiveness of corporate compliance programs, it recently provided direction on what it considers when evaluating the effectiveness of a corporate compliance program.[56] As mentioned earlier, the guidance from these organizations is remarkably consistent yet informs the discussion below.

A. Governance, Leadership, and Resources

Most laws, regulations, and international standards make clear that the leaders of an organization must be committed to complying with laws and making ethical business decisions not only for the organization but also when managing its third parties and suppliers. Beyond this, organizations are required to assure that the compliance and ethics function is adequately resourced with competent, experienced professionals. Finally, to demonstrate commitment to an ethics and compliance program, leaders must demand accountability by receiving information necessary to be effective stewards of an organization's reputation, its social responsibility, and its compliance with laws—in addition to managing its operations. This accountability and commitment includes transparently messaging its commitment to compliant, ethical, and socially responsible practices to its stakeholders.

1. Leadership Commitment

An ethics and compliance program should be strategically managed by the board of directors with specific responsibility assigned to someone within the organization who is high-level enough to provide effective oversight, a voice for the program, and the authority to execute the program's initiatives.[57] This includes providing regular reports to the board on legal risk assessments, company internal reporting of concerns, internal audit findings, and other mechanisms developed to detect, prevent, and mitigate noncompliant behavior.

Leaders must demonstrate their commitment to ethical and compliant decision-making not only in their communications but in the actions they take when performing their own duties at the organization. Brazil's law for establishing ethics and compliance programs to mitigate the risk of bribery provides that leaders must prove they back the

---

55. *See, e.g.*, *Compliance*, THE U.S. DEP'T OF JUSTICE (Oct. 12, 2019), https://www.justice.gov/criminal-fraud/strategy-policy-and-training-unit/compliance; *Good Practice Guidance on Internal Controls, Ethics and Compliance*, OECD (Feb. 18, 2010), https://www.oecd.org/daf/anti-bribery/44884389.pdf; UK Serious Fraud Office, *Joint Prosecution Guidance on Corporate Prosecutions* (Mar. 30, 2011), https://www.sfo.gov.uk/publications/guidance-policy-and-protocols/codes-and-protocols/.

56. *Evaluation of Corporate Compliance Program*, THE U.S. DEP'T OF JUSTICE, https://www.justice.gov/criminal-fraud/page/file/937501 (last visited Feb. 19, 2019).

57. *See, e.g., Id.*

program with "clear and unequivocal support."[58] One organization, ECI, emphasizes that ethics and compliance should be central to business strategy.[59]

Directors, executives, and managers are expected to speak to the organization's commitment to making ethical and legally compliant decisions.[60] Recent guidance suggests that leadership also should demonstrate through concrete actions that they support the program.[61] Some examples of leadership's actionable commitment to an ethics and compliance program include

- having board members who have applicable experience directing an organization's ethics and compliance program; identifying risks; and who have industry knowledge to enable independent informed oversight;
- developing performance metrics that include leadership's accountability for enforcing and following policies and procedures; encouraging open and frank communications; training and communicating to employees the organization's expectations for ethical decision-making;
- assuring procedures to encourage open communication, to include encouraging employees to raise concerns;
- developing processes to quickly and objectively review and address employee concerns;
- as part of performance reviews, providing opportunity for legal, internal audit, HR, and other controlling functions to opine on the ethical and compliance practices of leaders; and
- developing performance goals and objectives for ethical and compliant behavior as well as financial incentives to execute these goals.[62]

Recent guidance also indicates that a company's leadership should engage with other stakeholders to promote an ethical and compliant culture.[63] This may include collaborating with business partners to facilitate their ethical and compliant behavior; developing cooperative methods when responding to prosecutors or regulations in the course of an investigation; and developing trust with employees and customers.

2. Resourcing a Compliance and Ethics Program

The ethics and compliance framework requires resources to execute its mission. Thus, the board and leadership need to assure themselves that the auditors, HR personnel, compliance professionals, and lawyers have the resources and independence necessary to fulfill program mandates.[64]

---

58. Brazil Federal Executive Branch issued Decree No. 8,420/15, Mar. 2015.
59. *High-Quality E&C Programs (HQP) Standards, supra* note 14.
60. *Evaluation of Corporate Compliance Program, supra* note 56.
61. *Id.*
62. *Id.*
63. *Id.*
64. *Id.*

Starting at the board level, whether public, private, nonprofit, or for-profit, an independent Audit Committee of the board should be responsible for oversight of an organization's ethical decision-making and compliance with laws. The Audit Committee should be staffed with independent members who have not only industry knowledge but also the knowledge and experience to identify and manage risk, a commitment to integrity, and experience furthering that commitment in an organization, as well as an understanding of the entity's most significant legal compliance requirements. The Uber case study demonstrates these requirements.

Authority for strategic or tactical execution of an ethics and compliance program may be delegated to others within the organization but those with the authority for the program should have adequate resources and the necessary discretion to manage the program.[65] Additionally, laws, regulations, and guidance make clear that the ethics and compliance framework should be supported by experienced, qualified people with the independence to execute the organization's compliance goals and objectives.[66] Board members, executives, and those with responsibility over the program must have not only the commitment to the program but the knowledge and expertise to execute the program and to monitor it.[67]

3. Informed and Accountable Leadership

Reporting is crucial: legal, compliance, financial, internal audit professionals should have some mechanism for directly reporting to the board on matters related to ethics and compliance. The board should receive periodic briefings on the ethics and compliance program including topics such as: identified risks; risk mitigation plans; third-party due diligence; issues that have been reported; resolutions of those issues; updates on investigations; and statistics on training and communication.[68]

Further, the Audit Committee should develop procedures for receiving concerns and reports from legal, finance, auditors, and human resources and even directly from concerned employees and third parties, thus assuring legal and ethical risks are reviewed and addressed by the independent committee. When faced with a compliance or ethics issue, the board should have established practices for reviewing and making decisions related to the issue. This should include a defined process to obtain an objective and thorough investigation of the concern, as well as methods to obtain guidance from professionals with the competence to inform appropriate remediation.[69] For example, if the matter is related to financial controls, the board would want to be sure it has the knowledge and expertise to develop an appropriate remediation plan.

---

65. *Id.*
66. *Id.*
67. *Id.*
68. *Id.*
69. *Id.*

Finally, governance manifests itself in an organization's external engagement with governments, industry groups, nongovernmental organizations, and third parties to work holistically to further CSR best practices. Engaging external stakeholders is a vital part of an effective CSR program because it provides transparency into its operations and a measure by which stakeholders can hold the organization accountable. As part of this engagement, the socially responsible organization should develop appropriate methods to communicate its expectations through its website and other communication methods.[70]

B. Risk Assessment

Laws, regulations, and international standards mandate that organizations should develop a risk management process to identify, prioritize, and mitigate risks.[71] Part of that process is conducting a risk assessment which then informs the organization on its needs when designing and implementing its ethics and compliance program. The risk assessment should be done with the goal of identifying gaps and weaknesses in the organization's compliance and ethics structure, to include how it manages its third parties.[72] With its potential for noncompliant behavior quantified, the organization can construct a response in the form of a program. It defines for the organization the proportional response it needs to mitigate the risks—driving needed policies, procedures, training, communication, and most significantly, resourcing needs such as human capital or IT systems.[73] The risk assessment is an ongoing process that should be done regularly, and risks should be identified and prioritized; then, mitigation plans can be developed to address them.[74]

A risk assessment may be done in a formal, prescriptive manner using risk assessment questionnaires and tools. However, regularly surveying and discussing concerns with employees, managers, suppliers, third parties, and leaders can also bubble up areas of risk that need to be addressed. So too can staying informed on industry and jurisdictional issues such as prosecutions, investigations, civil law suits, and political turmoil. The Uber case study demonstrates one method for performing a risk assessment.

When initiating a risk assessment, an organization should initially evaluate the legal risks it may be exposed to and categorize those risks. This book's substantive chapters provide a workable list of an organization's risks as well as programmatic methodologies to assess those risks. Additionally, for a practical, holistic example of a corporation's efforts to define its legal risk exposure, a review of GE's Code of Conduct, *The Spirit and the Letter*, provides a workable list of risk areas, despite an entity's operational profile:

---

70. *See, e.g.,* OECD Due Diligence Guidance for Meaningful Stakeholder Engagement in the Extractive Sector, http://www.oecd.org/publications/oecd-due-diligence-guidance-for-meaningful-stakeholder-engagement-in-the-extractive-sector-9789264252462-en.htm; EU Guidance Non-Financial Reporting, https://ec.europa.eu/info/publications/170626-non-financial-reporting-guidelines_en.
71. *Id.*
72. *Id.*
73. *See, e.g.,* UK Bribery Act.
74. *Id.*

- Regulatory compliance
- Improper payments
- Supplier relationships
- International trade compliance
- Anti-money laundering
- Working with governments
- Competition law
- Fair employment practices
- Environment, health, and safety
- Securing facilities
- Intellectual property
- Cyber security and privacy
- Controllership
- Conflicts of interest
- Insider trading and stock tipping
- Integrity.[75]

Once risks are identified, the organization's leadership needs to consider those risks and prioritize the risks to identify its actions to mitigate the most serious risks of noncompliance facing the organization. An organized and comprehensive way to approach the entire ethics and compliance program is to use the risks an organization has identified as essentially its checklist for risk assessments, risk mitigation plans, needed policies and procedures, as well as training and communications that should be developed to educate on the program. The risk mitigation plans for each subject risk area should be owned by one person, with reports on executing the mitigation strategy provided regularly to leadership.[76]

It is the risk mitigation strategies that drive the ethics and compliance program, spark process improvement, potentially save costs, direct training, enhance communications, and identify resource needs such as human capital, IT solutions, and cost allocation.[77]

C. Code of Conduct, Policies, Procedures

An effective ethics and compliance program needs to have a clear code of conduct defining for all stakeholders that the organization is committed to following the law and making ethical choices. Uber provides a clear example on how to refine and adapt a code of conduct not only to reflect the mission and character of an organization but also to state plainly its commitment to making ethical and legal choices as it adds value.

---

75. *The Spirit and the Letter, GE Code of Conduct*, https://www.ge.com/in/sites/www.ge.com.in/files/TheSpirit&TheLetter.pdf (last visited Feb. 19, 2019).
76. *Id.; Evaluation of Corporate Compliance Program*, *supra* note 56.
77. *Evaluation of Corporate Compliance Program*, *supra* note 56.

Generally, a code of conduct is high level—the aspirational goals, commitment, and mission of an organization and those the organization does business with. Companies are required to have more than this, however. They need policies and procedures that operationalize ethical and compliant choices.[78] In other words, they need to provide employees and business partners with the discrete direction on how to comply with laws, regulations, and standards. To achieve this objective, organizations should rely on the findings of their risk assessment to identify the policies and procedures necessary to address the specific risks the company faces and build the policies and procedures into the organization's operations in a seamless manner designed to give employees the tools to mitigate the risk of noncompliance.[79]

British prosecutors describe why effective policies are so vital when discussing the fact that pursuant to the UK Bribery Act, a company commits a criminal offense if it fails to prevent bribery. The UK Bribery Act mandates that a responsible corporation have "reasonable or adequate procedures" in place. This statutory construct neuters the organization's typical defense to bribery. As UK prosecutors explain:

> "We didn't know anything about the conduct" and that those associated with it "were acting without authority." Such a statement would now amount to an admission and not a defense. The corporation instead has to demonstrate adequate procedures, which those associated with it, nonetheless subverted and circumnavigated.[80]

To be effective, policies and procedures should be readily accessible to the employees who will need them to execute their duties and the suppliers and third parties who will be expected to comply with them.[81] Further, a best practice is to assign an owner to each policy and procedure. The owner should have the knowledge, expertise, experience, and authority to update the policies and procedures based on some clearly determined process and time line for updating, to include reviewing policies regularly to assure they do not go stale and adapting policies and procedures in response to changing laws and regulations and a company's risk profile.[82] Finally, the policy owner needs to have the resources available to answer employee questions about the policy or to resolve concerns quickly, objectively, and transparently. The owner must work with auditors or others to regularly audit compliance with the policy as well as the policy's effectiveness.[83]

A review of the other chapters in this book informs the subject matter policies and procedures that should be developed as should the risk areas that a company has identified given its unique operations. However, a few core policies are the backbone of an effective compliance program:

---

78. *See, e.g., id.*
79. *See, e.g., id.*
80. Camilla de Silva, joint head of Bribery and Corruption, *Herbert Smith Freehills Corporate Crime Conference 2018 Speech,* June 21, 2018.
81. *Evaluation of Corporate Compliance Program, supra* note 56.
82. *Id.*
83. *Id,*

- Reporting concerns: A policy requiring employees to bring forward instances of noncompliant or unethical conduct.
- No retaliation: A policy making it clear that those who raise genuine concerns or questions will not be retaliated against in any way.
- Investigative procedures: Procedures defining how the organization will conduct investigations.
- Discipline for violating policies: Policies should clearly state that violations of the policy will result in discipline.
- Policy on policies: It seems bureaucratic, but to effectively manage policies and to keep them current, organizations should have a defined process for identifying new policies and revising old policies.

Beyond operationalizing an organization's ethics and compliance program, the establishment of these core policies and procedures, along with the means to easily and anonymously report concerns and ask questions, is an effective way to establish trust with employees and mitigate the risk of having the employee reach outside the organization to the government to have their concerns addressed.

D. Training and Communications

A corporation's commitment to ethics and compliance with laws, as well as the policies and procedures it has in place to affect these commitments, must be communicated to impacted stakeholders. To that end, laws, regulations, and industry standards demand that organizations, as part of an effective program, train and communicate not only employees but also other stakeholders, such as business partners and suppliers, on their program.[84]

A training and communications program should mirror an organization's identified legal risks. Developing a training and communications schedule on an annual basis, documenting that schedule, and executing as planned create a defined plan for the organization on training and communications.[85] It avoids repetition. And it also focuses training to the employees and third parties who are exposed to the particular risk.

Those who develop and execute the training should have familiarity with the subject matter and be able to answer questions as they arise.[86] Further, insisting that business leaders deliver training, particularly on ethical expectations, is a concrete way to establish their commitment to the organization.

Training should cover how to raise issues, concerns, and questions as well as make explicit that people need not fear raising a concern because the organization will not permit retaliation for doing so.[87] Communicating this principle in training, in addition to demonstrating the organization's commitment to an open and transparent culture, also mitigates the risk of employees taking unresolved concerns to the government as whistleblowers.

---

84. *Id.*
85. *Id.*
86. *See, e.g., id.*
87. *See, e.g., id.*
88. *High-Quality E&C Programs (HQP) Standards, supra* note 14.

Effective training and communication on ethics and compliance builds trust between leaders and employees. The case study on Uber demonstrates its leaders' approach to open communication on Uber's past issues and its plans to address them. This type of transparency combined with a demonstrated commitment to ethics and compliance instill the confidence employees need to respect their organization.

E. Internal System to Report Concerns

The socially responsible organization should encourage, protect, and value the reporting of concerns and suspected wrongdoing.[88] Compliance and ethics programs generally mandate that employees have specific methods to report concerns and ask questions without fear of reprisal, and do so anonymously.[89] In some jurisdictions, companies are required to make their reporting channels available to third parties.[90]

Once raised, concerns should be reviewed quickly and objectively, and the employee or third party who raised the issue should be informed, to the extent possible, of how the issue was resolved. Employees should be able to raise concerns through an anonymous reporting system and to multiple channels such as human resources, legal, financial, or their managers.[91] Retaliation must be forbidden, and that message should be clearly shared across an organization.[92]

As part of any issue-reporting process, guidelines should clearly establish when a complaint requires additional investigation. Policies should identify who needs to review more serious concerns, including when legal support is required. Protocols should define who needs to know about an issue that has been raised and how that is done. Protocols should also define how an organization will execute an internal investigation.

In addition to having multiple channels for employees to raise concerns and ask questions, organizations should train those in their structure who are likely to be the ones receiving an employee's concern or question—human resources, legal, internal audit, finance, compliance, and managers on receiving concerns. Training should provide those in an organization most likely to receive employee concerns or questions on how to listen to employees' concerns and questions, how to document what they have learned, and how to respond to the concerns or questions, even if that means taking the matter to another professional. Having a receptive, competent professional to receive employee concerns is vital to fostering a culture of compliance, transparency, and open communication.

In addition to making professionals in established functions available to receive employee concerns and questions, many organizations have effectively developed ombuds systems that provide yet another avenue for employees to raise issues.[93] Ombuds

---

89. *See, e.g.*, *Evaluation of Corporate Compliance Program*, *supra* note 56.
90. *See, e.g.*, Brazil Federal Executive Branch issued Decree No. 8,420/15, Mar. 2015.
91. *See, e.g.*, *Evaluation of Corporate Compliance Program*, *supra* note 56.
92. *See, e.g., id.*

can be assigned by facility, by function, or by geographic areas. An ombuds person need not have any compliance-related job duties but instead should be a well-known, well-respected colleague who others in the organization already trust with issues. Selected ombuds persons should also be trained on how to handle complaints. Many organizations have also found ombuds persons are a valuable resource in delivering training such as a basic lunch and learn on the need for employees to raise issues and to engage in difficult conversations that can identify noncompliance.

Whatever an organization's size, the information that is gathered through the reporting channels should be compiled and recorded in an organized manner. One way would be to organize the reported concerns by risk areas or by policy/regulation and to leverage technical databases to support due diligence. With the information packaged in a reportable manner, the corporation can implement a more efficient, effective, and auditable compliance and ethics program.

F. Monitoring and Auditing

Once a compliance and ethics program is instituted, the organization must regularly monitor and audit the program to make sure it is providing the systemic structure to aid the organization in compliance with laws and in ethical decision-making.[94] Organizations are also required to have monitoring and auditing plans to detect instances of misconduct.[95] These reviews may take a variety of forms.

Internal audits should be designed to review the effectiveness of the program overall. Internal audit plans should be developed at a strategic level, focused on the policies and compliance risks that pose the greatest concern for the organization. Thought should be given to whether these audits will reveal or expose criminal behavior; if so, the auditors should work at the direction of counsel to protect privileged information. The internal audit should, however, also undertake reviews of training completion, closing out risk mitigation plans, and other processes designed to facilitate the compliance and ethics program.

Monitoring data and information that is communicated to the organization through helplines as well as concerns raised directly to persons within the organization such as human resources, legal, finance, compliance, managers, and ombuds persons should be reviewed and evaluated to determine any trends or issues that may be percolating. Helplines should include a case management system to allow concerns to be tracked and systematically reviewed and closed.[96] The system should allow for running different types of reports by geography, time frame, and policy, for example.

Certifications are another method for a company to assess its employees' perception of the compliance program. When rolled out, the certification should be traceable to the employee and the organization should assure each person completes the certification. It is

---

93. *See, e.g.,* United Technologies Ombuds Program, http://www.utc.com/How-We-Work/Ethics-And-Compliance/Pages/Ombudsman-Program.aspx (last visited Feb. 19, 2019).
94. *Evaluation of Corporate Compliance Program, supra* note 56.
95. *See, e.g., id.*
96. *See, e.g., id.*

a concrete method to determine whether employees understand policies and procedures. However, care should be taken in crafting the certification to make sure it is not asking employees to admit to criminal conduct or regulatory violations. Certifications should also provide the employee the option of not making the certification but instead having the opportunity to talk with a legal or compliance professional confidentially.

Employee surveys, both through informal discussions and through a more formal electronic survey process, are also useful tools for pulsing the effectiveness of a program. The Uber case study demonstrates how employee discussion may be used to identify risk and to monitor employee perception of an organization.

G. Responding and Remediating

Organizations are required to identify and address noncompliant and unethical behavior. DOJ has made clear that the organization needs to determine why the noncompliant or unethical behavior occurred.[97] For example, was it intentional misconduct, lack of procedures, lack of training and awareness, or ineffective procedures or controls?[98] Along with this, the organization should identify why it may have missed risk indicators that the behavior was likely or even warning signs that the behavior was occurring. For example, did internal audit fail to identify the problem, and if so, why?[99]

Once the behavior is identified, responsible organizations with an effective ethics and compliance program should develop a defined remediation plan to mitigate the risk of the behavior occurring in the future.[100] The remediation plan should have one owner and, if need be, have the resources to execute the remediation plan to completion. To assure organizations effectively remediate findings, the organization should have the contractual means to terminate third-party relationships expeditiously; it should have the right to report the third party's improper behavior to government authorities if it legally required to do so or if it chooses to do so; and obvious controls should be in place to assure that any third parties who have been terminated for misconduct are not signed up by another division at a later date without appropriate approval and mitigation.

The organization should also develop reports on completing any remediation through to closure. Finally, the organization should take other measures to address the compliance miss and to otherwise hold itself accountable for why the wrongdoing occurred.[101]

---

97. *See, e.g., id.*
98. *See, e.g., id.*
99. *Id.*
100. *See id.*
101. *High-Quality E&C Programs (HQP) Standards, supra* note 14.

H. Managing Third Parties: Assessing Risk, Conducting Due Diligence, and Mitigating Risk

1. Assessing Third Party and Supplier Risk

To effectively comply with applicable laws and regulations and to further CSR objectives, organizations need to develop methods to manage third parties and suppliers, which requires specific plans to assess compliance risks, conduct traceable due diligence, and mitigate identified risk.[102] Given the risk third parties and suppliers pose to an organization's legal compliance, an organization should devote considerable thought and sufficient resources to its third party and supplier management programs.

Evaluation should include the types of external relationships an organization has and where around the globe those parties operate. For example, a business needs to consider whether its third-party risks occur as a result of a global supply chain sourcing from regions known for human trafficking, if restricted materials may be in a product sourced from a supplier, or whether risks occur due to the handling of export-controlled information. The below defines one approach to assuring an organization's third parties execute ethically and legally.

Step 1: Scoping: How Extensive Should the Due Diligence Be?
Scoping is the first step for any effective third party or supply chain compliance program. Consideration needs to be given to the due diligence an organization will conduct on a third party, what questions will be asked, and what steps will be taken upon receipt of responses or non-responses. For third parties that are suppliers, an organization must acquire information that does not exist within its organization and it is often best to look for and rely on industry standards as formats to exchange this information. Indeed, as discussed in chapters 4 and 6 on reporting and labor practices, some laws and regulations require that an organization disclose its work to acquire safety, substance, and labor practices engaged in by suppliers toward the end goal of completing a finished product.

For third parties such as customers, sales agents, consultants, and distributors an organization should start with determining how products go to market and how the organization will leverage sales agents, consultants, and distributors in all regions of the world.

Regardless of the nature of the third-party relationships that a business has, when evaluating third-party relationships the following factors should be considered in determining the level of due diligence:
- What are the applicable laws to include those laws in the nation where the third party will be working as well as any laws that the business may be subject to?

---

102. *See, e.g.*, DOJ Compliance Guidance, https://mneguidelines.oecd.org/OECD-Due-Diligence-Guidance-for-Responsible-Business-Conduct.pdf (last visited Feb. 16, 2019).

- Are there industry standards or guidance documents that define the nature of the relationship with the third party, the product/services provided, and how it should be managed?
- Has the third party or supplier been able to provide industry standard responses to compliance inquiries in a timely and accurate fashion in the past?
- Have competitors or others in the industry been investigated, prosecuted, or sued because of the actions of their third parties or suppliers? If so, why and what was the outcome?
- Where is the third party located—in a country or region known for corruption, human rights abuses, poor quality materials/production, and political instability or is the region more stable with a defined and honored rule of law?
- Does the organization have an existing relationship with the third party? If so, how long has that relationship been in place and how has the third party performed when audited?
- How much due diligence has been executed on the third party previously?
- How closely will the third party interact with the organization and its employees?
- Is it clear who owns and controls the third party? Could ownership have governmental ties or relationships?
- Is there indications that the third party is owned, controlled, or otherwise associated with politically exposed person, a state-owned or controlled enterprise, a sanctioned person or entity, or a person or entity with relationships in sanctioned countries that may be seeking to move money or goods into that country?
- Does the third party's leadership and executive team demonstrate a commitment to ethical decision-making and compliance with laws, regulations, and industry standards?
- Does the third party have a demonstrated history of capably performing the type of contract being considered and delivering quality results?[103] This type of assessment will inform an organization of the nature of the risks it faces as well as the laws, regulations, and global standards it needs to address to formulate an effective CSR program when managing its third parties.

Step 2: Execute Due Diligence
Once the appropriate level of due diligence is identified, the due diligence needs to be performed, documented, and updated and referenced regularly. Based on the risk analysis, a tiered due diligence may consist of the following:

---

103. *See, e.g.*, UK Bribery Act 2010; *Bribery Act Guidance,* SERIOUS FRAUD OFFICE, https://www.sfo.gov.uk/publications/guidance-policy-and-protocols/bribery-act-guidance/ (last visited Apr. 9, 2019); U.S. DEPARTMENT OF STATE, https://2001-1009.state.gov/e/eeb/cba/176.html (last visited Apr. 9, 2019); A Resource Guide to the U.S. Foreign Corrupt Practices Act, *supra* note 35.

- Survey: The third party completes a detailed application and submits a declaration of conformity and supporting documentation to support due diligence.
- Records search: A search of court filings, government, commercial databases, and media searches to determine if an entity or its management and owners are political exposed persons; or to determine if any entity or its management and owners are involved in litigation that suggests corrupt or fraudulent behavior; or negative media reports that demonstrate a lack of compliance with laws or a commitment to ethics, for example.
- Obtain references: Request the third party to provide references from its bankers, lawyers, accountants, clients, and other business partners.
- Phone interviews: Question the third party either via video or phone based on its application, the records it has provided, and commitment to compliance with laws and social responsibility.
- In-person interviews, audit, and site visits: Meet at the third party's location and interview executives, owners, and employees about the information provided in their application or that was discovered in the course of a records search; review the third party's manufacturing processes and other operational processes; and discuss the third party's commitment to compliance with laws and social responsibility expectations.
- Investigation: Review any identified red flags and take corrective action steps to close identified noncompliance issues.
- Ongoing monitoring: Subscribe to services that provide alerts to regulations and industry standards of concern, conduct annual declaration refreshes, and provide updates on third parties related to negative media reports, criminal and civil actions against the third parties, and its owners, leaders, or employees.[104] Supply chain monitoring and auditing should include visits to supplier sites including offices, manufacturing facilities, and worker housing. It should also include worker interviews, document review, and compliance system reviews.[105] The socially responsible organizations, depending on their risk exposure, should also consider using these same methods to monitor and audit lower tier suppliers and recruiters.[106]

Step 3: Remediating Risk with Contracts

An effective and practical way to execute a company's commitment to legal compliance and to social responsibility is to design third-party contracts so that the company's ethical expectations, social responsibility standards, and policies and procedures

---

104. *Doing Business Abroad*, U.S. DEPARTMENT OF STATE, https://2001-2009.state.gov/e/eeb/cba/176.htm (last visited Apr. 9, 2019).

105. KnowTheChain, https://knowthechain.org/ (last visited Apr. 10, 2019); *Office to Monitor and Combat Trafficking in Persons*, U.S. DEPARTMENT OF STATE, https://www.state.gov/j/tip/ (last visited Apr. 10, 2019).

106. KnowTheChain, *supra* note 105.

are integrated into the contract and are defined as material. By incorporating social responsibility requirements in third-party contracts, the organization clearly messages to its stakeholders, particularly to its third parties, that social responsibility is tied directly to how it conducts business.[107] Further, by including social responsibility mandates in contracts, a business is taking concrete steps to define and assure its policies are followed and it is assuring compliance with these policies through contract law to include effective remedies in the event of a breach.[108]

Companies should evaluate their third-party contracts to determine how they can be adapted to manage third-party compliance with laws, regulations, as well as its own policies and procedures that have been developed to further CSR and ethical decision-making while still allocating risk between the parties.

Governments, international organizations, and bar associations have all developed guidance for drafting contracts that manage the third-party relationship.[109] For example, through its opinion process, the U.S. Department of Justice has provided guidance on contract clauses that it expects the compliant organization to use when contracting with third parties to avoid or mitigate the risk of corrupt behavior and improper payments in violation of the FCPA.[110] Similarly, the ABA recently drafted model Uniform Commercial Code (UCC) contract clauses to manage the risk of human trafficking and forced labor.[111]

Guidance on contractual controls for third parties is consistent in recommending that organizations seek representations and certifications from the third party regarding its compliance with laws, social responsibility requirements, and ethical decision-making. As an initial matter, a business facilitates its own compliance with laws and that of its third parties by making sure contracts clearly define the goods or services to be provided.[112] This includes assuring appropriate payment terms not only based on the nature of the contract but also based on market conditions and industry standards. Incentive compensation to third parties should be structured to assure it is consistent with the market, industry standards and does not create perverse motivations for the third party to act improperly.[113]

---

107. Guiding Principles on Business and Human Rights, UNITED NATIONS HUMAN RIGHTS, OFFICE OF THE COMMISSIONER, https://www.ohchr.org/Documents/Publications/GuidingPrinciplesBusinessHR_EN.pdf (last visited Apr. 10, 2019); UN GLOBAL IMPACT, https://www.unglobalcompact.org/ (last visited Apr. 10, 2019); *Training Lawyers on Business and Human Rights*, INTERNATIONAL BAR ASSOCIATION, https://www.ibanet.org/LPRU/Business-and-Human-Rights-for-the-Legal-Profession.aspx (last visited Apr. 10, 2019).

108. *Id.*

109. David V. Snyder & Susan A. Maslow, *Human Rights Protections in International Supply Chains-Protecting Workers and Managing Company Risk*, ABA, BUSINESS LAW SECTION (Nov. 28, 2018), https://businesslawtoday.org/2018/11/human-rights-protections-international-supply-chains-protecting-workers-managing-company-risk/; DOJ Opinion 06-2, Dec. 2006; Opinion 08-01, Jan. 2008; Opinion 10-02, July 2010; KnowTheChain, *supra* note 105; *Guiding Principles on Business and Human Rights*, *supra* note 107.

110. DOJ Opinion 06-2, Dec. 2006; Opinion 08-01, Jan. 2008; Opinion 10-02, July 2010.

111. Snyder & Maslow, *supra* note 109.

112. KnowTheChain, *supra* note 105; *DOJ Compliance Guidance,* https://mneguidelines.oecd.org/OECD-Due-Diligence-Guidance-for-Responsible-Business-Conduct.pdf (last visited Apr. 10, 2019); *A Resource Guide to the U.S. Foreign Corrupt Practices Act*, *supra* note 35.

113. *Id.*

However, drafters should be sure that the contract does not unreasonably expand legal definitions related to such terms as conflicts of interest, improper payment, or human trafficking. So the contract should clearly define terms related to industry standards, guidance documents, and compliance with laws and ethics policies with precision either in the contract or through the requirement that the third party follow policies and procedures that define these terms.

Likewise, an organization should consider whether it will require proof of a third parties' compliance and social responsibility policies and procedures; or if it will require the third party to comply with their policies; or if it will require the third party to take any training on legal compliance, ethical, and social responsibilities. Finally, organizations should carefully draft the right to terminate the contract in the event the organization has reasons to believe that the third party may not be complying with applicable laws and regulations or corporate policies and procedures. The guidance also recommends assuring the right to audit the third party; requirements that the third party flow down certain contract terms to their business partners; and the right to immediately terminate the contract in the event legal or ethical risks are identified.[114] Some recommended approaches to developing contracts with third parties that effectively further CSR are included here, but the resources from the ABA, DOJ, the UN, and other entities cited in the endnotes should be consulted for detailed guidance.

Step 4: Cease Business Relationships with Noncompliant Third Parties

An often overlooked first step in mitigating the risk of working with a third party contributing to an organization's commitment to social responsibility and compliance with laws is the thoughtful evaluation of whether the organization even needs to use a third party or is it capable of performing the duties the third party would perform itself or with a more compliant third party.[115] Once the decision is made to use the third party, the organization should document its business reasons for employing a third party to define the nature and purpose of the relationship.[116] If a third party or supplier cannot or refuses to become compliant, then it may make the most sense to cease business with the third party or supplier.

Case Study Uber

I. History of Uber

The idea of Uber as a ride-sharing company was hatched in 2009 by Garrett Camp and Travis Kalanick, who had both successfully founded other companies. Nine years later, Uber had 16,000 employees globally and operated in over 600 cities.[117] In October 2018,

---

114. KnowTheChain, *supra* note 105.
115. *See, e.g.*, KnowTheChain, *supra* note 105.
116. *See, e.g.*, *A Resource Guide to the U.S. Foreign Corrupt Practices Act*, *supra* note 35.
117. Samantha M. Kelly, *Inside Uber: How the Company Attracts Top Talent Despite Its Reputation*, CNN BUSINESS (Feb. 22, 2009, 3:39 AM), https://money.cnn.com/2017/02/14/technology/uber-corporate-culture/index.html.

as Uber was making plans for an initial public offering (IPO), investment banks valued it around $120 billion.[118] Despite this high valuation, media reports and civil lawsuits—along with criminal and regulatory investigation—suggested that Uber exemplified a corporate culture that was without concern for following the law, acting ethically, or otherwise being a socially responsible corporate citizen. Starting in early 2018, however, Uber had begun adjusting its corporate culture to pivot toward being an organization committed to being ethically and socially responsible. Its journey is an informative case study for organizations that either need to reset their corporate culture or are in the process of developing a culture of social responsibility, ethics, and legal compliance.

II. Uber Scandals

A. Uber's Relationship with Competitors

One indication of Uber's culture before 2018 was the actions it took related to its competitors. Two examples illuminate Uber's approach to competition. First, in late summer 2015, media reported that Uber competitor Lyft claimed that people associated with Uber, over the course of almost a year, had ordered and then cancelled about 5,500 Lyft rides in an effort to try to tie up Lyft drivers so they could not respond to potential riders.[119]

Then, in February 2017, Google affiliate Waymo sued Uber, claiming a company that Uber had purchased was established using trade secrets its founder had taken while a Google employee. In May 2017, courts ruled that Uber had to return the documents to Waymo. Ultimately, Uber settled the matter by paying Waymo $244 million in Uber equity and agreeing not to infringe on Waymo's intellectual property.[120]

B. Uber's Relationship with Regulators

As Uber expanded operations across the country and around the world, its policy seemed to be to ignore local regulations and simply start operating in a jurisdiction. If regulators challenged Uber, the company would launch an aggressive public campaign, prompting its users to bombard regulators with e-mail messages and calls asking them to allow Uber to operate in the jurisdiction; it also hired lobbyists to influence regulators.[121] The

---

118. Alex Barinka Eric & Newcomer, *Uber Valued at $120 Billion in an IPO? Maybe*, BLOOMBERG (Oct. 16, 2018, 7:32 PM), https://www.bloomberg.com/news/articles/2018-10-16/uber-valued-at-120-billion-in-an-ipo-maybe; UBER NEWSROOM, https://www.uber.com/newsroom/company-info/ (last visited Feb. 11, 2019).

119. Erica Fink, *Uber's Dirty Trick Quantified: Rival Counts 5,560 Canceled Rides*, CNN BUSINESS (Aug. 12, 2014, 3:11 PM), https://money.cnn.com/2014/08/11/technology/uber-fake-ride-requests-lyft/index.html.

120. Alexandria Sage et al., *Waymo Accepts $245 Million and Uber's "Regret" to Settle Self-driving Car Dispute*, REUTERS (Feb. 9, 2018, 11:00 AM), https://www.reuters.com/article/us-alphabet-uber-trial/waymo-accepts-245-million-and-ubers-regret-to-settle-self-driving-car-dispute-idUSKBN1FT2BA.

121. Lori Aratani, *Uber Mobilizes Its Users to Fight Ban in Virginia*, THE WASHINGTON POST (June 6, 2014), https://www.washingtonpost.com/news/dr-gridlock/wp/2014/06/06/uber-mobilizes-its-users-to-fight-ban-in-virginia/?noredirect=on&utm_term=.8b4ffcc99669.

company was so aggressive that in 2014 as Uber tried to break into the Portland, Oregon, market, local politicians referred to Uber's leadership as "a bunch of thugs."[122]

When regulators began attempting to oversee Uber's actions, Uber developed technology that enabled its drivers to hide from riders Uber believed to be law enforcement investigating it.[123] Uber was alleged to use this technology in cities around the globe such as Portland, Oregon, which was investigating Uber's practices as was the U.S. Department of Justice.[124,125] Around the same time, the media began reporting that Uber had developed a software tool to alert its employees when government regulators may be raiding its offices so that employees could either change passwords or even remove damaging information.[126] Ultimately, Uber agreed to stop these practices. But other issues arose, and #deleteuber began trending in response to the company's stance on the U.S. immigration ban, the Waymo lawsuit, and charges of rampant sexism.[127]

C. Uber's Relationship with Its Employees

In February 2017, a *New York Times* investigation into Uber's culture uncovered an environment in which workers were pitted against one another and sexual harassment was tolerated.[128] The investigation was prompted by the allegations of a former Uber employee who claimed she had been sexually harassed by a manager while she was employed there. She claimed that when she raised concerns about the harassment, she was told she would be terminated if she continued to persist in her accusation. There were also allegations that then CEO and Uber founder Travis Kalanick knew the employee was being harassed but failed to act, which was alleged to be typical of Uber's general practice of overlooking this type of managerial misconduct. Around the same time, a leading Uber executive engineer faced allegations that he had been involved in sexual harassment while at a former employer.[129]

---

122. Aaron Mesh, *10 Things You Need to Know about Uber in Portland*, WILLAMETTE WEEK (Jan. 24, 2017), https://www.wweek.com/portland/blog-32551-10-things-you-need-to-know-about-uber-in-portland.html.

123. Mike Isaac, *How Uber Deceives the Authorities Worldwide*, THE N. Y. TIMES (Mar. 3, 2017), https://www.nytimes.com/2017/03/03/technology/uber-greyball-program-evade-authorities.html.

124. Elliot Njus, *Portland to Investigate Uber's 'Greyball' Scheme to Thwart Regulators*, THE OREGONIAN, https://www.oregonlive.com/commuting/2017/03/ubers_greyball_scheme_to_thwar.html (last updated Jan. 11, 2019).

125. Dan Levine & Joseph Menn, Exclusive: *Uber Faces Criminal Probe over Software Used to Evade Authorities*, REUTERS (May 4, 2017, 7:07 PM), https://www.reuters.com/article/us-uber-tech-crime-exclusive/exclusive-uber-faces-criminal-probe-over-software-used-to-evade-authorities-idUSKBN1802U1.

126. Olivia Zaleski & Eric Newcomer, *Uber's Secret Tool for Keeping the Cops in the Dark*, BLOOMBERG BUSINESSWEEK (Jan. 11, 2018), https://www.bloomberg.com/news/articles/2018-01-11/uber-s-secret-tool-for-keeping-the-cops-in-the-dark.

127. Marco della Cava, *Uber Admits Its Ghost Driver "Greyball" Tool Was Used to Thwart Regulators, Vows to Stop*, USA TODAY (Mar. 9, 2017, 7:08 AM), https://www.usatoday.com/story/tech/talkingtech/2017/03/08/uber-stop-using-greyball-target-regulators/98930282/.

128. Mike Isaac, *Uber Investigating Sexual Harassment Claims by Ex-Employee*, N.Y. TIMES (Feb. 19, 2017), https://www.nytimes.com/2017/02/19/business/uber-sexual-harassment-investigation.html.

129. Steven Overly, *Uber Hires Eric Holder to Investigate Sexual Harassment Claims*, LOS ANGELES TIMES (Feb. 21, 2017), https://www.latimes.com/business/technology/la-fi-tn-uber-eric-holder-20170221-story.html.

Uber's relationship with its employees was also impacted by its lack of infrastructure. Specifically, media reported that Uber lacked the infrastructure of an established business. That is, there was no chief financial officer or chief operating officer, which was unusual for a firm of such size operating in a heavily regulated industry and which surely created a perception for employees that the organization did not provide the structure they needed to perform.[130]

IV. UBER'S STEPS TO DEVELOP AN ETHICAL CULTURE

A. Overview

Uber's approach has recently started to change. Uber brought in a new CEO; and Uber's former culture now seems to be eroding, and in its place a culture of compliant and ethical behavior appears to be emerging. The concrete steps Uber has taken and plans to take provide a roadmap for any company on how to evolve its culture toward ethical and socially responsible behaviors.

B. Conducting a Risk Assessment

One of the first steps for Uber in its journey of remediating its compliance and ethics challenges was to essentially conduct a risk assessment. For Uber, this risk assessment came in the form of a Uber board mandate to hire a law firm to conduct an independent investigation into the claims of sexual harassment. To that end, Uber hired the law firm Covington & Burling to conduct a thorough and objective review of the harassment allegations. Ultimately, Covington & Burling's report was presented to Uber's board of directors. Uber's board of directors unanimously approved a resolution establishing a Special Committee of the board to oversee implementing all the report's recommendations which were designed to improve Uber's culture of compliance and ethics, particularly in respecting its employees.[131]

The report to Uber provides insight on conducting a risk assessment, regardless of the subject matter. For it is ultimately Covington & Burling's comprehensive review of Uber's operations that led it to make the recommendations it did to Uber's board to start Uber down a path of remediating its risks.

In conducting its assessment, Covington reviewed over 3 million documents.[132] Covington also interviewed individuals with knowledge of the alleged harassment to include both current and former members of the executive teams as well as others in the Uber organization.[133] As part of its review, Covington also gathered input from

---

130. Sheelah Kolhatkar, *At Uber, A New C.E.O. Shifts Gears*, THE NEW YORKER (Apr. 9, 2018), https://www.newyorker.com/magazine/2018/04/09/at-uber-a-new-ceo-shifts-gears.

131. Miguel Helft, *Here's the Full 13-Page "Holder Report" Aimed at Resetting Uber's Management and Culture*, FORBES (June 13, 2017, 01:48 PM), https://www.forbes.com/sites/miguelhelft/2017/06/13/heres-the-full-13-page-holder-report-aimed-at-resetting-ubers-management-and-culture/#7f6dae9b2c00.

132. Liane Hornsey, chief HR officer, *Statement on Covington & Burling Recommendations*, UBER NEWSROOM (Jan. 13, 2017), https://www.uber.com/newsroom/covington-recommendations/.

133. *Id.*

anonymous online focus groups about their Uber experiences in order to "[gather] broad-based data about employee perceptions concerning Uber's workplace environment and culture."[134] Covington recommended in its report that this type of focus group input continue going forward so Uber could assess its culture.[135]

Covington's approach demonstrates that when assessing the risk an organization faces, it is important to gather information from multiple sources. Covington interviewed employees directly, conducted anonymous focus group interviews and reviewed documents. But, Covington's methods also show that to truly stay informed on risks, an organization must engage in ongoing assessment of its risks—thus, Covington's recommendation for Uber to continue using focus groups to pulse employee experiences. Finally, the report crystalizes the need for any risk assessment, internal audit, or internal investigation to be thorough, objective, and conducted by knowledgeable professionals in order for any findings to carry the credibility necessary to foment change.

C. Ousted Uber Leadership

As the internal investigations into Uber employees' harassment claims continued, other challenges began to mount: government investigations into Uber business practices, complaints about how it dealt with its regulators, and accusations about how it treated its competitors. Uber's board and shareholders began insisting on action. The governance dispute for control of the company played out in the media, with founder and CEO Kalanick attempting to retain control of the company while directors and shareholders pressured him to depart.

The internal investigation uncovered a somewhat loosely organized company that failed to respect its employees. Having a report containing specific factual findings based on an objective and intensive investigation gave the board and shareholders the information needed to assess what governance and leadership changes were necessary. Without these changes, they knew Uber's legal and reputational expenses would continue to rise, threatening to destroy the company. Strong board member and shareholder pressure, backed by the report's findings, resulted in the departure of more than 20 employees in June 2017.[136]

Under pressure from the board and shareholders, Kalanick resigned as CEO the same month.[137] Along with Kalanick, another executive, Uber's senior executive for business, was ousted amid allegations he had attempted to share a victimized Uber rider's medical records, engaged in sexually harassing behavior, and sought to gather negative information on any reporter writing unfavorable stories about Uber.[138] These

---

134. *Id.*
135. *Id.*
136. Olivia Solon, *Uber Fires More Than 20 Employees after Sexual Harassment Investigation*, THE GUARDIAN (June 6, 2017, 23 52 EDT), https://www.theguardian.com/technology/2017/jun/06/uber-fires-employees-sexual-harassment-investigation.
137. Mike Isaac, *Uber Founder Travis Kalnick Resigns as C.E.O.*, THE N.Y. TIMES (June 21, 2017), https://www.nytimes.com/2017/06/21/technology/uber-ceo-travis-kalanick.html.
138. Alison Griswold, *Uber's Most Scandal-ridden Exec Is Out—And It's Not Travis Kalanick*, QUARTZ (June 12, 2017), https://qz.com/1003453/emil-michael-ubers-most-scandal-ridden-exec-is-reportedly-out/.

separations were the first critical step in moving Uber's toxic environment toward a more ethical and responsible culture.

Additionally, the report made clear that independent and experienced board members to include an independent chairperson were necessary to lead the company.[139] The report noted this would send a message to stakeholders that Uber was serious about reform.[140] Further, the report recommended that internal auditors and others with compliance responsibility report directly to a committee of the board.[141]

In changing a culture, one of the first steps is to assess the existing leadership's commitment to an ethically and socially responsible organization. If this commitment is lacking, as Uber's story demonstrates, the challenges may continue to grow, and change will not occur. When assessing whether corporate leadership should be replaced, counsel must appreciate their role as fiduciaries to the organization and operate by the legal mandates to foster a culture of ethics and integrity.[142] Failing to do so exposes the organization to more significant penalties in the event it is prosecuted.[143] As for refining a culture, lawyers can effectively do so when they take their fiduciary role seriously as stewards of the organization, teaming with directors and shareholders to move leaders out and encouraging directors and shareholders to ultimately own the decision to bring in new leaders.

D. New Leadership Brought In

Once leadership and others who are not committed to the ethical culture of a company have been ousted, new leadership needs to not only be committed to fostering a culture of integrity but also must have the ability to execute on developing a more ethical culture. Uber's case demonstrates this requires both a leader with the characteristics and temperament to lead the change and the support of directors and shareholders to make the change.

Uber's new CEO, Dara Khosrowshahi, who took the helm in 2018, exhibited both the characteristics and temperament to accomplish the needed changes. Based on his own statements and those who have worked with him, he was an experienced, capable, ethical business leader who is easygoing but also determined. These qualities enable a CEO to foster an ethical and compliant culture by modeling ethical decision-making. Khosrowshahi's nature could permit him to stay focused and directed, yet open, willing to listen, and approachable. Thus he seemed well suited to make the change.

---

139. Liane Hornsey, chief HR officer, *supra* note 132.
140. *Id.*
141. *Id.*
142. *See, e.g., Evaluation of Corporate Compliance Programs, supra* note 3.
143. U.S. Attorney Manual 9.28.300, https://www.justice.gov/jm/jm-9-28000-principles-federal-prosecution-business-organizations#9-28.300.

Uber also brought in a new general counsel, Tony West. Attorney West had been a high-ranking DOJ official and then general counsel at Pepsi. Upon taking the job, West declared: "I'm not the first to recognize that the company over-indexed on growth without putting in the appropriate guardrails ... Fostering a culture of compliance is going to be one of my top priorities."[144]

A strong, courageous, experienced general counsel needs to provide the guardrails that Attorney West referred to so that the organization is given clear, direct legal and compliance guidance. But in addition to a strong general counsel, an organization seeking to either change its culture or improve it requires experienced and courageous legal, financial, audit, compliance, and HR teams for they are the ones who will police the organization, whether to foster an ethical and compliant culture or to foster other qualities.

These guardrails also included limiting the role of Uber's founder and former CEO. This too was an important step when an organization has a larger-than-life leader like Kalanick, who could not seem to grasp that part of running a business includes following the law and making ethical choices, especially since often the leadership team follows that approach.[145]

With an independent review in hand and a process of implementation under way that included an active effort to remove and replace key members of its leadership, Uber was poised to embrace a newly ethical and compliant culture when its new CEO arrived. Board and shareholder support was evident, and the organization was confident he was capable of leading the efforts.

E. Communicating Expectations

Newly installed as CEO, Khosrowshahi began messaging Uber's commitment to ethical decision-making and to corporate social responsibility. But Uber's board had demonstrated its commitment to change even before he was hired when it adopted and then presented the Covington & Burling report recommending actions to employees. In the presentation to employees, Uber as an organization made clear that its goal was to improve its culture, "promote fairness and accountability," and "establish processes and systems to ensure the mistakes of the past will not be repeated."[146] It acknowledged that it would take time to build trust with its stakeholders.[147]

Even before CEO Khosrowshashi took over, Uber's board was working to communicate its goal of moving toward a more ethical and compliant organization. For

---

144. Hamza Shaban, *Uber Hires PepsiCo's Tony West as General Counsel*, THE WASHINGTON POST (Oct. 27, 2017), https://www.washingtonpost.com/news/the-switch/wp/2017/10/27/uber-hires-pepsicos-tony-west-as-general-counsel/?utm_term=.28e3afc658d1.

145. Tim J. Smith, *Uber Is Finally Growing Up*, FORTUNE (Aug. 22, 2018), http://fortune.com/2018/08/22/uber-ceo-new-york-london/.

146. Liane Hornsey, chief HR officer, *supra* note 132.

147. *Id.*

example, employees were provided Covington & Burling recommendations once the board had approved them. In a public message on its site, Uber stated:

> Implementing these recommendations will improve our culture, promote fairness and accountability, and establish processes and systems to ensure the mistakes of the past will not be repeated. While change does not happen overnight, we're committed to rebuilding trust with our employees, riders and drivers.[148]

When CEO Khosrowshahi took over, he took the time to communicate with his employees to learn that they were in fact interested in changing. Next, he implemented changes to help his employees improve the culture by recrafting Uber's cultural norms. In revealing the new tenets, he acknowledged Uber's global presence, and its impact on local communities, through the riders and drivers it serves each day. With this as a backdrop, some of the norms he developed in response to Uber's ethical expectations included:

- **"We celebrate differences."** This norm requires welcoming people of all backgrounds, encouraging different opinions, encouraging speaking up and working together.
- **"We do the right thing."** This norm is about rule following, but also treating others rightly and fairly.
- **"We act like owners."** This norm requires that all employees identify and solve problems, owning up to mistakes they make.

The new cultural norms also kept true to Uber's history of disruption: "We make big bold bets."[149]

Finally, CEO Khosrowshahi regularly spoke publicly about how he was changing the culture and that integrity is crucial to every decision Uber makes. He acknowledged he was brought in to remedy the mistakes of the past because, as he explained it, Uber's culture was "completely effed up."[150]

F. Settling Up with Regulators and Others

In addition to the internal changes, Uber took concrete actions to build trust and demonstrate integrity and its commitment to be socially responsible with its regulators and with the communities where it operated. CEO Khosrowshahi dropped the "win at all costs" strategy. In its place developed a more transparent, collaborative approach.

---

148. *Id.*
149. Dara Khosrowshahi, *Uber's New Cultural Norms*, UBER NEWSROOM (Nov. 8, 2017), https://www.uber.com/newsroom/ubers-new-cultural-norms/.
150. Kolhatkar, *supra* note 130.

First, around the time Khosrowshahi took over, London had revoked Uber's license to operate for, among other things, failing to report allegations of sexual assault. Several months later, Khosrowshahi apologized for Uber's behavior and convinced the courts to give Uber a temporary license to operate based on his representations that Uber was changing its ways.[151] Second, in April 2018, Uber reached a settlement with the FTC around a series of privacy breaches and failures to disclose the breaches that had angered the FTC. In reaching the settlement, acting FTC commissioner Maureen K. Ohlhausen explained:

> After misleading consumers about its privacy and security practices, Uber compounded its misconduct by failing to inform the Commission that it suffered another data breach in 2016 while the Commission was investigating the company's strikingly similar 2014 breach.[152]

Uber's settlement included requirements that it report breaches and that it regularly provide the FTC the reports of third-party audits on the security of its systems.[153]

V. SUMMARY AND TAKEAWAYS

Although directed by laws, regulations, and stakeholder expectations, developing and maintaining a culture that embraces ethical decision-making and corporate social responsibility are challenging. Yet, the benefits from that program, as Uber's case demonstrates, lead to not only compliance with laws and ethical decision-making but also increased value brought through a program of corporate social responsibility.

---

151. Julia Kollewe & Gwyn Topham, *Uber Apologizes after London Ban and Admits "We Got Things Wrong,"* THE GUARDIAN (Sept. 25, 2017, 09.11 EDT), https://www.theguardian.com/business/2017/sep/25/uber-tfl-concerns-vows-keep-operating-london-licence.

152. *Uber Agreed to Expanded Settlement with FTC Related to Privacy, Security Claims*, FED. TRADE COMM'N (Apr. 12, 2018), https://www.ftc.gov/news-events/press-releases/2018/04/uber-agrees-expanded-settlement-ftc-related-privacy-security.

153. *Id.*

Chapter 11

Impact Investing

Susan H. Mac Cormac, Jesse M. Finfrock, and Benjamin T.R. Fox

I. INTRODUCTION

With the rapid growth of the impact investment sector, it has become increasingly important for legal practitioners to gain fluency in the types of legal structures and investment instruments favored by both investors and social enterprises. While what constitutes impact may vary depending on a particular investor, impact investing is generally defined as investing for the purpose of generating social and environmental benefits alongside financial returns. The size of the impact investment sector has continued to expand—respondents to the Global Impact Investing Network's annual survey reported assets under management of approximately $228 billion.[1] The sector also remains incredibly diverse; food and agriculture, financial services, and energy were among the most popular sectors in 2018.[2]

In advising impact investors, it is essential to first understand the target financial returns that the investor seeks alongside its impact goals. In general, there are three classes of impact investor:

1. impact-first or impact-only investors—often charitable foundations—who prioritize impact over financial returns either relatively or absolutely (this is also known as concessionary capital)
2. impact and returns investors who place approximately equal priority on impact and financial returns
3. return-first investors who are focused primarily on market-rate financial returns but seek impact as an ancillary benefit of their investments.

---

1. *See* Global Impact Investing Network, *2018 Annual Impact Investor Survey*, ii, https://thegiin.org/assets/2018_GIIN_Annual_Impact_Investor_Survey_webfile.pdf.
2. *See* Global Impact Investing Network, *supra* note 1, 25. Note that financial services exclude microfinance, which was measured as its own separate category. *Id.*

Note that one impact investor may seek different impact versus financial returns weighting among multiple vehicles. For example, many impact investors have both for-profit investment vehicles and nonprofit foundations that, while pursuing the same mission, may tolerate different levels of return risk.[3]

While the impact investment sector is dynamic and evolving quickly, we note a few recent trends. First, foundations are moving larger portions of their endowments to impact investments, shifting their grant-making strategies to include program-related impact investments and establishing wholly owned investment funds that are intended to invest only in furtherance of the nonprofit's tax-exempt purpose. Second, family offices (investment management firms that manage assets for wealthy individuals and families) are becoming more creative with the structure of their impact investments and transactions. In particular, those with living donors are moving away from locking capital in private foundations and are creating or seeking impact-first fund structures. Third, hybrid funds (discussed further below), which seek funding from both for-profit and nonprofit enterprises and may themselves be structured partially as nonprofits and partially as profit-seeking entities, are growing in popularity. Fourth, for-profit funds are increasingly establishing affiliated entities ("side cars") focused on impact investments. Finally, traditional private equity and other mainstream investors have increased focus on impact investment.

II. IMPACT INVESTMENT INSTRUMENTS

In a social enterprise, both impact investors and the company are aligned in pursuit of such company's mission. As a result, mission-preserving provisions can be layered upon common investment structures (equity investments, debt investments, bonds, etc.) to ensure that the company continues to pursue its mission and does not fall victim to "mission drift."

A. Convertible Debt

Convertible debt—debt that converts to equity at a specified ratio when certain conditions are met—is a common financing mechanism for early-stage entrepreneurs and investors, whether impact-driven or otherwise.[4] Convertible debt instruments offer social entrepreneurs and investors a number of options to ensure the preservation of an early-stage social enterprise's mission. Social entrepreneurs and investors may require

---

3. An example of this is the Omidyar Network (ON). ON relies on a hybrid structure to make grants out of its nonprofit foundation and a for-profit LLC to make for-profit investments in early-stage start-up companies. *See generally*, https://www.omidyar.com/sites/default/files/file_archive/Omidyar%20Network%20Approach.pdf.

4. Another widely used impact investment instrument is regular debt (in contrast to convertible debt). For foundation investors focused on mission, that debt may include more favorable terms, such as lower interest, longer term, or partial or complete forgiveness triggered by achievement of mission-related milestones. In general, the impact mechanics in regular debt are similar to convertible debt, which we focus on here.

that the company's mission be memorialized at the time of the investment (e.g., in a new corporate form, corporate charter documents, shareholders' agreement, voting agreement, or in the debt instrument itself). They may also include affirmative covenants (e.g., borrower shall use the proceeds of an investment only in a mission-aligned fashion) or negative covenants (e.g., borrower shall not change its mission-aligned business plan; borrower shall not incur any material capital expenditures for activities that conflict with mission). Another option is to include material deviation from the company's defined mission as an event of default. To avoid cross-default with other debt instruments, which can be catastrophic for an early-stage company, mission-related provisions can be structured to trigger prepayment of the outstanding debt, as opposed to default, as well as mission-protective contractual remedies for the debtholder, such as a board takeover, if the borrower entity fails to prepay. Investors may also provide that a higher interest rate or prepayment will automatically apply if the borrower takes certain actions inconsistent with its mission, or that equity conversion will not apply automatically in the next round of financing if the borrower takes certain actions inconsistent with the mission, along with requiring detailed reporting by the company to debtholders on mission and impact.[5]

It is important to note that where deviation from the company's mission carries significant penalties, a key question is who determines the threshold of permissible deviation and whether such threshold has been breached. For example, the debtholder can have the right to determine that there has been a material deviation from the mission agreed upon at the time of investment, with the company having the right to object to this determination. The dispute is then resolved by a designated third party. In addition, the company can appoint a standing special committee of the board tasked with oversight of mission that reports to the board and the investors if there has been material deviation or the company and the investors can agree to establish the company's mission with reference to third-party standard. The third party then conducts audits of the company's compliance with the standard on a regular basis.[6]

B. Preferred Equity

Preferred equity—stock that has superior economic and governance rights as opposed to holders of a company's common stock—is also a common source of financing for early-stage social enterprises. There are several options for preserving mission in a preferred equity issuance. Shareholder voting agreements may require that certain investors approve actions which are mission- (or not-mission-) aligned. Another method is to create separate classes of stock for mission-aligned investors and founders, in conjunction with class approval rights for certain key items, e.g., material changes in the company's business plan, including changes to mission; a sale of the company, along with triggers for drag-along rights; or any action out of the ordinary course that could have a material impact on mission. Companies may also guarantee board representation

---

5. *See* Susan Mac Cormac, Morrison & Foerster LLP, *Preserving and Enhancing Impact: Corporate Forms*, Presentation at IMPACT.TECH (Oct. 2016), slides 14–15, https://www.slideshare.net/Impactdottech/preserving-and-enhancing-impact-corporate-forms.

6. *See* Susan Mac Cormac, Morrison & Foerster LLP, *supra* note 5, at slide 16.

for mission-aligned investors or have an impact investor board designee have specific veto rights at the board level. A company can also include redemption rights in the event of a material deviation from mission—for example, if the company deviates from its mission, it must repurchase investors' shares or face specified penalties, such as ceding board control to the unredeemed investors until the redemption price is paid or to grant a right of sale to a co-investor who serves as a guarantor in the event of mission deviation.[7]

Other strategies include having an investor rights agreement with information rights related to mission and impact reporting, changes to the conversion formula or conversion ratio from preferred stock to common stock in the event of a material deviation from mission (which would result in more common shares upon conversion of an investor's preferred shares), or specifying that dividends to preferred shareholders will become cumulative (i.e., will have to be paid regardless of the company's profitability) in the event of a material deviation from mission. Finally, investors can request preferential waterfall provision rights for mission-aligned investors, which afford priority in cash distributions. A related mechanism is to change the waterfall and/or the return (e.g., change the liquidation preference from 1x to 2x or from non-participating to participating preferred stock, in the event of deviation from mission).[8]

C. SAFEs

The Simple Agreement for Future Equity (SAFE) is a relatively new but popular financing instrument for many early-stage companies.[9] Like a convertible debt instrument, a SAFE converts into equity under specified circumstances—usually when a later financing round is raised with equity and generally at a discount.[10] However, a SAFE is an equity instrument and, consequently, has no fixed maturity date or interest rate, which offers greater flexibility to an early-stage company.[11]

SAFEs offer social enterprises a number of the same options for preserving mission focus as convertible debt instruments, including affirmative and negative covenants (such as material deviation from mission as an event of default), and requirements for conversion into a new corporate form (such as a Delaware public benefit corporation) prior to conversion into equity.

D. Bonds

Bonds are a widely used source of financing for corporations of all sizes in all sectors. As with the other traditional investment instruments described in this section, traditional

---

7. It is important to note that these types of redemption provisions may create barriers to co-investment options, particularly outside of the impact investing sector.
8. Provisions adjusting the waterfall may be problematic from a tax-planning perspective if foundation or nonprofit investors have a lower priority in the waterfall than for-profit investors.
9. *See* Thomson Reuters Foundation and Morrison & Foerster LLP, "Which Legal Structure Is Right for My Social Enterprise: A Guide to Establishing a Social Enterprise in the United States," May 2016, revised version forthcoming in 2019, 44, https://www.trust.org/contentAsset/raw-data/1b34bbc3-de52-477a-adae-850a56c2aabe/file.
10. *See id.*
11. *See id.*

bonds can be structured to account for the social mission of the issuing company. Two common examples are green bonds and social impact bonds. With respect to green bonds, there is no uniform definition, but in general green bonds are traditional debt securities, the proceeds of which are designated for use in business ventures that advance environmental objectives, e.g., investments in renewable energy generation, energy efficiency, or climate change mitigation or adaptation activities.[12] Green bond issuances have grown at a significant rate—in 2018, green bond issuances were expected to surpass $250 billion, far exceeding the prior high-water mark of $155 billion set in 2017.[13] With respect to social impact bonds, these bonds can take any number of legal forms, but in general they are a multiparty, pay-for-performance contract that pays investors financial returns contingent on the level of social impact created by a nonprofit organization. For example, a government or private entity may contract to pay for social outcomes that save money or create social value. Investors fund a nonprofit organization, which is the counterparty to the contract, to produce the desired social outcomes. If the social outcomes are achieved, the government or private entity pays investors back their principal with a predetermined level of return.[14] While social impact bonds have lagged behind green bonds in terms of adoption, total capital invested in impact bonds in 2017 exceeded $300 million.[15]

III. IMPACT INVESTOR STRUCTURES

A. For-Profit Funds Designed to Promote Impact

There are a number of key decisions that must be made when forming a for-profit impact investment fund.[16] First, *defining the scope of the fund's mission to include impact-related requirements is critical.* While most funds are set up with a very general investment focus, impact-focused funds can use the "purpose and powers" section of their fund agreements to mandate a more tailored purpose or mission. It is important that the mission be specific enough to permit meaningful measurement and reporting but not so narrow as to restrict the ability of the fund's general partner (GP) to adjust the fund's strategy in order to adapt to changing market conditions. It is also critical that the fund agreement specify a remedy in the event of a material deviation from the mission and an agreed mechanism for determining whether a material deviation has occurred.

Second, it is important to determine how investment decisions will be made and by whom. Related issues include the extent and nature of shareholder rights, including the

---

12. *See, e.g.,* https://www.icmagroup.org/green-social-and-sustainability-bonds/green-bond-principles-gbp/.
13. https://www.forbes.com/sites/gauravsharma/2018/02/01/global-green-bond-issuance-set-to-eclipse-250b-in-2018/#ee0a40c56693.
14. *See, e.g.,* https://www.gov.uk/guidance/social-impact-bonds.
15. https://www.brookings.edu/blog/education-plus-development/2018/01/17/paying-for-social-outcomes-a-review-of-the-global-impact-bond-market-in-2017/.
16. As a general citation for this section and the hybrid fund section, see https://impact.mofo.com/measuring/impact-investing-fund-mechanisms-to-incentivize-impact/.

exercise of preemptive rights; what exit options will be available to investors and under what circumstances; whether investment proceeds will be reinvested or distributed to investors and under what circumstances; and who will propose and have approval rights over the fund's budget.

Third, an impact investor must decide how costs will be shared among the investors and the fund. Specified costs may be paid out of investors' existing commitments or from additional payments due from investors. Potentially significant costs include expenses associated with forming the fund; annual operating expenses; indemnification, litigation, and tax audit expenses; and deal expenses, including broken-deal fees.

Finally, investors must determine how conflicts among the fund, its managers, and its investors will be handled. Investors and managers of the fund may be required to present relevant investment opportunities to the fund before pursuing them independently.

1. Length of Fund

Impact-oriented funds often employ a longer term than traditional investment funds in order to promote investments that may take longer than usual to reach profitability. Many impact investments also require significantly longer terms to yield appropriate returns on capital.

A long-term fund might have, for example, a 12-year term with a 3-year roll over, for a total duration of 15 years. Funds can also be structured as "evergreen funds," meaning that they have an indefinite lifetime in conjunction with redemption options for investors, e.g., allowing investors to opt-in or opt-out on an annual basis; allowing redemption following a formal notice process; or allowing redemption at will, with another impact investor or a foundation functioning as guarantor to the fund. Note that a fund that receives program-related investments (PRIs) from tax-exempt entities will require a mechanism permitting the tax-exempt entity to exit if the fund's mission changes in a way that could jeopardize the PRI's tax exemption or the tax-exempt status of the investor itself.

2. Impact-Based Compensation

Impact funds can be structured to tie the GP's compensation to the level of impact achieved in order to maintain alignment of interest between the GP and the fund's limited partners (LPs). For example, the GP could earn the typical 20 percent portion of the fund's returns, but with a portion of that percentage tied to impact performance, e.g., 15 percent through the financial performance of investment and 5 percent tied to impact performance. Alternatively, a fund could employ bonus-based compensation, with the bonus earned partially through financial performance and partially through impact performance.

3. Governance

A fund's governance structure may account for impact promotion and preservation. For example, an impact fund can create an advisory committee consisting of its LPs (an LPAC) with approval rights over investments or a duty to review the fund's mission and impact on an annual basis, possibly for purposes of determining the GP's compensation (see above). Note that nonprofit entities may be LPs (generally with certain protective provisions), in which case they are often members of an LPAC or may be a member of the impact fund's GP.

4. Protective Provisions

LPs who prioritize impact over profitability can be awarded certain rights relating to mission, information, and material deviations from mission. For example, the fund agreement could award "impact first" investors weighted voting rights or rights of first offer or require the consent of "impact first" investors, an LP board, or an advisory in order to deviate materially from the fund's mission or formally redefine the mission.

5. Distributions

Distributions can be structured to incentivize the pursuit of mission by a fund. For example, impact investors and/or nonprofit investors can be awarded preference in cash distributions. Alternatively, distributions can be structured to first return money to traditional investors so that the impact investors or charitable funds bear the losses in order to de-risk the investment for traditional investors, in the interest of allowing the fund to access a deeper pool of capital. Finally, the fund could be structured to donate a certain percentage of returns to charity once specified financial goals are met.

6. Monitoring Impact

It is vital that an impact fund measure, monitor, and report on its impact on a regular basis. These three activities require relevant metrics, measurement standards, and a reporting framework. With respect to relevant metrics, metrics are typically fund-specific but monitored on a portfolio-wide basis. It is important to use metrics tailored appropriately to the fund's desired impact, i.e., neither so broad that they overstate the level of impact nor so narrow that they fail to capture significant impacts. It is also important to use metrics based on data that can be gathered without significant additional expense of resources by the portfolio companies' or the fund's managers.

For measurement standards, benchmarks should be set, either externally or internally, that can be used to measure success consistently across time. When it comes to a reporting framework, a fund must determine the best way to communicate its level of success to both portfolio companies and LPs. It is increasingly common for impact funds to integrate their mission-related reporting with their traditional financial reporting (see example below).

7. Example

Pacific Community Ventures, LLC, a Delaware limited liability company, is an impact fund investing across a wide range of industries. Headquartered in San Francisco, CA, its funds provide capital and resources to high growth California businesses that bring significant economic gains to low-to-moderate income employees, as well as delivering financial returns to business owners and to its investors. Pacific Community

Ventures, LLC, is a hands-on investor that partners with management to provide capital and expertise to ensure the long-term success of its portfolio companies. It builds, develops, and maximizes the value within these organizations for the benefit of owners, management, and employees. Pacific Community Ventures, LLC, manages over $60 million and is currently investing out of Pacific Community Ventures Investment Partners III, LLC, a $40 million fund that closed in 2007. For more information, please visit http://pcvfund.com.

B. Foundations

1. Overview

Private foundations may make significant investments focused on impact in promotion of the foundation's charitable purpose. Such investments may be made directly or through other specific instruments described below. Foundation investments are also subject to a number of specific restrictions, including matters related to excess business holdings, self-dealing, and jeopardizing investments. Private foundations, together with their "disqualified persons,"[17] generally are limited to holding not more than 20 percent of a business entity (with certain exceptions).[18] With respect to self-dealing, foundations are barred from making investments or engaging in transactions that would be self-dealing to a disqualified person.[19] Finally, foundations are prohibited from making unduly risky investments.[20]

Foundations are required to distribute each year an amount equivalent to approximately 5 percent of the fair market value of the foundation's non-charitable assets. Traditionally, foundations have invested the remaining 95 percent of their endowment to achieve market-rate returns. However, in recent years, a number of prominent foundations have publicly stated their support for investing larger portions of their endowments in impact investments, therefore focusing on social returns in both their charitable distributions and investment strategies.[21]

2. Program-Related Investment (PRI)

In addition to traditional grants that serve their charitable exempt purposes, which is the typical primary charitable activity of private foundations, private foundations may make program-related investments (PRIs).[22] PRIs are investments made in lieu of grants and count toward a foundation's 5 percent annual distribution requirement. PRIs are

---

17. For purposes of the excess business holding rules, "disqualified persons" include substantial contributors; officers, directors, and trustees of the foundation, and an owner of more than 20 percent of a business that is a substantial contributor; a family member of any of those individuals; any business of which any of those individuals owns more than 35 percent; and another private foundation that is directly or indirectly controlled by, or receives substantially all of its contributions from, any of those individuals. I.R.C. §4946.
18. I.R.C. §4943.
19. I.R.C. §4941.
20. I.R.C. §4944.
21. *See, e.g.*, https://www.nytimes.com/2017/04/13/business/ford-foundation-mission-investment.html.
22. Treas. Reg. §53.4944-3.

subject to strict Internal Revenue Service (IRS) rules. The Internal Revenue Code's test for a PRI looks to the foundation's intent and purposes in making the investment, not simply the stated purpose of the entity receiving the funds, and the IRS also requires due diligence and oversight as to the actual use of funds for exempt purposes.[23] The primary purpose of the investment must be to accomplish a charitable purpose of the foundation. Financial returns cannot be a significant purpose of the investment, although the foundation may receive investment returns, which are typically below market, and any guaranteed returns must be limited to return of capital.

Typical PRI terms, which are usually documented in the PRI investment documents or a side letter, include: (a) investment purpose—the investment is made pursuant to the mission of the foundation and in furtherance of its tax-exempt purpose; (b) use of proceeds—the investment proceeds are limited to the prescribed activities that will further the foundation's tax-exempt purpose (and no funds shall be used for lobbying or partisan political activities); (c) reporting—a narrative summary of the use of proceeds (including with respect to progress in achieving the purpose of the investment) and audited financial statements are required; and (d) redemption—in the event that the company has not complied with the PRI requirements, the foundation shall have a right to redeem the foundation's investment.

3. Mission-Related Investment (MRI)

Mission-related investments (MRIs) are commercial investments made by foundations that are not charitable in nature, but still further a foundation's mission. Unlike PRIs, MRIs are made from a foundation's endowment funds and do not count toward a foundation's 5 percent distribution requirement. MRIs are permitted to seek investment returns, although some foundations are willing to accept below-market returns in exchange for substantial impact. Mission-related terms in investment documents or a side letter may be required by the foundation under certain circumstances, but unlike PRIs, there are no legal criteria that require linking the investment to charitable activities.

4. Traditional Investment

Traditional investments by foundations are, like MRIs, made from endowment funds. Such investments also do not count toward a foundation's 5 percent distribution requirement and may or may not further the foundation's mission.

5. Donor-Advised Fund (DAF)

Donor-advised funds (DAFs) are a popular vehicle for wealthy individuals to make tax-deductible charitable donations. Individuals can use one or more DAFs and advise DAFs to make investments or to select a third-party investment advisor. An impact investment fund can establish a relationship with a DAF. Like foundations, DAFs may make grants, PRIs, MRIs, and traditional investments.

---

23. Treas. Reg. §53.4945-5(b)(4). See Thomson Reuters Foundation and Morrison & Foerster LLP, *supra* note 9, 62, http://www.trust.org/contentAsset/raw-data/171b5a61-eb36-43d9-8049-7cebe575491f/file.

6. Examples

The Rockefeller Foundation is a nonprofit, 501(c)(3) tax-exempt private foundation. The Rockefeller Foundation maintains assets in excess of $4 billion and provides grants and makes investments in furtherance of its mission to expand opportunities for poor or vulnerable people and to help ensure that globalization's benefits are more widely shared. In addition to traditionally grant-making, the Rockefeller Foundation is also committed to use of PRIs. For instance, the Rockefeller Foundation's Zero Gap initiative intends to seed blended capital vehicles using PRI funds to help address the UN Sustainable Development Goals. For more information, please see https://www.rockefellerfoundation.org/our-work/initiatives/innovative-finance/.

The ImpactAssets Giving Fund is an impact investment-focused DAF. The Giving Fund accepts tax-deductible contributions of cash or securities and then permits the donor to advise how such contributions are deployed as impact investments—options include public and private debt and equity investments as well as directed grants. For more information, please see http://www.impactassets.org/our_products/giving_fund.

C. Hybrid Funds

Hybrid funds, or investment vehicles that aggregate nonprofit and for-profit assets with the goal of financing social enterprises, are a growing development in impact investing. These funds take a variety of forms, but at a high level, they require adherence to the tax-exempt purpose of the nonprofit while generating investment opportunities for for-profit investors. However, given the prohibitions on improper private benefit and private inurement, these funds are complicated structures that require careful consideration.

1. Benefits

The principal benefit of hybrid fund structures is that they can be used to aggregate nonprofit and for-profit capital, which can be in a blended pool structure (combining all capital into a single investment fund used for the same purpose) or a stacked deck structure (establishing a tiered fund of concessionary nonprofit capital and market-return capital). Nonprofit capital can be in the form of grants, PRIs, MRIs, and traditional investment. As discussed in greater detail above, if the nonprofit is providing grant or PRI funding, then there are strict rules around how the capital can be used, with less constraints around the use of MRI or traditional investment funds.

Other major benefits of a hybrid fund are that the nonprofit can provide an important advisory role to the for-profit in terms of impact assessment and reporting, which is required for PRI investments and standard practice for MRI investments and nonprofit funding generally. In addition, the inclusion of a nonprofit can also provide significant credibility in the impact investing marketplace, demonstrating a dedication to mission over (or in alignment with) financial returns. The combination of these attributes offers a hybrid fund unique opportunities to influence the market by seeding the pipeline of investment-ready enterprises that may attract market-return investors.

2. Role of the Nonprofit

The nonprofit can play a variety of roles in a hybrid fund structure. At the most basic level, it can simply be an advisor to the fund manager, counseling the fund on impact assessment and providing market and sector guidance. The nonprofit can also be a limited partner of the hybrid fund if it provides capital to the fund. If that is the case, then the fund will have certain limits, in particular around the types of investments it makes and how returns are structured. The nonprofit may also be the general partner itself, tasked with the management of the hybrid fund's operations, which is often coupled with the nonprofit as a limited partner. In each scenario, the nonprofit must carefully monitor how its assets are being used to ensure that it is not improperly benefiting the private parties involved and corporate blocker entities may need to be used to protect the tax-exempt status of the nonprofit.

3. Potential Issues and Trends

One key issue that arises in a hybrid fund structure is private benefit and private inurement. With respect to the first, a nonprofit cannot use its assets (which are held in public trust) to benefit a private party in a manner that does not fulfill its tax-exempt purpose. In a hybrid fund situation, a nonprofit cannot provide capital to an investment fund with for-profit limited partners if the nonprofit's funds are being used as loss capital or to subsidize the for-profit investors. However, a nonprofit can use its assets to invest in companies that are furthering the nonprofit's tax-exempt purpose. For this reason, it is critical that the nonprofit maintains control over how investments are made.

As with for-profit impact funds, hybrid funds also may be set up as evergreen funds to pursue impact outside of a typical ten-year venture capital fund structure. Hybrid funds also increasingly use compensation, specifically carry, to incentivize the managers of funds to pursue maximum impact.

IV. IMPACT MEASUREMENT AND REPORTING

One of the enduring challenges faced by the impact investment sector is how impact returns are measured, reported, and verified. Because the impact investment cuts across sectors and impact is measured differently by each investor, many investors have their own bespoke reporting processes and metrics. However, a number of important standards and corporate governance requirements have emerged to streamline and normalize impact reporting procedures and tools.

A. ESG Factors for Existing Public Companies

Publicly traded corporations in the United States and overseas already provide disclosures related to environmental, social, and governance (ESG) issues. U.S. corporations are required by law to disclose material risks to their businesses, which often include social and environmental risks, in their annual (10-K) and quarterly (10-Q) filings with Securities and Exchange Commission (SEC).[24] Some companies also issue voluntary ESG reporting, often using the Global Reporting Initiative[25] or another third-party standard. In addition, new U.S. Department of Labor guidance for ERISA plan fiduciaries noted that such fiduciaries should consider ESG factors when such factors reasonably impact an investment's financial return or risk profile and may consider such factors as tie-breakers when deciding between investment alternatives that are otherwise equal in terms of risk and return.[26]

B. Integrated Reporting

A growing number of companies provide integrated reporting, wherein they include additional, non-mandatory ESG-related disclosures within their mandatory financial reporting, rather than issuing a separate ESG report.

A number of organizations have been formed to research and disseminate information on, and standards for, best-practice integrated reporting. These include the Task Force on Climate-related Disclosures (TFCD)[27]; the Sustainability Accounting Standards Board (SASB),[28] which seeks to develop sustainability accounting standards comparable to the GAAP for financial accounting; and the International Integrated Reporting Council (IIRC),[29] which also develops standards for integrated reporting. Some stock exchanges now require integrated reporting for companies listed on their exchanges. The Long-Term Stock Exchange (LTSE), an organization formed in 2015, is promoting listing standards for U.S. companies pursuing an initial public offering and is focused on encouraging shareholders, directors, and managers to pursue long-term goals, including addressing community, diversity, and environmental issues.[30]

C. New Corporate Forms

A number of U.S. states have created new types of corporate organizational entities with structural features intended to promote the balancing of profitability and social mission (see chapter 12). These include benefit corporations, social purpose corporations (SPCs), and the Delaware public benefit corporation (PBC). In many states, benefit corporations and SPCs are required to make annual public disclosures relating to their pursuit of social mission. PBCs are required to make similar disclosures to shareholders and are permitted, but not required, to make them public.[31] Furthermore, many companies that are certified B Corps provide mission-related reporting in order to adhere to the B Corp standard developed by B Labs, a nonprofit, third-party certification organization.[32]

---

24. *See, e.g.*, https://www.sec.gov/rules/interp/2010/33-9106.pdf.
25. *See* www.globalreporting.org.
26. https://media2.mofo.com/documents/151112departmentoflaborclarifieserisa.pdf.
27. *See* https://www.fsb-tcfd.org/.
28. *See* https://www.sasb.org/.
29. *See* http://integratedreporting.org/.
30. *See* https://ltse.com/listings.
31. *See* Thomson Reuters Foundation and Morrison & Foerster LLP, *supra* note 9, 61–103, http://www.trust.org/contentAsset/raw-data/171b5a61-eb36-43d9-8049-7cebe575491f/file.
32. *See* https://bcorporation.net/about-b-lab.

D. New Delaware Statutes

Delaware has passed legislation allowing Delaware organizations to become certified as sustainability reporting entities.[33] Certification is voluntary, and the regime is highly flexible, permitting organizations to largely develop their own sustainability reporting regimes.[34] The key requirement of the regime is that the governing body—usually its board of directors or functional equivalent for non-corporate entities—must approve the adoption of specified standards and metrics for assessing the organization's sustainability, and that these standards and metrics must be made public. Reporting-entity status must be renewed annually.[35]

V. SUMMARY AND TAKEAWAYS

As this chapter demonstrates, existing traditional legal tools and structures are evolving at a rapid pace to support the demands of investors and entrepreneurs in the impact investment space. As the impact investment sector continues to grow, legal practitioners have a unique role to play in advising both investors and entrepreneurs on the investment instruments, legal structures, and reporting mechanisms that support the achievement of positive social returns alongside traditional financial returns. In fact, many believe that a focus on ESG factors will yield higher financial returns as compared with traditional investment.

VI. PRACTITIONER'S RESOURCE LIBRARY

A. List of Relevant Organizations

- **Toniic Institute**, a membership-based impact investing platform for exchanging knowledge and investment opportunities: https://www.toniic.com/.
- **NPX**, an impact fund manager that connects nonprofit organizations seeking to raise capital for long-term impact initiatives, private donors seeking to make impact-based donations to nonprofits, and impact investors who are willing to finance upfront risk in exchange for realizing impact-linked returns: https://npxadvisors.com/.
- **CREO Syndicate**, a platform for investors to share experiences, discuss common interests, and explore investment opportunities across the global environmental, sustainability, and impact marketplace: http://creosyndicate.org/.
- **Confluence Philanthropy**, an international platform focused on advancing mission-aligned investing: https://www.confluencephilanthropy.org/.

---

33. *See* https://corpgov.law.harvard.edu/2018/07/15/delawares-voluntary-sustainability-certification-law/.
34. *See* https://corpgov.law.harvard.edu/2018/07/15/delawares-voluntary-sustainability-certification-law/.
35. *See* https://corpgov.law.harvard.edu/2018/07/15/delawares-voluntary-sustainability-certification-law/.

- **Ceres**, a sustainability nonprofit organization working to advance global investments in clean energy and sustainable food and water: https://www.ceres.org/.
- **ImpactAssets**, a facilitator of direct impact investing within DAFs: http://www.impactassets.org/.
- **GIIN**, Global Impact Investing Network, a resource for impact investors regarding reporting and impact investment assessment: https://thegiin.org.
- **Omidyar Network (ON)**: https://www.omidyar.com/sites/default/files/file_archive/Omidyar%20Network%20Approach.pdf.
- **B Lab**: https://bcorporation.net/about-b-lab.
- **Task Force on Climate-Related Financial Disclosures**: https://www.fsb-tcfd.org/.
- **Carbon Disclosure Project and Carbon Tracker**: https://www.carbontracker.org/.
- **Sustainability Accounting Standard Board**: https://www.sasb.org/.
- **Integrated Reporting**: http://integratedreporting.org/.
- **LTSE**: https://ltse.com/listings.

B. Articles and Reports

- Global Impact Investing Network, "2018 Annual Impact Investor Survey," https://thegiin.org/assets/2018_GIIN_Annual_Impact_Investor_Survey_webfile.pdf.
- Susan Mac Cormac, Morrison & Foerster LLP, "Preserving and Enhancing Impact: Corporate Forms," Presentation at Impact.tech, October 2016, https://www.slideshare.net/Impactdottech/preserving-and-enhancing-impact-corporate-forms.
- Thomson Reuters Foundation and Morrison & Foerster LLP, "Which Legal Structure Is Right for My Social Enterprise: A Guide to Establishing a Social Enterprise in the United States," http://www.trust.org/contentAsset/raw-data/171b5a61-eb36-43d9-8049-7cebe575491f/file.
- International Capital Market Association, "Green Bond Principles," https://www.icmagroup.org/green-social-and-sustainability-bonds/green-bond-principles-gbp/.
- Guarav Sharma, "Global Green Bond Issuance Set to Eclipse $250B in 2018," *Forbes*, February 1, 2018, https://www.forbes.com/sites/gauravsharma/2018/02/01/global-green-bond-issuance-set-to-eclipse-250b-in-2018/#ee0a40c56693.
- Government of the United Kingdom, "Social Impact Bonds," November 16, 2012, https://www.gov.uk/guidance/social-impact-bonds.
- Emily Gustafsson-Wright and Izzy Boggild-Jones, "Paying for Social Outcomes: A Review of the Global Impact Bond Market," Brookings, January 17, 2018, https://www.brookings.edu/blog/education-plus-development/2018/01/17/paying-for-social-outcomes-a-review-of-the-global-impact-bond-market-in-2017/.

- Kristen Hiensch, "Impact Investing—Fund Mechanisms to Incentivize Impact," August 16, 2016, https://impact.mofo.com/measuring/impact-investing-fund-mechanisms-to-incentivize-impact/.
- James Stewart, "Ford Foundation Is an Unlikely Convert to 'Impact' Investing," *New York Times*, April 13, 2017, https://www.nytimes.com/2017/04/13/business/ford-foundation-mission-investment.html.
- Susan Mac Cormac, Paul Borden, Kristin Hiensch, and Jesse Finfrock, "Department of Labor Clarifies ERISA Fiduciary Requirements with Respect to Economically Targeted Investments and Environmental, Social, and Governance Goals," Morrison & Foerster LLP, November 12, 2015, https://media2.mofo.com/documents/151112departmentoflaborclarifieserisa.pdf.
- John Zeberkiewicz, "Delaware's Voluntary Sustainability Certification Law," Harvard Law School Forum on Corporate Governance and Financial Regulation, July 15, 2018, https://corpgov.law.harvard.edu/2018/07/15/delawares-voluntary-sustainability-certification-law/.

Chapter 12

Alternative Legal Entities

Susan H. Mac Cormac, Jesse M. Finfrock, and Benjamin T.R. Fox

I. INTRODUCTION

Alternative legal entities for social enterprises and impact investors have gained significant attention and acceptance in recent years, and they offer many new tools for aligning social or environmental impact and financial returns. However, before discussing alternative legal entities, it is important to note that the ordinary corporation and LLC forms in many states, and particularly in Delaware, offer a variety of means to preserve an organization's focus on a social mission, some of which exist by default and some of which can be included in charters, financing documents, or other agreements at the entity's discretion.

For corporations, these mechanisms include charter provisions, constituency statutes, the business judgment rule,[1] voting rights and shareholder agreements, and intellectual property licensing. With respect to charter provisions, ordinary corporations are permitted to include mission-related provisions in their corporate charters. However, where these provisions conflict with the traditional fiduciary duties of directors and officers, all things being equal, fiduciary duties will prevail.[2] With respect to constituency statutes, 31 states (but neither Delaware nor California) have legislation in place that permit or require a corporation to consider factors such as its impact on employees, society, and the community in its decision-making. However, constituency statutes have limited legal enforceability and, like mission-related charter provisions, cannot override traditional

---

1. *See* chapter 2.
2. *See* Susan Mac Cormac, Morrison & Foerster LLP, "Preserving and Enhancing Impact: Corporate Forms," Presentation at Impact.tech (Oct. 2016), slides 6–7, https://www.slideshare.net/Impactdottech/preserving-and-enhancing-impact-corporate-forms.

corporate fiduciary duties.[3] With respect to the business judgment rule, under Delaware law, the business judgment rule functions as a presumption that the decisions of directors are in the best interests of the corporation unless a specific breach of fiduciary duty can be shown by a party challenging the directors' decisions.[4] Fiduciary duties do *not* mandate that all management decisions be made for the purpose of maximizing the immediate value of the corporation's shares.[5] Consequently, the business judgment rule provides Delaware corporate directors and officers with significant latitude to pursue mission-aligned activities that are in the best interests of the shareholders and the corporation, e.g., activities that improve both the corporation's brand and its long-term profitability.[6] With respect to voting rights and shareholder agreements, ordinary Delaware corporations can choose to include special voting provisions in their articles of incorporation, including requirements that a supermajority of voting shares, or certain classes of shares, approve specified fundamental decisions. The shareholders of a corporation can also enter into voting agreements among themselves that specify similar requirements.[7] Finally, with respect to intellectual property (IP) licensing, where valuable IP is important to a corporation's pursuit of its mission, a structure can be created wherein the IP is held by a mission-aligned founder or affiliated nonprofit entity and licensed to the corporation. Such licensing agreement may include provisions whereby the licensor can increase royalty rates or terminate the license if the licensee violates certain terms of the agreement or acts inconsistent with the prescribed mission of the corporation.[8]

These strategies for preserving mission in an ordinary corporation are viable where the corporation is conducting normal business operations. However, their effectiveness may be compromised if the sale of the corporation appears imminent and inevitable. Under such circumstances, the *Revlon* doctrine may require that the directors maximize shareholder value by selling to a bidder willing to forgo mission but pay the highest price or face shareholder activism.[9]

In addition to corporations, limited liability companies (LLCs) in most states are specifically designed to permit a high degree of contractual flexibility. In Delaware, for example, mechanisms for preserving mission in an ordinary LLC in the articles of organization or operation agreement include: explicit prioritization of mission over return to investors and elimination of traditional fiduciary duties—note, however, that some

---

3. *See* Thomson Reuters Foundation and Morrison & Foerster LLP, "Which Legal Structure Is Right for My Social Enterprise: A Guide to Establishing a Social Enterprise in the United States," May 2016, revised version forthcoming in 2019, 40, https://www.trust.org/contentAsset/raw-data/1b34bbc3-de52-477a-adae-850a56c2aabe/file.
4. *See* Susan Mac Cormac, Morrison & Foerster LLP, *supra* note 2, slide.
5. *See* M. Todd Henderson, *Everything Old Is New Again: Lessons from Dodge v. Ford Motor Company*, U. Chicago John M. Olin Law & Economics Working Paper No. 373, 27 (2007).
6. *See* Susan Mac Cormac and Heather Haney, *New Corporate Forms: One Viable Solution to Advancing Environmental Sustainability*, 24 J. App. Corp. Fin. 49, 50 (2012); *see also* Shlensky v. Wrigley, 237 N.E.2d 776 (Ill. App. 1968).
7. *See* Susan Mac Cormac, Morrison & Foerster LLP, *supra* note 2, slide 5.
8. *See* Susan Mac Cormac, Morrison & Foerster LLP, *supra* note 2, slide 8.
9. *See* Revlon, Inc. v. MacAndrews & Forbes Holdings, Inc., 506 A.2d 173 (Del. 1986).

states, including California, do not permit LLCs to eliminate certain traditional fiduciary duties by contract; waterfall structures requiring that profits be distributed to affiliated nonprofits or mission-aligned members before other investors; guaranteed management roles for mission-aligned members; membership class voting and protective provisions related to mission; and mission-related "tag-along," "drag-along," and change-of-control approval rights for mission-aligned members.[10]

II. OVERVIEW

A. Understanding the Driving Forces behind the Proliferation of the New Corporate Forms

Although there are many ways that social enterprises can embed an impact focus into traditional corporate forms such as corporations and LLCs, or integrate commercial operations into traditional nonprofit forms, traditional structures of for-profit and not-for-profit entities do not always effectively meet the unique needs of social entrepreneurs and impact investors. For instance, increasingly, founders, employees, and consumers alike are pushing companies to promote their social or environmental efforts, to embrace a social enterprise entity, to secure a "B Corp" certification,[11] and/or to establish a relationship with a nonprofit, all of which can bolster the credibility of companies. In addition, young investors are driving change in investor circles as they merge their philanthropic efforts with their investment activities, and more established and mainstream investors are increasingly seeing the financial benefit of a focus on positive social and/or environmental impact. In response, entrepreneurs, investors, and their legal counsel are innovating novel hybrid legal structures. Further, a growing number of states have created new types of entities with the goal of helping enterprises access a wider variety of financing options while pursuing both profitability and purpose.

B. Marrying Nonprofits with For-Profits (Hybrid or Tandem Structures)

Hybrid or tandem entities, where separate nonprofits and for-profits operate synergistically with shared ownership, governance, or assets, have existed in a variety of forms for decades. One classic early example is a corporate foundation, which may engage in charitable distribution of the affiliated corporation's products. Another example is

---

10. *See* Chapter 11.
11. *See* Chapter 4. A benefit corporation is a legal entity, while "B Corp" is a certification (similar to organic or fair trade), which is promulgated by the nonprofit B Lab (https://bcorporation.net/about-b-lab). Other third-party reporting organizations include Global Reporting Initiative (GRI) (http://www.globalreporting.org), Ceres (http://www.ceres.org), and the International Organization for Standardization (https://www.iso.org/iso-26000-social-responsibility.html). In addition, SustainAbility's report "Rate the Raters" includes further resources on reporting organizations (http://sustainability.com/our-work/reports/rate-the-raters-phase-two).

for-profit spinout from a nonprofit university. Under this model, the university develops valuable intellectual property, which it believes is commercializable, and then it spins out a for-profit operating entity to which it licenses the intellectual property, often in return for initial equity. Generally, the university would not assign or transfer the intellectual property due to the complicated and expensive process of valuing and transferring nonprofit assets into a for-profit. Rather, the license of intellectual property and equity ownership would create a hybrid structure given the close relationship of entities.

Hybrid structures are gaining popularity because of the following reasons: substantial flexibility in the types of activities in which each entity can engage, the ability to raise both investment and philanthropic capital, credibility in impact circles by including the nonprofit arm to engage in charitable activities, and cost-shifting strategies related to nonprofit activities that may benefit the for-profit's business and operation (provided that appropriate protections are built in to avoid private benefit and private inurement). Specifically, each of these structures creates complicated issues, particularly concerning protection of the nonprofit entity's tax-exempt status—for instance, monitoring for unrelated business income tax, protecting against private benefit and private inurement, ensuring that nonprofit activities and the use of nonprofit assets are in furtherance of the nonprofit's tax-exempt purpose, and protecting directors from exposure to personal liability. Although they are popular, and receiving significant attention at the moment, due to the complexity involved in structuring and managing hybrid entities, entrepreneurs are usually better served initially establishing a single entity (typically a for-profit) and growing into the hybrid as their business model matures.

C. Overview of the New Types of Alternative Legal Entities—L3C, SPC/PBC, Benefit Corporations, Benefit LLCs

While a dual profit-mission mandate is permissible in certain traditional entity structures, the primary purpose of new organizational forms is to make a dual focus mandatory, to varying degrees, for the organization. These new forms include social purpose corporations (SPC), public benefit corporations (PBC), benefit corporations, low-profit limited liability companies (L3C), benefit limited liability companies (BLLC), and public benefit limited liability companies (PBLLC).

However, alternative legal entities face a number of challenges. They are not available in all states (although it is possible to incorporate in a state with such a statute and register as a foreign entity in another, albeit with additional costs and administrative responsibilities), and the nature of their legal rights and obligations varies significantly among states. Many state statutes creating benefit corporations and L3Cs are not well integrated with existing state statutory law regulating traditional for-profit entities, leading to potential conflicts and liability for management and investors. Furthermore, the novelty of many alternative forms means that there is not an established body of case law upon which entrepreneurs and investors can rely when interpreting statutes and regulations to make business decisions. There is, for example, ambiguity in many states regarding the fiduciary duties of officers and directors of alternative legal entities (see below). Alternative legal entities do not receive federal tax benefits as a feature of their organizational form—they are taxed as either traditional corporations or traditional limited liability companies.

Furthermore, some of these organizational forms were designed to simplify access by for-profit entities to equity investments by private foundations, in particular L3Cs, in part by streamlining compliance with the rules of private foundation investments.[12] However, the effectiveness of this effort in practice is subject to debate among practitioners, and critics have voiced concerns that some new structures may create a false impression among private foundations that the organization's legal structure can substitute for legally mandated analysis. Consequently, these structures have not facilitated foundation investment to the degree that their advocates originally intended.[13]

III. HYBRID (TANDEM) ENTITIES[14]

A. Overview

Hybrid structures come in all shapes and sizes depending on the specific needs of the entrepreneurs and investors. The most common forms of structures are: (i) a contractual relationship between a for-profit and a nonprofit; (ii) a nonprofit as a minority investor in a for-profit; (iii) a for-profit as a wholly owned subsidiary of a nonprofit; (iv) a nonprofit with a for-profit as a sole member; and (v) nonprofit investment into a for-profit impact fund.[15] The form with which most lawyers are familiar is a for-profit entity which establishes a related nonprofit—the typical large corporation (or law firm) foundation. However, for some social entrepreneurs, it may be preferable to start with a nonprofit and spin out commercializable activities into for-profit operations or companies, which in turn can help drive revenue back to the nonprofit and provide a steady funding stream and alternative to grant funding. The hybrid structure that is best for a given situation largely depends on two key factors: the source of funding and the functions of each entity.

---

12. In addition to traditional investments intended to make financial returns, private foundations may make "program-related investments," which are subject to strict IRS rules (see chapter 11 for more information).

13. *See* Thomson Reuters Foundation and Morrison & Foerster LLP, *supra* note 3, 62–63. *So You Want to Start a Social Enterprise?*, A NEW YORK LAWYERS FOR THE PUBLIC INTEREST COMMUNITY GUIDE (Oct. 2015), https://www.americanbar.org/content/dam/aba/directories/pro_bono_clearinghouse/ejc_2016_104.authcheckdam.pdf; *Operating in Two Worlds: Tandem Structures in Social Enterprise*, Ingrid Mittermaier and Joey Neugart. THE PRACTICAL TAX LAWYER, Fall 2011; *Using New Hybrid Legal Forms: Three Case Studies, Four Important Questions, and a Bunch of Analysis*, Robert A. Wexler and David A. Levitt, 69 EXEMPT ORG. TAX REV. 63 (Jan. 2012).

14. *Id.*

15. Examples include Medicines360 (http://www.medicines360.org/), Kepler's Books (https://www.keplers.com/), Year-Up (https://www.yearup.org/), Public Radio Exchange (PRX) (https://www.prx.org/), Omidyar Network (https://www.omidyar.com/), Salesforce (https://www.salesforce.com/), Crisis Text Line (https://www.crisistextline.org/), and Pacific Community Ventures (https://www.pacificcommunityventures.org/).

B. Benefits of Hybrid Structures

There are myriad practical reasons to form a hybrid entity, but the mantra should remain: Form follows function. For instance, social entrepreneurs may see an opportunity to raise capital from a variety of sources that include return-seeking investors (that may want to invest in a for-profit business), philanthropic organizations (that would be able to fund either a nonprofit or a for-profit), or government finance organizations (that might prefer to fund nonprofit entities). In addition, a hybrid structure provides substantial flexibility in the types of activities that can be engaged in at the various entities; in fact, to be successful and avoid liability, the nonprofit and for-profit must perform different functions or serve different markets (as discussed below). While these may be the two most important reasons, there are several other factors that often drive social entrepreneurs to consider hybrid entities, including creating mission lock, generating credibility in stakeholder communities, and offsetting costs.

Impact-oriented social entrepreneurs often form hybrids to lock in the mission of the for-profit. This can be achieved by assigning or maintaining a valuable piece of intellectual property at the nonprofit, with a license to the for-profit to use the intellectual property. The licensing agreement may then contain provisions whereby if the licensee violates certain agreement terms or acts inconsistently with the prescribed mission of the corporation or operates in a way that runs contrary to the tax-exempt purpose of the nonprofit, the licensor can either increase royalty rates or terminate the license. However, it is important to consider the impact on valuation or M&A transactions (i.e., the "spurn-out").[16]

Nonprofits must remain committed to furthering their social or environmental tax-exempt purpose, and this simple requirement generates credibility within their stakeholder communities. In particular, this provides assurance that the nonprofit is not operating to benefit private individuals or maximize revenues. Because of this, a for-profit that aligns itself with a credible nonprofit can benefit from the brand and position the nonprofit holds in the marketplace and broader community.

A hybrid entity can also benefit from certain cost-shifting strategies related to nonprofit activities that benefit the for-profit's business or operations. Note, however, that in the case of research, the nonprofit's research products should be published or otherwise made public to avoid a private inurement issue (as discussed below). In the case of other services provided by the nonprofit, the for-profit must pay at least fair market value.

C. Legal and Practical Issues with Hybrid Structures

Despite the benefits, there are many complicated issues and risks that arise when structuring and managing a hybrid, particularly if a nonprofit holds equity in a for-profit that has other outside investors and if there are overlapping officers and directors. The complications are such that forming a hybrid is generally expensive, as doing so often

---

16. *See* Susan Mac Cormac, Morrison & Foerster LLP, *supra* note 2, slide 6.

requires multi-stakeholder negotiations, generally more than one law firm, and often engaging independent accountants and valuation experts. Similarly, maintaining a hybrid after formation creates ongoing compliance efforts and additional costs, and potentially demands the engagement of a sophisticated chief financial officer (CFO).

Perhaps the most critical issue facing hybrids is the protection and maintenance of the nonprofit's tax-exempt status and the avoidance of excise taxes. Tax exemption can be jeopardized if the nonprofit's commercial activities are too substantial, if the nonprofit's assets are being used to benefit private individuals (known as private benefit or private inurement), if the entities fail to maintain separate functions between the nonprofit and the for-profit, and/or if the nonprofit strays from the pursuit of its tax-exempt purpose and activities. In some cases, if the Internal Revenue Service determines private inurement has occurred, then the entity can be required to pay substantial excise taxes.[17] Other key issues nonprofits must consider include: protecting against the unintentional generation of Unrelated Business Taxable Income (UBTI); exposing directors to personal liability; guarding against "mission drift" or the failure of the nonprofit to further its tax-exempt purpose; establishing the appropriate governance, oversight, and control mechanisms; ensuring that each entity is able to fundraise adequately so that one entity does not languish; considering whether the for-profit should be a corporation or a pass-through entity for tax purposes; maintaining the branding and credibility of the nonprofit; and implementing an employee structure that will endure over time without causing issues with respect to reasonable compensation limits of the nonprofit.

D. General Requirements and Best Practices for Hybrid Structures

To mitigate the risks and issues related to hybrid formation and operations, a variety of best practices should be considered and implemented. In each of the various hybrid models, the nonprofit, for-profit, and investors must take into account various considerations as outlined below.

First, the entities must negotiate all transactions on an "arm's length" basis. This becomes a potential issue when the directors and officers of the nonprofit are also set to become the directors and officers of the new for-profit. Initial high-level talks involving these persons are acceptable, but executives who are transitioning or sharing roles between the two entities should largely be limited to assisting with development of the business plan and other work unaffiliated to the inter-entity relationship. To negotiate at arm's length, at a minimum: (a) each entity should be represented by independent legal counsel; and (b) it is necessary to appoint at least two disinterested directors to the governing bodies of each of nonprofit and for-profit. Even better would be to establish standing special committees of disinterested directors for each entity to negotiate a term sheet, compensation, and other material matters, approve transactions, and generally oversee the relationship after it has been established. Note that a director is disinterested with respect to an entity if she or he has no financial interest or other material relationship with such entity.

---

17. If the nonprofit is a private foundation, additional federal tax law restrictions and potential excise tax penalties may apply. These will not be discussed here.

Second, both entities must track and document the flow of funds, the flow of services and resources, and the flow of intellectual property between the nonprofit and the for-profit. Although in many cases, one entity can make loans to the other, such loans may be prohibited if they qualify as self-dealing transactions under state or federal law. If permitted, interest on loans should be at market rate, and depending on the hybrid structure, the interest on loans may be UBTI to the nonprofit. Other revenue flows include dividends on the equity held by the nonprofit in a for-profit subsidiary and royalties paid pursuant to license agreements (which also may be UBTI depending on the relationship). Furthermore, it is good practice to hire a sophisticated CFO and finance team to manage the relationship and the flow of funds, assets, services, and resources. The CFO, directors, and other officers must ensure that: (a) the for-profit always pays at least "fair market value" rates to the nonprofit for services, resources, and assets provided by the nonprofit to the for-profit; and (b) the for-profit pays at least "fair value" to the nonprofit for any nonprofit assets that are transferred or assigned to the for-profit. Note that if the nonprofit is deemed to be generating revenue from commercial activities that are not substantially related to its tax-exempt purpose, then the nonprofit will be required to pay tax on that income. Further, if that unrelated business activity and revenue become more than insubstantial, such activity will jeopardize the nonprofit's tax exemption. There is no bright-line threshold for this risk, but a rule of thumb of practitioners is that unrelated income should not exceed approximately 20 percent of the nonprofit's income; if that level is approached, the nonprofit should consider moving that activity to a taxable corporate subsidiary in order to protect the nonprofit's tax exemption. Indeed, this is a common reason for a nonprofit to create a corporate subsidiary.[18]

Third, the hybrid must monitor for unreasonable compensation at executive levels. Under state law, directors of the nonprofit can be personally fined and barred from being involved in nonprofits in the future if they allow or enable the nonprofit's assets to be used for the benefit of private individuals. Under federal law, directors and executives may be subject to penalty excise taxes if they receive excessive benefits from a nonprofit.[19] One area in which this issue arises is around compensation for executives at the nonprofit, which is limited to a reasonable level as compared to other similarly situated nonprofits (unlike in the for-profit sector). For directors and officers who are employed by both the nonprofit and the for-profit, the compensation such persons derive

---

18. *See, e.g., Does My Nonprofit Need to Pay Tax? Understanding Unrelated Business Income Tax*, Dec. 2011, https://nonprofitquarterly.org/2011/12/25/does-my-nonprofit-need-to-pay-tax-understanding-unrelated-business-income-tax/. Note, however, that much lower thresholds (even 5 percent) can be problematic if the activity or revenue is significant. From the IRS perspective, 5 percent of a $1 million charity may not raise exemption concerns, but 5 percent of a $100 million charity might, especially if that activity showed continued or rapid growth.

19. I.R.C. §4958. In extreme cases, allowing nonprofit assets to be used for the benefit of individuals or other entities can ultimately jeopardize the nonprofit's tax exemption. If the nonprofit is a private foundation, a transaction with or compensation to "disqualified person" may be prohibited and result in excise taxes, unless it comes within a self-dealing exception. See IRC §§4941, 4946.

at the nonprofit can be aggregated together with the compensation they receive at the for-profit, including equity compensation, for purposes of this analysis. To avoid this pitfall, compensation arrangements should be negotiated by disinterested individuals, the entities should be represented by separate legal counsel, certain board review procedures should be followed, and an independent valuation analysis may need to be conducted.[20] Nonexecutive employees can create additional issues, and the founders should determine early on where the employees will reside. There are dual employment models (in which employees work for both entities) or employee "leasing" models (where one entity employs all personnel and then leases them to the other entity). The reason this is important to consider is that over time, a "brain drain" effect occurs in which employees at a nonprofit will gradually shift over into the for-profit in order to benefit from high-pay and equity incentives, leaving behind a nonprofit that struggles with staff retention or low morale.

Fourth, documentation governing the relationship between the entities may take the form of inter-entity agreements, including an intellectual property license agreement, services agreement, or resource-sharing agreement. These agreements should be drafted in such a way as to be easily refreshed and amended as the relationship between the entities evolves over time. Furthermore, it is critical to maintain a clear distinction between the function of nonprofit and the function of for-profit such that the entities avoid selling competing goods and services. For instance, a distinction might be that the for-profit sells a product at market prices in certain geographical regions, which provides revenue to back to the nonprofit, and the nonprofit distributes that product for free in other geographical regions. These distinctions can be included in the inter-entity agreements.

In addition, if the nonprofit is deemed to be generating revenue from commercial activities that are unrelated to its tax-exempt purpose, then the nonprofit will be required to pay tax on that income. Finally, if the nonprofit is a private foundation, then such a nonprofit (together with its substantial contributors, directors, officers, and their family members and businesses) cannot in the aggregate own more than 20 percent of an active trade or business, with certain exceptions.[21]

E. Hybrid Fund Structures

Increasingly, there is interest among impact investors, particularly private foundations, to form hybrid investment funds. To date, these have largely remained small scale; however, there are several active negotiations under way to create large-scale funds. These structures are discussed in chapter 11.

---

20. *See, e.g.*, *Operating in Two Worlds: Tandem Structures in Social Enterprise*, https://www.adlercolvin.com/wp-content/uploads/2017/12/Operating-in-Two-Worlds-Tandem-Structures-in-Social-Enterprise-00403192xA3536.pdf.

21. *See Excess Business Holdings and 4943(g): A New and Narrow (but Important) Exception*, Feb. 9, 2018, https://www.adlercolvin.com/wp-content/themes/adlercolvin/pdf/Excess-Business-Holdings-and-4943g-A-New-and-Narrow-but-Important-Exception.pdf.

IV. FOR-PROFIT ENTITIES

A. Overview

1. History

Vermont became the first state to introduce an alternative for-profit legal entity intended to benefit social enterprises when it passed its L3C statute in April 2008.[22] Maryland passed the first benefit corporation statute in April 2008.[23] California introduced the SPA (originally named a flexible purpose corporation) when the legislature passed the Corporate Flexibility Act in 2011, as amended by the Social Purpose Corporation Act in 2014.[24] Delaware passed legislation creating its PBC in July 2013[25] and most recently enacted its PBLLC statute as of August 2018. Today, the majority of social enterprises using one of these forms are incorporated in Delaware.

2. Current State

As of August 2018, 33 states[26] had enacted benefit corporation or benefit company statutes, including Delaware's PBC statute and PBLLC statute. Of the 33 states, 8 states had passed L3C statutes; 5 states had passed SPC statutes; and 3 states had passed BLLC statutes.[27] In total, 38 states have created at least one alternative legal entity targeted at social enterprises, and 7 additional states are considering creating at least one of these types of alternative entity.[28] However, note that the names of these entities can be misleading; for instance, some benefit corporations resemble the PBC while others are different breeds altogether.

B. Benefit Corporation

1. Model Legislation

Benefit corporations are for-profit entities.[29] Some state benefit corporation statutes are based on model legislation promulgated by B Labs, a nonprofit, third-party certification organization. The key features of the model legislation are

- a requirement of adherence to a general public purpose, which is generally defined as pursuing a material positive impact on society and the environment,

---

22. *See* Elizabeth Schmidt, *Vermont's Social Hybrid Pioneers: Early Observations and Questions to Ponder*, 35 (1) VT. L. REV., 163–209 (Fall 2010).
23. *See* http://www.csrwire.com/press_releases/29332-Maryland-First-State-in-Union-to-Pass-Benefit-Corporation-Legislation.
24. *See* https://www.ftb.ca.gov/Archive/professionals/taxnews/2014/October/02.shtml.
25. *See* https://news.delaware.gov/2013/07/17/governor-markell-signs-public-benefit-corporation-legislation/.
26. "States" incudes the District of Columbia.
27. There is some disagreement among practitioners as to how to categorize these entities. For example, the Social Enterprise Law Tracker describes Colorado's legislation as a benefit corporation, not an SPC. However, while CO's bill may be based on the benefit corporation model legislation, it deviates substantially so as to be more similar to the DE PBC.
28. *See* https://www.socentlawtracker.org.
29. Example is Patagonia (https://www.patagonia.com).

taken as a whole, as assessed against a third-party standard, from the business and operations of a benefit corporation;
- an option to include a specific public purpose in the benefit corporation's charter or articles of incorporation. Generally, the benefit corporation may adopt one or more of the following seven purposes: (i) providing beneficial products or services to low-income or underserved individuals or communities; (ii) promoting economic opportunity beyond job creation; (iii) preserving the environment; (iv) improving human health; (v) promoting the arts, sciences, or knowledge; (vi) increasing capital flow to public benefit entities; and (vii) accomplishing other particular benefits for society or the environment;
- a requirement that the benefit corporation's directors, in discharging their duties, consider the interests of the benefit corporation's shareholders, as well as the interests of its customers, its employees and communities and the employees and communities of its subsidiaries and suppliers, and the local and global environment;
- a requirement that amendments to the benefit corporation's specific public purpose be adopted by a two-thirds vote of the shareholders entitled to vote on the matter; and
- a requirement that the benefit corporation issue to shareholders an annual benefit report including
  - a narrative description of the general and specific public benefits created by the benefit corporation during the year and how they were achieved, as well as any circumstances that hindered the achievement of benefits;
- an evaluation of the benefit corporation's social and environmental performance during the year, prepared in accordance with a third-party standard selected by the benefit corporation and applied consistently with benefit reports issued in prior years, along with an explanation of any inconsistency.[30]

However, since the model benefit corporation code was developed, states have increasingly gone their own way and adopted statutes that deviate significantly from the model desired outcome, and the model language itself has seen several revisions.

2. Benefits

The benefit corporation form offers several advantages for a social enterprise. Benefit corporation status brands an entity as having a social purpose beyond profit maximization, which may provide access to third parties, consumers, strategic partners, investors, and other stakeholders whose interests are aligned with that purpose. For entrepreneurs and investors focused on creating general public benefits (in contrast to a specific public benefit), the benefit corporation form may help to lock in that mission. Third-party certifications may also provide some level of certainty to potential investors and strategic partners that the benefit corporation is actually pursuing its stated social purpose, and by design the benefit corporation forms generally synchronize well with

---

30. *See* http://benefitcorp.net/attorneys/model-legislation.

the B Corp certification requirements.[31] In fact, B Lab requires conversion to a benefit corporation or similar form for a company to maintain its license to the B Corp mark.

3. Risks

The benefit corporation form also has risks, including fiduciary conflicts, new shareholder enforcement rights, and issues with scaling.

Some state statutes require that benefit corporations appoint an independent benefit director with special powers and duties related to the preparation of the annual benefit report (as discussed below). Under certain circumstances, the fiduciary duties applicable to a benefit director may conflict with the traditional fiduciary duties applicable to corporate directors generally.[32] It is also not clear to what extent fiduciary duties apply to the pursuit of a general public purpose, but they could potentially be viewed as quite extensive. Furthermore, corporate boards have both substantive and procedural duties, and while a shareholder challenge on substantive grounds falls under the lenient "business judgment rule" (providing substantial deference to the board), a challenge on procedural grounds requires a more strict adherence to formal process.[33] In other words, "an additional procedural duty [lurks] beneath the surface of the benefit corporation statute."[34] As of August 2018, there have been no cases addressing this question, and thus there remains a risk of uncertainty. Finally, embedding into charter documents a long list of social and environmental goals for directors to consider creates a conflict issue of "too many masters" that will ultimately dilute effectiveness and increase liability, particularly given the strength of the traditional duty of loyalty that directors owe to their companies.

Almost all benefit corporation statutes expressly provide for a right of action against directors and officers of benefit corporations for a violation of their duties under the statute (see below). This right of action, most commonly termed a "benefit enforcement proceeding," generally grants certain identified parties, including directors and shareholders, the right to bring direct or derivative claims against directors or officers of a benefit corporation in order to enforce the general or specific public benefit purposes of the benefit corporation and the statutorily defined standards of conduct for the directors and officers. Some states, whether intentionally or by virtue of poor drafting, also allow unrelated third parties to bring benefit enforcement proceedings.[35] If liability protections for directors under the relevant state's law are insufficient, potential directors and officers may be deterred from joining the benefit corporation's board or management team.[36]

---

31. *See* Thomson Reuters Foundation and Morrison & Foerster LLP, *supra* note 3, 78.

32. *See* Thomson Reuters Foundation and Morrison & Foerster LLP, *supra* note 3, 86–87.

33. Jesse Finfrock and Eric Talley, *Social Entrepreneurship and Uncorporations*, 2014 U. ILL. L. REV. 1867 1881–82 (2014), https://scholarship.law.berkeley.edu/facpubs/2453/.

34. Ian Kanig, *Sustainable Capitalism through the Benefit Corporation: Enforcing the Procedural Duty of Consideration to Protect Non-Shareholder Interests*, 64 HASTINGS L.J. 863, 898 (2013).

35. *See, e.g.*, the Connecticut Benefit Corporation Act, https://www.cga.ct.gov/2014/TOB/S/2014SB-00023-R00-SB.htm.

36. *See Model Benefit Corporation Legislation*, version of Apr. 17, 2017, http://benefitcorp.net/sites/default/files/Model%20benefit%20corp%20legislation%20_4_17_17.pdf; Thomson Reuters Foundation and Morrison & Foerster LLP, *supra* note 3, 83–84.

In some cases, the statutory restrictions on pursuit of profit maximization, particularly where benefit enforcement proceedings are allowed and the high shareholder vote threshold required in order to amend a benefit corporation's social purpose, may inhibit a benefit corporation's ability to attract additional investors and strategic partners and thus limit its ability to grow through mergers and acquisitions (M&A) or an initial public offering (IPO).[37]

C. Certain State Differences

1. Benefit Director

As noted above, some state statutes require that benefit corporations appoint a benefit director. Each state that imposes this requirement mandate that the benefit director be independent (as defined by the benefit corporation statute) and provide that a benefit corporation may stipulate additional qualifications for the benefit director in its corporate charter. The benefit director generally has the same powers and duties as ordinary directors, as well as specific powers and duties relating to the preparation of the benefit corporation's annual benefit report. In each state that requires a benefit director, the benefit director must provide, for inclusion in the benefit report, a statement or opinion on whether the benefit corporation acted in accordance with its general and, where applicable, specific public benefit purposes during the year covered by the report and whether the directors and officers of the benefit corporation complied with their respective duties in connection with creating these public benefit during that year. Additionally, if the benefit director believes that the benefit corporation or its directors or officers failed to act in accordance with the public benefit purposes of the benefit corporation, then the statement or opinion must include a description of these failures. Some legal experts believe that such statements will cause the director to breach her or his traditional fiduciary duties. Most states that require the appointment of a benefit director protect the benefit director from personal liability for acts performed in his or her capacity as benefit director, customary exceptions for acts that constitute self-dealing, knowing violations of law, etc., but these protections vary between states.[38]

2. Enforcement Rights

As noted above, nearly all states with benefit corporations provide for benefit enforcement proceedings. In many states, a benefit enforcement proceeding is the only type of action, proceeding, or claim that may be brought or asserted against a benefit corporation or its directors or officers to enforce that state's benefit corporation law. The parties entitled to bring a benefit enforcement proceeding generally include: (i) the benefit corporation itself, (ii) the shareholders of the benefit corporation, (iii) the directors of the benefit corporation, (iv) the holders of at least 5 percent of the stock or other equity ownership of an entity of which the benefit corporation is a subsidiary, or (v) other classes of

---

37. *See* Thomson Reuters Foundation and Morrison & Foerster LLP, *supra* note 3, 87.
38. *See* Thomson Reuters Foundation and Morrison & Foerster LLP, *supra* note 3, 86–87.

individuals specifically identified in the benefit corporation's charter documents; however, there are exceptions to and variations among these enumerated groups in different states. States also provide different degrees of protection from personal liability for corporate directors and officers for acts performed in an official capacity.[39] While this may provide some assurance that the benefit corporation will adhere to its public benefit purposes, it also creates additional risks associated with managing and operating the benefit corporation, including distractions from building the business, dispersed control and decision-making, and conflicting preferences for how to best achieve the entity's public benefit purposes.

3. Social Purpose Corporation (CA, WA, also versions in CO, FL, MI)

Following California, four other states—Washington, Colorado, Florida, and Texas—have introduced some form of SPC that are substantially similar to California.[40]

Like the benefit corporation, the SPC is a for-profit entity that shares many fundamental characteristics with an ordinary corporation.[41] The specific statutory requirements to form and operate an SPC vary by state. The key features of California's SPC statute, for example, include

- a requirement that the SPC's articles of incorporation specify that the organization is dedicated to one or more of the following enumerated special purposes:
    - one or more charitable or public purpose activities that may be carried out by a California nonprofit public benefit corporation; or
    - the purpose of promoting positive effects of, or minimizing adverse effects of, the SPC's activities upon any of (i) the SPC's employees, suppliers, customers, and creditors; (ii) the community and society; or (iii) the environment, provided that the SPC considers the purpose in addition to or together with the financial interests of the shareholders and compliance with legal obligations and takes action consistent with that purpose.
- a requirement that directors and officers of an SPC operate in furtherance of all of the purposes to which the SPC is dedicated, including special purposes, and consider the special purpose or purposes (in addition to traditional shareholder economic interests) when determining what is in the best interests of the SPC and its shareholders;
- a requirement that any amendment to or elimination of a special purpose specified in the SPC's articles of incorporation be adopted by at least a two-thirds vote of each class of the SPC's voting shares. Note that a higher threshold may be specified in the SPC's articles of incorporation; and

---

39. *See* Thomson Reuters Foundation and Morrison & Foerster LLP, *supra* note 3, 83–84.
40. *See* https://www.socentlawtracker.org/#/spcs.
41. Examples include Kepler's 2020 (http://www.keplers2020.com), Hydrobee (http://www.hydrobee.com), and Purism (https://puri.sm/).

- a requirement that the management and directors of the SPC specify objectives for measuring the impact of the SPC's efforts relating to its special purpose or purposes. A discussion and analysis of these efforts must be included in the SPC's annual report, which must be delivered to shareholders at least 15 days prior to the SPC's next annual meeting and made publicly available, e.g., by posting on the SPC's website. The annual report must include certain information on the SPC's efforts relating to its special purposes, including the following:
  - identification and discussion of the overall objectives of the SPC relating to its special purpose or purposes and an explanation of any changes made in the special purposes during the fiscal year;
  - identification and discussion of the material actions taken by the SPC during the fiscal year to achieve its special purpose objectives, the impact of those actions, and the extent to which those actions achieved the special purposes during the fiscal year;
  - identification and discussion of material actions, including the intended impact of those actions, that the SPC expects to take in the short and long term with respect to achievement of its special purposes;
  - discussion and analysis of the financial, operating, and other measures used by the SPC to evaluate its performance in achieving its special purposes, including any changes made to the evaluation measures during the fiscal year; and
  - discussion of any material expenditures incurred by the SPC during the fiscal year in furtherance of achieving the special purpose or purposes and a good faith estimate of future expenditures over the next three fiscal years.[42]

The SPC form presents several benefits to social entrepreneurs and investors. It provides shareholders with a means of shaping the social mission of the entity, as well as erecting barriers to dilution or elimination of that social mission. It also provides directors and officers with significant flexibility in determining how to pursue the SPC's social purpose. As with benefit corporations, SPC status brands an entity as having a social purpose beyond profit maximization, which may provide access to third parties, consumers, strategic partners, investors, and other stakeholders whose interests are aligned with that purpose. The mandatory reporting requirements provide additional accountability and certainty to existing and potential investors and strategic partners that the SPC is pursuing a social mission.[43] Importantly, unlike benefit corporations, SPC statutes do not include benefit enforcement proceedings that may create distractions, control issues, or other conflicts or risks.

As with the benefit corporation form, there is still potential for conflict between the directors' fiduciary duties of profit-seeking and pursuit of the social mission. However, this risk may be lower for SPCs than for benefit corporations, since SPCs are generally subject to substantially the same rules as ordinary corporations and thus

---

42. *See* California Corporations Code §2500–3503.
43. *See* Thomson Reuters Foundation and Morrison & Foerster LLP, *supra* note 3, 64.

benefit from greater clarity surrounding the duties of directors and how their conduct is evaluated. For example, existing corporate governance case law in most states imposes a reasonableness and materiality standard that applies to the prioritization by directors and managers of one or more of the stated special purposes over others, including, under certain circumstances, favoring the achievement of a stated special purpose over the economic interests of the shareholders.[44]

As with the various benefit corporation forms, the use of the SPC form also has the potential to create some confusion among investors and shareholders as to requirements imposed on the entity and their rights as shareholders as compared with ordinary corporations and benefit corporations, which also exist in most jurisdictions that allow SPCs. For example, shareholders of ordinary California corporations have the right to decline to participate in certain corporate transactions and receive fair value for their equity (dissenters' rights), such as mergers. In addition to standard dissenters' rights, shareholders of an SPC may also have dissenters' rights in the event of any material change in the special purposes set forth in the entity's articles of incorporation that is subject to a supermajority voting requirement (see discussion above). The main concern here is that a company may be required to cash out shareholders when it has undertaken no liquidity or financing event. SPCs may also merge with other SPCs or other corporate entities, and the SPCs may either survive or terminate in such a merger, but any merger or reorganization materially altering or eliminating an existing SPC's special purposes will also be subject to shareholder supermajority voting rights. This may make mergers and acquisitions more difficult and suppress the ability of companies to effectively scale. Furthermore, SPC statutes do not require a benefit director or provide for benefit enforcement proceedings, unlike benefit corporation statutes, but SPC shareholders have the same rights to elect and remove directors and to bring a claim for breach of fiduciary duties under applicable state law as shareholders in an ordinary corporation.[45]

4. Delaware Public Benefit Corporation

Alternative social enterprise entities became more broadly accepted once Delaware's public benefit corporation statute was passed in July 2013, as amended in 2015.[46] As with the SPC and benefit corporation forms, a PBC is a for-profit entity that includes a specific social or environmental purpose within its charter documents.[47] Because of Delaware's strong, management-friendly corporate legal system and the familiarity of investors with the state's laws, more PBCs have been incorporated in Delaware than

---

44. *See* Thomson Reuters Foundation and Morrison & Foerster LLP, *supra* note 3, 68.
45. *See* Thomson Reuters Foundation and Morrison & Foerster LLP, *supra* note 3, 67–69.
46. *See* https://news.delaware.gov/2013/07/17/governor-markell-signs-public-benefit-corporation-legislation.
47. Examples include Allbirds (https://www.allbirds.com/), Open Invest (https://www.openinvest.co/), Kickstarter (https://www.kickstarter.com/), King Arthur Flour (https://www.kingarthurflour.com/), New Resource Bank (https://newresourcebank.com/), Seventh Generation (https://www.seventhgeneration.com/), Year-Up (https://www.yearup.org/), and This American Live (https://www.thisamericanlife.org/).

benefit corporations or SPCs in any other state.[48] In addition, to date Delaware PBCs have attracted more investment than either benefit corporations or SPCs.[49]

A Delaware PBC shares many of the fundamental characteristics of an ordinary Delaware corporation. The key distinguishing features of the Delaware PBC statute include
- a requirement that the PBC's certificate of incorporation identify one or more specific public benefits that the PBC will promote. A public benefit is defined in the statute as "a positive effect (or reduction of negative effects) on one or more categories of persons, entities, communities or interests (other than stockholders in their capacities as stockholders) including, but not limited to, effects of an artistic, charitable, cultural, economic, educational, environmental, literary, medical, religious, scientific or technological nature";
- a requirement that the PBC's directors and officers manage the PBC in a manner that balances stockholders' economic interests, the interests of those materially affected by the PBC's conduct, and the PBC's specified public benefit(s). This balance requirement is deemed to satisfy a PBC director's fiduciary duties to stockholders and the PBC if the director's decision is both informed and disinterested and not such that no person of ordinary, sound judgment would approve, which affords a high degree of discretion to the directors and officers;
- a requirement that any amendment to or elimination of a public benefit specified in the certificate of incorporation be approved by at least two-thirds of the outstanding voting stock (originally 90 percent, but amended in 2015); and
- a requirement that the PBC provide its stockholders with a report on the PBC's pursuit of its public benefit(s) at least every two years. The report must include: (i) the objectives set forth by the PBC's board of directors to promote the public benefit(s); (ii) the standards adopted by the board of directors to measure progress in promotion of the public benefit(s); (iii) objective, factual information based on those standards regarding the success of the PBC in meeting its public benefit objectives; and (iv) an assessment of the PBC's success in meeting its objectives and promoting its enumerated public benefit(s). The PBC is not required to publish this report, but PBCs may elect to require in their certificate of incorporation or bylaws that the report be published or that a third-party certification be used.[50]

The Delaware PBC form shares many of the benefits of the SPC form: it provides stockholders with a means of shaping the social mission of the entity and significant protection against dilution or elimination of the specified public benefit, and it affords directors and officers a very high degree of flexibility in determining how to pursue public benefit. It also brands an entity as having a social purpose beyond profit maximization,

---

48. *See* https://data.world/blab/benefit-corporations-list.
49. *See* https://data.world/blab/investors-in-benefit-corporations.
50. *See* 8 Del. C. §362(b).

which may provide access to third-parties, consumers, strategic partners, investors, and other stakeholders whose interests are aligned with that purpose. The mandatory reporting requirements provide additional accountability and certainty to stockholders that the PBC is pursuing a social mission, as well as to potential investors that they will benefit from the required reporting if they buy the PBC's shares (in cases where the PBC has not elected to make its report publicly available).[51] In addition, like the benefit corporation forms, the PBC also works well for B Corp certification.

The Delaware PBC also shares some of the risks of the SPC form and to a lesser degree the benefit corporation forms. There remains a degree of uncertainty regarding the fiduciary duties of PBC directors and officers due to the lack of Delaware case law specifically addressing this issue. However, directors and officers of Delaware PBCs benefit not only from the statute's explicit mandate that they reasonably balance stockholders' economic interests with other factors but also from the considerable deference afforded to directors' and officers' business judgment under well-developed Delaware corporate case law (see discussion below).[52]

In addition, there remains potential for confusion among stockholders and potential investors about the characteristics of the PBC form as compared to ordinary Delaware corporations. For example, as with SPCs, mergers and acquisitions involving a PBC as target or acquirer must be approved by two-thirds of the outstanding voting stock of the PBC, which is not necessarily the case in mergers or acquisitions involving ordinary Delaware corporations, and both SPC and PBC offer dissenters rights on conversion from an existing corporate entity to the new form (see discussion above). Delaware PBC status may be confused with benefit corporation status in other states despite the significant differences between the forms, e.g., the lack of a general public purpose requirement, benefit director, benefit enforcement proceedings, or benefit report public disclosure requirement in the PBC. In addition, the term "public benefit corporation" refers in many states, including California, to a type of nonprofit corporate entity, creating potential for confusion.[53]

Delaware PBC status offers social entrepreneurs and investors a number of additional advantages over other social enterprise forms. The Delaware PBC statute is well integrated with the preexisting Delaware General Corporate Law and consequently benefits from many of the entrepreneur- and investor-friendly characteristics that have made Delaware the primary state of choice for U.S. incorporations generally, including the ease of the incorporation process as well as access to the Delaware courts and their highly developed body of corporate case law.[54] Importantly, as noted above, the Delaware PBC statute also lacks a benefit enforcement proceeding and the requirement of a benefit director found in many state benefit corporation statutes (see above), which eliminates the particular fiduciary risks that those requirements raise for directors and officers.[55]

---

51. See Thomson Reuters Foundation and Morrison & Foerster LLP, *supra* note 3, 103.
52. See Thomson Reuters Foundation and Morrison & Foerster LLP, *supra* note 3, 107.
53. See Thomson Reuters Foundation and Morrison & Foerster LLP, *supra* note 3, 103–04.
54. See Susan Mac Cormac, Morrison & Foerster LLP, *supra* note 2, slide 4.
55. See Thomson Reuters Foundation and Morrison & Foerster LLP, *supra* note 3, 106–07.

5. Low-Profit Limited Liability Company (L3C)

Low-profit limited liability companies (L3Cs) are for-profit entities that share many of the same features as ordinary LLCs, including the central feature of pass-through taxation. In addition to satisfying the general requirements applicable to LLCs in its state of formation, the articles of organization or the operating agreement of an L3C must enumerate an appropriate purpose. Most L3C statutes require that

- the L3C have or significantly further a charitable or educational purpose within the meaning of Section 170 of the Internal Revenue Code;
- the L3C would not have been formed but for the charitable or educational purpose;
- the production of income or appreciation of property not be a significant purpose of the L3C; and
- the L3C have no political or legislative purpose.[56]

At present, the L3C form has not been widely adopted by social enterprises.[57] This low level of uptake is likely due to three factors. One factor is that few states have implemented the L3C form. As of August 2018, 11 states have enacted or proposed L3C legislation (the most popular states are Michigan and Vermont); however, LC3 legislation has failed in New York and was repealed in North Carolina.[58] The second factor is that the ordinary LLC form is itself highly flexible and can accommodate the incorporation of the functional elements of an L3C, such as a charitable purpose, into its articles of organization and operating agreement, which makes L3C status superfluous under many circumstances (see below). Third, while L3Cs are ostensibly designed to accept program-related investments from foundations, in practice the L3C form does not make doing so any easier—all of the technical requirements remain in place (see chapter 11).

5. Benefit Limited Liability Company (BLLC)

As of August 2018, five states—Connecticut, Maryland, Oregon, Pennsylvania, and Utah—have proposed or enacted benefit limited liability company statutes.[59] These BLLC statutes largely track the model benefit corporation legislation, including the requirement of pursuing a general public purpose and allowing for enforcement proceedings. While Maryland passed the first BLLC statute in 2011, BLLCs remain relatively uncommon.[60] The generally understood reasons for this are similar to the low use of the L3C form, namely that the LLC form is inherently flexible and impact can be embedded without reliance on a statutory form (see above).

---

56. *See* Thomson Reuters Foundation and Morrison & Foerster LLP, *supra* note 3, 74–75.
57. Examples include H2OforHumanity (http://www.h2oforhumanity.com/) and interSector Partners (https://www.intersectorl3c.com/).
58. *See* https://www.socentlawtracker.org/#/l3cs; *see also* https://www.intersectorl3c.com/l3c.
59. *See* https://www.socentlawtracker.org/#/bllcs; example is New Brooklyn Farms (https://www.newbrooklynfarms.com/).
60. *See* a list of Maryland BLLCs: http://www.dat.state.md.us/businesses/Documents/Benefitcorpllc.pdf.

6. Delaware Statutory Public Benefit Limited Liability Company (Proposed)

In July 2018, Delaware approved an amendment to its LLC statute that allows for the formation of public benefit limited liability companies (PBLLCs).[61] The legislation took effect on August 1, 2018, and there were no PBLLC formations within the first month.[62] The new PBLLC statute shares many of the key features of the Delaware PBC statute, including

- a requirement that the PBLLC's certificate of formation identify one or more specific public benefits that the PBC will promote;
- a requirement that the PBLLC's managers or managing members manage the PBLLC in a manner that balances members' economic interests, the interests of those materially affected by the PBC's conduct, and the PBC's specified public benefit(s);
- a requirement that any amendment to or elimination of a public benefit specified in the certificate of formation approved by at least two-thirds of holders of at least two-thirds of the percentage or other interest in the profits of the PBLLC; and
- a requirement that the PBLLC report biennially to its members with respect to its promotion of the public benefit specified in its certificate of formation, including reporting on the objectives, standards, measurements, and assessments of the PBLLC's efforts.[63]

Given Delaware's strong business law traditions and institutions, the PBLLC is arguably the most likely LLC form to be utilized on a large scale. However, it remains to be seen how the PBLLC may be adopted by the social enterprises and impact investors for the same reasons as the L3C and BLLC.

V. SUMMARY AND TAKEAWAYS

Ultimately, there is no ideal entity choice for social entrepreneurs and investors seeking to balance mission and profitability. Rather, the optimal corporate form depends on a number of factors, including

1. the relationship between mission and profitability in the business. i.e., Is mission an absolute priority relative to profitability, is the converse the case, or is balance somewhere in between those two absolutes?
    - whether and how the business plans to grow, e.g., through franchising, M&A, or an IPO;

---

61. *See* http://delcode.delaware.gov/title6/c018/sc12/index.shtml.
62. *See* https://www.cogencyglobal.com/blog/delaware-enacts-limited-liability-company-act-amendments. Examples are limited because the legislation is newly enacted.
63. *See* https://legis.delaware.gov/BillDetail/26554.

- the profile of the investor base, and whether any investors have special tax situations, e.g., foundations making program-related investments;
2. the relationship between management and investors, e.g., Do the founders have a significant or majority ownership interest in the organization?
    - employee goals and expectations, e.g. Will the employees be seeking equity compensation, top-of-market pay, or other performance incentives?
    - governance structure, e.g., Do the founders or any of the investors intend to have a significant role in the actual management of the business?

VI. PRACTITIONER'S RESOURCE LIBRARY

A. Articles

"Does My Nonprofit Need to Pay Tax? Understanding Unrelated Business Income Tax," Dec. 2011, https://nonprofitquarterly.org/2011/12/25/does-my-nonprofit-need-to-pay-tax-understanding-unrelated-business-income-tax/.

Elizabeth Schmidt, "Vermont's Social Hybrid Pioneers: Early Observations and Questions to Ponder," Vt. L. Rev., Vol. 35, No. 1, pp. 163–209, Fall 2010.

"Excess Business Holdings and 4943(g): A New and Narrow (but Important) Exception," Feb. 9, 2018, https://www.adlercolvin.com/wp-content/themes/adlercolvin/pdf/Excess-Business-Holdings-and-4943g-A-New-and-Narrow-but-Important-Exception.pdf.

Ian Kanig, "Sustainable Capitalism through the Benefit Corporation: Enforcing the Procedural Duty of Consideration to Protect Non-Shareholder Interests," 64 HASTINGS L.J. 863, 898 (2013).

Jesse Finfrock and Eric Talley, "Social Entrepreneurship and Uncorporations," 2014 U. Ill. L. Rev. 1867 (2014), pp. 1881–2, https://scholarship.law.berkeley.edu/facpubs/2453/.

M. Todd Henderson, "Everything Old Is New Again: Lessons from Dodge v. Ford Motor Company," U. Chicago John M. Olin Law & Economics Working Paper No. 373, 27 (2007).

"So You Want to Start a Social Enterprise?," A New York Lawyers For the Public Interest Community Guide, October 2015, https://www.americanbar.org/content/dam/aba/directories/pro_bono_clearinghouse/ejc_2016_104.authcheckdam.pdf.

"Operating in Two Worlds: Tandem Structures in Social Enterprise," Ingrid Mittermaier and Joey Neugart, The Practical Tax Lawyer, Fall 2011.

Susan Mac Cormac, Morrison & Foerster LLP, "Preserving and Enhancing Impact: Corporate Forms," Presentation at Impact.tech, October 2016, slides 6–7, https://www.slideshare.net/Impactdottech/preserving-and-enhancing-impact-corporate-forms.

Susan Mac Cormac and Heather Haney, "New Corporate Forms: One Viable Solution to Advancing Environmental Sustainability," 24 J. APP. CORP. FIN. 49, 50 (2012); see also Shlensky v. Wrigley, 237 N.E.2d 776 (Ill. App. 1968).

"Using New Hybrid Legal Forms: Three Case Studies, Four Important Questions, and a Bunch of Analysis," Robert A. Wexler and David A. Levitt, 69 Exempt Org. Tax Rev. 63 (Jan. 2012).

B. Books and White Papers

John Montgomery, *Great From the Start: How Conscious Corporations Attract Success*, Morgan James Publishing (May 1, 2012).

Rick Alexander, *Benefit Corporation Law and Governance: Pursuing Profit with Purpose*, Berrett-Koehler Publishers; 1 edition (October 16, 2017).

Thomson Reuters Foundation and Morrison & Foerster LLP, "Which Legal Structure Is Right for My Social Enterprise: A Guide to Establishing a Social Enterprise in the United States," p. 40, http://www.trust.org/contentAsset/raw-data/171b5a61-eb36-43d9-8049-7cebe575491f/file.

C. Instruments and Standards

- Impact Terms Project: https://impactterms.org/.
- Model Benefit Corporation Legislation: http://benefitcorp.net/attorneys/model-legislation.
- Social Enterprise Law Tracker: https://www.socentlawtracker.org.
- See also Reporting (below).

D. Reporting

- B Lab affiliated reporting resources: www.benefitcorp.net, www.bcorporation.net, https://bthechange.com/, www.giirs.org, http://b-analytics.net/giirs-funds.
- Carbon Disclosure Project and Carbon Tracker: https://www.carbontracker.org/.
- Foundation Center's TRASI Database: http://trasi.foundationcenter.org.
- Global Reporting Initiative: www.globalreporting.org.
- Global Impact Investing Network: www.thegiin.org, http://iris.thegiin.org.
- International Integrated Reporting Council: http://integratedreporting.org/.
- Sustainability Accounting Standards Board (SASB): https://www.sasb.org/.
- SustainAbility: www.sustainability.com.
- Task Force on Climate-related Financial Disclosures: https://www.fsb-tcfd.org/.
- UL: www.ul.com.

Chapter 13

Cybersecurity Risk Management Is a Corporate Responsibility

Megan Brown, Moshe Broder, Michael Diakiwski,
Matt Gardner, Kat Scott, and Matt Solomson

I. INTRODUCTION

Cybersecurity risks include far more than consumer data breaches. Threats from hacktivists, nation-states, and criminals affect companies, customers, employees, competitors, and third parties. Attacks can result in system outages, disruption of services, theft and manipulation of data, and possible physical harm.

There are no simple answers or compliance checklists. Responsible cybersecurity requires a mind-set that prioritizes risk management. As a result, cybersecurity can be considered a corporate responsibility. After reviewing this chapter, counsel and management will understand the cybersecurity challenge and the shifting U.S. legal landscape.

II. WHAT IS CYBERSECURITY?

Cybersecurity is one of the most challenging issues facing organizations. Cybersecurity once was considered an offshoot of privacy. It is not. Cybersecurity goes beyond data control, integrity, and confidentiality. It involves the protection of networks and data from intrusions and disruptions. Statistics are sobering. Eighty-five percent of companies suffer some form of cyberattack each year.[1] Fifty-eight percent of victims are small businesses. In terms of perpetrators, 50 percent of breaches were carried out by organized criminal groups. Twelve percent of breaches involved nation-state or state-affiliated actors.[2]

Federal definitions are not comprehensive, but they do shed light on the risks. The Cybersecurity Information Sharing Act of 2015 defines a cybersecurity threat as "an action ... on or through an information system that may result in an unauthorized effort to adversely impact the security, availability, confidentiality, or integrity of an information system or information that is stored on, processed by, or transiting an information system."[3] The federal definition of "significant activities undermining cybersecurity" includes efforts "to deny access to or degrade, disrupt, or destroy an information and communications technology system or network; or to exfiltrate, degrade, corrupt, destroy, or release information from such a system or network without authorization for purposes of conducting influence operations; or causing a significant misappropriation of funds, economic resources, trade secrets, personal identifications, or financial information for commercial or competitive advantage or private financial gain; significant destructive malware attacks; and significant denial of service activities."[4]

The government recognizes that "cyberattacks will happen. According to the Department of Homeland Security's Science and Technology Directorate, 70 percent of hacking utilizes lost, stolen or weak credentials, and 60 percent of malware uses privilege escalation or stolen credentials."[5] The tactics used by adversaries rapidly evolve. "Spear-phishing emails emerged as by far the most widely used infection vector, employed by 71 percent of groups."[6]

Motives vary. Bad actors steal intellectual property and data; they interrupt operations or critical services; they seek ransom to release seized data or computers. In Verizon's experience, ransomware was the "most prevalent variety of malicious code" the company saw in its 2017 data.[7] And malware can spread rapidly across the world:

> The release of NotPetya was an act of cyberwar ... Within hours of its first appearance, the worm raced beyond Ukraine and out to countless machines around the world ... It crippled multinational companies including Maersk,

---

1. Kroll, *Global Fraud and Risk Report 2016/2017*, at 4 (2017), https://www.kroll.com/en-us/intelligence-center/reports/global-fraud-risk-report.
2. Verizon, *2018 Data Breach Investigations Report*, 11th ed., at 5 (2018), https://enterprise.verizon.com/resources/reports/dbir/ ("Verizon DBIR").
3. 6 U.S.C. §1501(5)(A). The Act excludes "any action that solely involves a violation of a consumer term of service or a consumer licensing agreement." *Id.* at §1501(5)(b).
4. 22 U.S.C. §9524.
5. National Security Telecommunications Advisory Committee, *NSTAC Report to the President on Internet and Communications Resilience*, at 13 (Nov. 16, 2017), https://www.dhs.gov/sites/default/files/publications/NSTAC%20Report%20to%20the%20President%20on%20ICR%20FINAL%20%2810-12-17%29%20%281%29-%20508%20compliant_0.pdf ("NSTAC Report to the President").
6. Symantec, *Internet Security Threat Report*, Vol. 23, at 28 (Mar. 2018), https://www.symantec.com/content/dam/symantec/docs/reports/istr-23-2018-en.pdf.
7. *Verizon DBIR* at 14.

pharmaceutical giant Merck, FedEx's European subsidiary TNT Express, French construction company Saint-Gobain, food producer Mondelēz, and manufacturer Reckitt Benckiser. In each case, it inflicted nine-figure costs.[8]

Distributed denial of service (DDoS) attacks are another serious concern. A DDoS attack is a malicious effort to use multiple compromised computer systems or devices to disrupt a server or network by flooding the target with Internet traffic.[9] They can be achieved using a botnet, which is "a network of internet-connected end-user computing devices infected with bot malware and are remotely controlled by third-parties for nefarious purposes."[10] Cyberattacks can wreak havoc on businesses, making it vital to think beyond prevention to response and resilience.

III. WHICH COMPANIES AND ORGANIZATIONS ARE AFFECTED?

All organizations need to address cybersecurity. The legal landscape is an expanding patchwork of federal and state statutes, regulations, data breach notification requirements, "soft" law, and consumer protection enforcement and litigation.

A. Critical Infrastructure

Cybersecurity law and policy in the United States generally take a risk-based approach. Because the private sector manages the majority of vital products and services, policymakers pay special attention to the entities on which citizens are most reliant.

As outlined in the 2013 Presidential Policy Directive 21 (PPD-21), the government has long believed that *responsibility for cybersecurity is a shared one*. PPD-21 sets out a "national policy on critical infrastructure security and resilience. This endeavor is a shared responsibility among the federal, state, local, tribal, and territorial entities, and public and private owners and operators of critical infrastructure."[11] The Directive established 16 critical infrastructure sectors, "whose assets, systems, and networks, whether physical or virtual, are considered so vital to the United States that their incapacitation or destruction would have a debilitating effect on security, national economic security, national public health or safety, or any combination thereof."[12] Key sectors include communications, energy, financial services, information technology, and transportation, among others.[13]

---

8. A. Greenberg, *The Untold Story of NotPetya, The Most Devastating Cyberattack in History*, WIRED (Aug. 22, 2018), https://www.wired.com/story/notpetya-cyberattack-ukraine-russia-code-crashed-the-world/.
9. *Verizon DBIR* at 23.
10. *NSTAC Report to the President* at 5 (citation omitted).
11. Press Release, White House, *Presidential Policy Directive—Critical Infrastructure Security and Resilience*, PRESIDENTIAL POLICY DIRECTIVE/PPD-21 (Feb. 12, 2013), https://obamawhitehouse.archives.gov/the-press-office/2013/02/12/presidential-policy-directive-critical-infrastructure-security-and-resil.
12. *See* DHS, *Critical Infrastructure Sectors*, https://www.dhs.gov/critical-infrastructure-sectors (updated Aug. 22, 2018).
13. *See id.*

For critical infrastructure, the Department of Homeland Security (DHS), in coordination with sector-specific agencies, maintains a risk-based list of entities that meet criteria in Executive Order (EO) 13636, "Improving Critical Infrastructure Cybersecurity," Section 9(a). These Section 9 entities are those for which "a cybersecurity incident could reasonably result in catastrophic regional or national effects on public health or safety, economic security, or national security."[14] The list is updated annually and DHS has produced recommendations for government engagement and how to foster cybersecurity among these entities.[15]

B. Regulated Industries

Regulated industries, like health care, financial services, energy, and the government contracting community, have heightened obligations. Whether by statute or agreement, their responsibilities exist because of the role they play in society—providing or supporting essential operations and the delivery of public services.

Critical industries have legal obligations, in addition to "softer" expectations such as best practices. In the energy sector, regulatory standards outline security controls, in addition to guidance for cyber frameworks and coordination.[16] For example, the Federal Energy Regulatory Commission (FERC) issued a final rule in April 2018, clarifying obligations for electronic access control of certain systems. The rule requires, among other things, mandatory security controls for transient electronic devices (e.g., thumb drives, laptop computers, and other portable devices frequently connected to and disconnected from systems).[17] In 2018, FERC finalized a rule on supply chain risk management, which includes cybersecurity for electronic security perimeters and vulnerability assessments.[18]

For financial services, cybersecurity is a focus of many regulators, including the Financial Industry Regulatory Authority (FINRA) and the Securities and Exchange Commission (SEC). FINRA monitors firms' ability to protect the confidentiality, integrity, and availability of customer information. This includes reviewing compliance

---

14. *See, e.g.*, DHS, *Presidential Executive Order (EO) 13800, Strengthening the Cybersecurity of Federal Networks and Critical Infrastructure, Support to Critical Infrastructure at Greatest Risk ("Section 9 Report") Summary* (May 8, 2018), https://www.dhs.gov/sites/default/files/publications/EO-13800-Section-9-Report-Summary-20180508-508.pdf.

15. *See id.*

16. U.S. Dep't of Energy, *Energy Sector Cybersecurity Framework Implementation Guidance* (Jan. 2015), https://www.energy.gov/sites/prod/files/2015/01/f19/Energy%20Sector%20Cybersecurity%20Framework%20Implementation%20Guidance_FINAL_01-05-15.pdf.

17. Revised Critical Infrastructure Protection Reliability Standard CIP-003–7—Cyber Security—Security Management Controls, 83 Fed. Reg. 17913 (Apr. 19, 2018), https://www.gpo.gov/fdsys/pkg/FR-2018-04-25/pdf/2018-08610.pdf.

18. Supply Chain Risk Management Reliability Standards, 83 Fed. Reg. 53992 (Oct. 26, 2018), https://www.gpo.gov/fdsys/pkg/FR-2018-10-26/pdf/2018-23201.pdf.

with SEC regulations, such as the requirement for firms to adopt written policies to protect customer information.[19]

The health care industry is primarily regulated under the Health Insurance Portability and Accountability Act of 1996 (HIPAA), which requires covered entities to ensure the confidentiality of health-related information. In regulations promulgated by the Department of Health and Human Services (HHS), the HIPAA Privacy Rule establishes standards to protect individuals' medical records and other personal health information (PHI).[20] The HIPAA Security Rule also establishes standards to protect electronic personal health information.[21]

IV. SOURCES OF LAW

A. Key Statutes

Businesses face an evolving mosaic of statutes, executive orders, and regulations. A few statutes should be familiar to practitioners:

- The Computer Fraud and Abuse Act (CFAA) provides criminal penalties for, broadly speaking, "hacking" as well as for committing traditional crimes through the use of a computer.[22] The CFAA prohibits accessing a computer without authorization, as well as exceeding authorized access.[23] This broad language has enabled the government to charge defendants in a variety of circumstances, ranging from disgruntled employees intentionally interrupting network traffic to corporate information systems[24] or deleting computer files and executing computer viruses[25] to nation-state actors hacking into networks to steal trade secrets.[26] While indictments under the CFAA are uncommon, considerable civil litigation takes place, often between competitors.[27]

---

19. *See* Regulation S-P (17 C.F.R. §248.30), which requires firms to adopt written policies and procedures to protect customer information against cyberattacks and other forms of unauthorized access; Regulation S-ID (17 C.F.R. § 248.201–202), which outlines a firm's duties regarding the detection, prevention, and mitigation of identity theft; and The Securities Exchange Act of 1934 (17 C.F.R. §240.17a-4(f)), which requires firms to preserve electronically stored records in a non-rewriteable, non-erasable format.
20. *See* 45 C.F.R. §§160.101–552; 45 C.F.R. §§164.102–106; 45 C.F.R. §§164.500–534.
21. *See* 45 C.F.R. §§160.101–552; 45 C.F.R. §§164.102–106; 45 C.F.R. §§164.302–318.
22. 18 U.S.C §1030.
23. *Id.*
24. United States v. Brown, 884 F.3d 281, 283 (5th Cir. 2018).
25. United States v. Thomas, 877 F.3d 591, 592 (5th Cir. 2017).
26. United States v. Dong, No. 2:14cr118 (W.D. Pa. filed May 1, 2014).
27. LabMD, Inc. v. Tiversa, Inc., 719 F. App'x 878, 879 (11th Cir. 2017) (security company downloaded patient data from corporate website and then solicited business from company); Facebook, Inc. v. Power Ventures, Inc., 844 F.3d 1058, 1063 (9th Cir. 2016), *cert. denied*, 138 S. Ct. 313 (2017) (social media company attempted to solicit users for its site using automated script run on another social network website).

- The Electronic Communications Privacy Act of 1986 (ECPA), which includes the Wiretap Act and the Stored Communications Act (SCA), was enacted to extend privacy protections to content and non-content information held or processed by electronic communications service providers.[28] ECPA generally prohibits the unlawful access to or interception of communications that are stored or in transit, though certain procedures are provided for voluntary or compelled disclosure. ECPA's prohibitions are criminal in nature but the statute also provides for civil liability.[29]
- In 2015, Congress enacted the Cybersecurity Information Sharing Act of 2015, which authorizes private entities to engage in monitoring, defensive measures, and information sharing activities for a "cybersecurity purpose."[30] The Act does not authorize offensive "hack backs," though the line between such activity and defensive measures is somewhat unclear.[31] Private entities receive protection from liability for monitoring information systems and sharing or receiving cyber threat information.[32]

B. Regulation of Federal Systems

Federal government cybersecurity and IT systems have been the frequent subject of Executive Orders and other directives. In 2017, the Trump administration issued Executive Order 13800 to modernize federal IT infrastructure and improve resilience of critical infrastructure to protect against botnets. In September 2018, President Trump issued the National Cyber Strategy, which builds upon EO 13800 and outlines numerous streams of effort for the federal government. It also anticipates the private sector playing a prominent role in securing critical infrastructure and establishing international norms.[33] The Federal Information Security Modernization Act of 2014 (FISMA 2014) updates the FISMA of 2002 and authorizes DHS to administer federal information security policies for federal Executive Branch civilian agencies.[34]

---

28. Electronic Communications Privacy Act of 1986, Pub. L. No. 99–508, 100 Stat. 1848 (1986) (codified as amended at 18 U.S.C. §§2510–2522, 2701–2712, 3121–3126 (2012)).

29. *See, e.g.*, Skapinetz v. CoesterVMS.com, Inc., No. CV PX-17–1098, 2018 WL 805393, at *1 (D. Md. Feb. 9, 2018) (plaintiff stated claim for violation of SCA where former employer accessed personal e-mail account of former employee without authorization).

30. 6 U.S.C. §§1501–1510.

31. M. Gardner, M. Broder, *CISA: Hope for More Cybersecurity, Challenges in Implementation and Interpretation*, The Procurement Law (ABA), Spring 2016, at 1, 23–28.

32. 6 U.S.C. §1505.

33. The White House, *National Cyber Strategy of the United States of America* (Sept. 2018), https://www.whitehouse.gov/wp-content/uploads/2018/09/National-Cyber-Strategy.pdf.

34. 44 U.S.C. §§3551, *et seq.*

V. REGULATION OF FEDERAL CONTRACTORS

Contractors doing business with the government face a wide-ranging set of cybersecurity obligations. First, contractors must comply with FAR 52.204–21, which provides safeguarding requirements and security control obligations derived from National Institute of Standards and Technology (NIST) Special Publication (SP) 800–171. Second, all Department of Defense (DoD) contracts now contain DFARS 252.204–7012, which requires that defense contractors that have "Covered Defense Information" residing on or transiting across their information systems comply with NIST SP 800–171 to safeguard that information and "rapidly" report incidents to the DoD.[35] Companies that cannot demonstrate compliance with the SP 800–171 requirements must, at the least, establish a system security plan (SSP), which identifies the current state of compliance and any gaps, and prepare a plan of actions and milestones (POAM) for completing implementation.[36]

Defense contractors must comply with DFARS 252.204–7008, which requires that contractors implement DFARS 252.204–7012 on covered systems used in support of the contract, as well as specifically represent that the security requirements of NIST SP 800–171 will be implemented, unless a variance is granted. Defense contractors are subject to DFARS 252.204–7009, which restricts the access, use, or dissemination of information obtained from a third-party's reporting of a cyber incident pursuant to DFARS 252.204–7012. Contractors using cloud computing to provide information technology services under a DoD contract must comply with additional security, reporting, and access requirements in DFARS 252.239–7009 and 252.239–7010.

These requirements present unique risks. If a solicitation requires a contractor to demonstrate compliance with a cybersecurity regulation at the time of proposal submission, and the contractor can be shown not to meet the standard, such a failure could support a bid protest.[37] And because of the specific representation requirement in DFARS 252.204–7008, under the implied certification theory recognized by the Supreme Court in *Universal Health Services Inc. v. United States et al. ex rel. Escobar*,[38] practitioners have recognized the possibility of False Claims Act liability, in suits brought by the government or a *qui tam* relator, alleging a violation of a material cybersecurity requirement.[39]

---

35. DFARS 252.204–7012 (revised May 30, 2018).

36. DoD Guidance for Reviewing System Security Plans and the NIST SP 800–171 Security Requirements Not Yet Implemented, 83 Fed. Reg. 17807–01 (Apr. 24, 2018).

37. *Cf. Discover Technologies LLC*, B-412773, 2016 CPD ¶ 142 (Comp. Gen. May 27, 2016) (denying protest challenging awardee's lack of FISMA compliance where solicitation made compliance with cybersecurity requirements mandatory post-award, but not at the time of source selection).

38. 136 S. Ct. 1989 (2016).

39. Counsel are looking for cases to press False Claims Act (FCA) theories based on cyber incidents. "Whether hackers succeed or not in acquiring sensitive information, any breach in cybersecurity that goes unreported could violate the False Claims Act." *See* Mahan Law, *Failure to Report Cybersecurity Breach*, https://www.mahanyertl.com/failure-to-report-cyber-hacking-or-apply-cybersecurity/ (last visited Oct. 31, 2018). Few cases have been litigated, but there are indicators that cyber claims and omissions can provide the basis for FCA cases. *See, e.g.*, United States ex rel. Sheldon v. Kettering Health Network, 816 F.3d 399 (6th Cir. 2016) (affirming dismissal of FCA case on other grounds, after plaintiff brought a *qui tam* lawsuit).

VI. REGULATION OF THE PRIVATE SECTOR

In addition to sector-specific approaches, for public companies, the SEC has begun enforcing cybersecurity violations through a new cyber unit.[40] The SEC in September 2018 charged a financial firm for deficient cybersecurity procedures, in violation of the Safeguards Rule and Identity Theft Red Flag Rule, which are designed to protect confidential customer information and protect customers from identity theft.[41]

As noted above, the FTC is a key regulator of cybersecurity, using its authority under Section 5 of the FTC Act over unfair or deceptive trade practices.[42] Additionally, it enforces the Gramm-Leach-Bliley Act (GLBA) and the Safeguards Rule, under which financial institutions must secure information with a "comprehensive information security program."[43] The FTC also enforces the Children's Online Privacy Protection Rule (COPPA), which imposes data security requirements on operators of online services directed to or serving children under 13 years old.[44]

VII. STATE LAWS AND ENFORCEMENT

Multiple states have data security laws, creating an evolving patchwork. Some laws provide for private rights of action, while others limit enforcement to the attorney general. California passed the first Internet of Things (IoT) cybersecurity law, which imposes security requirements on manufacturers.[45] Other states, including Maryland, impose requirements on businesses that possess personal information to "implement and maintain *reasonable security procedures* and practices that are appropriate to the nature of the personal information owned or licensed and the nature and size of the business and its operations."[46] On the other extreme, Oregon provides that a person is in compliance with the law only if particular actions are taken, including employee training, monitoring, detecting, preventing, responding to attacks or system failures, and protecting personal information against unauthorized access.[47] Some states have enforced their cybersecurity laws against corporations.[48]

---

40. Press Release, SEC, *SEC Announces Enforcement Initiatives to Combat Cyber-Based Threats and Protect Retail Investors* (Sept. 25, 2017), https://www.sec.gov/news/press-release/2017-176.

41. *See* Press Release, SEC, *SEC Charges Firm with Deficient Cybersecurity Procedures* (Sept. 26, 2018), https://www.sec.gov/news/press-release/2018-213; *see also Voya Financial Advisors, Inc.*, Administrative Proceeding File No. 3–18840, 2018 WL 4627393 (SEC Sept. 26, 2018) (order instituting administrative and cease-and-desist proceedings).

42. 15 U.S.C. §45. One successful challenge has been asserted against the FTC's application of its broad enforcement power to cybersecurity violations. LabMD, Inc. v. Fed. Trade Comm'n, 894 F.3d 1221, 1234 (11th Cir. 2018).

43. 16 C.F.R. §314.3(a).

44. 15 U.S.C. §6501, *et seq.*; 16 C.F.R. §312.8.

45. Cal. S.B. 327 (2018).

46. Md. Code Ann., Com. Law §14–3503(a) (emphasis added).

47. Or. Rev. Stat. §646A.622.

48. *See, e.g.*, Commonwealth v. Equifax, Inc., No. 1784CV03009BLS2 (Mass. Super. Ct. Sept. 19, 2017), http://www.mass.gov/ago/docs/press/2017/equifax-complaint.pdf.

States also regulate specific sectors. For example, financial service firms in New York must comply with Department of Financial Services regulation which requires, among other things, a cybersecurity plan and the disclosure of cyber incidents within 72 hours.[49]

VIII. "SOFT" LAW

U.S. policymakers promote a risk-based approach to cybersecurity. This favors soft law, like voluntary frameworks, over inflexible statutes and regulations. While they generally lack the force of law, partnerships and voluntary frameworks are a preferred model for addressing cybersecurity.

These quasi-legal elements are favored for several reasons. First, technology evolves rapidly. Second, threats are constantly changing. Third, best practices and guidance allow for the flexibility to adapt. A traditional compliance model that locks in standards is generally ill-suited to address changes occurring at the speed of technology.

A. Where Does Soft Law Come From?

Nearly every discussion of cybersecurity at the federal level includes the National Institute for Standards and Technology (NIST) within the Department of Commerce. The agency has been charged with, among other things, "stimulating cooperative work among private industrial organizations in efforts to surmount technological hurdles."[50] NIST has core responsibilities under the Federal Information Security Management Act of 2002 "for developing information security standards and guidelines, including minimum requirements for federal information systems."[51] NIST publishes guidance, including handbooks, NIST interagency or internal reports (NISTIRs), special publications, technical notes, white papers, and bulletins. NIST has taken on an influential role over private sector activity in privacy and security.

Beyond NIST, industry best practices, global standards, and government guidance shape the direction of cybersecurity law and policy, and may become de facto legal standards.

1. NIST's *Cybersecurity Framework* and Other Publications

In 2013, President Obama issued an EO on Improving Critical Infrastructure Cybersecurity.[52] It tasked NIST with developing a voluntary cybersecurity framework through an open, consultative process, which culminated in the 2014 *Framework for Improving Critical Infrastructure Cybersecurity* ("Cybersecurity Framework" or

---

49. *See* 23 NYCRR §500.00, *et seq.*
50. 15 U.S.C. §271(a)(5).
51. *See* 44 U.S.C. §§3501, *et seq.*; *see also* NIST, *Risk Management FISMA Background*, https://csrc.nist.gov/projects/risk-management/detailed-overview (last visited Oct. 31, 2018).
52. Exec. Order No. 13636, 78 Fed. Reg. 11739 (Feb. 12, 2013).

"Framework").[53] The Framework is voluntary guidance to help organizations manage cybersecurity risks. While it was developed to improve cybersecurity risk management in critical infrastructure, it has been adopted by organizations across sectors due to its voluntary nature and flexibility. In April 2018, NIST updated this flagship document with Version 1.1.[54]

In Version 1.1, NIST expanded its reach, applying the Framework to organizations relying on technology, whether "information technology (IT), industrial control systems (ICS), cyber-physical systems (CPS), or connected devices more generally, including the Internet of Things (IoT)."[55] Among other changes, it expanded the discussion of supply chain risk management (SCRM), emphasizing communication among stakeholders up and down supply chains.

In addition, NIST offers dozens of special publications, NISTIRs, white papers, and bulletins with guidance for the private sector on risk management,[56] security and privacy controls,[57] digital identity lifecycle management,[58] and the IoT.[59] NIST has many other activities under way on cybersecurity. It is developing technical standards for everything from online authentication to encryption and risk management, and it is delving deeper into privacy. NIST's documents are revised at the agency's discretion.

NIST's work is incorporated by reference into federal regulations, often focused on federal IT systems and contractor compliance. But it would not be surprising to see NIST's security work included in federal regulation more often. The Office of the Federal Register (OFR), which is charged with approving agencies' incorporations by reference, issued a rule that "federal agencies may only enforce regulatory requirements that have been published in the *Federal Register* and codified in the *Code of Federal Regulations* ... agencies can fulfill this publication requirement by incorporating reference materials that have been published elsewhere. This is permitted so long as the materials are 'reasonably available to the class of persons affected' and the OFR has approved their incorporation. Materials that are properly incorporated by reference become part of 'the law.'"[60] We expect to see more incorporation by reference of NIST publications, frameworks, and controls on cyber-related topics.

---

53. NIST, *Framework for Improving Critical Infrastructure Cybersecurity*, Version 1.0 (Feb. 12, 2014), https://www.nist.gov/sites/default/files/documents/cyberframework/cybersecurity-framework-021214.pdf.

54. NIST, *Framework for Improving Critical Infrastructure Cybersecurity*, Version 1.1 (Apr. 16, 2018), https://nvlpubs.nist.gov/nistpubs/CSWP/NIST.CSWP.04162018.pdf ("Cybersecurity Framework").

55. *Id.*

56. NIST, SP 800–37, Revision 1, *Guide for Applying the Risk Management Framework to Federal Information Systems: A Security Life Cycle Approach* (Feb. 2010, updated June 5, 2014), https://csrc.nist.gov/publications/detail/sp/800-37/rev-1/final.

57. NIST, SP 800–53, Revision 4, *Security and Privacy Controls for Federal Information Systems and Organizations* (Apr. 2013, updated Jan. 22, 2015), https://csrc.nist.gov/publications/detail/sp/800-53/rev-4/final.

58. NIST, SP 800-63B, *Digital Identity Guidelines, Authentication and Lifecycle Management* (June 2017, updated Dec. 1, 2017), https://nvlpubs.nist.gov/nistpubs/SpecialPublications/NIST.SP.800-63b.pdf.

59. NIST, NISTR 8228 (Draft), *Considerations for Managing Internet of Things (IoT) Cybersecurity and Privacy Risks* (Sept. 2018), https://nvlpubs.nist.gov/nistpubs/ir/2018/NIST.IR.8228-draft.pdf.

60. E. Bremer, *New Rules on Incorporated Standards Encourage Necessary Public-Private Collaboration*, THE REG. REV. (Jan. 27, 2015), https://www.theregreview.org/2015/01/27/bremer-public-private-collab/.

2. Industry Best Practices and Codes of Conduct

Industry has long practiced self-regulation in security. Recent efforts on IoT security offer an example. In 2018, CTIA—The Wireless Association announced the creation of the CTIA Cybersecurity Certification Program for cellular-connected IoT devices.[61] A CTIA representative noted that "America's wireless industry has long been a leader in cybersecurity best practices and establishing an industry-led cybersecurity certification program for IoT devices is a major step in building a trusted, secure wireless ecosystem for the Internet of Things."[62] GSMA, which represents mobile operators globally, produced *IoT Security Guidelines*;[63] ISCA Labs, an independent division of Verizon, published an *IoT Security Testing Framework*;[64] and Symantec published an *IoT Reference Architecture White Paper*.[65]

In 2018, the Financial Services Sector Coordinating Council, with trade associations, published the *Financial Services Sector Cybersecurity Profile*, Version 1.0.[66] The profile is based on the NIST *Cybersecurity Framework* and other guidance, including ISO/IEC 27001. The *Profile* is intended to align:

> cybersecurity regulatory expectations and authorities [and provide] a flexible structure to absorb future supervisory expectations within its organization, vocabulary, and taxonomy. Institutions and supervisory agencies and organizations can focus on the core elements of their cybersecurity risk management missions. With the efficiencies gained, more resources can then be applied to cybersecurity.[67]

Other efforts led by private coalitions are enhancing security in the cloud,[68] the Internet,[69] the ICT supply chain,[70] and cybersecurity generally.[71]

---

61. Press Release, CTIA, *Wireless Industry Announces New Cybersecurity Certification Program for Cellular-Connected IoT Devices* (Aug. 21, 2018), https://www.ctia.org/news/wireless-industry-announces-internet-of-things-cybersecurity-certification-program.

62. *Id.*

63. GSMA, *IoT Security Guidelines Overview Document*, Version 2.0 (Oct. 31, 2017), https://www.gsma.com/iot/wp-content/uploads/2018/08/CLP.-11-v2.0.pdf.

64. ICSA Labs, *Internet of Things (IoT) Security Testing Framework*, Version 2.0 (Oct. 26, 2016), https://www.icsalabs.com/sites/default/files/body_images/ICSALABS_IoT_reqts_framework_v2.0_161026.pdf.

65. Symantec, *An Internet of Things Reference Architecture* (2016), https://www.symantec.com/content/dam/symantec/docs/white-papers/iot-security-reference-architecture-en.pdf.

66. FSSCC, *The Financial Services Sector Cybersecurity Profile*, Version 1.0 (Oct. 25, 2018), https://www.fsscc.org/files/galleries/Financial_Services_Sector_Cybersecurity_Profile_Overview_and_User_Guide_2018-10-25.pdf.

67. *Id.* at 2.

68. *See, e.g.*, Cloud Security Alliance, https://cloudsecurityalliance.org/ (last visited Oct. 31, 2018).

69. *See, e.g.*, Internet Governance Coalition, http://internetgovernancecoalition.com/ (last visited Oct. 31, 2018); Internet Security Alliance, https://isalliance.org/ (last visited Oct. 31, 2018); The Vendor Security Alliance, https://www.vendorsecurityalliance.org/index.html (last visited Oct. 31, 2018).

70. *See, e.g.*, U.S. Chamber of Commerce, *Supply Chain Security Working Group*, https://www.uschamber.com/issue-brief/supply-chain-security-working-group (last visited Oct. 31, 2018).

71. *See, e.g.*, Council to Secure the Digital Economy, https://securingdigitaleconomy.org/ (last visited Oct. 31, 2018); Coalition for Cybersecurity Policy and Law, https://www.cybersecuritycoalition.org/ (last visited Oct. 31, 2018); Coalition to Reduce Cyber Risk, Inc., https://crx2.org/ (last visited Oct. 31, 2018); Global Cyber Alliance, https://www.globalcyberalliance.org/ (last visited Oct. 31, 2018).

3. Global Technical Standards

Corporate counsel should be aware of international efforts to set standards for cybersecurity and appreciate how these efforts may impact business. Several global standards organizations develop and promote technical security standards and best practices. Notable organizations and examples include: the International Organization for Standardization's (ISO) ISO/IEC 27000 family—Information security management systems;[72] the Institute of Electrical and Electronics Engineers (IEEE) standards and best practices;[73] and Underwriters Laboratories (UL) Cybersecurity Assurance Program.[74]

4. Government Guidance

The government has produced a plethora of guidance documents to assist organizations. Products are generally aimed at moving the private sector toward more secure and resilient cyber practices. Navigating the volume of materials can be overwhelming, especially for small and mid-sized organizations. This section refers to a small selection of documents and efforts that the government has recently initiated or updated.

In early 2018, the SEC refreshed its guidance for publicly traded companies on disclosing cybersecurity risk.[75] Like the previous guidance from 2011, the SEC stated that companies must inform investors about "material cybersecurity risks and incidents in a timely fashion."[76] While materiality is still the lynchpin of disclosure, the SEC's guidance significantly expands on what it expects from companies, including information about how the board manages cyber risk as well as information about past incidents. Further, the SEC emphasized the role a company's cybersecurity policies and procedures play in identifying and managing risk. The SEC also underscored its view that insiders are prohibited from trading on non-public material information related to cyber risk.

The FTC offers a series of documents to help companies of all sizes protect consumer data and information they maintain. The FTC's core cybersecurity publications include *Start with Security: A Guide for Business*,[77] *Data Breach Response: A Guide for Business*,[78] *Protecting Personal Information: A Guide for Business*,[79] and the "Stick with

---

72. ISO, *ISO/IEC 27000 Family—Information Security Management Systems*, https://www.iso.org/isoiec-27001-information-security.html (last visited Oct. 31, 2018).

73. *See, e.g.,* IEEE Standards Association, https://standards.ieee.org/standard/index.html (last visited Oct. 31, 2018) (such as IEEE 2413—Standard for an Architectural Framework for the Internet of Things (IoT)); and IEEE, *Internet of Things (IoT) Security Best Practices* (Feb. 2017), https://internetinitiative.ieee.org/images/files/resources/white_papers/internet_of_things_feb2017.pdf.

74. UL, *UL Cybersecurity Assurance Program (UL CAP)*, https://services.ul.com/service/ul-cybersecurity-assurance-program-ul-cap/ (last visited Oct. 31, 2018).

75. SEC, *Commission Statement and Guidance on Public Company Cybersecurity Disclosures* (Feb. 26, 2018), https://www.sec.gov/rules/interp/2018/33-10459.pdf.

76. *Id.* at 4.

77. FTC, *Start with Security: A Guide for Business, Lessons Learned from FTC Cases* (June 2015), https://www.ftc.gov/system/files/documents/plain-language/pdf0205-startwithsecurity.pdf.

78. FTC, *Data Breach Response: A Guide for Business* (Sept. 2016), https://www.ftc.gov/system/files/documents/plain-language/pdf-0154_data-breach-response-guide-for-business.pdf.

79. FTC, *Protecting Personal Information, A Guide for Business* (Oct. 2016), https://www.ftc.gov/system/files/documents/plain-language/pdf-0136_proteting-personal-information.pdf.

Security" blog series.[80] In April 2018, FTC staff produced *Engage, Connect, Protect: The FTC's Projects and Plans to Foster Small Business Cybersecurity*.[81]

The FTC has held public hearings examining whether broad-based changes in the economy, evolving business practices, new technologies, or international developments might require adjustments to competition and consumer protection law, enforcement priorities, and policy. The FTC sought engagement from all stakeholder groups, including industry, academia, and civil society organizations and plans to produce reports summarizing its findings and recommendations in 2019.[82]

The U.S. Department of Justice (DOJ) has also engaged on a variety of cybersecurity issues. In 2018, the attorney general ordered the formation of a Cyber-Digital Task Force to produce a report assessing the many ways that the department is combatting the global cyber threat and "to identify how federal law enforcement can more effectively accomplish its mission in this vital and evolving area."[83] The report outlines DOJ's role in securing the digital ecosystem, but also emphasizes the important role that *all* sectors play. In September 2018, DOJ released Version 2.0 of its *Best Practices for Victim Response and Reporting of Cyber Incidents*.[84] The updated document aims to "help organizations prepare a cyber incident response plan and, more generally, to better equip themselves to respond effectively and lawfully to a cyber incident." Version 2.0 discusses incident response considerations, including ransomware, information sharing under the Cybersecurity Information Sharing Act of 2015, cloud computing, and working with incident response firms. DOJ notes that "it was drafted primarily for smaller organizations and their legal counsel; however, it may be useful for larger organizations with more experience in handling cyber incidents as well."[85]

The Department of Energy (DOE) is engaged with the energy sector. In 2018, DOE established the Office of Cybersecurity, Energy Security, and Emergency Response (CESER) "to make the nation's electric power grid and oil and natural gas infrastructure resilient to cyber threats." CESER underscored that "with 90 percent of the nation's power infrastructure privately held, coordinating and aligning efforts between the government and the private sector is vital. To achieve its vision, CESER works closely with representatives of the energy sector, companies that manufacture energy technologies, the National Laboratories, universities, other government agencies, and other stakeholders."[86]

---

80. FTC, *Stick with Security: A Business Blog Series* (Oct. 2017), https://www.ftc.gov/tips-advice/business-center/guidance/stick-security-business-blog-series.

81. FTC, *Engage, Connect, Protect: The FTC's Projects and Plans to Foster Small Business Cybersecurity* (Apr. 2018), https://www.ftc.gov/system/files/documents/reports/engage-connect-protect-ftcs-projects-plans-foster-small-business-cybersecurity-federal-trade/ecp_staffperspective_2.pdf.

82. FTC, *Hearings on Competition and Consumer Protection in the 21st Century*, https://www.ftc.gov/policy/hearings-competition-consumer-protection (last visited Oct. 31, 2018).

83. DOJ, *Report of the Attorney General's Cyber Digital Task Force*, at 2 (July 2, 2018), https://www.justice.gov/ag/page/file/1076696/download.

84. DOJ, *Best Practices for Victim Response and Reporting of Cyber Incidents*, Version 2.0 (Sept. 2018), https://www.justice.gov/criminal-ccips/file/1096971/download.

85. *Id.* at 1.

86. Dep't of Energy, *Cybersecurity for Critical Energy Infrastructure*, https://www.energy.gov/ceser/activities/cybersecurity-critical-energy-infrastructure.

The Food and Drug Administration (FDA) has ramped up efforts on cybersecurity and medical devices. In April 2018, the FDA released the Medical Device Safety Action Plan that seeks to explore regulatory solutions to enhance patient safety and advance medical device cybersecurity.[87] This was followed, in October 2018, with a playbook on medical device cybersecurity[88] and a commitment to update the FDA's premarket guidance on cybersecurity.[89]

5. Contractual Obligations and Cyber Insurance

Corporate counsel must also review and survey third-party agreements, which increasingly require parties to implement security controls, make timely notifications, and adhere to certain expectations of business partners, vendors, and suppliers. Among these rising expectations are requirements to: update software and patch vulnerabilities; protect data by using certain levels of encryption or algorithmic keys; and maintain a cybersecurity insurance policy. Indeed, organizations should make a risk management assessment and consider whether requiring cyber insurance for critical vendors is something to include in their own vendor contracts.

Cyber insurance is no longer novel, nor should it be looked at as optional by major companies. It is becoming a must have, like general liability and property insurance. It is important for corporate counsel to be aware that policies may limit the choice of outside counsel or third-party incident response teams. Depending on the nature of business operations, a cyber policy may need to cover operational and enterprise systems.

IX. GLOBAL CHALLENGES

Global expectations are on the rise, especially in relation to personal data that is collected or maintained and the security procedures implemented to protect such information. Laws have trended toward having extraterritorial reach and mandating data localization, i.e., requiring that certain data be collected, processed, and stored inside a country's borders. This section identifies introductory considerations and emerging trends.

---

87. FDA, *Medical Device Safety Action Plan Protecting Patients, Promoting Public Health*, https://www.fda.gov/downloads/AboutFDA/CentersOffices/OfficeofMedicalProductsandTobacco/CDRH/CDRHReports/UCM604690.pdf.

88. Mitre, *Medical Device Cybersecurity, Regional Incident Preparedness and Response Playbook*, Version 1.0 (Oct. 2018), https://www.mitre.org/sites/default/files/publications/pr-18-1550-Medical-Device-Cybersecurity-Playbook.pdf.

89. *See, e.g.*, FDA, *Content of Premarket Submissions for Management of Cybersecurity in Medical Devices: Guidance for Industry and Food and Drug Administration Staff* (Oct. 2, 2014), https://www.fda.gov/downloads/MedicalDevices/DeviceRegulationandGuidance/GuidanceDocuments/UCM356190.pdf; *see also* Press Release, FDA, *Statement from FDA Commissioner Scott Gottlieb, M.D. on FDA's Efforts to Strengthen the Agency's Medical Device Cybersecurity Program as Part of Its Mission to Protect Patients* (Oct. 1, 2018), https://www.fda.gov/NewsEvents/Newsroom/PressAnnouncements/ucm622074.htm.

A. Asia

China's Cybersecurity Law came into effect in June 2017, and subsequent regulations are forthcoming. The Cybersecurity Law promotes the Chinese principle of cyberspace sovereignty or the ability to regulate the Internet within its borders. It requires network operators and providers of network products and services to adhere to personal information protection obligations, including notice and consent requirements, and the law imposes specific cybersecurity obligations. Network operators are generally obligated to safeguard their networks against disruption, damage or unauthorized access, and to prevent data leakage. Providers of network products and services must comply with certain Chinese national standards and ensure the security of their products, including by providing an opportunity for the Chinese government to test and evaluate prior to introduction to the Chinese market. Additionally, citizens' personal information and other business data must be stored within China's borders. China is pursuing regulations related to the Cybersecurity Law.

In Vietnam, a cybersecurity law, effective in January 2019, requires technology companies to store personal data on users, locally in Vietnam. It also has certain requirements to cooperate with the Vietnamese government in removing "offensive content."

In 2016, the Government of Japan released a *General Framework for Secure IoT Systems*, which "aims to clarify the fundamental and essential security requirements for secure IoT systems."[90] Japan's efforts to build upon this *General Framework* and enhance security more generally remain ongoing. In July 2018, Japan released an updated version of its *Cybersecurity Strategy*, which hews more closely to the approach American policymakers have taken thus far. It highlights a focus on advancing security within the supply chain and IoT ecosystems and utilizing public and private sector cooperation to protect critical infrastructure.[91]

B. Europe

Europe generally takes a more regulatory approach to cyber and data security than the United States. In May 2018, the European Union's (EU) General Data Protection Regulation (GDPR) became effective.[92] It is extraterritorial, applying to all companies processing and maintaining personal data of subjects residing in the EU, regardless of the company's location. Along with new privacy and security obligations, the GDPR brings significant monetary penalties.[93] Fines for noncompliance can be up to €20 million or 4 percent of an organization's total worldwide annual turnover, whichever is higher.

---

90. Japan, National Center of Incident Readiness and Strategy for Cybersecurity, *General Framework for Secure IoT Systems*, at 1 (Aug. 26, 2016), https://www.nisc.go.jp/eng/pdf/iot_framework2016_eng.pdf.

91. *See* Japan, National Center of Incident Readiness and Strategy for Cybersecurity, *Cybersecurity Strategy* (July 27, 2018), https://www.nisc.go.jp/eng/pdf/cs-senryaku2018-en.pdf.

92. Council Directive 2016/679, General Data Protection Regulation, 2016 O.J. (L 119) 1 (EU), https://eur-lex.europa.eu/legal-content/EN/TXT/?qid=1540584420394&uri=CELEX:32016R0679 ("GDPR").

93. *See id.*

Several elements of the GDPR are worth noting, because of their divergence from expectations in America. In the United States, the definition of a "breach" typically means the unauthorized acquisition of computerized data that compromises the security, confidentiality, or integrity of personal information maintained by the data collector.[94] Under the GDPR, the scope of a breach is broader and includes accidental or unlawful destruction or loss, alteration, and unauthorized disclosure of or access to personal data. Domestically, "personal information" is some combination of a person's name with another identifier, such as a Social Security Number.[95] But the GDPR defines "personal data" as "*any* information *relating* to an identified or identifiable natural person."[96] There are also special provisions for the management of particularly sensitive data, such as race, religion, or ethnic background and aggressive notification deadlines after a breach.[97]

Beyond the GDPR, other EU regulations extend to regulated entities which the United States has traditionally defined as "critical infrastructure" operators. Adopted by the European Parliament, the "Directive on security of network and information systems" (NIS Directive) is part of the European Commission's (EC) cybersecurity strategy and is designed to increase security standards and cooperation among EU Member States.[98] Like the GDPR, the NIS Directive may apply to U.S. organizations doing business in the EU, including EU-based subsidiaries of critical infrastructure operators as well as U.S.-based e-commerce and cloud computing companies. Penalties for noncompliance are determined by Member States, and countries have contemplated stiff penalties.

The NIS Directive encourages specific standards to raise the bar on security:

> [Standardization] of security requirements is a market-driven process. To ensure a convergent application of security standards, Member States should encourage compliance or conformity with specified standards so as to ensure a high level of security of network and information systems at Union level. ENISA [the European Union Agency for Network and Information Security] should assist Member States through advice and guidelines.[99]

In September 2017, the EC introduced a "Cybersecurity Package," which includes a stringent certification scheme for connected devices.[100] The EC proposed to establish rules to create certification schemes for particular Internet-connected devices and services. Presently, EU Member States may have varying requirements, and this framework seeks

---

94. *See, e.g.*, 815 Ill. Comp. Stat. §§530/1–25.
95. *See, e.g.*, Wis. Stat. §134.98.
96. *GDPR*, art. 4, §1 (emphasis added).
97. *GDPR*, at art. 33, §1.
98. *See* Council Directive 2016/1148, *Directive on Security of Network and Information Systems*, 2016 O.J. (L 194) 1 (EU), https://eur-lex.europa.eu/legal-content/EN/TXT/?uri=uriserv:OJ.L_.2016.194.01.0001.01.ENG&toc=OJ:L:2016:194:TOC ("NIS Directive").
99. *Id.*, at §66.
100. Commission Proposal for a Regulation of the European Parliament and of the Council on ENISA, the "EU Cybersecurity Agency," and repealing Regulation (EU) 526/2013, and on Information and Communication Technology cybersecurity certification ("Cybersecurity Act"), COM (2017) 477 final (Sept. 13, 2017), https://eur-lex.europa.eu/legal-content/EN/TXT/?qid=1540585269424&uri=CELEX:52017PC0477.

to coalesce around a more uniform certification. Under the proposal, the certification schemes would be voluntary, "unless otherwise provided in Union legislation laying down security requirements of ICT [information and communications technology] products and services."[101]

Specific EU Member States and other countries have adopted their own rules and guidance documents. The United Kingdom published a *Code of Practice for Consumer IoT Security* providing organizations guidelines to produce devices that are "secure by design."[102] Updates to the guidance are expected.

Diffuse efforts around the world introduce additional complexity in the marketplace. With the prospect of compliance with multiple standards and regulatory regimes, multinational corporations should encourage U.S. government efforts to support and develop international standards aimed at harmonizing varied approaches to regulating technology.

X. HOW SHOULD A RESPONSIBLE ORGANIZATION MANAGE CYBERSECURITY RISK?

As companies approach cybersecurity, they need to think about not only their own security but also the role they play in the broader economy. A few of the key elements are addressed below.

A. Key Task: Risk Management and Planning

Several elements of risk management have emerged as basics, many derived from the NIST Framework,[103] now in its second iteration. The Framework emphasizes five functions, which "provide a high-level, strategic view of the lifecycle of an organization's management of cybersecurity risk:" Identify, Protect, Detect, Respond, Recover.[104] Under each function, the Framework provides outcomes and references—standards, guidelines, and best practices.[105] By using the Framework, an organization can manage risk.

Organizations should start with a risk assessment. This can be done internally or with an outside expert. If the latter, consider doing it through counsel to maximize applicable legal privileges. A gap assessment, particularly if it is done against regulatory demands like the DFARS, NIST 800–171, or HIPAA, may raise questions. For example, many regimes contemplate some use of encryption, but do not mandate particulars.

---

101. *Id.*
102. United Kingdom, Dep't for Digital, Culture, Media & Sport, *Code of Practice for Consumer IoT Security*, https://www.gov.uk/government/publications/secure-by-design/code-of-practice-for-consumer-iot-security (updated Oct. 14, 2018).
103. *Cybersecurity Framework.*
104. *Id.* at 10.
105. *Id.*

These decisions should be discussed internally, recognizing trade-offs between user experience, cost, and security.

Every organization needs an incident response plan. "Because performing incident response effectively is a complex undertaking, establishing a successful incident response capability requires substantial planning and resources."[106] Plans can be robust and detailed or fairly high level, depending on the size, function, and sophistication of the organization. Plans must be tested or reviewed so they are understood and can be adjusted. Many organizations conduct "tabletop" exercises that simulate a cyber incident to test responsiveness and policies. A mature cybersecurity posture may include regular security testing. These too may be most prudently done with counsel to maximize applicable privileges.

Companies need a cyber risk governance structure. The federal government has been emphasizing corporate accountability for cybersecurity. Public companies are expected to have and publicly describe board and management engagement.[107] All organizations should ensure that the senior levels of the organization are informed and exercise appropriate oversight. This can include regular updates to the board.

Organizations are expected to foster a culture of security. Employees should receive routine training on best practices, cyber hygiene, and compliance. A hot topic is insider trading.[108] Organizations need to ensure that product development, marketing, and sales teams keep security top of mind. The same is true for third-party risk managers and contracting professionals. Each new product, service, or relationship may have cyber implications. Law departments need to set expectations and support this culture.

B. Key Task: Handling Incidents

Almost every organization will have some sort of security incident, either directly or because a business partner suffers an attack or business interruption. Organizations need to be prepared to deal with an attack. Questions to ask before you are in a crisis include:

- Who has authority to shut down e-mail or take a website offline?
- Do you have backups of key data and systems in case you have to take databases offline?
- Do you have an insider threat program to spot risky behavior?
- Do you have a good relationship with your Internet service provider (ISP) and other providers of security services? Many organizations have DDoS mitigation and other services already in place.
- Do you have a policy in place for decisions about payment of ransomware?
- Do you have a relationship with law enforcement?

---

106. NIST, SP 800–61, Revision 2, *Computer Security Incident Handling Guide*, at 10 (Aug. 2012), https://csrc.nist.gov/publications/detail/sp/800-61/rev-2/final.

107. SEC, *Commission Statement and Guidance on Public Company Cybersecurity Disclosures*, 83 Fed. Reg. 8166, 8170–71 (Feb. 26, 2018).

108. *Id.* at 8167.

- Do you know which regulators, customers, and partners you are obligated to notify in the event of an attack? SEC or other regulatory disclosures are important, and there may be requirements for notice in short periods of time, such as 72 hours for covered contractors.[109]

C. Key Task: Handling Vulnerabilities in Products, Services, or Websites

Government and industry are focused on vulnerabilities in software, products, services, and supply chains. The defense contracting community has long operated under Security Technical Implementation Guides (STIGs), which are configuration standards for some DoD devices and systems. STIGs are put out by the government to enhance security posture by offering "technical guidance" including "to 'lock down' information systems/software that might otherwise be vulnerable to a malicious computer attack."[110]

Companies of all sizes need to understand that their enterprise software and systems, industrial controls, and product lines will likely face security issues and need to be updated. This can have significant security consequences. For example, the flaw that enabled a well-known Microsoft Windows exploit—EternalBlue—was "fixed" by Microsoft in March 2017; however, "outdated and unpatched systems still permit the exploit to flourish in the hands of threat actors."[111]

Companies' products can have vulnerabilities, creating challenges for manufacturers and users. The security community is regularly claiming to identify security flaws in products and websites. Some are "white hat" hackers, while others have less noble motives.[112] Organizations should factor vulnerability disclosure into risk management. An emerging expectation is that companies will make use of vulnerability disclosure programs, which outline how third parties can communicate security vulnerabilities to organizations.[113]

These programs can be complex and have trade-offs. One concern about vulnerability disclosure programs is premature disclosure, which may facilitate cyber

---

109. DFARS 252.204–7012(c)(1)(ii).

110. *See, e.g.,* Information Assurance Support Environment (IASE), *Security Technical Implementation Guides (STIGs),* https://iase.disa.mil/stigs/Pages/index.aspx (last visited Oct. 31, 2018).

111. C. Osborne, *Why the "Fixed" Windows EternalBlue Exploit Won't Die,* ZDNET (Sept. 17, 2018), https://www.zdnet.com/article/why-the-fixed-windows-eternalblue-exploit-wont-die/.

112. C. Barrett, St. Jude Medical, Inc. vs. Muddy Waters Consulting LLC, et al.*: Who Bears the Burden to Disclose Discovered Software Vulnerabilities in Medical Devices?*, ABA HEALTH eSOURCE (Aug. 2017), https://www.americanbar.org/groups/health_law/publications/aba_health_esource/2016-2017/august2017/medicaldevices/ (describing what "is believed to be the first time a private firm—MedSec, a cyber-security research firm—leveraged discovered cybersecurity vulnerability information [in this case, vulnerabilities in medical devices, including pacemakers] to gain private profits rather than inform the manufacturer per the FDA guidance governing post-market management of cybersecurity in medical devices").

113. *See* M. Brown, M. Gardner, and A. Rice, *An Invitation to Hack: The Benefits and Risks of Vulnerability Disclosure Programs* (July 14, 2017), https://www.youtube.com/watch?v=-xb87hEt_Ws.

attacks, create consumer fear, and expose a company to liability.[114] They may not be right for every organization; however, the government is encouraging them, adding new information related to vulnerability disclosure to the NIST Framework.[115] The DOJ published *A Framework for Vulnerability Disclosure Program for Online Systems*, which is "assistance, not authority" for "organizations interested in instituting a formal vulnerability disclosure program."[116] The National Telecommunications and Information Administration (NTIA) convened a multistakeholder process which brought together "security researchers and software and system developers and owners to address security vulnerability disclosure."[117]

D. Key Task: Establishing and Maintaining Privilege

Because of the litigation, regulatory, and compliance risks associated with cybersecurity, prudent organizations should ask themselves what activities can and should be conducted under attorney-client privilege. Several categories of activities may be privileged so advance planning is wise.

Employees should be educated on when to involve legal departments, both in incidents and more generally when discussing risks, gaps, and compliance. Engineers and security professionals should be counseled on the risks of sharing sensitive information outside the company.

Risk assessments by consulting firms and security experts can be valuable. But they can also create a record of recommendations and findings, so engagements should be structured to maximize and not waive applicable privileges. In the right circumstances, third parties can be retained by counsel (in-house or outside) and managed by attorneys, particularly where their expertise is needed to help the legal team to advise the company.

In incident response, it is vital to preserve attorney-client privilege. Working with third parties can waive privilege, so care must be taken in engaging communications firms, security vendors, and forensics experts. So too, care must be taken when dealing with the government. In the heat of the moment, organizations must balance speed of disclosure with care to avoid making public or other statements that can be used as admissions or evidence of negligence.

Organizations and their lawyers should take care to maximize privilege in communications with senior management and the board of directors. As boards demand information about the organization's cybersecurity posture and risk management, attorneys should help determine what information goes to the board and under what circumstances.

---

114. *Id.*
115. *See Cybersecurity Framework* at *iii*.
116. DOJ, *A Framework for a Vulnerability Disclosure Program for Online Systems*, Version 1.0, at 1 (July 2017), https://www.justice.gov/criminal-ccips/page/file/983996/download.
117. NTIA, *Multistakeholder Process: Cybersecurity Vulnerabilities* (Dec. 15, 2016), https://www.ntia.doc.gov/other-publication/2016/multistakeholder-process-cybersecurity-vulnerabilities.

E. Key Task: Communicating with Customers and Others

Communications about security should be undertaken with care and accuracy. Public communications and statements to vendors and customers about security can form the predicate for claims of deception, such as under the deceptive trade practices authority wielded by the FTC under Section 5 of the FTC Act. The FTC has brought dozens of security-related cases that rest on theories of deception from omissions or claims related to security and privacy.[118]

There is increasing focus on disclosures to other businesses about the security attributes of software and services. This relates to supply chain integrity and product lifecycle management. Government agencies are looking at whether products and services need to contain a "software bill of materials" that explains the code and derivation of software elements.[119]

Those doing business with the government face unique concerns. NIST's *Special Publication 800–171, Revision 1* (*SP 800–171*) outlines 110 security requirements for use by federal agencies when contracting with nonfederal organizations.[120] As of December 31, 2017, covered DoD contractors have been required to implement *SP 800–171*, pursuant to the DFARS.[121] Under *SP 800–171*, contractors must have a "system security plan" where the contracting organization describes "how the specified security requirements are met or how organizations plan to meet the requirements."[122] Contractors should take extra care when making any statements to the federal government about their cyber posture, especially given the potential for risk associated with breach of contract claims and False Claims Act liability. In light of these risks, it is important that contractors document good faith efforts to comply with the voluminous, and often ambiguous, requirements of *SP 800–171*. Communicating cybersecurity practices and posture to the government should be top of mind for all contractors doing business with the government.

---

118. *See, e.g.*, Complaint for Injunctive and Other Equitable Relief, *Wyndham*, No. 2:13-cv-01887, 2012 WL 12146600 (D.N.J. June 26, 2012) (alleging that the company's privacy policy misrepresented security measures); Complaint, *BLU Products, Inc.*, No. 172–3025, 2018 WL 2042045, at *2 (F.T.C. Apr. 30, 2018) (alleging that the company's privacy policy misrepresented security when it claimed to use "appropriate physical, electronic, and managerial security procedures to help protect the personal information that [customers] provide to [the company]").

119. NTIA, *NTIA Software Component Transparency*, https://www.ntia.doc.gov/SoftwareTransparency (updated Oct. 30, 2018) (convening a multistakeholder process to consider software bill of material (SBOM) issues, including how SBOM production and consumption, and how SBOM data might be shared).

120. *SP 800–171, Revision 1*.

121. DFARS 252.204–7012(b)(2)(ii) ("The Contractor shall implement NIST SP 800–171, as soon as practical, but not later than December 31, 2017.").

122. *SP 800–171, Revision 1* at 25 ("The plan describes the system boundary; the operational environment; how the security requirements are implemented; and the relationships with or connections to other systems. Nonfederal organizations should develop plans of action that describe how any unimplemented security requirements will be met and how any planned mitigations will be implemented. Organizations can document the system security plan and plan of action as separate or combined documents and in any chosen format.").

F. Key Task: Information Sharing and Interacting with Government

The federal government has touted collective defense and suggested that companies must step up to their responsibilities to combat shared threats. On November 16, 2018, President Trump signed into law the Cybersecurity and Infrastructure Security Agency Act of 2018. This legislation reorganized and established a new operational agency within DHS, the Cybersecurity and Infrastructure Security Agency (CISA). CISA houses several offices, including the National Risk Management Center (NRMC), which is focused on facilitating cross-sector information sharing and collaboration on threats.[123]

> [The NRMC] is where the expertise of the private sector comes in, to help us contextualize the threat both in the planning phase as well as in the response and recovery. The private sector also knows its operational environment better than we will ever know in the government, so we will look to their expertise to help us understand how the pieces fit together.[124]

A cornerstone of collective defense is information sharing, with the government and among private organizations. While most information sharing is voluntary, the government is pressing companies to do more: "Organizations should consider leveraging external guidance obtained from Federal government departments and agencies, Information Sharing and Analysis Centers (ISACs), Information Sharing and Analysis Organizations (ISAOs), existing maturity models" and other resources.[125] Information sharing is part of the NIST Framework[126] and benefits the whole ecosystem, so it should be considered by responsible organizations.

Because private systems are the targets of attacks, companies interact with the government in several ways. Companies may need the assistance of government in an incident and can contact experts in the DHS, which manages several private-facing support activities. Many companies also work with the FBI or DHS on incidents or emerging threats. One thing to consider is how to protect information from public or other disclosure, as under Freedom of Information Act requests. Organizations should explore programs like the Protected Critical Infrastructure Information (PCII) program,[127] described above, with the advice of counsel.

Several venues exist for information sharing. Notable constructs are ISACs and ISAOs. ISACs are "are non-profit, member-driven organizations formed by critical infrastructure owners and operators to share information between government and industry."[128] Today, there are sector-specific ISACs for critical infrastructure, including the Automotive ISAC, the Aviation ISAC, the Communications ISAC, and the

---

123. *See* DHS, *About CISA*, https://www.dhs.gov/cisa/about-cisa (last visited Jan. 11, 2019).

124. Secretary Kirstjen M. Nielsen, Remarks at the National Cybersecurity Summit (Jul. 31, 2018), https://www.dhs.gov/news/2018/07/31/secretary-kirstjen-m-nielsen-s-national-cybersecurity-summit-keynote-speech.

125. *Cybersecurity Framework* at 15.

126. *See id.* at 26 ("ID.RA-2: Cyber threat intelligence is received from information sharing forums and sources.").

Financial Service ISAC.[129] ISAOs have similar goals as ISACs—"to gather, analyze, and disseminate cyber threat information;"[130] ISAOs are not sector-specific. Trade associations often support information sharing efforts.

At the federal level, DHS "has developed and implemented numerous information sharing programs."[131] These programs are now consolidated within its newest agency—CISA.

- The National Cybersecurity and Communications Integration Center (NCCIC) "is a 24/7 cyber situational awareness, and incident response center that is a national nexus of cyber and communications integration for the federal government, intelligence community, and law enforcement. The NCCIC shares information among public and private sector partners to build awareness of vulnerabilities, incidents, and mitigations."[132]
- DHS's Cyber Information Sharing and Collaboration Program (CISCP) is a platform for "DHS and participating companies [to] share information about cyber threats, incidents, and vulnerabilities. Information shared via CISCP allows all participants to better secure their own networks and helps support the shared security of CISCP partners."[133]
- DHS's Automated Indicator Sharing (AIS) initiative, which is available through the NCCIC, "connects participating organizations to a DHS-managed system that allows bi-directional sharing of cyber threat indicators, helping to build a common, shared knowledge of current cyber threats."[134]

The government has systems to promote information sharing and protect information that is shared. The PCII program, created by the Critical Infrastructure Information Act of 2002, implements "uniform procedures on the receipt, validation, handling, storage, marking, and use of CII voluntarily submitted to [DHS]."[135] Similarly, the Cybersecurity Information Sharing Act of 2015 encourages two-way information sharing, with and from the government:

> The Act promotes the goal of sharing while simultaneously providing privacy protections in two ways: first, by specifying the types of cyber threat

---

127. Critical Infrastructure Information Act of 2002, 6 U.S.C. §131 *et seq.*; *see also* 6 C.F.R. §29 *et seq.*

128. DHS, *Information Sharing*, https://www.dhs.gov/topic/cybersecurity-information-sharing (last visited Sept. 27, 2016).

129. National Council of ISACs, *Member ISACs*, https://www.nationalisacs.org/member-isacs (last visited Oct. 31, 2018).

130. DHS, *Information Sharing*, https://www.dhs.gov/topic/cybersecurity-information-sharing (last visited Oct. 31, 2018).

131. DHS, *supra* note 130.

132. *Id.*

133. DHS, *supra* note 130.

134. *Id.*

135. DHS, *Protected Critical Infrastructure Information (PCII) Program*, https://www.dhs.gov/pcii-program (updated Oct. 4, 2018).

information that can be shared under the Act between and among non-federal and federal entities; and, second, by limiting sharing under the Act only to those circumstances in which such information is necessary to describe or identify threats to information and information systems. Effectively, the only information that can be shared under the Act is information that is directly related to and necessary to identify or describe a cybersecurity threat.[136]

Thanks in part to these protections, industry has grown increasingly comfortable sharing information. "There's still caution from industry, but industry does appreciate the access to government information [and is] getting more comfortable with these interactions."[137]

Still, there are gaps in these protections which corporate counsel should consider. For example, the Act's protections extend only to sharing "cyber threat indicators" and "defensive measures,"[138] and not explicitly to other information that may be shared, such as best practices. These risks are illustrated by litigation spurred by the Jeep hacking incident in 2015.[139] In that case, the Auto-ISAC, a nonparty, was subpoenaed to produce documents, including materials related to the Auto-ISAC's cybersecurity best practices.[140] Although this subpoena was quashed,[141] the prospect of company information shared with an ISAC being subject to disclosure "could chill information sharing that is vital to national security."[142]

G. Key Task: Handling Investigations and Litigation

Cyber risks and incidents can lead to government oversight, investigations, and enforcement by a number of players including federal regulators, inspectors general, congressional committees, state attorneys general, and the plaintiffs' bar.

There are a number of steps that organizations should consider in dealing with government oversight. Organizations in the midst of an incident should involve

---

136. DHS, DOJ, *Guidance to Assist Non-Federal Entities to Share Cyber Threat Indicators and Defensive Measures with Federal Entities under the Cybersecurity Information Sharing Act of 2015*, at 5 (June 15, 2016), https://www.us-cert.gov/sites/default/files/ais_files/Non-Federal_Entity_Sharing_Guidance_%28Sec%20105%28a%29%29.pdf.

137. *Hearing on Telecommunications, Global Competitiveness, and National Security before the H. Subcomm. on Commc'ns & Tech.*, 115th Cong. (2018), https://docs.house.gov/meetings/IF/IF16/20180516/108301/HHRG-115-IF16-Wstate-ClancyC-20180516-U11.pdf (testimony of Charles Clancy, director and professor, Hume Center for National Security and Technology, Virginia Polytechnic Institute and State University).

138. *Id.* §§1501–1510.

139. Flynn v. FCA U.S. LLC, No. 16-mc-00078, 2016 WL 6996181 (S.D. Ill. Nov. 30, 2016).

140. Memorandum of Law of Non-Party Auto-ISAC in Support of Motion to Quash Third-Party Subpoena at 2, 6, *Flynn v. FCA U.S. LLC*, No. 16-mc-00078 (S.D. Ill. Sept. 27, 2016).

141. Order, Flynn v. FCA U.S. LLC, No. 16-mc-00078, 2016 WL 6996181 (S.D. Ill. Nov. 30, 2016).

142. Non-Party Auto-ISAC, Inc.'s Reply in Support of Motion to Quash Third-Party Subpoena at 17, *Flynn v. FCA U.S. LLC*, 16-mc-00078 (S.D. Ill. Oct. 21, 2016).

professionals, including the organization's insurer(s) (if the company has cyber coverage) and counsel (in-house, outside, or both). These professionals can provide expertise in dealing with regulators or investigators. In a breach, it is critical to preserve the attorney-client privilege. It will also be important to be able to convey the organization's story regarding the incident. And, to the extent possible, ensure that the organization keeps a record of events and preserves evidence.

XI. SUMMARY AND TAKEAWAYS

Organizations of all types need to address cybersecurity as an enterprise risk. This requires engagement by executive management and counsel, as well as human resources, IT infrastructure, procurement, product development, marketing, physical security, and technical experts. There is no single solution or compliance manual. To manage cyber risk, companies need resources—including technical and legal expertise—and a commitment from senior executives to address these risks. Frameworks and best practices abound, so responsible and prudent organizations should seek out guidance and third-party assistance as needed to customize their approaches.

XII. PRACTITIONER'S RESOURCE LIBRARY

A. Select Federal Guidance and Resources

U.S. Department of Homeland Security (DHS), *Cybersecurity and Infrastructure Security Agency*, https://www.dhs.gov/CISA.

DHS, *Protected Critical Infrastructure Information (PCII) Program*, https://www.dhs.gov/pcii-program; *see also* 6 C.F.R. Part 29 (Sept. 1, 2006).

U.S. Department of Justice (DOJ), *Best Practices for Victim Response and Reporting of Cyber Incidents*, Version 2.0 (Sept. 2018), https://www.justice.gov/criminal-ccips/file/1096971/download.

DOJ, *Report of the Attorney General's Cyber Digital Task Force*, at 2 (July 2, 2018), https://www.justice.gov/ag/page/file/1076696/download.

Federal Trade Commission (FTC), *Start with Security: A Guide for Business, Lessons Learned from FTC Cases* (June 2015), https://www.ftc.gov/system/files/documents/plain-language/pdf0205-startwithsecurity.pdf.

FTC, *Data Breach Response: A Guide for Business* (Sept. 2016), https://www.ftc.gov/system/files/documents/plain-language/pdf-0154_data-breach-response-guide-for-business.pdf.

FTC, *Protecting Personal Information, A Guide for Business* (Oct. 2016), https://www.ftc.gov/system/files/documents/plain-language/pdf-0136_proteting-personal-information.pdf.

FTC, *Stick with Security: A Business Blog Series* (Oct. 2017), https://www.ftc.gov/tips-advice/business-center/guidance/stick-security-business-blog-series.

FTC, *Engage, Connect, Protect: The FTC's Projects and Plans to Foster Small Business Cybersecurity* (Apr. 2018), https://www.ftc.gov/system/files/documents/reports/engage-connect-protect-ftcs-projects-plans-foster-small-business-cybersecurity-federal-trade/ecp_staffperspective_2.pdf.

National Institute of Standards and Technology (NIST), *Framework for Improving Critical Infrastructure Cybersecurity*, Version 1.1 (Apr. 16, 2018), https://nvlpubs.nist.gov/nistpubs/CSWP/NIST.CSWP.04162018.pdf.

NIST, SP 800–37, Revision 1, *Guide for Applying the Risk Management Framework to Federal Information Systems: A Security Life Cycle Approach* (Feb. 2010, updated June 5, 2014), https://csrc.nist.gov/publications/detail/sp/800-37/rev-1/final.

NIST, SP 800–53, Revision 4, *Security and Privacy Controls for Federal Information Systems and Organizations* (Apr. 2013, updated Jan. 22, 2015), https://csrc.nist.gov/publications/detail/sp/800-53/rev-4/final.

National Security Telecommunications Advisory Committee, *NSTAC Report to the President on Internet and Communications Resilience* (Nov. 16, 2017), https://www.dhs.gov/sites/default/files/publications/NSTAC%20Report%20to%20the%20President%20on%20ICR%20FINAL%20%2810-12-17%29%20%281%29-%20508%20compliant_0.pdf.

Revised Critical Infrastructure Protection Reliability Standard CIP-003–7—Cyber Security—Security Management Controls, 83 *Fed. Reg.* 17913 (Apr. 19, 2018), https://www.gpo.gov/fdsys/pkg/FR-2018-04-25/pdf/2018-08610.pdf.

U.S. Securities and Exchange Commission, *Commission Statement and Guidance on Public Company Cybersecurity Disclosures* (Feb. 26, 2018), https://www.sec.gov/rules/interp/2018/33-10459.pdf.

Supply Chain Risk Management Reliability Standards, 83 Fed. Reg. 53992 (Oct. 26, 2018), https://www.gpo.gov/fdsys/pkg/FR-2018-10-26/pdf/2018-23201.pdf.

U.S. Department of Energy, *Energy Sector Cybersecurity Framework Implementation Guidance* (Jan. 2015), https://www.energy.gov/sites/prod/files/2015/01/f19/Energy%20Sector%20Cybersecurity%20Framework%20Implementation%20Guidance_FINAL_01-05-15.pdf.

The White House, *National Cyber Strategy of the United States of America* (Sept. 2018), https://www.whitehouse.gov/wp-content/uploads/2018/09/National-Cyber-Strategy.pdf.

The White House, *Presidential Policy Directive—Critical Infrastructure Security and Resilience*, Presidential Policy Directive/PPD-21 (Feb. 12, 2013), https://obamawhitehouse.archives.gov/the-press-office/2013/02/12/presidential-policy-directive-critical-infrastructure-security-and-resil.

B. Select Private Sector Guidance and Resources

CTIA-The Wireless Association, IoT Cybersecurity Certification Program Management Document, Version 1.0 (Oct. 2018), https://api.ctia.org/wp-content/uploads/2018/10/ctia_IoT_cybersecurity_pmd_ver-1_0.pdf.

Financial Services Sector Coordinating Council, *The Financial Services Sector Cybersecurity Profile*, Version 1.0 (Oct. 25, 2018), https://www.fsscc.org/files/

galleries/Financial_Services_Sector_Cybersecurity_Profile_Overview_and_User_Guide_2018-10-25.pdf.

GSMA, *IoT Security Guidelines Overview Document*, Version 2.0 (Oct. 31, 2017), https://www.gsma.com/iot/wp-content/uploads/2018/08/CLP.-11-v2.0.pdf.

Symantec, *Internet Security Threat Report*, Vol. 23, (Mar. 2018), https://www.symantec.com/content/dam/symantec/docs/reports/istr-23-2018-en.pdf.

Verizon, *2018 Data Breach Investigations Report*, 11th ed., (2018), https://enterprise.verizon.com/resources/reports/dbir/.

Chapter 14

Working with Governments

Margaret M. Cassidy, Daniel Portnov, and Kwame Boateng

I. INTRODUCTION

Businesses engage with governments through every facet of their operations—obtaining licenses to operate, paying taxes, pursuing government contracts, influencing government policy, importing and exporting products, recruiting and hiring from the government, and in many other ways. These engagements expose a business, its employees, and its business partners to the risk of corrupt activity.

Over the past decade or so, organizations have become proactive in managing corruption risks because of an increase in corruption investigations and enforcement around the globe. Many businesses have embraced the notion that corrupt actions will result in costs to the organization, a decrease in its value, and damage to its reputation. As a result, businesses have engaged boards, leaders, employees, and third parties to prevent, identify, and mitigate the risk of corruption through defined anticorruption programs operated within the organization. These efforts are designed to decrease the "supply" of improper payments. However, given the impact that corruption has on economies and governments, as well as emerging trends in corporate social responsibility, there is a call for businesses to look externally, beyond their third parties, to mitigate corruption risks by developing programs designed to address the "demand" for improper payments from corrupt government officials.

This chapter will discuss the business case for using corporate social responsibility (CSR) principles to manage and mitigate corruption risk from the demand side. It will also discuss the laws and regulations that should drive an organization's approach to developing a program to compliantly, ethically, and responsibly work with governments. It will also cover norms, standards, and guidance that have been developed to help organizations identify and mitigate corruption risks and how those norms may facilitate an organization in developing socially responsible methods for mitigating corruption.

Finally, this chapter will provide actionable approaches to developing a CSR program to compliantly work with governments.

II. THE CASE FOR CSR WHEN WORKING WITH GOVERNMENTS

Corrupt behavior weakens economies, enables poverty, distorts the distribution of income, destabilizes governments, impedes the rule of law, and ultimately "hinders both public and private sector productivity."[1] Corrupt governments impact a business by reducing the quality of basic government services and increasing the costs of government services that a business needs to operate and that citizens need to live safe and secure lives.[2] Corruption distorts competition and rewards those who cannot compete in an open and fair market.[3] Companies may also find themselves at a competitive disadvantage if they refuse to pay bribes. Therefore, business and foreign direct investment decrease their interest in corrupt nations.[4]

Conversely, ethical governments foster democracy, the rule of law, and stable economies. CSR requires that organizations conduct their business in a fair and ethical manner which includes acting responsibly by following and respecting laws as well as ethical and cultural norms even in countries where the rule of law may not be adequately enforced.[5] Operating an organization fairly includes avoiding corrupt or improper interactions with governments and other organizations.[6] It also includes responsibly engaging in the political process.[7]

Given this, a corporation benefits by developing a defined anticorruption CSR program for essentially two reasons. First, by working to diminish the demand for corrupt payments, a business assures not only that the communities in which it works are more stable and economically viable but that the organization itself benefits from stable and effective governments. Second, decreasing the supply for corrupt payments mitigates the business' exposure to corruption investigations and prosecutions.

A company's fight against corruption has been a business issue because it impacts the bottom line as a result of the costs to the business not only for investigations that result in no penalty but also for prosecutions. Investigations and prosecutions bring staggering costs for lawyers, accountants, program managers, as well as monetary sanctions and court-ordered compliance monitors. For example, Siemens paid an estimate of

---

1. *OECD Recommendation on Public Integrity,* OECD, http://www.oecd.org/gov/ethics/recommendation-public-integrity/ (last visited Apr. 10, 2019).
2. Greg Hills et al., *Anti-Corruption as Strategic CSR: A Call to Action for Corporations* (May 2009), https://www.fsg.org/publications/anti-corruption-strategic-csr#download-area.
3. Hills et al., *supra* note 2.
4. *Id.*
5. *Guidance on Social Responsibility, ISO 26000:2010 Clause 4.6.*, https://www.iso.org/obp/ui/#iso:std:iso:26000:ed-1:v1:en (last visited Apr. 10. 2019).
6. *Id.*
7. *Id.*

$1.4 billion in bribes to officials around the world to win government contracts such as a national ID card project in Argentina and mass transit work in Venezuela. As a result, it was responsible for paying $1.6 billion in fines to American and European authorities to settle the bribery charges, and that does not include the cost of legal counsel, forensic accountants, and others Siemens had pay to handle the investigation.[8] Additionally, organizations subject to corruption investigation or prosecution also often face shareholder lawsuits as well as internal turmoil as it identified and disciplined those responsible. Finally, as governments, standard-setting organizations, industries, employees, and consumers have focused more on influencing organizations by leveraging the unique power each stakeholder has to influence socially responsible behavior, organizations that demonstrate a commitment to socially responsible behavior often reduce their risk of reputational damage, to include consumer boycotts and negative press which may also impact a business' bottom line.

A strong compliance program that is focused internally mitigates a business' risk of a corruption investigation and prosecution by decreasing the supply of corrupt payments into a market.[9] "Companies should be able to identify and mitigate against bribes and corrupt payments not only to ensure compliance with the law, but also to keep markets competitive and to ensure that their activities are benefiting the societies in which they operate."[10] When businesses turn their actions externally in an attempt to decrease the demand for improper payments, they enable strong government institutions "making economies more productive, public sectors more efficient, societies and economies more inclusive."[11] This in turn breeds trust not only in the government but in the corporations that operate in the market.[12]

Similarly, a CSR program for working with governments limits a government's demand for corrupt payments. By engaging externally with local, state, and national governments to develop anticorruption enhancements within the government, organizations will decrease their risk of liability for corrupt behavior when engaging with those governments with whom they have worked. Just as with well-developed corporate anticorruption programs, these efforts will likely protect a business' bottom line by mitigating corruption risk.

When businesses turn their actions externally by developing and executing a strong anticorruption compliance program but also by undertaking efforts to decrease a government's demand for corrupt payments, it enhances value for a variety of stakeholders—shareholders, employees, local communities, consumers, and governments.[13]

---

8. *Siemens to pay $1.34 Billion in Fines*, N.Y. TIMES (Dec. 15, 2008), https://www.nytimes.com/2008/12/16/business/worldbusiness/16siemens.html.

9. *What Are the Costs of Corruption*, TRANSPARENCY INTERNATIONAL, https://www.transparency.org/what-is-corruption#costs-of-corruption (last visited Apr. 10, 2019).

10. Amol Mehra & Ajoke Agbool, *The Corporate Responsibility to Prevent Corruption*, FORBES (July 1, 2011).

11. *What Are the Costs of Corruption*, *supra* note 9.

12. *OECD Recommendation on Public Integrity*, *supra* note 1.

13. *Id.*

III. SELECT LAWS AND REGULATIONS WHEN WORKING WITH GOVERNMENTS

A. Overview

Most countries have laws and regulations designed to prohibit corrupt behavior and to assure transparency and objectivity in government decision-making, to include bribery laws, conflicts of interest laws, gift regulations, lobbying and campaign finance laws, as well as government procurement. Although countries each take their own approach to preventing corruption, and assuring government transparency and objectivity, the principles that guide these laws and regulations are similar. A business seeking to develop an anticorruption CSR program should familiarize itself with the principles that these laws embody; and in doing so, a business will have informed itself on the framework for its CSR program to foster ethically working with governments.

Regardless of the country or law at issue, common definitions are used in the laws that are designed to facilitate a transparent and objective government. These definitions need to be considered when evaluating these laws.

Government Official: Most laws and regulations define a government official as any person acting on behalf of or for an organization controlled wholly or partially by the government.[14] Generally, these laws and regulations do not differentiate between elected officials, appointed officials, civil servants, unpaid or part-time government employees or officials; nor do they differentiate between higher and lower ranking government officials or employees. Some laws and regulations also consider officials or employees of public international organizations, such as the United Nations or the World Bank, to be government officials.[15] Political party members and officials of a political party, as well as candidates for public office, are also often considered government officials.

In some countries, the distinction between commercial and government is blurred or even nonexistent. In these nations, the government owns, controls, or manages what appear to be commercial or private enterprise. Accordingly, many laws include those who own, control, manage, or even work in these entities, often referred to as "state-owned enterprise," to be a government official.[16] Further, any person, to include private individuals, acting on behalf of a government entity or government agency or state-owned enterprise may also be considered, under many laws and regulations, a government official.[17] A comprehensive way to conceptualize who a government

---

14. *See, e.g.,* French Criminal Code Articles 435-1; 435-1; A Resource Guide to the U.S. Foreign Corrupt Practices Act, https://www.justice.gov/sites/default/files/criminal-fraud/legacy/2015/01/16/guide.pdf (last visited Feb. 17, 2019); *Codes and Protocols, Bribery Act 2010, Joint Prosecution Guidance of the Director of the Serious Fraud Office and the Director of Public Prosecutions*, SERIOUS FRAUD OFFICE (Mar. 30, 2011), https://www.sfo.gov.uk/publications/guidance-policy-and-protocols/codes-and-protocols.

15. *See, e.g.*, A Resource Guide to the U.S. Foreign Corrupt Practices Act, *supra* note 14.

16. *See, e.g., id.*

17. *See, e.g.,* 18 U.S.C. §§201–209; A Resource Guide to the U.S. Foreign Corrupt Practices Act, https://www.justice.gov/sites/default/files/criminalfraud/legacy/2015/01/16/guide.pdf (last visited Apr. 14, 2019); UK Bribery Act 2010.

official or employee may be is to consider anyone with a position of public trust or with government-related responsibilities to be a government official for purposes of corruption and improper activity.[18]

Finally, these laws and regulations also treat a government official's family members, members of their households, business partners, officers, directors, investors, or others who may share a common financial interest or business interest with a government official to be covered by the laws and regulations.[19]

Intent: Violations of the laws and regulations that define how to work with governments may not require the business or the individual to have intended to engage in improper behavior. Similarly, the laws and regulations do not require that the improper payment or improper influence be actually transmitted to the government official. Instead, the mere attempt, even if unsuccessful, may result in a violation of law.[20]

Further, many countries' laws permit the government to pursue not only individuals for engaging corrupt practices but also the corporation.[21] When pursuing the corporation, prosecutors use the actions of the employees or third parties to prove the corporation acted illegally.

Penalties: Consequences for violating laws and regulations that define how to interact with governments may carry criminal, civil, or administrative penalties depending on the law or regulation that is violated. If criminal, prosecutors may seek to incarcerate individuals, debar or suspend the individual from future government procurements, seek probation or fines. As for corporations that violate a criminal law, the company may be fined, required to disgorge its profits, ordered to pay for a compliance monitor, delisted from a public exchanging, suspended and/or debarred from government work, or the company may go bankrupt as a result of the weight of the penalties and reputational damage.[22] Civil and administrative penalties include fines as well as debarment and suspension from government business.

Reporting and Disclosure Requirements: See chapters 4 and 10.

Corruption: The term "corruption" covers a broad range of improper and illegal activities such as bribery, kickbacks, conflicts of interest, and procurement fraud. The OECD uses a basic definition of the term "corruption" to convey the improper activity: "abuse of public or private office for personal gain."[23]

---

18. *See, e.g.*, Dixson v. United States, 465 U.S. 482, 496 (1984).
19. *See, e.g.,* 18 U.S.C. §§201–209; A Resource Guide to the U.S. Foreign Corrupt Practices Act, *supra* note 17; UK Bribery Act 2010.
20. *See, e.g.*, *id.*
21. *See, e.g.*, *id.*
22. *See, e.g., id.; see also* Eric Lasry et al., *Anti-Corruption in France,* BAKER MCKENZIE GLOBAL COMPLIANCE NEWS, https://globalcompliancenews.com/anti-corruption/handbook/anti-corruption-in-france/ (last visited Apr. 14, 2019).
23. *Corruption: A Glossary of International Criminal Standards*, OECD (2007), http://www.oecd.org/corruption/anti-bribery/39532693.pdf; *See also* 18 U.S.C. §201; Saudi Arabia Regulations for Combating Bribery Royal Decree M/36 dated 29/12/1412H, corresponding to 27/6/1992G; Brazilian Criminal Code (Decree Law No. 2,848), Article 333 (individuals); Brazilian Anti-Bribery Law No. 12,846/2013 (legal entities).

B. Bribery

The crime of bribery occurs when an item of value is given, offered, promised, directly or indirectly to a government official with the intent to influence government action or inaction.[24] Or when a government official demands, solicits, receives, accepts, or agrees to receive anything of value with the intent to influence government action or inaction.[25] Further, generally, the mere offer or demand alone is sufficient to be considered a crime. That is, the attempt to bribe is as illegal as the bribe.[26] Additionally, many bribery statutes, the FCPA for example, do not except out what some may consider to be gifts or hospitality, if the gift or hospitality was provided to obtain new business or retain business.[27] Finally, as discussed in chapter 10, having a third party engage in these actions on behalf of the business also implicates the business in the crime of bribery.

Some countries prohibit "commercial bribery" that conceptually is the same as bribery of a government official, but rather than improperly offering, promising, or attempting to offer items of value to a government official in exchange for government action, it criminalizes improperly offering items of value to a private individual employed by a nongovernment enterprise to improperly influence the nongovernment entity to perform or not perform some action.[28]

Additionally, the bribery statutes of some countries, for example, the UK Bribery Act and France's new anticorruption law, require organizations to develop ethics and compliance programs that are designed to prevent or detect corruption. Failing to have such a program may itself be considered a crime.[29] For reporting requirements, see chapters 4 and 10.[30]

C. Gifts/Gratuities/Entertainment

Governments and international standard-setting organizations recognize that providing meals, gifts, entertainment, offers of jobs, or anything else of value to a government official may be in fact a bribe. But, if not, when designing an anticorruption CSR program, businesses should consider that providing anything of value to a government official may create an appearance of impropriety or the appearance that the government official is not objective in making decisions. In the United States, this is certainly the case and federal and state laws prohibit or limit what government officials may be provided.

---

24. *See, e.g.,* French Criminal Code Articles 435-1; 435-1; A Resource Guide to the U.S. Foreign Corrupt Practices Act, *supra* note 14; *Codes and Protocols, Bribery Act 2010, supra* note 14.
25. *Id.*
26. *See, e.g.,* A Resource Guide to the U.S. Foreign Corrupt Practices Act, *supra* note 17, UK Bribery Act; 18 U.S. Code §201.
27. *Id.*
28. UK Bribery Act; French Criminal Code, Articles 445-1, 445-2 and 445-3.
29. *Id.*
30. *See, e.g.,* UK Bribery Act; French Criminal Code, Articles 445-1, 445-2 and 445-3; Ghana: Criminal Offenses Act, 1960 (Act 29); Government Contracts (Protection) Act, 1979 (AFRCD 58); The Public Procurement Act 2003; Serious Fraud Office Act, 1993 (Act 466); The Financial Administration Act; Internal Audit Agency Act, 2003 (Act 658); Anti-Money Laundering Act, 2008 (Act 749).

As a result, gift regulations or ethics regulations often prohibit government officials, candidates for public office, and their immediate family members from directly or indirectly accepting or receiving items of value from persons or entities that interact with that government official or that government official's agency, or even simply interacting with the government in any manner.[31] Regulations often either completely prohibit or limit the value of gifts, meals, travel, and even admission to training or seminars.[32] The regulations may also prohibit government officials from fund-raising or otherwise asking for contributions to charities that the government official or their family support.[33]

D. Political Activity—Campaign Contributions and Lobbying

1. Overview

As the ISO anticorruption standard notes, responsibly engaging in the political process is a vital component to preventing corruption.[34] Lobbying and campaign finance laws are designed to further transparency in the political process by regulating interactions with governments to influence government policies, laws and procurements as well as support for political candidates or political and policy issues to mitigate corruption risks.

2. Lobbying Laws

Lobbying laws further transparency in the political process by requiring those who communicate with government officials in order to influence passage, defeat, or modifications of laws, regulations, policies, and budgets to register and disclose their lobbying efforts. Lobbying also includes communicating with government officials on acquisitions or purchasing decisions depending on who in the government the communication is with.[35] Lobbying laws require lobbyists, often the individual lobbyist and the lobbyists' employer, to make extensive disclosures about their communications with government officials as well as about the work that the lobbyist did to prepare for the communications such as researching, preparing position papers, and other related activities.[36] Lobbyists are generally required to register, and registration includes disclosing their clients, their expenses, time spent, and the nature of the communications. Lobbyists may have enhanced restrictions around providing gifts or items of value to government officials.[37]

Recently the U.S. Foreign Agent Registration Act[38] (FARA) has attracted media attention because of high-profile prosecutions for violating FARA. FARA is similar

---

31. *See, e.g.,* Iowa Code §68B.22.
32. *See id.*
33. *See, e.g,* 5 CFR 2635.808.
34. International Organization for Standardization (ISO), https://www.iso.org/standards.html (last visited Apr. 14, 2019).
35. *See, e.g.,* The Lobbying Disclosure Act, 2 U.S.C. 2 U.S.C §1601; Miami-Dade County, Miami-Dade Code §2–11.1(b).
36. *See, e.g., id.*
37. *See, e.g.,* The Lobbying Disclosure Act, 2 U.S.C. 2 U.S.C §1601.
38. *22 U.S.C. §611 et seq.; 28 CFR Part 5.*

to other lobbying laws because it requires registration and disclosure of lobbying activities.[39] However, FARA's focus is on lobbyists working at the direction of a foreign entity to try and influence the U.S. government on U.S. law or policy. FARA also requires registration and disclosure if a U.S. person or entity is representing a foreign entity before a U.S. government agency, to include merely trying to facilitate a meeting between a foreign entity and the U.S. government.[40] Similarly, working at the direction of a foreign entity, to try and to influence public opinion in the United States, also requires registration under FARA.[41] Public relations activities under FARA include advising a foreign entity on matters related to topics of interest to the public as well as advising on U.S. politics and policies.[42] FARA also requires registration if publishing or disseminating information verbally or in writing about the benefits of a foreign entity's political, economic, social, cultural, or any other advantages the foreign entity may have.[43] Finally, soliciting, collecting, or dispersing any item of value for a non-U.S. entity, such as loans or political contributions, also requires registration.[44]

3. Campaign Finance Laws

Just as lobbying laws are designed to bring transparency to the work of the government, so too do campaign finance laws by regulating contributions to candidates' political campaigns, political parties, and political action committees. As a result, campaign finance laws also require extensive disclosures about the entity or person making the contribution. Laws and regulations may limit amounts of contributions; types of contributions such as in-kind or monetary; and whether businesses may even make political contributions at all. Any campaign contribution provided in exchange for government action would be an illegal act, even if a seemingly permitted contribution.[45] Businesses seeking government work may be prohibited from making any political contributions or may be required to disclose those contributions.[46] Some state lobbying laws prohibit a company's board members, executives, sales and business development professionals, and their family members from making political contributions.[47] Campaign finance laws may require disclosure of any campaign contributions a company, its leaders, and its leaders' immediate family members made before it was awarded a government contract and often the disclosures are required during the procurement process.[48]

---

39. *Id.*
40. *Id.*
41. *Id.*
42. *Id.*
43. *Id.*
44. *22 U.S.C. §611 et seq.; 28 CFR Part 5;* Foreign Agents Registration Act, U.S. Department of Justice, https://www.justice.gov/nsd-fara (last visited Apr. 14, 2019).
45. EU Law No. 88–227, of March 11, 1988, as amended.
46. *See, e.g.*, N.J. Executive Orders 117, 118; N.J.A.C. 19:25-24-1 et seq.; 19:25-25-1et seq.; 19:25-26-1et seq.
47. *See e.g., id.*
48. *See, e.g.,* New Jersey, Executive Orders 117, 118; N.J.A.C. 19:25-24-1et seq.; 19:25-25-1et seq.; 19:25-26-1et seq.

E. Conflicts of Interest Laws

Another legal and regulatory tool that governments use to assure transparency, objectivity, and to prevent corruption are conflict of interest laws. Most conflict of interest laws are designed to address the fact that even an appearance of a conflict is as damaging as an actual conflict.

A conflict of interest generally occurs when the government officials' ability to perform their duties objectively would be impaired. Generally, these laws define a conflict as a situation where, as a result of an official's family relationships, business relationships, or financial interest, they would not be able to objectively perform their duties or there may be the appearance that they may not be able to perform their duties objectively.[49]

To address conflicts of interest, government employees are often required to disclose their financial and business interests. These financial disclosures are designed to provide transparency into the government employees' finances to both prevent conflicts of interest and identify potential conflicts.[50]

Additionally, conflict of interest laws and regulations limit a government employee from using their position to further their own interests, the interests of their families, friends, and business relationships. Government employees are prohibited from accessing or using nonpublic government information that may enable their use of this information to their personal benefit.[51]

Conflict of interest laws also often regulate government employees' outside activities by prohibiting such activity whether that be another job or volunteer work, for example, one that conflicts with the employee's official duties.[52] Government officials are generally prohibited from engaging in political activity while at work for the government.[53]

When government employees decide to search for employment outside of the government, they are often restricted in doing so and may be required to recuse themselves from some of their government duties, if their government duties required them to make or oversee acquisition decisions; or if they were a high-ranking government official with substantial authority in the organization.[54] A former government employee may be restricted in how they can engage with the government on behalf of their new employer after having left government.[55]

For businesses, conflict of interest laws may require the business to disclose any business or financial relationship its employees, directors, owners, or third parties have with government officials. Laws may also restrict businesses from recruiting a government employee while the government employee has duties related to that business or when the government employee is responsible for making government acquisition decisions.[56] In

---

49. *See, e.g.* 8 U.S.C. §§202–209; 41 U.S.C. §423; 5 U.S.C. §3110.
50. *See, e.g.* 5 C.F.R. part 2635; Preventing Conflicts of Interest in the Executive Branch, U.S. Office of Government Ethics, https://www2.oge.gov/web/oge.nsf/Statutes (last visited Apr. 14, 2019).
51. *See, e.g., id.*
52. *See, e.g., id.*
53. *See, e.g., id.*
54. *See e.g.*, 18 U.S.C. §§202–209; MA Code §268A, sec. 5.
55. *See, e.g.*, Preventing Conflicts of Interest in the Executive Branch, U.S. Office of Government Ethics, https://www2.oge.gov/web/oge.nsf/Statutes (last visited Apr. 14, 2019).
56. *See, e.g., id.*

the United States, violating these requirements may be considered a crime.[57] Similarly, even if permitted to recruit and hire a government official, the government official may be statutorily prohibited from interacting with the government on behalf of their new employer or from receiving compensation that originated from government work while they were still employed with the government.[58]

F. Procurement Laws

OECD reports that about 13 percent of GDP in OECD signatory countries comes from public procurement.[59] Government procurement by its nature is highly vulnerable to corruption.[60] Given this, many countries have developed complex procurement processes to manage government procurement to further integrity, transparency, stakeholder participation, accessibility, and oversight.[61]

Governments may have a defined process for soliciting work and for awarding contracts which often requires public notice about the solicitation and award. Regulations protect both government and bidder procurement sensitive information in an effort to avoid a bidder obtaining nonpublic information to use to its advantage.[62] Government employees, contractors, or anyone acting on behalf of a government with access to procurement sensitive information may not disclose it or seek to obtain it unless legally permitted to do so.[63]

Government employees who may have a personal, financial, or business interest in the company seeking the award may be required to disclose that interest and to recuse themselves.[64] Procurement regulations usually have extensive rights for the government to audit contractors and to demand how contractors select their subcontractors.[65]

Likewise, companies executing or pursuing government work are often required to disclose any relationships the company, its leaders, owners, managers, employees, and family members of these individual may have with a government employee; or the type of work the company is performing for the government.[66] Businesses pursuing government work may be required to certify their compliance with lobbying, campaign finance, bribery, gifts, and other laws and regulations. Procurement laws also often require that the business pursuing government work have a reputation for integrity and compliance with laws, to include at times being required to have an ethics and compliance program.[67]

---

57. 18 U.S.C. §§202–209.
58. *See, e.g.*, 18 U.S.C. §§202–209; Executive Order 12674 of 1989 modified by EO 12731; 41 U.S.C. §423; 5 CFR 2635.
59. *Public Procurement Toolbox*, OECD, http://www.oecd.org/governance/procurement/toolbox/principlestools/integrity/ (last visited Apr. 14, 2019).
60. *Id.*
61. *Id.*
62. *See, e.g.* 48 C.F.R. §3.104-1-11; *Procurement Integrity*, U.S. DEPARTMENT OF JUSTICE, https://www.justice.gov/jmd/procurement-integrity (last visited Apr. 14, 2019).
63. *See, e.g.*, 48 CFR 3.104-4(a-b).
64. *See, e.g.*, 5 C.F.R. 2635.502, 502.
65. *See, e.g.*, 48 CFR 52.215-2.
66. *See, e.g.*, 48 C.F.R. Part 9.
67. *See, e.g.*, 48 CFR 52.203-13.

G. Trade Sanctions and Export Regulations

Most nations restrict doing business or engaging in financial transactions with certain countries, organizations, and individuals, and these restrictions are often directed to those who are government officials or who otherwise have some connection to the government of the country. In the United States, the U.S. Treasury's Office of Foreign Asset Controls (OFAC) enforces sanctions programs primarily by blocking assets and restricting trade of the sanctioned country, organization, or individual.[68] Sanctions essentially make it illegal for a corporate to do business with the sanctioned nation. Similarly, the sanctions may be directed at an industry, certain entities, and even individuals. Trade sanctions are designed to protect a country's economic and national security interests; and as a result countries will develop guidance to facilitate compliance with trade laws. For example, Nigeria will be publishing registrations of who owns the companies in its country to facilitate identification of possible sanctioned persons and entities; and in the United States, OFAC provides extensive guidance on trade laws.[69]

In addition to trade laws, governments also regulate the export of certain products and services that have or may have a military, intelligence, or law enforcement use.[70] Exporting includes shipping, carrying, transferring, disclosing through any means, to include verbal communication or e-mails, information, services, technology, and goods.[71] Similar to trade sanctions, export regulations are designed to protect a country's national security interests by preventing certain governments from accessing information, services, technology, and goods.

Even non-U.S. products may be considered an export after brought into the United States and then exported.[72]

These laws and regulations are challenging to manage because trade sanctions and export regulations change quickly as a result of shifting political relationships between nations. The repercussions of noncompliance may result in civil or criminal sanctions. This creates the need for businesses to not only develop compliance programs to manage these requirements but also manage how their business partners and customers handle export-controlled items and how they comply with trade sanctions. Organizations may be held civilly or criminally liable if they know or have reason to know that their actions violate the law—accordingly due diligence is mandatory (see chapter 10).

Additionally, trade laws and import regulations control goods that enter a nation to protect a nation's interests and policies. For example, U.S. trade and import laws

---

68. 18 U.S.C. §2332(d); 31 CFR §501; *Office of Foreign Assets Control—Sanctions Programs and Information,* U.S. DEPARTMENT OF TREASURY, http://www.treasury.gov/resource-center/sanctions/Pages/default.aspx (last visited Apr. 13, 2019).

69. *The Road Map on the Implementation of Beneficial Ownership Disclosure in Nigeria,* https://eiti.org/sites/default/files/documents/neiti-bor-281216.pdf (last visited Apr. 13, 2019).

70. *See, e.g., Overview of U.S. Export Control System,* A Resource on Strategic Trade Management and Export Controls, https://www.state.gov/strategictrade/overview/ (last visited Apr. 2014).

71. *Id.*

72. 15 CFR 730.5; *Overview of U.S. Export Control System,* A Resource on Strategic Trade Management and Export Controls, https://www.state.gov/strategictrade/overview/ (last visited Apr. 2014).

and regulations allow the government to seize and forfeit goods entering the United States if the goods "have been introduced, or attempted to be introduced, into the United States contrary to law."[73] This prohibition is expansive and covers goods that enter the United States if those goods are, for example, counterfeit, contraband, fail to have proper licenses or permits, violate trademark laws.[74] Goods entering the United States may also be prohibited if they do not comply with health, safety, or conservation laws and regulations that may include goods produced with forced labor.[75]

IV. STANDARDS AND GUIDANCE WHEN WORKING WITH GOVERNMENTS

A. Overview

Given the evidence demonstrating that in countries where corruption is strong and the rule of law is weak economic opportunities are limited, economic growth is stymied, and human rights are not respected, many organizations beyond governments provide guidance, standards, and norms to assist organizations and governments in mitigating the risk of corruption and improper interactions with government officials.

As countries have been more active in passing laws and regulations to eradicate corrupt behavior, international organizations, nonprofits, and governments have developed standards and guidance for governments to mitigate the demand side for improper payments, as well as the supply side by directing organizations that interact with governments on mitigating corruption risks. This guidance is generally consistent and reflects the methods for developing effective ethics and compliance programs, as discussed in chapter 10. However, the guidance and standards provide for not only managing compliance with corruption laws but also recommend how socially responsible organizations should develop approaches for managing its interactions when working with governments.

The International Organization for Standardization (ISO), Organisation for Economic Co-operation and Development (OECD), and the United Nations all provide specific standards for anti-corruption compliance to multinational corporations. Management and counsel seeking to establish or update their compliance programs should consider each as a starting point, along with government developed guidance such as the Resource Guide for the Foreign Corrupt Practices Act and UK Bribery Act.[76]

While not black letter law, these standards do form the bases of several countries' anti-corruption regulatory regimes and are flexible enough to be tailored to companies of different size, business, and geographic focus. Some of these organizations provide concrete tools for assessing corruption risks globally. For example, Transparency

---

73. *See, e.g.*, Tariff Act 19 U.S.C. §§1595, 1595a; 19 C.F.R. §§12.42–.45; Trade Facilitation and Trade Enforcement Act of 2015 (TFTEA).
74. *Id.*
75. *Id.*
76. A Resource Guide to the U.S. Foreign Corrupt Practices Act, 54–55; UK Bribery Act 2010.

International has designed a "Corruption Perceptions Index" which measures the perceived corruption in any given country.[77]

B. International Organization for Standardization (ISO)

The ISO develops and publishes best practices and standards for multinational corporations seeking to stay on the forefront of a dynamic compliance landscape. It is comprised of national standards bodies from 163 member countries and has developed over twenty thousand voluntary international standards.

In October 2016, ISO published ISO 37001:16—Anti-bribery Management Systems (ISO 37001)—the first and only standard designed to help organizations establish, implement, maintain, and improve their anti-bribery compliance program.[78] The standard was written for organizations large and small, public and private, and headquartered in any country.[79] Its measures, or best practices, may be integrated with existing management processes and controls, following ISO's common high-level structure for management system standards. Further, its requirements make it accessible to independent certification by third parties.

ISO 37001 echoes guidance issued by the U.S. Department of Justice and the Securities and Exchange Commission on the Foreign Corrupt Practices Act—specifically "A Resource Guide to the U.S. Foreign Corrupt Practices Act (FCPA)," issued in 2012. Since its publication, ISO 37001 has been used by foreign governments such as Singapore and Peru and major corporations like Walmart and Microsoft to form the basis of their anti-bribery policies and procedures.

ISO 37001 is focused on both bribery *by* the organization, its personnel, or agents and bribery *of* the organization, its personnel, or agents.[80] The standard applies a generic definition of bribery, since its legal definition and criminalization vary by country.[81]

C. The Organisation for Economic Co-operation and Development (OECD)

The OECD Anti-bribery Convention of 1997 established legally binding standards among its signatory nations that criminalized bribery of foreign officials in international business transactions.[82] The Convention touts itself as the first anti-bribery instrument that focuses on the "supply side" of bribery.[83] That is, having the "suppliers" of improper

---

77. *FAQS On Transparency International*, TRANSPARENCY INTERNATIONAL, https://www.transparency.org/whoweare/organisation/faqs_on_transparency_international/9 (last visited Apr. 9, 2019).
78. *ISO 37001—Anti-bribery Management Systems,* INTERNATIONAL ORGANIZATION FOR STANDARDIZATION, https://www.iso.org/iso-37001-anti-bribery-management.html (last visited Apr. 9, 2019).
79. *Id.*
80. *Id.*
81. *Id.*
82. *OECD Convention on Combating Bribery of Foreign Public Officials in International Business Transactions,* OECD, http://www.oecd.org/corruption/oecdantibriberyconvention.htm (last visited Apr. 9, 2019).
83. *Id.*

payments punished and providing them the tools and guidance to mitigate the risk of the organization making improper payments.[84] Signatory countries to the Convention now number 44 and include all G-8 countries.[85]

Upon coming into force in 1999, the Convention created the OECD Working Group on Bribery, a peer-driven monitoring body that rigorously examines and makes recommendations on member countries' implementation of international anti-bribery obligations.[86] The Working Group issued further findings and recommendations on anti-bribery controls in 2009 and subsequently issued Good Practice Guidance on Internal Controls, Ethics, and Compliance (Good Practice Guidance), addressed to small and medium companies, in 2010.[87] OECD continues to provide further guidance and resources for managing public integrity, to include developing a public integrity toolbox.[88]

D. United Nations Convention against Corruption

The United Nations Convention against Corruption is the only legally binding universal anti-corruption instrument which UN member states have signed. In addition to providing guidance preventing corruption, it also provides guidance and support for law enforcement on recovering assets, cooperating internationally to combat corruption, as well as technical support. A highlight of the Convention is a specific chapter on asset recovery, aimed at returning assets to their rightful owners, including countries from which they had been taken illicitly. The vast majority of UN member states are parties to the Convention.[89]

V. GOVERNANCE AND COMPLIANCE WHEN WORKING WITH GOVERNMENTS

A. Developing a CSR Program for Working with Governments

Whether building a CSR program to compliantly work with governments or improving an existing program, approaching the risk of corruption when working with governments, businesses should take a strategic and holistic approach to assure efficiencies and effectiveness. A strategic, holistic approach provides the context for leaders by demonstrating to both directors and executives why the organization needs a compliance program around working with governments.

---

84. *Id.*
85. *Id.*
86. *Id.*
87. *Id.*
88. *Public Procurement Toolbox*, OECD, http://www.oecd.org/governance/procurement/toolbox/principlestools/integrity/ (last visited Apr. 9, 2019).
89. *United Nations Convention against Corruption*, UNODC, https://www.unodc.org/unodc/en/treaties/CAC/ (last visited Apr. 9, 2019).

It is vital to convey why a business needs a program to mitigate against the risk of corruption because many directors and executives respond to the notion of establishing an anti-corruption program by explaining that their organization is ethical and would simply not engage in corrupt behavior. That may be true but corruption is insidious and without a holistic, strategic perspective, it is hard for leaders to appreciate how a business may be at risk for exposure to corruption. A more holistic approach to mitigating corruption risks and building a CSR program for compliantly working with governments provides leadership the context for why a CSR program is necessary which then allows leadership to provide strategic direction and to actually understand a program's overall structure and effectiveness.

Without a strategic approach, businesses often focus on gifts, meals, and entertainment resulting in business leaders spending their time reviewing and approving requests for gifts, meals, or other entertainment. Similarly, directors may wonder why they are getting reports about which customers were taken out to dinner in a quarter or reports that simply state the organization uses a certain number of consultants to sell its products—neither report gives context. Either way, leadership lacks context for the compliance program focused on working with governments and as a result will likely not be engaged in supporting the program.

A holistic approach to a CSR program designed to compliantly work with governments helps assure that different functions in an organization follow the same policies and have the same appreciation for the organization's commitment to avoiding the risk of corruption. For example, a company's social responsibility team may support the state senator's favorite charity, which his wife runs and pays herself $550,000 a year to do so, by contributing $10,000 to the charity's annual fund-raiser. Meanwhile, the same company's business development team is denied their request to buy a $30 mooncake for a client. Employees will quickly discover these inconsistencies as will a government should the organization find itself under investigation. Employees who do not understand policies or who learn of inconsistent policies will not follow policies and processes because the processes do not make sense to them.

A strategic, holistic approach manages the corruption risk throughout all geographies where the business operates and throughout all functions in the organization. Many well-intentioned anticorruption programs myopically focus on mitigating the risk of violating the Foreign Corrupt Practices Act while forgetting that interacting with U.S. federal, state, and local government officials also expose the business to corruption risks; and that other countries also have an array of corruption laws, as discussed earlier, that must be followed.

B. Developing a Strategic View to Compliantly Work with Governments

The first step for an organization to take a more strategic and holistic view of how it works with governments is to identify how it interacts with governments. This includes analyzing the sales and delivery process: how the business goes to market; how it identifies its clients; how it delivers its goods and services, and how it gets paid. This should also include identifying the geographic markets within which the business operates as well as the level of corruption risk in that geography using the guidance and assessment of international organizations like Transparency International. Once those markets are identified, the business needs to determine how it interacts with governments in those markets. This includes how it: obtains government licenses and permits; pays taxes; obtains visas or work permits; and engages in any government inspections; etc.

Without conducting an initial risk assessment of this type, the anticorruption program is not tethered to how the business operates. Once a business identifies how it interacts with governments, it should then identify what laws apply. With a comprehensive understanding of how the business interacts with governments and the laws that apply to those interactions, a business is able to develop a holistic, strategic plan to build a compliance and CSR program when working with governments. Chapter 10 on ethics and compliance should be consulted for further guidance on developing processes, policies, and training.

Questions to get started on determining how a business interacts with governments:

1. How does the organization obtain or retain business?

    - Does it use third parties like sales agents, consultants, or others to develop customers?
    - Does it use an internal business development or sales team?
    - Does it sell to governments? Do the business' customers sell to governments?
    - Regardless of whether the business uses third parties or its own team to obtain and retain business, exactly how does the business sell?
    - Does it host seminars, trainings, social events to engage with customers or potential customers?

2. How does the organization identify, recruit, and hire talent?

    - Does the business recruit from governments because the business benefits from having former government officials or government employees knowledge and expertise?
    - Does it get resumes from government officials and government employees because the business is attractive to government officials?
    - Does it bring on interns or employees at the recommendation of customers?
    - Does it have a program for recruiting from state and local universities and colleges?

3. Does the organization try to influence policy, participate in the political process, or support political candidate?

    - Does it have a political action committee?
    - Do it have internal lobbyists or does it retain outside lobbying support?
    - Does it have a strong interest in policy or in particular laws and regulations? If so, does it engage in policy debate, policy influence, or in influencing laws and regulations?

- Are business leaders active politically as individuals—supporting candidates or causes?
- Does the organization host events to support political candidate or political causes?

4. How does the organization comply with laws and regulations that require interacting with government officials?
    - What is the process for obtaining permits? Licenses? Visas? Paying taxes? Disputing taxes?
    - Who in the organization is responsible for getting permits, licenses, visas, paying taxes?

5. What is the organization's process for responding to government requests for information subpoenas, audits, letters requesting information, representations, and certifications?
    - Does it have a process for responding?
    - Who is responsible for managing the response and for interacting with the government?

6. Do employees and leaders regularly socialize with government officials or employees?
    - Are any employees close friends or family with government officials or employees?
    - Are any employees themselves a government official?

7. If the business has government contracts, grants, loans, or any type of agreement with the government:
    - How are these agreements executed?
    - How are invoices paid?
    - How are expenses identified and accounted for?
    - How are disputes over the agreements handled?

8. If merging, acquiring, forming joint ventures, or other partnerships, how are these organizations involved with governments?

C. External Engagement

Although a business ethics and compliance program as discussed above and in chapter 10 is necessary to manage the risk of anticorruption, these internal compliance programs are designed to combat the supply of improper payments. However, to engage as a responsible corporate citizen in the fight against corruption, the demand side of corruption must be considered as part of a governance and compliance program. To impact the demand side of corruption, an organization should undertake initiatives to engage externally. Engaging with external stakeholders will position a company to influence the demand for corrupt payments in a community.

First, it is vital for a business to communicate with external stakeholders on the topic of combatting corruption, to include signing on formally to anticorruption pacts or initiatives.[90] Specifically, this may entail the business engaging with organizations like the OECD and the UN, organizations that have developed these pacts, as well as engaging with others in the business industry and with trade associations around best practices to combat corruption.[91]

External engagement also includes working with governments on policy and legislation to further initiatives that will combat corruption and further the rule of law. For example, the Merck Company Foundation has established programs, guidance, and support for ethics and anti-corruption work in emerging markets and participates and funds thought leadership and training in the area. Although most companies will not have the resources for such an endeavor, participating in organizations that combat corruption with thought leadership, training, and interactions with government and nongovernment organizations is possible.[92] When making this commitment to engage externally, it's important that the organization actually assign employees the responsibility to undertake the engagement and to provide them the resources to actively engage.

Second, the organization should make clear to industry, its third parties, and to governments that it is committed to combatting corruption and that it will hold itself, its business partners, and governments accountable for behavior that is inconsistent with this commitment, even in nations where the rule of law is not enforced or is weak.[93] This demonstrated commitment may be exhibited by requiring its business partners to contractually agree to ethical and compliant behavior as discussed further in chapter 10. It should also be made clear through an organization's websites and other corporate literature as well as regularly discussed by its leaders in public forums and in internal corporate events. Finally, some organizations with robust ethics and compliance programs and training have offered training externally to their business partners, industry, and even governments to externally reach stakeholders.[94]

---

90. *See, e.g.*, OECD, http://www.oecd.org/unitedstates/?; https://oecdonthelevel.com/2018/12/05/taking-the-fight-against-corruption-to-the-demand-side-of-bribery/.

91. *See, e.g.*, Transparency International, https://www.transparency.org/; UN Convention against Corruption, https://www.unodc.org/unodc/en/treaties/CAC/index.html; OECD, http://www.oecd.org/unitedstates/?; https://oecdonthelevel.com/2018/12/05/taking-the-fight-against-corruption-to-the-demand-side-of-bribery/; Extractive Industries Transparency Initiative (EITI), https://eiti.org/who-we-are.

92. The Merck Company Foundation, https://www.msdresponsibility.com/ethics-transparency/.

93. *See, e.g.*, International Organization for Standardization (ISO), https://www.iso.org/standards.html (last visited Apr. 14, 2019).

94. *See, e.g., Combating International Corruption: A Work in Progress*, The Metropolitan Corporate Counsel (July 2008), http://www.metrocorpcounsel.com/pdf/2008/July/19.pdf.

VI. SUMMARY AND TAKEAWAYS

As a result of increased prosecutions for corrupt behavior as well as more countries passing anti-corruption laws, businesses have been more diligent in developing internal programs to mitigate the risk of corrupt behaviors which decreases the supply of improper payments. However, given a corporation's unique ability to provide capital, create jobs, and be a source of tax revenue, the socially responsible corporation is well positioned to influence governments to combat corruption and support the rule of law which will decrease the demand for improper payments.[95] As a result, corporations need to continue to develop, manage, and improve their internal corporate ethics and compliance program to mitigate corruption risks but they also need to focus externally to combat improper behavior.

To accomplish this, businesses first need to appreciate when assessing their risk of corrupt behavior to consider that business functions beyond business development and finance may be exposed to the risk of improper behavior when working with governments. Upon assessing the risk of corruption strategically and holistically, beyond the functions that are traditionally thought to expose a business to this risk, the organization needs to develop ethics and compliance approaches to mitigate the risk.[96] See chapter 10 on ethics and compliance for further guidance on developing ethics and compliance programs. However, the socially responsible company, in addition to its internal commitment to identify and mitigate corruption risks when working with governments, needs to act externally by engaging with industry, trade associations, standard-setting organizations, and even governments to impact the demand for improper behavior. It is through committing to work both internally and externally that a corporation develops an effective CSR program when working with governments.

---

95. *Id.*
96. *Guidance on Social Responsibility*, *supra* note 5.

About the Editors

Alan S. Gutterman is the Founding Director of the Sustainable Entrepreneurship Project (www.seproject.org). In addition, Alan's prolific output of practical guidance and tools for legal and financial professionals, managers, entrepreneurs and investors has made him one of the best-selling individual authors in the global legal publishing marketplace. His cornerstone work, Business Transactions Solution, is on online-only product available and featured on Thomson Reuters' Westlaw, the world's largest legal content platform, which includes almost 200 book-length modules covering the entire lifecycle of a business. Alan has also authored or edited over 80 books on sustainable entrepreneurship, management, business law and transactions, international law business and technology management for a number of publishers including Thomson Reuters, Practical Law, Kluwer, Aspatore, Oxford, Quorum, ABA Press, Aspen, Sweet & Maxwell, Euromoney, Business Expert Press, Harvard Business Publishing, CCH and BNA.

Alan has over three decades of experience as a partner and senior counsel with internationally recognized law firms counseling small and large business enterprises in the areas of general corporate and securities matters, venture capital, mergers and acquisitions, international law and transactions, strategic business alliances, technology transfers and intellectual property, and has also held senior management positions with several technology-based businesses including service as the chief legal officer of a leading international distributor of IT products headquartered in Silicon Valley and as the chief operating officer of an emerging broadband media company. He has been an adjunct faculty member at several colleges and universities, including Boalt Hall, Golden Gate University, Hastings College of Law, Santa Clara University and the University of San Francisco, teaching classes on a diverse range of topics including corporate finance, venture capital, corporate law, Japanese business law and law and economic development. He received his A.B., M.B.A., and J.D. from the University of California at Berkeley, a D.B.A. from Golden Gate University, and a Ph. D. from the University of Cambridge.

For more information about Alan and his activities, please contact him directly at alangutterman@gmail.com, follow him on LinkedIn (https://www.linkedin.com/in/alangutterman/) and visit his website at alangutterman.com, which includes an extensive collection of links to his books and other publications and resource materials for students and practitioners of sustainable entrepreneurship.

Margaret M. Cassidy is the principal and founder of Cassidy Law. She counsels businesses on legal and ethics matters when dealing with foreign, federal, state, and local governments in the areas of corruption, FCPA, fraud, international trade, the False Claims Act, government ethics, procurement, and national security. Prior to launching Cassidy Law, Margaret held positions as PricewaterhouseCoopers' Government Ethics & Compliance Leader, GE Transportation's Global Ethics & Compliance Counsel, and as a state court prosecutor. Margaret currently chairs the ABA Business Law Section Corporate Compliance Committee.

Travis Miller is an international trade and compliance attorney specializing in ITAR/EAR/Sanctions, global anti-corruption, anti-slavery, code of conduct, environmental, health and safety, product stewardship (RoHS/REACH/Conflict Minerals), and corporate social responsibility (corporate ethics, CSR/CDP reporting, SEC filings). He manages Assent's worldwide legal activities, such as advising the board of directors on legal matters and overseeing corporate compliance, governance initiatives and other commercial transactions. Travis provides legal support and insight to every team at the company, from sales to services and partner organizations.

Ashley C. Walter is a business lawyer who specializes in advising technology and life sciences companies regarding strategy and compliance with respect to corporate social responsibility-related legal requirements. Ashley's practice also includes representing clients before government agencies in connection with competition and national security filings, and he has experience advising on a wide variety of corporate matters including formations, intellectual property and employment matters, venture capital financings, and mergers and acquisitions.

As Chair of the CSR Governance & Compliance Practice Group of Fenwick & West, Ashley provides value to clients by bringing to bear a firm grounding in corporate social responsibility (CSR) issues, sector-specific knowledge, a deep familiarity with current and proposed CSR-related legal requirements, a practical understanding of technology company supply chains, and significant experience in the design and implementation of responsibility management systems, such as CSR policies and standards.

Ashley is a co-founder and a former Chair of the Corporate Social Responsibility Law Committee of the ABA Business Law Section and has published and lectured on CSR, including at Stanford Law School, where he has taught the course "Corporate Social Responsibility" and has served as a panelist for the Stanford Directors' College.

About the Authors

Fernanda Beraldi (Chapter 6: Labor and Supply Chain Practices) works for Cummins Inc. in Indianapolis as Senior Director, Ethics and Compliance. Fernanda has fifteen years of legal experience and started at Cummins in 2015 after having worked for more than six years for Embraer SA. She is dual-licensed as an attorney in Brazil and Indiana. Fernanda graduated from Mackenzie University in São Paulo, Brazil, and completed a Master of Laws program in Corporate and Commercial Law at Robert H. McKinney School of Law in Indianapolis (cum laude). Fernanda's past work experience exposed her to a broad array of foreign countries, a variety of cultures, and a number of compliance related areas of practice such as export control, anti-bribery regulations and enforcement, interacting with government officials and state-owned entities, conflicts of interest, creating worldwide sales agents policies, and developing content and providing global and/or customized training to employees and third parties on these important matters. Specific subject matters also include corporate compliance program structure, risk assessment, strategy, and internal investigations. Currently, she has direct accountability for Cummins corruption prevention, third-party compliance program, anti-money laundering and antislavery programs, and implementation of compliance program globally. She has worked on deal teams conducting due diligence reviews, developing global compliance strategy, and negotiating compliance terms and policies, and compliance integration for newly closed deals. In 2019, Fernanda was one of the recipients of the Top 10 "30-somethings" by the Association of Corporate Counsel, the first Brazilian to receive such honor.

Moshe B. Broder (Chapter 13: Cybersecurity Risk Management Is a Corporate Responsibility) is an associate in the Government Contracts, National Security, and Privacy & Cybersecurity practices at Wiley Rein LLP. Moshe counsels and represents government contractors in a broad range of legal issues, including bid protests, contract claims, and prime-subcontractor disputes litigated in federal and state courts. Moshe graduated *cum laude* from the Georgetown University Law Center, where he served as Assistant Managing Editor on the *Georgetown Immigration Law Journal*, and received his B.A. in psychology from Yeshiva University.

Ed Broecker (Chapter 6: Labor and Supply Chain Practices) is a partner at Quarles & Brady LLP in Indianapolis. Ed has a great depth of experience in supply chain matters, international trade, investigations, compliance program creation, improvement and related training, counseling, and assessment. He represents a broad array of national and international clients with concentration in the fields of advanced manufacturing, IT and life sciences, sales and distribution, and hospitality and gaming industries. He balances business results and mitigation of legal risks, concentrating his practice on commercial agreements, corporate and board governance, software licenses, finance and equipment leases and helping clients in transitional situations including asset monetization, business expansion, and capitalization. Ed is a member of the American Bar Association, Business Law Section, and a member of the Corporate Compliance Subcommittee.

Renée Brooker (Chapter 10: Building a CSR Program through an Ethics and Compliance Program) is the former Assistant Director for Civil Frauds at the Justice Department, where she had oversight for hundreds of settlements and judgments, with nearly $6 billion in False Claims Act and FIRREA recoveries. Renée left the Justice Department in 2017 to expand Finch McCranie's whistleblower practice to Washington, D.C., and to serve as part of the team for Larry Thompson, Independent Corporate Compliance Monitor, and Auditor for Volkswagen AG, under its plea agreement and consent decree.

Emily C. Brown (Chapter 6: Labor and Supply Chain Practices) is an associate at Green and Spiegel LLC in Philadelphia, PA. She earned her J.D. and M.A. at American University and is barred in the District of Columbia. Focusing her practice on immigration compliance, she advises companies on proper onboarding and Form I-9 procedures and supports companies during government investigations.

Emily is developing resources for the International Supply Chain Initiative to advise companies on how to identify and remediate the risk of forced labor in the global supply chain. She has been a speaker on human trafficking and works to raise awareness of how to eliminate forced labor. Emily also volunteers in her community, as a sexual assault victim advocate in South Jersey. During law school, Emily worked as a law clerk for U.S. Immigration and Customs Enforcement in the Human Rights Law Section, strengthening protections and legal remedies for victims of human trafficking. During her graduate program, she prepared a Human Rights Impact Assessment for the American Bar Association Center for Human Rights, which analyzed international trade agreements' effect on labor laws in Asia and how to protect workers' rights. Emily has studied human rights, migration, and international affairs in the Middle East and Europe.

Megan Brown (Chapter 13: Cybersecurity Risk Management Is a Corporate Responsibility) is a partner leading Wiley Rein LLP's Cybersecurity and Data Privacy practice, where she has practiced for 15 years. She served as Counsel to two U.S. Attorneys General at the Department of Justice and also works as Cybersecurity Program Director at the National Security Institute at the George Mason Antonin Scalia Law School. Megan graduated from Harvard Law School and the College of William and Mary, and clerked on the U.S. Court of Appeals for the Fifth Circuit.

Radha Curpen (Chapter 9: Corporate Social Responsiblity and Indigenous Rights) has over 25 years of experience, often in high-profile matters in North America, including provinces across Canada and in the United States. She specializes in environmental, Aboriginal and regulatory matters, and the transportation of dangerous goods. Radha provides strategic counsel to clients on regulatory compliance, the management of environmental risks, the defense of environmental litigation, the avoidance and defense of environmental related prosecutions, crisis prevention and management, mitigating business disruption, and reputation management.

Within her Aboriginal practice, Radha advises on comprehensive and specific land and property compensation claims; the duty to consult, treaty claims and interpretation; Aboriginal self-government; the fiduciary relationship between governments and Aboriginal peoples; claims to renewable and non-renewable natural resources; hunting, fishing, and trapping rights; government relations; economic development; and various public policy issues.

Radha has been repeatedly recognized as one of Canada's top lawyers in Aboriginal law, energy law and environmental law, as well as a leading environmental lawyer in the United States. She practices in both English and French.

Michael L. Diakiwski (Chapter 13: Cybersecurity Risk Management Is a Corporate Responsibility) is an associate in the Privacy & Cybersecurity, National Security, and Telecom, Media & Technology practice groups at Wiley Rein LLP. Michael draws on his experience as a former official with the U.S. Department of Homeland Security, where he advised the Secretary, General Counsel, and senior leadership on high-profile legal, political, and security matters. He graduated from Georgetown Law and earned his undergraduate degree at Providence College.

Richard Duda (Chapter 3: Stakeholder Engagement) currently serves as Associate General Counsel, Operations and Regulatory Affairs at Ingredion Incorporated. He previously held the positions of Associate General Counsel, South America, and Counsel, Asia-Pacific. Rick, who joined Ingredion in 2005 as Counsel, Litigation, received his law degree from Loyola University Chicago School of Law and his bachelor's degree in Information and Decision Science from the University of Illinois at Chicago.

Jesse M. Finfrock (Chapter 11: Impact Investing; Chapter 12: Alternative Legal Entities) is an associate in the San Francisco office of Morrison & Foerster and is a member of the firm's Corporate Group. Mr. Finfrock's practice focuses on "impact" investing and social entrepreneurship. Mr. Finfrock counsels family offices, foundations, venture capital investors, charities, startups and emerging companies on structuring, early-stage and late-stage financings, and general transactional matters. He works with clients across a broad range of industries, including technology, healthcare, life sciences, education, media, social services and consumer products. He currently serves as co-chair of the firm's San Francisco sustainability committee. Mr. Finfrock earned his B.A. in Anthropology from the University of California, Santa Cruz in 2005 and received his J.D. from the University of California, Berkeley–School of Law in 2014, where he launched a student social venture group and ran a social enterprise he cofounded. Jesse is a member of Echoing Green's Legal Advisory Group, Start Small Think Big's Founding Partner Advisory Council, and the Impact Investing Legal Working Group, among others. Prior to joining Morrison & Foerster, Mr. Finfrock was corporate counsel at a local law firm headquartered in San Francisco.

Benjamin T.R. Fox (Chapter 11: Impact Investing; Chapter 12: Alternative Legal Entities) is an associate in Morrison & Foerster's Corporate Department in the San Francisco office. Mr. Fox is a member of the firm's Social Enterprise and Impact Investing and Energy and Clean Technology Groups. Mr. Fox's practice focuses on the representation of clients in the clean technology, renewable energy and sustainability space. Mr. Fox counsels startup to late-stage private companies, venture capital and private equity investors, as well as family offices, private foundations and public charities in a broad range of transactional matters including early-stage and late-stage equity and debt financings, mergers, acquisitions, asset purchases and sales, joint ventures and hybrid or "tandem" structuring arrangements between non-profit and for-profit entities. He currently serves as member of the San Francisco Young Professionals in Energy events committee. Mr. Fox earned his J.D. from the University of California, Berkeley, School of Law (Boalt Hall), with a certificate of specialization in both Environmental Law and Energy and Clean Technology Law. At Boalt, he served as an executive editor of *Ecology Law Quarterly*, a member of the *California Law Review*, and a judicial extern for the Honorable Edward M. Chen of the U.S. District Court for the Northern District of California.

Matthew Gardner (Chapter 13: Cybersecurity Risk Management Is a Corporate Responsibility) is a partner in the Privacy & Cybersecurity and White Collar practice groups at Wiley Rein LLP. Matt has extensive experience working with critical infrastructure companies to manage cyber risk and routinely advises clients on complicated issues involving the intersection of law and emerging technologies. Prior to private practice, Matt was a federal prosecutor focused on investigating computer crimes.

Kwame Gyamfi Boateng (Chapter 14: Working with Governments) currently works as a law clerk with Cassidy Law PLLC. Kwame is a recent graduate of George Washington University's LLM program and prior to that obtained a Bachelor of Laws degree from the University of London and a Bachelor's degree in Sociology with History from the University of Ghana. Kwame has extensive experience in corporate and international law from his time working at Trustee Services Limited, a subsidiary of Bentsi-Enchill, Letsa & Ankomah Law Firm (BELA) in Accra, Ghana. Among his proudest achievements are having served as President of the Rotaract Club of Accra (a Rotary International Youth Program of Accra, Ghana) where he led volunteers to include creating a scholarship to sponsor underprivileged youth.

Julie Kendig-Schrader (Chapter 5: Environment) has practiced environmental and land use law with the international law firm of Greenberg Traurig for over twenty years.

She previously worked as counsel for the South Florida Water Management District. Her practice includes representation of local, national and international corporations providing guidance regarding environmental and land use regulatory and permitting issues.

E. Christopher Johnson, Jr. (Chapter 6: Labor and Supply Chain Practices) is CEO and Cofounder of Center for Justice, Rights & Dignity; retired General Motors North America Vice President; and General Counsel and Chair, Corporate Social Responsibility Committee, ABA Business Law Section. Johnson, a West Point graduate and decorated Army veteran, is dedicated to fighting human trafficking. At the outset, he acknowledges Jesus Christ for always being the guiding light in his life and for bringing into his life all the people mentioned below and many other family members, colleagues, and friends who have contributed to his success. This includes his parents and his two wives, Sheryl, whose life was claimed by breast cancer, and his current wife, Rhonda, for her faithful and unrelenting love and support, and Erin, Chip, and Souluna who have made him a proud father and grandfather; also his diligent and dedicated coauthors, and Susan Maslow, Elise Groulx Diggs, his daughter Erin Preston-Johnson Bevel, Esq., Bill Minick, Bo Delp, Tom Mackall, Michael Torrence, Nelson Miller, and Alisia Jones who have made significant contributions to this work; together with the Working Group to Draft Human Rights Protections in International Supply Contracts led by David V. Snyder, chair, and Susan Maslow, vice chair, and Working Group members, Jennifer Martin and Ramona Lampley. In addition, the author also acknowledges the support of past ABA president Laurel Bellows and other colleagues on the ABA Business Law CSR Subcommittee to implement the ABA Model Policies on Labor Trafficking and Child Labor now led by Deborah Walker Kool and formerly led by Co-Chairs Bill Johnston, Denise Kraft, and Brad Newman; and the editors of this chapter, particularly Margaret M. Cassidy and Alan Gutterman, who not only contributed significantly to this chapter but also the other chapters in this book and have extended much grace to the author.

Michael R. Littenberg (Chapter 4: Reporting and Disclosure) is a partner at Ropes & Gray, in the Securities and Public Companies practice. He is based in the New York office. As part of his practice, for almost thirty years, Michael has been active in advising leading public and private companies, asset managers, and asset owners on CSR, ESG, and supply chain compliance matters, and he is widely viewed as one of the leading practitioners in this emerging area.

Carmen X.W. Lu (Chapter 2: ESG, Sustainability, and CSR: Governance and the Role of the Board) received a B.A. summa cum laude in Political Science from Yale University in 2012, where she was a member of Phi Beta Kappa and received the Arthur Twining Hadley Prize as the highest ranking graduate. She received her J.D. from Yale Law School in 2016, where she was articles and essays editor of the *Yale Law Journal* and executive editor of the *Yale Journal on Regulation*.

Susan H. Mac Cormac (Chapter 11: Impact Investing; Chapter 12: Alternative Legal Entities) is a corporate partner in the San Francisco office of Morrison & Foerster, where she co-chairs the firm's Social Enterprise + Impact Investing Group and Energy Group. Her practice focuses on using corporate law to develop creative capital market solutions to pressing environmental problems. She represents top investors dedicated to impact as well as a range of social enterprises. She co-led the drafting group for the first of the new corporate forms (the Social Purpose Corporation in California). Ms. Mac Cormac also advises on corporate governance, particularly the intersection of fiduciary duties with sustainability. Her practice also includes representing mainstream investors in late-stage investments and counseling startup to late-stage private companies in the clean technology and renewable energy space in capital raising and project acquisitions.

Ms. Mac Cormac has been recognized as *California Lawyer* Attorney of the Year in both 2012 and 2016 and was named the Most Innovative Lawyer in North America in 2015 by the *Financial Times*. Ms. Mac Cormac was a founding board member of the Sustainability Accounting Standards Board, is a member of the board of directors of Business for Social Responsibility, the Ceres President's Council, and the Earth Genome Project, and is an advising board member of the Committee Encouraging Corporate Philanthropy's Strategic Investor Initiative. She has joined the faculty at both the Stanford Director's College and the Northwestern Corporate Counsel Institute and is an adjunct professor at UC Berkeley School of Law.

Susan Maslow (Chapter 6: Labor and Supply Chain Practices), a cofounder and partner of Antheil Maslow & MacMinn LLP since 1992, is Vice Chair of the Working Group to Draft Human Rights Protections in International Supply Contracts, ABA Section of Business Law, and Vice Chair of the ABA Section of the Business Law Subcommittee to Implement the ABA Model Principles on Labor Trafficking and Child Labor. She concentrates her practice primarily in general corporate transactional work and finance documentation and represents entrepreneurial individuals and privately held companies in a variety of business negotiations and arrangements.

Sabastian V. Niles (Chapter 2: ESG, Sustainability, and CSR: Governance and the Role of the Board) is a partner at Wachtell, Lipton, Rosen & Katz where he focuses on rapid response shareholder activism and preparedness, takeover defense and corporate governance; risk oversight, including as to cybersecurity and crisis situations; U.S. and cross-border mergers, acquisitions, buyouts, investments, divestitures, and strategic partnerships; and other corporate and securities law matters and special situations. Sabastian advises worldwide and across industries, including technology, financial institutions, media, energy and natural resources, healthcare and pharmaceuticals, construction and manufacturing, real estate/REITs and consumer goods and retail.

Daniel Portnov (Chapter 14: Working with Governments) is an experienced litigator who defends both individuals and companies in white collar, regulatory, and complex civil matters. Prior to joining the Law Office of Sara Kropf, Dan was Counsel in the Division of Enforcement at the Securities and Exchange Commission. While at the SEC, Dan was a member of the Asset Management Unit, a specialized group investigating potential misconduct involving registered investment advisors, investment companies, and private funds, with a particular focus on violations of the Investment Advisers Act.

Dan has also worked in the New York offices of two large international law firms and clerked for the Honorable Joan A. Lenard, U.S. District Court Judge in the Southern District of Florida. Additionally, he teaches legal research and writing at the George Washington University Law School.

Margaret Richardson (Chapter 5: Environment) has over twenty years of legal experience with a significant focus on regulatory issues and the operational impacts of local, state, federal, and international regulations. Margaret is currently General Counsel and Executive Vice President of Government and Investor Relations with Anuvia Plant Nutrients. Margaret has supported several global organizations that required the ability to understand and navigate regulatory concerns and drive effective business and legal solutions.

Michael B. Runnels (Chapter 3: Stakeholder Engagement) is Associate Professor of Law & Social Responsibility in the Sellinger School of Business at Loyola University Maryland. His research focuses on the nexus between good business and good ethics. Professor Runnels received his B.A. from the University of Georgia, during which he had the opportunity to study at the University of Oxford, England, and received his J.D. from the Fordham University School of Law. While at Fordham, Professor Runnels served as Senior Articles Editor of the *Fordham Journal of Corporate and Financial Law*. Professor Runnels teaches law, ethics, and social responsibility to undergraduate and graduate business students, and spends summers teaching business ethics to Chinese nationals at the Beijing Institute of Technology. He also works with the National Jesuit Committee on Investment Responsibility as a stakeholder engagement adviser and participant.

Nicholas J.C. Santos (Chapter 3: Stakeholder Engagement) is Assistant Professor of Marketing in the College of Business at Marquette University, Wisconsin. He is a member of the Board of Directors of Marquette University High School, Milwaukee, and a trustee of Creighton University, Omaha. Currently, he is President of the Colleagues of Jesuit Business Education (CJBE) and is a member of the National Jesuit Committee on Investment Responsibility (NJCIR) and the policy board for the Society of Macromarketing. He has published widely in a number of journals such as *Business and Politics*, *Journal of Business Ethics*, *Journal of Catholic Social Thought*, *Journal of Macromarketing*, *Journal of Public Policy & Marketing* and is an invited reviewer for a number of journals.

Kathleen E. Scott (Chapter 13: Cybersecurity Risk Management Is a Corporate Responsibility) is Senior Associate at Wiley Rein LLP. Kat counsels technology clients on regulatory, transactional, and compliance matters, and she also advises clients on FCC, FTC, NIST, NTIA, and state law issues. She is a Certified Information Privacy Technologist (CIPT), and she uses that perspective to advise technology companies and others on privacy, cybersecurity, and other issues. Her areas of focus include FTC privacy and data security standards as well as consumer protection laws like the Telephone Consumer Protection Act.

Randal M. Shaheen (Chapter 7: Product and Customer Responsibility) has more than 30 years of experience as an advertising attorney. A member of BakerHostetler's Advertising, Marketing and Digital Media team, he represents clients before a variety of regulatory agencies, including the Federal Trade Commission (FTC), Consumer Financial Protection Bureau (CFPB), National Advertising Division (NAD), and state attorneys general, and he is sought after for his handling of multijurisdictional matters. Mr. Shaheen has also handled matters related to privacy and data security, marketing to children, "green" claims, dietary supplements, claims of weight loss and health and performance, comparative claims, the use of surveys, and "Made in the USA" claims. Mr. Shaheen is a graduate of Harvard Law School.

David M. Silk (Chapter 2: ESG, Sustainability, and CSR: Governance and the Role of the Board) joined Wachtell, Lipton, Rosen & Katz in 1988 and became partner in the Corporate Department in 1995. His practice focuses on hostile and negotiated merger and acquisition transactions, private equity transactions, corporate governance, proxy contests, restructurings, joint ventures and securities laws. He represents public and private companies and private equity funds in a wide variety of industries. Mr. Silk is a graduate of the University of Pennsylvania School of Law, where he was a member of the editorial board of the University of Pennsylvania Law Review and the Order of the Coif. He has lectured frequently on governance and transactional topics and has served as an adjunct faculty member at the University of Pennsylvania Law School teaching a course on mergers and acquisitions.

Sharon Singh (Chapter 9: Corporate Social Responsibility and Indigenous Rights) focuses her practice on the resources and infrastructure sector, with an emphasis on Aboriginal law, Indigenous relations, governance, regulatory, and environmental law. She advises clients on Aboriginal law and policy issues including treaty rights and land claims; negotiating agreements with Indigenous communities for project development and ongoing operations; Aboriginal due diligence on project development and M&A transactions; regulatory approval processes; and emerging issues in Indigenous relations.

Before joining Bennett Jones, Sharon was with Rio Tinto for 10 years, based in Australia and Canada, holding senior positions across many fields including commercial, legal, regulatory, government, and community relations. She has a built a reputation for her ability to progress issues through creating trusting relationships between industry groups, associations, governments, Indigenous and local communities, and the not-for-profit sector.

Sharon is a senior policy advisor to the Mining Association of Canada, and serves on Aboriginal and environmental advisory committees with the Association of Mineral Producers and the British Columbia Business Council.

W. Stanford Smith (Chapter 7: Product and Customer Responsibility) is Senior Vice President and General Counsel-Americas for Software AG USA, Inc., a global provider of software products and services. Mr. Smith's responsibilities include providing legal counsel on a broad range of global and regional issues, particularly in the areas of licensing, M&A, product development, employment, competition, corporate governance, CSR, contract management, and litigation. Mr. Smith and his team have developed in-house solutions to optimize in-house legal resources, including automatic contract generation applications and tools to track analytics concerning the efficiency, accuracy, rapidity, and customer satisfaction of services provided to Software AG's teams. The Association of Corporation Counsel named Software AG and Mr. Smith's team as 2018 Value Champions in recognition of their development of these applications and tools. Mr. Smith has lectured on legal topics relating to in-house practice and building relationships with outside legal service providers, and is a member of several professional committees and practice groups, including the ABA Business Law Section's Corporate Social Responsibility Law Committee. Mr. Smith is a graduate of the University of Virginia School of Law.

Matthew H. Solomson (Chapter 13: Cybersecurity Risk Management Is a Corporate Responsibility) is Chief Legal Officer, Federal Government Solutions, Anthem, Inc., a Fortune 30 company, where he leads the legal team supporting the company's federal contracting business unit and where he also has managed the compliance and contracts management groups. Mr. Solomson teaches Government Contracts Law as Adjunct Professor at the University of Maryland School of Law and received his J.D. and M.B.A. from the University of Maryland. In addition to his prior experience in private practice (Arnold & Porter LLP and Sidley Austin LLP) and with the U.S. Department of Justice, he is the author of *Court of Federal Claims: Jurisdiction, Practice, and Procedure*, the only comprehensive legal treatise focused on that court, published by Bloomberg BNA in 2016.

Charlotte Teal (Chapter 9: Corporate Social Responsibility and Indigenous Rights) maintains a regulatory practice with a focus on environmental and aboriginal law. She has experience with regulatory compliance issues, environmental investigations, contaminated sites, and transportation of dangerous goods. She has effectively represented clients in front of the British Columbia Supreme Court.

Charlotte summered and articled with Bennett Jones prior to joining the firm as an associate in the regulatory group in Vancouver. She is a member of the Canadian Bar Association and Vancouver Bar Association.

Keith T. Vernon (Chapter 3: Stakeholder Engagement) is a strategic advisor in CSR stakeholder engagement matters and an accomplished litigator holding an AV Preeminent Peer Rating with Martindale-Hubbell. Mr. Vernon has led a variety of subject matter/issue CSR stakeholder engagements including human rights and environmental matters. Mr. Vernon received his J.D. from Loyola University, New Orleans, and his undergraduate degree from Saint Joseph's University.

Index

A

Accountable Capitalism Act, 16
administrative law judge (ALJ), 125
ADS. *See* Automated Driving Systems (ADS)
ALJ. *See* administrative law judge (ALJ)
alternative legal entities
  corporate forms, driving forces of, 251
  for-profit entities
    benefit limited liability company, 267
    benefits, 258–60
    Delaware public benefit corporation, 264–6
    Delaware statutory public benefit limited liability company, 268
    director, benefit, 261
    enforcement rights, 261–2
    low-profit limited liability companies, 267
    overview, 258
    risks, 260–1
    social purpose corporation, 262–4
  hybrid/tandem entities, 251–2
    benefits of, 254
    fund structures, 257
    legal and practical issues, 254–5
    overview, 253
    requirements and practices, 255–7
  L3C, SPC/PBC, benefit corporations, benefit LLCs, 252–3
American National Standards Institute (ANSI), 126
ANSI. *See* American National Standards Institute (ANSI)
assessments practices, employees, 110
Australian federal Modern Slavery Act, 62–3
Automated Driving Systems (ADS), 132

B

BBB. *See* Better Business Bureau (BBB)
behavioral ground rules, 39
behavioral regulations, 5–6
benefit limited liability companies (BLLC), 252, 267
Better Business Bureau (BBB), 136
Biometric Information Privacy Act (BIPA), 144
BIPA. *See* Biometric Information Privacy Act (BIPA)
BLLC. *See* benefit limited liability companies (BLLC)
board composition and capacity, 18
board oversight, ESG governance, 16–17

boards of directors
  challenges and opportunities (*see* management teams, challenges and opportunities)
  on ESG issues, 21
  goals, 21
  stakeholder engagement, 21
bonds, impact investment, 236–7
Brazil data protection law, 148–9

C

CAA. *See* Clean Air Act (CAA)
California Consumer Privacy Act of 2018, 143
California Transparency in Supply Chains Act, 60–1
Calvert Research and Management, 22
campaign finance laws, 306
Canada data protection law, 148
Canadian Extractive Sector Transparency Measures Act, 68
CAN-SPAM. *See* Controlling the Assault of Non-Solicited Pornography and Marketing Act (CAN-SPAM)
Carbon Disclosure Project, 60
CDP. *See* Carbon Disclosure Project
CDRH. *See* Center for Devices and Radiological Health (CDRH)
CDSB. *See* Climate Disclosure Standards Board Framework
Center for Devices and Radiological Health (CDRH), 130
CERCLA. *See* Comprehensive Environmental Response, Compensation, and Liability Act (CERCLA)
CFAA. *See* Computer Fraud and Abuse Act (CFAA)
CGCPA. *See* Children's Gasoline Burn Prevention Act (CGCPA)

Chemical Safety Information, Site Security and Fuels Regulatory Relief Act (CSISSFRRA), 74
Children's Advertising Review Unit (CARU), 137
Children's Gasoline Burn Prevention Act (CGCPA), 125
Children's Internet Protection Act (CIPA), 134
Children's Online Privacy Protection Act (COPPA), 136, 141–2
CIPA. *See* Children's Internet Protection Act (CIPA)
Clean Air Act (CAA), 74–5
Clean Water Act (CWA), 76–7
Climate Disclosure Standards Board Framework, 60
CMR. *See* Conflict Minerals Report (CMR)
Code of Practice for ethical employment, 64
Commodity Futures Trading's (CFTC) Whistleblower Program, 209
Communications and Video Accessibility Act (CVAA), 134
community engagement
  charitable contributions, 158–9
  consultation requirements, 161
  events, 160
  Fair Labor Standards Act, 161–2
  governance and compliance, 164–7
  involvement practice
    businesses, start-ups and, 172
    development initiatives, 168–9
    investment, 169–71
    partnerships, 171–2
  philanthropic activities, 157–8
  reporting, 167–8
  voluntary standards, norms, and guidelines, 162–4
  volunteer programs, 159–60

community investment, 169–71
community partnerships, 171–2
compensation and benefits, employees, 108–9
compensation, impact-based, 238
Comprehensive Environmental Response, Compensation, and Liability Act (CERCLA), 74, 81–3, 89
Computer Fraud and Abuse Act (CFAA), 275
conditionally exempt small quantity generators (CESQGs), 80–1
Conflict Minerals Report (CMR), 65
Conflict Minerals Rule, 64–6
conflict of interest laws, 307–8
Consumer Product Safety Act (CPSA), 124
Consumer Product Safety Commission (CPSC), 124
   civil penalties, 127–8
   statutes, 124–5
   voluntary safety standards, 126
Consumer Product Safety Improvement Act (CPSIA), 125
Controlling the Assault of Non-Solicited Pornography and Marketing Act (CAN-SPAM), 136
COPPA. *See* Children's Online Privacy Protection Act (COPPA)
corporate social responsibility (CSR)
   behavioral regulations and disclosure, 5–6
   evolution of, 1–2
   manufacturing operations and point sources, 2–3
   practitioner's manual, 6–8
   product regulations, 4–5
   waste stream management, 4–5
corruption, 303
CPSA. *See* Consumer Product Safety Act (CPSA)
CPSC. *See* Consumer Product Safety Commission (CPSC)
CPSIA. *See* Consumer Product Safety Improvement Act (CPSIA)
CSISSFRRA. *See* Chemical Safety Information, Site Security and Fuels Regulatory Relief Act (CSISSFRRA)
CSR. *See* corporate social responsibility (CSR)
Cures Act, 128
customer privacy, international, 148–9
CVAA. *See* Communications and Video Accessibility Act (CVAA)
CWA. *See* Clean Water Act (CWA)
cyber insurance, 284
cybersecurity, 271–3
Cybersecurity Information Sharing Act, 276
cybersecurity risk
   federal contractors, 277
   global challenges, 285–7
   law, sources of, 275–6
   management of
      communications, 291
      government, interacting with, 292–4
      incidents handling, 288–9
      information sharing, 292
      investigations and litigation, 294–5
      privilege, maintaining, 290
      risk management and planning, 287–8
      vulnerabilities, 289–90
   organizations, affected, 273–5
   private sector, 278
   "Soft Law," 279
      contractual obligations, 284
      cyber insurance, 284
      global technical standards, 282
      government guidance, 282–4
      industrial best practices, 281
      National Institute for Standards and Technology, 279–80
   state laws and enforcement, 278–9

D

DAFs. *See* Donor-advised funds (DAFs)
decision-making process, employment, 110
Delaware Certification of Adoption of Transparency and Sustainability Standards, 57–8
Delaware public benefit corporation, 264–6
Delaware statutory public benefit limited liability company, 268
Department of Defense (DoD), 277
Department of Justice (DOJ), 201, 206
Department of Labor (DOL), 98
Dietary Supplement Health and Education Act (DSHEA), 139
Discharge Monitoring Report—Quality Assurance (DMR-QA), 77
disclosure
   climate change, 23–5, 58–9
   drivers, 48–50
   foreign instruments, 66
      EU Non-financial Reporting Directive, 67
      French Duty of Vigilance Law, 67
      International Integrated Reporting Council Framework, 68
      resource extraction, 68–9
      Stock Exchange Guidance, 67–8
   frameworks and standards
      Delaware Certification of Adoption of Transparency and Sustainability Standards, 57–8
      Global Reporting Initiative Standards, 54–5
      Sustainability Accounting Standards Board Standards, 55–6
      UN Global Compact, 56–7
      UN Guiding Principles, 50–2
   issue-specific instruments
      Conflict Minerals Rule, 64–6
      environmental disclosures, 58–60
      modern slavery, 60–4
      pay equity rules, 66
   "Soft Law" instruments
      OECD Guidelines, 52–3
      RBC Guidance, 53–4
      UN Guiding Principles, 50–2
   types of, 45–7
Division of Privacy and Identity Protection (DPIP), 141
DMR-QA. *See* Discharge Monitoring Report-Quality Assurance (DMR-QA)
DOD. *See* Department of Defense (DoD)
Dodd-Frank Act, 207–8
DOJ. *See* Department of Justice (DOJ)
DOL. *See* Department of Labor (DOL)
Donor-advised funds (DAFs), 241
DPIP. *See* Division of Privacy and Identity Protection (DPIP)
DSHEA. *See* Dietary Supplement Health and Education Act (DSHEA)
Dutch child labor legislation, 47

E

ECPA. *See* Electronic Communications Privacy Act (ECPA)
EEOC. *See* Equal Employment Opportunity Commission (EEOC)
EITI. *See* Extractive Industries Transparency Initiative; Extractive Industries Transparency Initiative (EITI)
Electronic Communications Privacy Act (ECPA), 276
Emergency Planning and Community Right-to-Know Act (EPCRA), 74
employee handbooks, 112
employment laws and practices. *See also* labor and supply chain practices
   agreements, 107–8
   assessments, 110

compensation and benefits, 108–9
decision-making process, 110
diversity, 110
employee handbooks, 112
health and safety, 111
noncompetition agreement, 109
non-solicitation agreements, 109
payment and scheduling practices, 109–10
performance reviews, 110
recruiting and hiring, 107
retaliation, 112
sexual harassment, 113–15
termination, 112–13
training and education, 111–12
union formation, 110–11
Endangered Species Act (ESA), 87–8
environment
  legal and regulatory issues, 72
  litigation trends, 92–4
  local regulations, 90–1
  state regulations, 89–90
  U.S. federal regulations, 73–4
    Clean Air Act, 74–5
    Clean Water Act, 76–7
    Comprehensive Environmental Response, Compensation, and Liability Act, 81–3
    Endangered Species Act, 87–8
    Hazardous Materials Transportation Act, 86–7
    Resource Conservation and Recovery Act, 79–81
    Safe Drinking Water Act, 77–8
    Toxic Substances Control Act, 83–6
  voluntary standards, 91–2
environmental disclosures
  Carbon Disclosure Project, 60
  Climate Disclosure Standards Board Framework, 60
  TCFD Recommendations, 59–60
  U.S. Securities and Exchange Commission Guidance, 58–9
environmental responsibility, 46
environmental, social, and governance. *See* ESG (environmental, social, and governance)
EPCRA. *See* Emergency Planning and Community Right-to-Know Act (EPCRA)
Equal Employment Opportunity Commission (EEOC), 98
ESA. *See* Endangered Species Act (ESA)
ESG (environmental, social, and governance), 9
ESG, sustainability and CSR governance
  boards of directors, 21
  case studies
    Peabody Energy and Exxon Mobil, 23–5
    Salesforce.Com, 22–3
  challenges and opportunities, 19–21
  components of
    board composition and capacity, 18
    board oversight, 16–17
    management, partnership with, 17–18
    shareholder and stakeholder engagement, 18–19
  influencing trends
    board composition and diversity, 13–14
    disclosure and ESG ratings, 14
    shareholder *versus* stakeholder models, 15–16
    stakeholder engagement, 14–15
  issues, 11–12
  legal framework, 10
ESTMA. *See* Extractive Sector Transparency Measures Act (ESTMA)
ETFs. *See* exchange-traded funds (ETFs)
ethics and compliance program
  CFTC Whistleblower Program, 209

development and implementation, 209–10, 216–17
   auditing process, 217–18
   code of conduct, 214–16
   governance, 210
   internal reporting system, 217–18
   leadership, 210–13
   managing third parties, 220–4
   monitoring process, 217–18
   policies, 214–16
   procedures, 214–16
   remediation plan, 219
   risk assessment, 213–14
   training and communications, 216–17
discretionary report, 205–6
federal False Claims Act, 207
international whistleblowers, 208–9
IRS Whistleblower Program, 209
jurisdictions and organizations, consistent across, 200–5
reports, mandatory, 205
resourcing, 211–12
state False Claims Acts, 207
whistleblower laws, 207
whistleblowers under FIRREA, 209
EU Accounting and Transparency Directives, 68
EU Conflict Minerals Regulation, 66
EU data protection rules, 147–8
EU Non-financial Reporting Directive, 67
exchange-traded funds (ETFs), 11
Extractive Industries Transparency Initiative (EITI), 68–9
Extractive Sector Transparency Measures Act (ESTMA), 68
Exxon Mobil, climate change risks, 23–5

F

FACA. *See* Federal Advisory Committee Act (FACA)
Fair Credit Reporting Act, 142
Fair Labor Standards Act (FLSA), 99
FALCPA. *See* Food Allergen Labeling and Consumer Protection Act (FALCPA)
False Claims Act, 207
FARA. *See* Foreign Agent Registration Act (FARA)
FAST. *See* Fixing America's Surface Transportation Act (FAST)
FCC. *See* Federal Communications Commission (FCC)
FCPA. *See* Foreign Corrupt Practices Act (FCPA)
FDA. *See* Food and Drug Administration (FDA)
FDAMA. *See* Food and Drug Administration Modernization Act (FDAMA)
FDASIA. *See* Food and Drug Administration Safety and Innovation Act (FDASIA)
FD&C Act. *See* Federal Food, Drug, and Cosmetic Act (FD&C Act)
Federal Advisory Committee Act (FACA), 133–4
Federal Communications Commission (FCC), 133–5
Federal Food, Drug, and Cosmetic Act (FD&C Act), 128
Federal Hazardous Substances Act (FHSA), 125
Federal Information Security Modernization Act of 2014 (FISMA 2014), 276
Federal Motor Vehicle Safety Standards (FFMVSS), 131
Federal Trade Commission (FTC), 135
   enforcement mechanisms, 137–8
   privacy legislation
      Children's Online Privacy Protection Act, 141–2
      enforced/administered statutes, 143
      Fair Credit Reporting Act, 142
      Gramm-Leach-Bliley Act, 142–3

Section 5(a), 141
statutes, 135–6
voluntary standards/resources, 136–7
FFA. *See* Flammable Fabrics Act (FFA)
FFMVSS. *See* Federal Motor Vehicle Safety Standards (FFMVSS)
FHSA. *See* Federal Hazardous Substances Act (FHSA)
Financial Institutions Reform, Recovery, and Enforcement Act (FIRREA), 209
FISMA 2014. *See* Federal Information Security Modernization Act of 2014 (FISMA 2014)
Fixing America's Surface Transportation Act (FAST), 132
Flammable Fabrics Act (FFA), 125
FLSA. *See* Fair Labor Standards Act (FLSA)
FMI. *See* Food Marketing Institute (FMI)
Food Allergen Labeling and Consumer Protection Act (FALCPA), 139
Food and Drug Administration (FDA), 128
statutes, 128–9, 138–9
voluntary standards, 130, 140
Food and Drug Administration Modernization Act (FDAMA), 128–9, 138–9
Food and Drug Administration Safety and Innovation Act (FDASIA), 128–9
Food Labeling Guide, 140
Food Marketing Institute (FMI), 140
Food Safety Modernization Act (FSMA), 128–9
forced labor, 102–4
audits, 117
contracts, business partners, 116
cooperating with government, 118
disclosure, 117–18
government, reporting to, 118
monitoring process, 117
recruiting and hiring, 116
risk assessment, 116–17

training and communications, 115–16
Foreign Agent Registration Act (FARA), 305–6
Foreign Corrupt Practices Act (FCPA), 206
foreign CSR disclosure instruments, 66
EU Non-financial Reporting Directive, 67
French Duty of Vigilance Law, 67
IIRC, 68
resource extraction, 68–9
Stock Exchange Guidance, 67–8
FSMA. *See* Food Safety Modernization Act (FSMA)
FTC. *See* Federal Trade Commission (FTC)
fund's governance structure, 238–9
funds, investment, 237–8

G

GDPR. *See* General Data Protection Regulation (GDPR)
General Data Protection Regulation (GDPR), 144–5
data processing agreements, 146–7
officer, appointment of, 145
rights, 145–6
Global Reporting Initiative (GRI), 14, 47
government guidance, cybersecurity risk, 282–4
governments, businesses with
anticorruption CSR program, 300–1
bribery statutes, 304
conflict of interest laws, 307–8
corruption, 303
export regulations, 309–10
gifts/gratuities/entertainment, 304–5
governance and compliance
CSR program development, 312–13
external engagement, 315–16
strategic view, developing, 313–15

government official, 302–3
penalties, 303
political activities
   campaign finance laws, 306
   lobbying laws, 305–6
procurement laws, 308
standards and guidance, 310–12
trade sanctions, 309–10
Gramm-Leach-Bliley Act, 142–3
GRI. *See* Global Reporting Initiative (GRI)
GRI 411, indigenous rights, 192
Guiding Principles, 50
   to protect/respect human rights, 51–2

H

Hazardous Materials Transportation Act (HMTA), 86–7
Health Insurance Portability and Accountability Act (HIPAA), 275
Hong Kong Stock Exchange
   Environmental, Social and Governance Reporting Guide, 67
human capital management, 46
human rights
   Guiding Principles, 50–2
   RBC Guidance, 54

I

IFC Performance Standard 7, indigenous rights, 192–3
IIRC. *See* International Integrated Reporting Council (IIRC)
ILO. *See* International Labour Organisation (ILO)
ILO Convention No. 169, indigenous rights, 189–90
indigenous rights
   Australia, 184–5
   awareness and recognition of, 195
   Canadian Aboriginal law, 178
      Aboriginal rights, 178–9
      Aboriginal Title, 179
      duty to accommodate, 180–1
      duty to consult, 180
      Treaty rights, 179–80
      United Nations Declaration on the Rights of Indigenous Peoples, 181–4
   Chile, 187
   employ practices, 196–7
   Mexico, 185–7
   norms, standards, and guidelines
      Canadian policy, 193–4
      human rights, 188
      international, 188–93
   resources, 194–5
Institutional Shareholder Services (ISS), 12, 14
International Integrated Reporting Council (IIRC), 14
International Labour Organisation (ILO), 102
International Organization for Standardization (ISO), 119, 311
international standards, cybersecurity, 281
investment funds, 237–8
investment, impact
   instruments
      bonds, 236–7
      convertible debt, 234–5
      preferred equity, 235–6
      SAFEs, 236
   measurement and reporting, 243–5
investor, impact, 233–4
investor structures, impact, 242
   foundations, 240
      donor-advised funds, 241
      examples, 241
      mission-related investments, 241
      program-related investment, 240–1
      traditional, 242

hybrid funds, 242–3
profit funds, 237–8
   compensation, 238
   distributions, 239
   example, 239–40
   governance, 238–9
   longer term, 238
   monitoring impact, 239
   protective provisions, 239
IPIECA, 69
IRS Whistleblower Program, 209
ISO. *See* International Organization for Standardization (ISO)
ISS. *See* Institutional Shareholder Services (ISS)

L

labor and supply chain practices, 97–8
  employment, 104–5 (*See also* employment laws and practices)
  forced labor mitigation compliance plan
    audits, 117
    contracts, 116
    cooperating with government, 118
    disclosure requirements, 117–18
    monitoring, 117
    recruiting and hiring, 116
    reporting to government, 118
    risk assessment, 116–17
    training and communications, 115–16
  human trafficking, 102–4
  issues, 119–21
  labor exploitation, 102–4
  U.S. labor and employment laws, 98–101
  voluntary standards, norms, and guidelines, 105–7

Labor Management Relations Act (LMRA), 100–1
large quantity generators (LQGs), 81
L3Cs. *See* low-profit limited liability companies (L3Cs)
leadership commitment, ethics and compliance program, 210–11
limited liability companies (LLCs), 250–1
LMRA. *See* Labor Management Relations Act (LMRA)
lobbying laws, 305–6
London Convention, environmental regulations, 72
London Stock Exchange Group, 68
low-profit limited liability companies (L3Cs), 252, 267
LSE Group. *See* London Stock Exchange Group

M

management teams, challenges and opportunities, 19–21
Manufactured Food Regulatory Program Standards (MFRPS), 130
Medical Device User Fee Act (MDUFA), 129
MFRPS. *See* Manufactured Food Regulatory Program Standards (MFRPS)
mission-related investments (MRIs), 241
MNE (multinational enterprises) Guidelines, 52–3
modern slavery disclosure, 60
  Australian federal Modern Slavery Act, 62–3
  California Transparency in Supply Chains Act, 60–1
  New South Wales Modern Slavery Act, 63–4
  UK Modern Slavery Act, 61–2
  Welsh Code of Practice, 64

Montreal Protocol, environmental regulations, 72
MRIs. *See* mission-related investments (MRIs)

N

NAAQS. *See* National Ambient Air Quality Standards (NAAQS)
NAD. *See* National Advertising Division (NAD)
Nasdaq ESG Reporting Guide, 67–8
National Advertising Division (NAD), 137
National Ambient Air Quality Standards (NAAQS), 74
National Highway Traffic Safety Administration (NHTSA), 131
   statutes, 131–2
   voluntary standards, 132–3
National Institute for Standards and Technology (NIST), 279–80
National Labor Relations Act (NLRA), 100–1
National Labor Relations Board (NLRB), 98, 101
National Pollutant Discharge Elimination Systems (NPDES), 76
New South Wales Modern Slavery Act, 63–4
NGOs. *See* nongovernmental organizations (NGOs)
NHTSA. *See* National Highway Traffic Safety Administration (NHTSA)
NIST. *See* National Institute for Standards and Technology (NIST)
NLEA. *See* Nutrition Labeling and Education Act (NLEA)
NLRA. *See* National Labor Relations Act (NLRA)
NLRB. *See* National Labor Relations Board (NLRB)
nongovernmental organizations (NGOs), 5
NPDES. *See* National Pollutant Discharge Elimination Systems (NPDES)
Nutrition Labeling and Education Act (NLEA), 138

O

Occupational Safety and Health Administration Act (OSHA), 100
OECD. *See* Organisation for Economic Co-operation and Development (OECD)
OEM. *See* original equipment manufacturer (OEM)
Oil Pollution Act (OPA), 74
Organisation for Economic Co-operation and Development (OECD), 311–12
   guidelines, 193
original equipment manufacturer (OEM), 5
OSHA. *See* Occupational Safety and Health Administration Act (OSHA)

P

Paris Accord, environmental regulations, 72–3
pay equity disclosure rules, 66
payment and scheduling practices, employees, 109–10
PBC. *See* public benefit corporations (PBC)
PBLLC. *See* public benefit limited liability companies (PBLLC)
PDMA. *See* Prescription Drug Marketing Act (PDMA)
Peabody Energy, climate change risks, 23–5
penalties, 303
performance reviews, employees, 110
Poison Protection Packaging Act, 125

Prescription Drug Marketing Act (PDMA), 128
PRIs. *See* program-related investments (PRIs)
product responsibility and customer care
    customer health and safety
        Consumer Product Safety Commission, 124–8
        Federal Communications Commission, 133–5
        Food and Drug Administration, 128–31
        National Highway Traffic Safety Administration, 131–3
    customer privacy
        EU data protection rules, 147–8
        Federal Trade Commission, 140–3
        General Data Protection Regulation, 144–6
        international protection laws, 148–9
        U.S. state law approaches, 143–4
        voluntary standards, 149
    governance and compliance, 149–50
    marketing and labeling
        Federal Trade Commission, 135–8
        Food and Drug Administration, 138–40
    reporting requirements, 150
program-related investments (PRIs), 240–1
public benefit corporations (PBC), 252
public benefit limited liability companies (PBLLC), 252

R

RBC Guidance. *See* Responsible Business Conduct (RBC) Guidance
RCRA. *See* Resource Conservation and Recovery Act (RCRA)
recruiting and advertising, employment, 107
Refrigerator Safety Act, 125
Regulation Fair Disclosure (Reg FD), 33–4
Resource Conservation and Recovery Act (RCRA), 79–81
Responsible Business Conduct (RBC) Guidance, 53–4

S

SAFE. *See* Simple Agreement for Future Equity (SAFE)
Safe Drinking Water Act (SDWA), 77–8
safety standards, employees, 111
Salesforce.Com, integrating ESG, 22–3
Sarbanes-Oxley Act, 207–8
SASB. *See* Sustainability Accounting Standards Board (SASB)
SDGs. *See* sustainable development goals (SDGs)
SDWA. *See* Safe Drinking Water Act (SDWA)
Securities and Exchange Commission (SEC), 29, 31
SEC Whistleblower Program, 207–8
shareholder *vs.* stakeholder models of governance, 15–16
Simple Agreement for Future Equity (SAFE), 236
small quantity generators (SQGs), 81
social purpose corporation (SPCs), 262–4
stakeholder engagement
    course of action, proposal
        assessing ability, dialogue, 33
        issues in proposal, 32
        Regulation Fair Disclosure, 33–4
        shareholder, information of, 33
    learning cycle, 37–8
        action plan, 40
        behavioral ground rules, 39
        representatives, flexible, 40
        subject matter experts, 38–9
        team leader, role of, 40

legal and regulatory requirements, 30–1
    filing shareholder resolution, 31
    proposal in dialogue, 32
    resolution, voting, 32
    shareholder proposal, to exclude, 31
practices in, 34
    guidelines for expectations and logistics, 37
    setting goals, 35
    staying engaged, 36
resolving impasses, 41
Stock Exchange Guidance, 67
supply chain practices. *See* labor and employment practices
Sustainability Accounting Standards Board (SASB), 14, 47
    voluntary disclosure standards, 55–6
sustainable development goals (SDGs), 47, 155

T

Task Force on Climate-related Financial Disclosures, 59–60
TCFD. *See* Task Force on Climate-related Financial Disclosures
termination, labor law compliance, 112–13
third parties, managing
    assessing risk, 220
    case study, 224–7
    due diligence, 220–2
    noncompliant relationships, 224
    remediating risk, 222–4
    supplier risk, 220
Title VII of the Civil Rights Act, 99
Tobacco Control Act, 139
Toxic Substances Control Act (TSCA), 84–6
training and education, employment, 111–12
Transportation Recall Enhancement, Accountability, and Documentation Act (TREAD), 132
TSCA. *See* Toxic Substances Control Act (TSCA)

U

Uber, 224–5
    competitors, relationship with, 225
    employees, 226–7
    ethical culture, to develop
        expectations, 230–1
        integrity, 231–2
        leadership, 228–30
        risk assessment, 227–8
    regulators, 225–6
UK Gender Pay Gap Information Regulations, 66
UK Modern Slavery Act, 61–2
UNDRIP. *See* United Nations Declaration on the Rights of Indigenous Peoples (UNDRIP)
UN Framework Convention on Climate Change (UNFCCC), 72
UN Global Compact, 56–7
UN Guiding Principles on Business and Human Rights, 50–2
union formation practice, employees, 110–11
United Nations Declaration on the Rights of Indigenous Peoples (UNDRIP), 181–4, 190–2
U.S. Conflict Minerals Rule, 47, 64–5
U.S. Fish and Wildlife Service (USFWS), 87
U.S. labor and employment laws, 98
    equal employment, 99
    Fair Labor Standards Act, 99
    Labor Management Relations Act, 100–1

Occupational Safety and Health Administration Act, 100
Title VII of the Civil Rights Act, 99
wage and benefits laws, 99
workers compensation laws, 100
U.S. Pay Ratio Rule, 66
U.S. Securities and Exchange Commission Guidance, 58–9
U.S. state law, consumer data privacy
California Consumer Privacy Act of 2018, 143
Colorado, 143–4
Illinois's Biometric Information Privacy Act, 144
state and local privacy legislation, 144
U.S. Trafficking Victims Protection Act, 102–4

V

ValueAct Spring Fund, 11
voluntary disclosure, 46–7

Delaware Certification of Adoption of Transparency and Sustainability Standards, 57–8
GRI Standards, 54–5
SASB's, 55–6
UN Global Compact, 56–7
voluntary environmental standards, 91–2

W

wage and benefits laws. *See* Fair Labor Standards Act (FLSA)
waste management system, 4–5
Welsh Code of Practice for Ethical Employment in Supply Chains, 64
Welsh public sector supply chains, 64
whistleblower laws, 207
workers compensation laws, 100
workers health and safety standards, 111